T0004152

DOMINA
THE WOMEN WHO
MADE IMPERIAL ROME

GUY DE LA BÉDOYÈRE

YALE UNIVERSITY PRESS
NEW HAVEN AND LONDON

For information about this and other Yale University Press publications, please contact:
U.S. Office: sales.press@yale.edu   yalebooks.com
Europe Office: sales@yaleup.co.uk   yalebooks.co.uk

Set in Adobe Garamond Pro by IDSUK (DataConnection) Ltd
Printed and bound by CPI Group (UK) Ltd, Croydon, CR0 4YY

Library of Congress Control Number: 2018946848

ISBN 978-0-300-23030-7 (hbk)
ISBN 978-0-300-25484-6 (pbk)

A catalogue record for this book is available from the British Library.

10 9 8 7 6 5 4 3 2 1

Dedicated to the imperial women of my own family: Rosemary, Sarah, Rochelle, Áine, Daniela, Nell and Willow-Rose, and my former students who inspired this book

CONTENTS

PLATES AND MAPS

Plates

All photographs are by the author unless otherwise stated.

16. Inscription of Lucius Caesar, Porticus of Gaius and Lucius, Rome.
17. Temple of Vesta, Roman Forum.
18. The Roman Forum.
19. Tombstone of Agrippina the Elder, Museo Capitolini, Rome.
20. Sestertius of Agrippina the Elder. Private collection.
21. Bronze coin of Messalina. Classical Numismatic Group, www.cngcoins. com.
22. Cistophoric tetradrachm of Claudius and Agrippina. Private collection.
23. The Gemma Claudia, Kunsthistorisches Museum Vienna. Photo and copyright: Gryffindor.
24. Agrippina crowns Nero, Aphrodisias, Turkey. Photo and copyright: Carole Raddato.
25. Nero's Golden House, Rome.
26. Tetradrachm of Nero and Poppaea. Private collection.
27. View of Oplontis.
28. Sestertius of the Temple of the Deified Augustus and Livia. Private collection.
29. The Severan Women. Private collection.
30. Julia Domna and Septimius Severus on the Arch of the Moneychangers (Porta Argentarii), Rome.
31. Sestertius of Julia Mamaea. Private collection.
32. Julio-Claudian dynastic relief, Ravenna, Museo Nazionale di Ravenna. Photo and copyright: John Pollini.

Maps

FOREWORD

The Roman world, whether writing or reading about it, watching epic movies, wandering amongst its prodigious weed-strewn ruined monuments or padding softly past museum cases packed with curious and remarkable artefacts, is something of a modern obsession. Indeed, it has been since the days of the Renaissance and the Enlightenment. However remarkable the physical remains, above all else it is the sheer force of the personalities that makes the Roman era so compelling. Recorded for us by Roman historians like Suetonius, Tacitus and Cassius Dio, individuals such as Augustus, Livia, Caligula, Messalina, Agrippina and Nero have long escaped the confines of those ancient chronicles. They remain well known today, serving as enduring symbols of power, opportunism, greed and folly. It is impossible to walk through the forums at Rome, or to read about their world, and not try to imagine what these remarkable people were really like.

With so many books written about the Roman world, what more could there possibly be to say? The women of the Julio-Claudian dynasty, the longest-lasting in Roman history, have proved popular topics in the past and present, either in the form of individual biographies or books that feature a series of shorter lives.[1] Even though the only reason the dynasty survived was because of the female bloodline, there has not, to this author's knowledge, been any attempt to write a narrative history of the period in terms of the women of the imperial Julio-Claudian family and their milieu.[2] Nor has it normally been noted that the second longest-lasting dynasty in Roman history, that of the Severans, was also largely dependent on the female bloodline for its existence. All these women emerge as agents in an ongoing process of change, both in the conflicting roles of mothers and as political players, through their fundamental roles as the backbone of the dynasty and symbols of Roman society. Inevitably their importance to their dynasties meant that they ended up in positions of exceptional significance. Their narrative is therefore synonymous with the history of the period. This does not mean that the men are prevented from intruding; their presence on centre stage is remorseless and inevitable, but they deserve to be pushed into the background a little more than is customary.

The inspiration for this book is the large silver coin, known as a cistophoric tetradrachm, of Claudius and his niece-wife empress Agrippina the Younger struck at Ephesus in around the year AD 51 (plate 22). The coin shows the emperor and empress as 'jugate' busts, alongside one another and slightly offset. The significance and symbolism are remarkable. In a world where women could not hold any legitimate political power, here is a coin that appears to show joint rulers, an 'Augustus' and an 'Augusta'. That a Roman empress had reached such a remarkable level of prominence was and remains truly startling. It was a mark of Agrippina's exceptional level of political guile and manipulative skills that she had achieved this. The coin was an unprecedented design and remained unmatched and unrepeated in the Roman period. Even more astonishingly, Agrippina managed to carry her status through Claudius' death in 54 and well into the reign of her son Nero. Her reign, and there is no better word for it, was the climax of female political power in the Roman world. Nobody else until Julia Maesa of the Severan era would come close to Agrippina. Understanding how Agrippina and others managed to achieve their grasp on power, and the price they paid for that, is at the heart of this book's purpose.

Many very interesting modern books have been written on women in the Roman world and it is important to pay them due credit. Richard Bauman's *Women and Politics in Ancient Rome* (1992) is an excellent survey of women in the days of the Republic and right through the Julio-Claudian period to the death of Nero. J.P.V.D. Balsdon's *Roman Women* (1962) is a classic work that covers women from the origins of Rome right through to the fourth century. Balsdon's book is especially recommended to readers looking for more information about women in Rome's earlier centuries. To them can be added Wood's survey of *Imperial Women: A Study in Public Images* (1999) and a number of biographies by other scholars such as Anthony Barrett that have focused most on Livia and Agrippina the Younger, or on several different women. Routledge's Classical Monographs and Women in the Ancient World series have generated some very stimulating titles. These include Emily Hemelrijk's *Matrona Docta* (2004), which covers the educated women of the elite from Cornelia Africana to Julia Mamaea, and Elaine Fantham's biography of Julia, Augustus' daughter. Other recent works, such as Nicholas Purcell's essay on Livia and the Womanhood of Rome (2009 edition), Catharine Edwards's analysis of the role immorality played in Roman politics (2010), and Rebecca Langlands's survey *Sexual Morality in Ancient Rome* (2009) amongst others were very useful sources of ideas and inspiration. Julie Langford's biography of Julia Domna, *Maternal Megalomania* (2013), has some interesting though controversial analysis not only of the nature of female power in the Roman world but also of the way women were deployed as rhetorical devices by Roman historians as part of their commentary on male rulers. It is an interesting reflection of the present age that whereas books on Roman women half a century ago tended to be written by men, they are now more usually written by women. This is in spite of a move to see women's history as part of mainstream historical scholarship.[3] But it is the ancient historians who are by far and away the most important resources used for this book. For all their faults they take us closer to the time than any modern authority possibly can. It is their sometimes outrageous prejudice that tells us most about the framework in which the women of the Julio-Claudians operated.

Anyone, however familiar with the Roman period, can find the vast range of names overwhelming. This can also cause problems for the most practised specialist. This derives from the Roman habit of eldest sons carrying usually the same name as their fathers, including in adoptive relationships. Daughters also acquired their names from their fathers, Agrippa's daughter Agrippina the Elder being a particularly obvious example. While it was normal for brothers to have a different *praenomen* (first name), it was common (but not obligatory) for sisters to have the same name. This way Octavia's daughters by Gaius Claudius Marcellus were both called Claudia Marcella and her daughters by Antony were both named Antonia. In this book a bewildering number of women called Julia appear. The normal custom in modern works with sisters is to call the elder Major and the younger Minor. Conversely, where the relationship is mother-daughter then the terms 'Elder' and 'Younger' are now usually used, such as Agrippina the Elder and Agrippina the Younger, even if using Latin and English terms seems inconsistent.[4] Wherever possible a person's identity has been specified as clearly as possible. The policy with male names is to use the name by which they are best known today. Octavian, for example, was more accurately Octavius before he became Augustus. However, he is usually now referred to as Octavian and that is how he appears in this book.

Analogies and comparisons from other eras are occasionally considered, though this is resisted by some scholars and not by others.[5] Roman society was of course very different from medieval or modern societies. However, there are not only similarities but also instances of self-conscious comparisons or even emulation. This can, with caution, help inspire lateral approaches rather than confining oneself to the parameters of a 'period' which can so easily restrict perceptions to stock positions. One of the most instructive ways of approaching history is to see how depictions of heroes and villains resemble one another across periods. The English Wars of the Roses (c. 1455–85) had three especially prominent female protagonists, two of whom were vilified by contemporary historians supporting their respective rivals.[6] Their treatment has conspicuous similarities to how women like Julia the Elder and Agrippina the Younger were depicted by Roman historians. This is a significant point. The explanations must include the manner in which medieval male historians were also inclined to portray powerful women who challenged the vested interests of their era, and the stylistic and rhetorical conventions established by Tacitus, Suetonius, Dio and others, which seem to have inspired them.

Readers can obviously use this book in any way they wish. As explained, the book is written largely as a narrative history of the Julio-Claudian period through the lives of the empresses and other imperial women. The Introduction and Chapter 1 (Virtue, Honour and Chastity) cover some of the important background to women's lives in the Roman world, particularly in the late Republic. This necessarily entails making references to women who feature later in the story. Some readers may prefer therefore to start at Chapter 2 and refer back to the earlier sections as needed.

The experience of writing this book has been both memorable and sobering. Power in the Roman world was determined, controlled and defined by men. Women were supposed to be respectful, compliant and honourable,

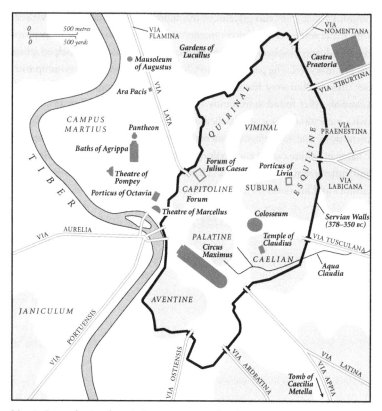

Map 1. Rome, showing the main locations mentioned in the text.

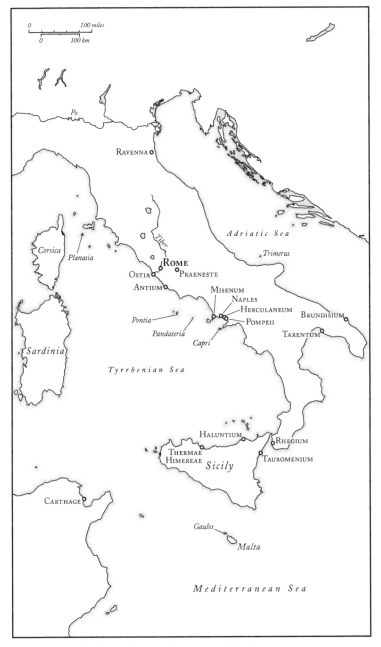

Map 2. Roman Italy, showing the main places mentioned in the text.

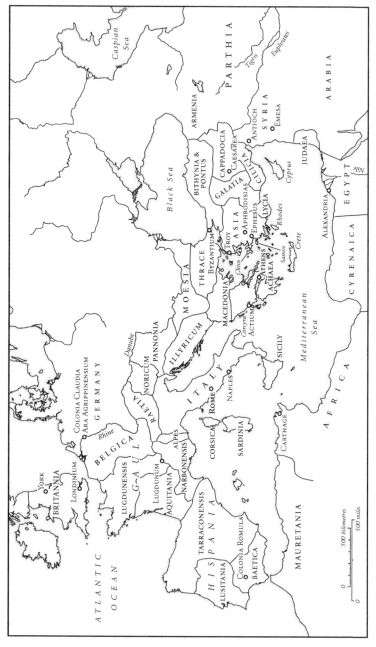

Map 3. The Roman Empire, showing the main places mentioned in the text.

INTRODUCTION

Descent through the female line was the crucial factor that enabled the exist-ence and survival of both the Julio-Claudian and Severan dynasties. Augustus engaged in a complicated series of experiments in establishing the identity of his own power and finding ways for his regime to continue after his death. Augustus from the outset made blood the key qualification for succession but the failure of the male line in his own time, which frustrated him so much, continued through the period and recurred under the Severans. This increased the importance of female members of the dynasties and with dramatic consequences. They were so important that it is possible to rewrite the history of the period in terms of their reigns and lives rather than the traditional approach. However, understanding what happened is dependent on the Roman written sources which are hugely complicated by ambiguities, gaps, bias and agendas. Above all, ancient historians were often critical of women in power and used them as 'proof' of the degeneracy and inadequacies of emperors. Modern historians therefore find themselves chal-lenged by the evidence available. To this we can add buildings, sculpture and coins to try and provide a balance.

In the year AD 65 in Rome a domestic tragedy took place. It was one of the most decisive events ensuring the final and chaotic collapse of a dynasty that had ruled the Roman world for almost a century. Most of the crises that had afflicted the Julio-Claudian imperial family were self-inflicted and this one was no different. It was also the final moment in the life of the last significant female member of the dynasty's court circle, Poppaea Sabina, empress of Rome and wife of the aimless aesthete and histrionic matricide emperor Nero. She fell to the ground, fatally wounded by her husband's kicks. She took with her their unborn child. It was the price she paid for admonishing him about the time he spent at the circus. It was the price Nero paid for his reckless and indulgent personality and a disaster for the Julio-Claudian dynasty, which would die with him three years later.

The Julio-Claudian emperors (27 BC–AD 68) and their exalted family members exerted enormous influence across the Roman world, establishing a template for imperial dynastic identity and that dynasty's control of power. They presided over a vast empire, operating a system of government that withstood the consequences of the family's cast of extraordinary characters and the tensions generated by their idiosyncratic response to the unique and unprecedented position in which they found themselves. The women involved were no less significant than the men whose stories have dominated the traditional perspective of the period. These women also used varying degrees of agility and success to experiment with how they could assert their power.

The Julio-Claudian emperors are so named because of their descent either from the Julii through Augustus' daughter Julia or his sister Octavia, or from the Claudii through Livia by her first husband. Tiberius (14–37) was descended from Livia, Caligula (37–41) from all three, Claudius (41–54) from Livia and Octavia, and Nero (54–68) once more from all three. There remains no doubt that their era was one of the most remarkable in world history. The evidence that has survived continues to bear witness to that fact. The century in which they ruled is already well documented in a variety of general histories and individual biographies. It was the Roman historian Suetonius, an equestrian who served on Hadrian's staff, who vividly defined the Julio-Claudian era in terms of the consecutive emperors with his idiosyncratic and occasionally outrageous individual biographies of their lives. This work has long been recognized as a haphazard mixture of broadly reliable but disorganized information collected together with scurrilous anecdotes. Historians have tended to see the period in terms of a succession of imperial male biographies ever since.

Suetonius could have also, or even instead, profitably explored the period through the equally remarkable and notorious lives of the empresses and other prominent female members of the family. Of course he did not and nor did any other Roman historian either of the Julio-Claudian era or later periods. The lives of empresses and imperial women have invariably to be pieced together from incidental references in the works of men like Tacitus and Dio or the biographies of emperors. Had he written biographies of the Julio-Claudian women Suetonius might very well have made the startling, albeit elementary, observation that the only reason there was a Julio-Claudian dynasty at all was because the bloodline was almost exclusively transmitted down through the women. Not one of the Julio-Claudian emperors was succeeded by his son.[1] In most cases there was no surviving son in the first place. When there was, as in the case of Claudius' son Britannicus, the succession passed him by. It was the female route that legitimized the claim to dynastic descent by the successive male rulers even if the details and nature of each succession differed according to circumstances. Oddly, the real extent of the dynastic implications of Poppaea's death appears to have excited little notice among ancient and even modern historians, as well as the more general issue of the vital importance of key female members of the imperial family to the dynasty's survival.[2] The failure of the male line was a major factor throughout Roman imperial history. Very few emperors succeeded their blood fathers to rule in their own right as opposed to serving as a co-ruler. Even fewer of these were succeeded in turn by their own sons. It was not until the fourth century and the reigns of the sons of Constantine I and then in the fifth century with the reign of Theodosius II that an emperor ruled in his own right after the reigns of his father and grandfather.[3]

The Julio-Claudian reliance on the female line was successfully obscured at the time because from the dictator Caesar right through to Nero the fiction of a father-son succession was manufactured with great success largely by using the system of adoption. The only exception was the accession of Claudius in 41 when the succession incongruously passed from a nephew to his uncle at the behest of the Praetorian Guard. Claudius' eligibility even then was only conferred on him through his descent from Augustus' wife Livia and Augustus' sister Octavia, and not Augustus himself.

The crux of the matter as far as this book is concerned is the process of succession during the two principal dynasties that emerged during the Roman imperial period up to 284.[4] As the first 'emperor', Augustus needed to find a way to secure his regime after his death. The circumstances of power being vested in one man were new, and in theory totally unacceptable within the Roman constitution. He therefore spent a great deal of time and energy on trying to find mechanisms that cloaked his control of the Roman world within the constitutional offices of the Republic. When it came to the succession Augustus came closest to exposing the monarchical nature of his regime. There was, by definition, no procedure for any such thing. Therefore he could not openly nominate a successor. In any case he had no son. Not having a son was a blessing in disguise. It prevented Augustus from making the obvious choice and thereby provoking allegations of a monarchy in the making. Instead, Augustus had to think laterally. He earmarked first the male offspring of his sister Octavia Minor, then his daughter Julia, and finally his wife Livia. This guaranteed his dependence on the female bloodline. Augustus never selected anyone for a successor who was not a relative, though he came close with his son-in-law Agrippa. These individuals were only marked out by their proximity to Augustus and the award of honours and offices that associated them with his. It was, at best, a tenuous and unavoidably oblique solution that created uncertainty and ambiguity.

The era of the Julio-Claudians has a great deal to tell us about how imperial women operated within the Roman state. There is much also to be learned from the Severans because they pushed their luck even further. Julia Domna, empress of Septimius Severus (193–211), brought with her a family of like-minded, highly intelligent, educated and ambitious wealthy women from Emesa (Homs) in Syria. After her death in 217 her widowed sister Julia Maesa used her position and connections to place first on the throne her eldest grandson Elagabalus (218–22), and then, after his murder, her second grandson, Severus Alexander (222–35), the sons of her daughters Julia Soaemias and Julia Mamaea.[5] Even their names were a legacy of the Julio-Claudian period. Spurious tales of adultery were used to fabricate legitimacy for the emperors Elagabalus and Severus Alexander by claiming they were really the illegitimate sons of Caracalla (211–17). The Severan empresses were publicly associated with Venus Genetrix, the mythical progenitor of the Julii. The Severan dynasty was also primarily a female one, and conspicuously more so than that of the Julio-Claudians. These women were, if anything, even more assiduous than the Julio-Claudian women in the way they tried to take over male power structures. The story about Soaemias being the first empress openly to attend the Senate was clearly linked by later Roman historians to the way Livia had managed the Senate from her own house without attempting to intrude on the male-only assembly. Maesa died in her bed, but both her daughters and grandsons had violent deaths, destroyed by their imperial ambitions. Their saga has many echoes of what happened in the Julio-Claudian era, helping us to understand why gaining and holding on to power was so difficult for women in the Roman world and continued to be so. Thereafter, no comparable dynasty occurred again though some individual empresses were able to play prominent roles in imperial affairs in much later ages.[6]

The Julio-Claudian era followed centuries of the Roman Republic, which was brought to an end at the Battle of Actium in 31 BC after decades of civil war, factionalism and chaos. The needs of peace, Tacitus said, determined from then on that power had to be concentrated in the hands of one man (Augustus). Tacitus echoed the geographer Strabo's much earlier observation during the reign of Tiberius that the Roman Empire was so big it had to be controlled by one man 'in the manner of a father'.[7] Tacitus had plenty of acerbic comments to make about how the emperors ruled and the change in Roman society the new system resulted in. Like almost everyone else at the time it would never have occurred to him or Strabo that anyone other than a man could be that person.

Each of the emperors also ruled very differently. Augustus, for example, focused all his attention on manufacturing a recreation of the Republican state. Tiberius struggled to assert his identity under the weight of Augustus' posthumous reputation and his mother Livia's domineering presence. Caligula relied far more on experimenting with a more despotic style of rule to compensate for his youth and lack of experience. Claudius operated a more bureaucratic court-centred style of rule. Nero had little interest in anything beyond his personal indulgence. The role of the imperial women therefore changed throughout the reigns of the emperors, but so also did their opportunities. These women's roles were far more important than just serving as peripheral components of the dynasty. They made substantial contributions to the political, social and cultural character of the regime, whether those were for the better or for the worse, sometimes determining the course of history. Some helped sustain the regime, others almost toppled it. Either way they made their mark. It was, as has been said, undoubtedly a 'partnership in power', but exactly what that meant is more of a challenge to understand than at first it appears.[8]

The ways in which elite Roman women acquired and used power depended on how women were positioned in Roman society and how the political system operated. Only men could hold office. Men from senatorial families were expected to progress through a series of magistracies, entering the Senate early in their careers. These magistracies made them eligible for administrative and military positions, climaxing in the consulship. There was therefore no official position that women could hold within the Republic's constitution. However, the Romans had a very clear idea about the importance and utility of women to society and the interests of the aristocracy.

Once Augustus came to power problems emerged in finding a definition of his position and role. There was technically no such thing as an 'emperor'. Supreme power in the Roman world under the emperors was vested in a strange mixture of conventional Republican magistracies and privileges held by only one person, the *princeps*, or, literally, 'first citizen'. The word *princeps* denoted simultaneously Augustus' membership of the senatorial elite on an equal footing with his peers as well as suggesting that he exceeded them. He did that through his *auctoritas*. The word meant literally 'authority' but in a much more all-encompassing way than the English word suggests.[9]

This made it possible for Augustus and almost everyone else to indulge in the fancy that the Republic was still in existence. As constitutional arrangements go the Republic was both disorganized and strangely brilliant. The disorganization meant that it was possible to view the system and see what one wanted to see. The Republic could be said to have survived intact, its offices and protocols all working properly and presided over by the Senate. It was equally easy to change the focus and see that while all this might be true there was a single man at the centre. His personal status and authority exceeded everyone else's and his sole control of those offices was the result, even though he was by definition supposed not to exist.

The brilliance of the Augustan regime was the stability this created out of a system that had become dangerously chaotic. It had almost torn the Roman world apart until Augustus defeated his enemies and took charge of a population sick of the disorder. Since only men were eligible for the constitutional positions and privileges it follows that women had neither a gateway to formal powers nor the necessary prestige other than as the wives and family members of men who possessed these. Women were generally restricted in public life to roles as priestesses or as members of the Vestal Virgins in charge of the cult of

Vesta. These were prestigious but were not vital front-rank political positions (plate 17). Although this system underwent enormous change the essential elements and the official exclusion of women from power remained in place throughout imperial Roman history.

The non-existence of the formal position of 'emperor' is very important to bear in mind when it comes to using terms like 'emperor' and 'empress'. Emperor is a word derived from *imperator*, best translated as 'general' and meaning literally having the power to command an army. That power was known as *imperium* and was granted in theory by the Senate. Imperium was supposed to be both temporary and conditional. The acclamation imperator was one of the titles emperors took. In time it became synonymous with supreme power but in the time of the Julio-Claudians it was still evolving into that meaning. This can easily be seen from coin legends. Until the reign of Nero (54–68), imperator was a subsidiary title featured towards the end of a coin legend, abbreviated to IMP. Only under Nero did it gravitate to the beginning in the manner of a forename, becoming more common thereafter and eventually permanent. It is convenient for us to use these words, for example considering what it was like 'to be empress in an empire that allowed only emperors', but they can help create a false sense of absolutes and opposites.[10] No one in Rome at the time spoke in the same way about their rulers. They had neither the terminology nor the conceptual framework to do so. Instead, the name 'Augustus' and its female equivalent 'Augusta' became the way the Romans referred to the emperor and his empress. Augustus adopted his new name when it was proposed by a senator called Munatius Plancus. It was derived from other words that denoted an increase in dignity (*auctus*) and the consecration of anything in a religious rite by an augur (a type of priest who looked out for and interpreted signs). The consecration gave them the quality of *augusta*.[11] Augustus was therefore a name without political associations but instead had a quasi-religious aspect that hinted at the special qualities which placed him above others.

The absence of any formal route to power for women did not prevent them either from finding different ways to exert power, or some from reaching for supreme power itself. The very vagueness of male imperial power in the Roman Empire was precisely what helped facilitate the creative approach to power adopted by women like Livia, Agrippina the Younger and Julia Maesa. They accomplished this through an ingenious number of routes, evading the

two particularly good examples. Both were extensively honoured after their deaths by their sons, Caligula and Claudius respectively. In their cases the process was as much about self-interest as genuine respect for their mothers' memories. Claiming to have had a mother of unimpeachable virtue was an integral component of the two emperors' public images. There was also a more general cultural tradition of reverence for past examples of exalted women. Cornelia Africana, mother of the reforming Gracchi brothers, was one of the best examples in the late Republic and on into the imperial era.[22] Long after her death she was being portrayed as a moral exemplar just as women like Agrippina the Younger who were regarded as villains served as moral warnings.

The ancient sources include extended narratives, passing references, or anecdotes written down from decades to hundreds of years after the time these women lived. Each Roman historian had his own agenda, and it is always the case that our sources are male. The record of the Julio-Claudian women was one invariably compiled by men. It was weighed down in varying degrees with the prejudices of a society that had such a specific idea of the separate sphere in which women lived, or should have lived. The instinctive bias of Roman historians forms one of the biggest obstacles to understanding the Julio-Claudian and Severan women, though it also tells us much about the political, legal and social environment in which these women lived.

Very few of the Roman historians we rely on for the Julio-Claudian period had known or seen any of the dynasty's women in person. Most, like Tacitus or Suetonius, found their material by scavenging through imperial archives or in histories and other books that have not survived. Apart from Augustus' *Res Gestae* we have no autobiographical material either by the emperors, empresses or any other members of the imperial family. Roman historians also habitually only showed any serious interest in aristocratic married women. That was once they had become conspicuous members of the elite and were participating in public life and family arrangements. Unmarried younger women and girls are virtually ignored.

Evidently thoroughly enjoying himself from the moment he picked up his stylus, Suetonius had an eye for his readership, both then and in the future. More useful as a history is what remains of Tacitus' *Annals*, though this only begins with the reign of Tiberius and has not survived intact. Gaps exist throughout, including parts of the reigns of Tiberius, Claudius and Nero and, most frustratingly of all, the entire reign of Caligula. In a statement that could be seen either as monumental arrogance, naivety or just disingenuous, Tacitus announced grandly at the start of his *Annals* that he would tell his history 'without anger or partiality' on the grounds that he was sufficiently removed from the events.[23]

It is, needless to say, apparent throughout that Tacitus had a very clear agenda. He used subtle means to direct his readers. Women were used as devices to drive his narrative themes. One was that Livia had systematically manipulated opportunities to ensure her son Tiberius became emperor instead of Augustus' grandsons.[24] This has been amply perpetuated in our own era by Robert Graves's novel *I Claudius*. Such sources present us with enormous challenges, not least because of the tendency either to idolize or condemn female characters.[25] Agrippina the Younger and Poppaea are presented in part as the personalities with the masculine attributes that, in the opinion of Tacitus, Claudius and Nero ought to have had. Agrippina's ambition as Claudius' empress was also seen as evidence of his inability, or unwillingness, to keep her under control. Likewise, her conduct helped 'explain' Nero's degenerate behaviour. Using female characters this way helped to amplify Claudius and Nero's failings, just as much later Dio's account of Julia Domna's agony when Caracalla killed his brother Geta in her arms served to emphasize the barbarity of Caracalla's vicious personality. The real focus of the Roman historians here was on Nero and Caracalla rather than the truth about the female personalities involved.

Dio's history makes good some of the lost passages of Tacitus, as do a few other sources such as Josephus. Dio, who like Tacitus was a senator, is also one of the two essential sources for most of the Severan period. The other is Herodian about whose occupation and origins we know almost nothing, though he does refer to having been in some sort of imperial service.[26] Both were contemporaries and eyewitnesses of the Severans (Dio died about 235, Herodian sometime in the 240s or a little later). However, their accounts differ in some detail and represent a far less substantial record. This is especially true where the women are concerned for the Severan era, unlike the more extensive collected sources for the Julio-Claudian period.[27]

Despite the separation in time both Tacitus and Dio viewed imperial history with a sense of moralizing dismay at what monarchy had brought the Roman world. They also bemoaned the reduction of senatorial authority.

They of course had been influenced themselves, Tacitus most by the republican tone of Sallust. Tacitus and the majority of the other sources for the Julio-Claudian period, such as Suetonius, wrote in the first few decades of the second century AD. They were attracted to demonstrating and even amplifying the contrast between the perceived excesses of the Julio-Claudian era and the more restrained and dignified reigns of Trajan and Hadrian.[28] Tacitus was also beguiled by the appeal of a narrative in which disastrous outcomes like Nero's later reign could be traced back to earlier events or, more often, the defective personalities of his villains such as Livia and Agrippina the Younger and their ulterior motives.[29] Ronald Syme, one of the greatest modern historians of the late Republic and early imperial period, conceded that he had been 'unable to escape from the influence' of Tacitus.[30] Where truth blurred into caricature is often very difficult to unravel.[31]

Using often unsatisfactory sources of evidence Roman historians could mix up events or even people. Only rarely do we know what evidence or resources our sources had to hand. We know that they relied on a mixture of official records, private documents, published works, anecdotal information, tradition and their own invention.[32] Appian and Plutarch for example plundered the history written by Gaius Asinius Pollio during the reign of Augustus, which is long lost. Similarly, Tacitus credits Pliny the Elder as a source for his information about Agrippina the Elder's activities in Germany in 15. In truth Pliny had written at the earliest several decades after the event and that particular work is lost too. Substantiating Tacitus' claims is therefore impossible but in the context of the period quite normal. Reconstructing the movements of some of the key women involved, for example whether Livia or Julia accompanied their respective husbands on journeys abroad, is like walking into an impenetrable fog. Their presence was often not recorded and if it was then the miasma clears to offer only occasional references which scarcely ever go hand in hand with any kind of verifiable date.[33] Some of our sources, such as Macrobius, wrote so long after the events they describe (several centuries in his case) that their reliability has to be questioned though not necessarily with any confidence about drawing a definitive conclusion one way or the other. Dio's long and essential history survives in large part only as a late antique epitome of what he had originally written.[34] Much was lost or confused in the process of abridgement. Letters from the Julio-Claudian period, if they exist at all, normally only survive when quoted all or in part by a Roman historian who included them in another work. Aulus Gellius refers to reading a 'volume of letters of the deified Augustus written to his grandson Gaius', and quotes from it, but the collection is otherwise unknown.[35] We have no way of knowing whether any of these quoted letter texts are bowdlerized.[36]

One of the features of academic studies of the ancient world, or indeed any period in history, is the very different positions adopted based on what seems to be absolutely certain interpretations of often quite indifferent, vague or insubstantial evidence. We also have to deal with sources written in either Latin or Greek. Anyone with even modest proficiency in either knows that ambiguities and other difficulties of meaning abound in both languages, resulting in translations that often subtly or even substantially differ. The potential also for allusions or other oblique references that we simply do not recognize is considerable. These complications are made worse by the errors in transmission from antiquity. The histories that we have are texts that escaped vaporization during the Middle Ages, being copied in monasteries whose archives were then plundered by the energetic and eagle-eyed printers of the Renaissance searching for material to publish throughout Europe. When more than one medieval copy survives it is instantly apparent that the texts usually differ in detail. Sometimes this has significant consequences for understanding the meaning. Often there is uncertainty about which text is the correct one, leading to inconclusive and arcane scholarly debate. Much else was lost along the way.

At best then the written evidence is often challenging, fragmented and ambiguous, if it exists at all. The chance of finding any new evidence that might resolve an issue once and for all is extremely small. Certainty will remain elusive. The problem continues on into modern works. Any historian of the ancient world, including this one, struggles to know how far to go with the evidence available. This becomes especially apparent with full-length biographies of prominent individuals such as Livia or Antonia Minor. These almost invariably stretch what we know beyond breaking point. Any evidence, however peripheral, is rounded up and incorporated, accepted or refuted as necessary to reconcile it with the theory being expounded.[37] This can also result in one author's speculations or assumptions being interpreted by others as facts and repeated as such.[38]

It is also quite possible that the more remarkable claims made by Tacitus and Suetonius, among others, had at least some and perhaps even a significant

ever existed. One thing, however, is certain. The Julio-Claudian and Severan dynasties were recognized to have been remarkable periods in their own times, and the women who played so important a part in them amongst the most memorable individuals in the history of the Roman Empire. Before we can start to explore their stories though we must begin by considering where women were positioned in society, what was expected of them, and how they were either venerated or condemned for the way they conducted themselves.

1

VIRTUE, HONOUR AND CHASTITY

The role of women in the Roman world was both sharply defined and strangely ambivalent. Women had no formal political role: they could not vote or hold office. They were defined by their relationship to the men in their families, as wives, mothers or sisters. Elite women were expected to live by the highest standards of moral and sexual virtue (pudicitia), qualities which enhanced them and their families. Women of high status were habitually used in arranged marriages to form social, political and economic alliances between families and had little say in what happened to them. However, women could also exert enormous informal power and control. By the late Republic some women were earning reputations for themselves as highly educated and influential players on the political stage. Some were seen as dangerous threats to order and stability. The lack of formal political status turned out in some ways to be an advantage under the Empire. Women in the imperial family became a prominent, even dominant, part of the regime's image but were not restricted by the limitations of office. Moreover, some of them began to challenge what was expected of them by the forces of conservatism.

'What business has a woman with a public meeting?' asked Valerius Maximus, who went on to answer his own question, 'If ancestral customs be observed, none.'[1] In public life women could normally only hold some honorific roles such as a priestess and even that was restricted to women of status. Otherwise they were expected to act as dutiful daughters, wives and mothers. Women could be venerated if they lived up to the exacting standards of chastity, virtue and honour expected of them and condemned if they did not.[2]

These traditions stretched back over centuries. There was a long-standing belief held by Roman traditionalists that women had the potential to undermine the state to a disastrous level because of their susceptibility to temptation and degeneracy. The 'rape of the Sabine women' took place in the earliest days of Rome's mythical history when Roman men seized neighbouring Sabine women in order to force them to become their wives. On the face of it the purpose was simply to increase the opportunity for procreation, which was becoming a crisis thanks to a shortage of suitable Roman women. It was also obviously an exercise in asserting power and using women as reproductive commodities. The best looking had even been previously earmarked for the leading senators and were carried off accordingly by gangs. A war followed when the Sabines set out to recover their women. Tarpeia, a young Roman woman, betrayed her city when she sought and accepted the promise of golden bracelets from Tatius, king of the Sabines, in return for letting some of his soldiers secretly into Rome. Once inside the Sabine troops killed her out of contempt for her treachery to her own people.

The message was clear: greed leads to betrayal. Pinning this on a woman's weakness suited the Roman sense of where the problem lay and reinforced the prejudice against women having power of any sort. The war was only brought to an end by the Sabine women's intervention in which they blamed themselves for the disorder. 'Turn your anger onto us. We are the cause of war,' they said, offering to die rather than be the reason for the conflict. Peace was almost immediately agreed and the Romans and Sabines settled down to a cooperative future.[3] Even if the story was pure fabrication there was also something prescient about the Sabine women's role as peacemakers and in their indispensability to the early men of Rome. Conversely, Tarpeia served as an allegorical warning about the damage women could do to Roman civilization, and therefore as the precise opposite of what a Roman woman should be.[4] At least Roman women of a later generation showed themselves to be made of sterner stuff. In the aftermath of the Gaulish capture of and withdrawal from Rome in around 390 BC the city was confronted by an alliance of enemies from other nearby cities demanding that Roman women be handed over. The population of the city fled in a rout called the *Poplifugia*. However, volunteer Roman maidservants were sent over to the enemy to get them drunk. They then climbed into wild fig trees (*caprifici*) to signal to the Romans to launch a surprise attack. This was so successful that the occasion was celebrated thereafter on 5 July with women sacrificing to Juno Caprotina under a wild fig tree.[5]

Roman male ambivalence about women was very resilient. In 195 BC Roman women mounted a protest against the lex Oppia of 215 BC which was supposed to prohibit their public displays of luxury in the form of purple and gold. It was a provision brought in during the Second Punic War (218–201 BC). The law limited women to owning half an ounce of gold or clothing with purple borders in order to stop them wasting money on luxuries during a national emergency. In the aftermath of the war it was felt by many women and some men that the return to prosperity meant that the law should be torn up. According to Livy the women's protests amounted to insubordination because they could not be controlled by the imperium ('command') of their husbands. Marcus Porcius Cato was described as speaking up for the law, observing that 'vices, avarice and extravagance' were the plagues that destroyed all great empires. He claimed he had only restrained himself when walking through the Forum through a 'swarm of women' (*frequentia mulierum*) out of respect for a few individual women who had been behaving properly. In other words, the inability of some women to control themselves, their refusal to be subject to their husbands, and their inclination to exhibit degenerate behaviour threatened the state. Cato also spelled out the proper place for women, outside the sphere of public affairs.[6] There was an alternative point of view, put by the tribune Lucius Valerius at the time: women should stay under the guardianship of men but not to the extent of enslaving them – they had after all willingly contributed financially to the defence of Rome. He even pointed out the absurdity of prohibiting women from wearing purple when that was the colour embellishing the togas of men holding office. He won. The law was repealed. Lucius Valerius and his supporters might have been more liberal but even they only went so far – equality was not on the table, and certainly not a formal role in public life. Livy, who recounted this story some two hundred years later, doubtless had in mind the increasingly assertive nature of some elite women in his own time. Valerius Maximus put the women's obsession with 'refining their personal adornment' on this occasion down to their *imbecillitas mentis*, 'mental weakness', though he was generous enough to suggest that 'denial of opportunity' had not helped.[7]

Women were thus depicted all too easily as chaste and modest heroines or self-indulgent and dangerous liabilities. Nothing had changed by the Julio-Claudian period as Valerius Maximus' comments illustrate. The notion of contrasting personalities to the point of caricature was a favourite trope of ancient Roman historians. It was by no means restricted to women but their depiction seems to have been more polarized. Female members or associates of the imperial house were useful when they could be depicted as stock characters. Favourite characters were the promiscuous and immoral, the schemers and the duplicitous, or the venerated and idolized Roman matrons. Augustus' granddaughter Agrippina the Elder was a woman whose exalted morality and popularity with the army earned her the undying admiration of traditionalists like Tacitus. Conversely, Agrippina the Younger was enthusiastically portrayed as the epitome of the decadent and opportunistic political self-server with the added titillation of the whiff of incest. These characteristics were fielded as thoroughly undesirable, while simultaneously serving as indispensable components of a gripping story. More complex, and beyond the scope of this book, is the extent to which the Roman world's preoccupation with the violent domination of women, slaves, prisoners and animals had a disturbing psycho-sexual foundation.[8]

Female attributes were identified as demeaning characteristics of certain men, especially those who fell prey to luxury and vice. They were damned for being 'effeminate' because they were threats to the Roman male sense of identity.[9] Accusations of effeminacy or allusions to men having the defects of fallen women were also part of the wider cut and thrust of Republican politics. They served as the basis of insulting jokes. Sometimes the victim gave as good as he got. Cicero recounted a tale about Quintus Opimius, consul in 154 BC. Opimius decided to tease a man called Egilius because he was considered effeminate, saying: 'What say you Egilia, my girl? When are you coming to me with your distaff and wool?' Egilius, a notorious wit, fired back with 'By Pollux, I do not dare for my mother has forbidden me to go near infamous women.' In this instance Cicero described Egilius as seeming *mollior*. Although the word meant literally 'tender' or 'delicate', it was also used disparagingly to suggest that a man was weak and womanly.[10]

The Latin word *effeminare*, 'to make feminine', meant far more than it does in modern English. It also suggested an enervating effect and a slide into luxurious self-indulgence. In other words, 'female' attributes were potential symbols of degeneracy. Nero was an emperor perceived as devoid of any of the necessary masculine characteristics of a Roman male authority figure. Dio created a speech for the British tribal leader Boudica in which she said that 'the Mistress Domitia Nero' was 'in fact a woman, as is proved by his singing, lyre-playing and beautification of his person'.[11] The 'speech', which included sneers at the Romans for being ruled by Messalina and Agrippina beforehand, was a complete fabrication. It served simply as a medium for Dio to denigrate Nero in terms his Roman readers would have understood and relished, and allowed him to pour scorn on the Roman people for allowing themselves to be ruled by Nero and two women. Boudica was presented as the precise opposite of Nero: a woman who had all the masculine characteristics he lacked and who led a rebellion in Britain that nearly lost the Empire a whole province. In her 'speech' Boudica celebrated the warrior qualities of her British men and women, and mocked Roman men in general for their effete indulgence in luxuries, homosexuality and enslavement to a poor-quality lyre player. The portrayal of Boudica is unsubstantiated but belonged to a tradition in which strong and assertive women closer to home could be used to make points about villainous or inadequate men.

Women in the Roman world were both trapped and liberated by the Roman political and legal system. This is evident under the Julio-Claudians and the origins of this contradiction stretch back to the earliest times. Women were supposedly controlled by men within the structure of the family. Exploring the dynamic between tradition and change when it came to the role of women as powerful and influential figures is an essential part of understanding the evolving nature of the Roman world. This is complicated by the fact that the Romans to a large extent did not themselves necessarily recognize how the political and social role of women was changing. If they did, then there is some evidence that they suppressed or ignored it. In polite society, traditional attitudes continued to prevail.[12] These old ideas were based on the belief that women suffered from weaker intellects and that they therefore needed to remain under the supervision of guardians. It was taken for granted that 'the male sex as a whole is far superior in skill and is cleverer'.[13] There was even the phrase *fecit errorem muliebrem*, 'he made a womanly error', meaning that a man had made a mistake only a woman would normally be capable of making.[14]

Women were also restricted by law in various other ways, including being prevented from inheriting more than 100,000 sesterces. 'Law, passed for men's

their number invited to select who was 'the most blameless of the sex'. The winner was Sulpicia, wife of Quintus Fulvius Flaccus, 'placed above them all for purity'.[24]

This must help explain the compromising of the ancient plebeian cult. A woman's success in achieving, maintaining and displaying her sexual virtue this way would not only reflect on her but also her family. It was correspondingly fragile. *Pudicitia* could be destroyed by anything from gossip, unexpected circumstance and infidelity to an error of judgement. 'The supreme honour of a woman's triumph' was how well and honourably she had performed in her marriage, said the Augustan poet Propertius.[25] Propertius also thought *pudicitia* was particularly vulnerable to the challenges of unsettled times because of the breakdown of social order. One of his elegies slated Tarpeia and her treachery. A century later Juvenal put down the outbreak of immorality to the destructive effects of luxury as Rome grew wealthy, indulging in a nostalgic fantasy that poverty and living in primitive huts 'in the good old days' had forced women to be chaste through lack of opportunity.[26] Valerius Maximus recounted the punishments meted out to women whose reputations had been damaged, such as the daughter of an equestrian called Pontius Aufidianus, who killed her after learning that she had lost her virginity to her tutor, a slave.[27] A woman with immaculate *pudicitia* was obviously an asset of enormous family prestige. No man wanted to be married to a woman whose *pudicitia* had been questioned.[28]

The annual ceremony of the Parentalia commemorated the ancestors with whose prestige their descendants were imbued. Roman society focused its emphasis on the durability of the *familia* of which the senior male, the *paterfamilias*, enjoyed virtually monarchical powers, yet did so in a society that refuted such an idea. He possessed complete power over all the members of his *familia*. This included his immediate family, his relatives and also the staff and slaves of his household. The identity of each family was explicitly male. Female members were generally named according to the *gens*, a word best translated as 'family' or 'clan' in our modern sense of an extended family. Thus the female members of the Julii were generally named Julia; those of the Cornelii were named Cornelia and so on.

The *materfamilias* ran the *domus* (the 'household') as the *domina* for her husband. The word *domina* means literally 'mistress' and was the title used to refer to the mistress of the household and ladies of status. This was how the women of the Julio-Claudians were referred to and addressed, whether empresses or not. The *domina* was central to the household's spiritual and everyday welfare, her identity being subsumed into that purpose. Educated and assertive women of high status could, and did, command remarkable influence, especially when it came to the interests of their family. Elderly women who had proved their standing were accorded the privilege of a public speech at their funerals.[29] It was expected that the *materfamilias domina*, far from retreating into the shadows as her Greek equivalent did, should take a full and active part in company and be a prominent part of the household. The contrast with Greek women was something first-century BC Romans were proud of.[30]

Cornelia Africana, the widow of Tiberius Sempronius Gracchus the Elder (d. 153 BC) and daughter of the celebrated general of the Second Punic War, Publius Cornelius Scipio Africanus and his wife Aemilia, oversaw the education and development of the three of her twelve children who survived to adulthood. Her parents were known for the way they had embraced new ideas about luxury and culture which resulted in an education Cornelia had greatly benefited from. It was this background that played such an important part in the rearing of Cornelia's children and the role she played in developing their political ambition.[31] The two boys were the reforming Gracchi brothers, and the third child was Sempronia, wife of the general Scipio Aemilianus.[32]

Cornelia was admired and respected in her own time and afterwards for her astute political judgement. She believed that her younger son Gaius' determination to seek revenge for his elder brother Tiberius' assassination by a senatorial mob in 133 BC threatened the stability of the state, though she had felt in principle that Tiberius' reforms were valid. In 124 BC she begged Gaius not to stand for the position of tribune of the plebs until after her death.[33] She also persuaded Gaius to abandon a law he had passed that meant a magistrate who had been deprived of his position by due process was prohibited from standing for office again. The law had been expressly made to prevent a tribune called Marcus Octavius, deposed by Tiberius Gracchus, from being re-elected. Cornelia saw that this obvious act of legal revenge could serve no useful purpose. The withdrawal of the law was welcomed by the people. Cornelia must have known that it would be. Her involvement only increased her standing.[34] Cornelia's actions in no sense damaged her relationship with her son. Gaius fiercely defended her against any critics, in one instance accusing an opponent of 'effeminate' tactics by daring to insult a woman of such enormous esteem. It was an example of scathing Republican political humour, used to excellent effect later against Antony.[35]

Cornelia's literary skills were well known. 'We have all read the letters of Cornelia, the mother of the Gracchi, and are satisfied, that her sons were not so much nurtured in their mother's lap, as in the elegance and purity of her language,' said Cicero more than half a century after her death.[36] Evidently her correspondence had been published to wide acclaim, though none has survived. Cicero proceeded to cite other women whose conversation he had admired. Cornelia's reputation for her 'extremely learned speech' and literary and intellectual abilities endured. She was also remembered for acting as a patron of intellectuals, and as a supreme example of Roman womanhood. In old age she held open house for 'literary men', recounted her sons' lives with pride and was esteemed for her nobility and magnanimity.[37] This helped her escape the opprobrium heaped on certain notorious women. It was acceptable for a Roman woman to be educated but only if she used it for the greater good of her family and Roman society, and continued to operate within the moral boundaries defined for women.

Cicero's point was that women were just as important for the education of their children in the home. Roman mothers, especially those of high status, were not supposed to act as indulgent and benevolent sources of emotional security. That was the job of household staff. Instead the responsibility of mothers was to supervise their offsprings' moral and intellectual development. They should challenge any misdemeanours, inappropriate conduct or other deficiencies with fierce admonishments even when it was not the child's fault. After all, as Horace said, 'It is only from the sturdy and the good that sturdy youths are born,' by which he meant not just the inheritance of resilient bodies but also morality.[38] Looking much further ahead, Antonia Minor's treatment of her daughter Livilla, following her affair and conspiracy with the treacherous praetorian prefect Sejanus, was therefore only to be expected. So also was her verbal cruelty to Claudius, her handicapped son.[39] Far from damaging her reputation, Antonia Minor was held in enormous esteem in her lifetime and posthumously in part precisely because of the way she handled her children. Claudius was one of the main agents in formalizing his mother's high standing in perpetuity.[40]

Cornelia Africana was an unusually conspicuous woman, but she still operated within the conventional framework of Roman female life. She willingly defined herself in terms of being her famous father's daughter, not least because that was how everyone else would have seen her. She was also defined by her mother Tertia Aemilia, a woman who had chosen to overlook her husband's interest in a slave girl of the household. This was thought noteworthy because a wife should not seek to damage her husband's mighty reputation by calling into question his self-control.[41] Cornelia's sons had had remarkable, indeed notorious, careers but left no descendants. Cornelia could be admired and respected without any later associations through her role as her father's daughter alone. Caesar was all too aware of how his career might affect his mother, Aurelia Cotta, in the eyes of posterity. On the day of the election for chief priest in 63 BC, a post he had used bribes and every other possible political manoeuvre, crooked or otherwise, to secure, he warned her that she would later that day see him either elected or an exile.[42]

Tales from earlier Roman history, like that of Tarpeia and the Sabines, could serve as warnings to women who failed to restrict themselves to being moral symbols and reproductive accessories. Around 420 BC a Vestal Virgin called Postumia was falsely accused of committing a sexual offence and put on trial. Postumia was known for dressing well and had a reputation for her witty conversation and talking freely. Her conduct, as far as Livy was concerned, was manifestly inappropriate for a young woman. Therefore it was quite understandable that the allegation of sexual impropriety had been made. In short, she 'deserved it'. Postumia escaped being found guilty but she was warned by the then chief priest (*pontifex maximus*) to dress more suitably in future and to cut out the wisecracks.[43] Postumia was lucky. Vestal Virgins who failed to observe their strict code of chastity were liable to drastic punishments ordered by the *pontifex maximus*. These could involve being buried alive in a small chamber and slowly starved to death. This method of punishing a Vestal Virgin was the only official method of condemning a woman's memory that existed in the Roman state during the Republic.[44] Under the principate some women of the imperial family, especially Livilla and Messalina, presented new challenges. They were posthumously treated accordingly with sanctions hitherto applied only to men.[45]

Livy wrote his history of Rome during the Augustan era. Incorporating Postumia's story and his judgement of it reflected the mood of the times in which he wrote just as much as it reflected fifth-century BC Rome. Moral warnings and all the other expectations of cast-iron probity formed the basis for Augustus' use of the women in his family, the way he depicted them to the Roman public, and his broader expectations of Roman aristocracy. One of the most impressive surviving funerary monuments of Rome is the Tomb of Caecilia Metella on the Via Appia close to the third milestone south of the city. She probably died during the earlier part of the reign of Augustus and had been married to one of Caesar's supporters, Marcus Licinius Crassus (d. 49 BC).[46] She was also the daughter of an ex-consul who had won a victory in Crete in 62 BC and been awarded a triumph. The substantial 11-metre- (about 36 foot-) high drum-shaped mausoleum sits on a prominent hill and owes its survival to its conversion into a fortress in the twelfth century. The tomb was, and remains, very conspicuous but its commemorative inscription is perfunctory, stating simply that it belonged to 'Caecilia Metella, daughter of Quintus (Caecilius Metellus) Creticus (wife of Marcus Licinius) Crassus' (plate 2). Caecilia Metella, whose achievements, skills or other edifying characteristics (whatever any of those were) are completely lost to history, was thus primarily celebrated as the wife and daughter of exalted men.[47] Their names would have been well known to other persons of quality, their clients, and their enemies. The tomb was therefore mainly about those men and their families, and the esteem their connection through marriage brought them. In short, even though the tomb was ostensibly Caecilia Metella's, it really served as an advertisement hoarding for her deceased father and husband's individual and collective status and the prestige it brought their families thereafter. One of the beneficiaries will have been Crassus' son of the same name who was consul with Octavian in 30 BC.

The same even applied to the far better-known Cornelia Africana. In certain contexts, despite her reputation for education, she too was liable to be defined to posterity by her role as a wife and mother rather than in her own right. The base of a statue of Cornelia displayed in the Porticus of Metellus and then its new guise as the Porticus of Octavia throughout antiquity labelled her simply as 'Cornelia, daughter of Africanus, [mother] of the Gracchi'. However, the reference to Africanus was a later addition used to obscure her motherhood of the Gracchi, which was how she had previously been commemorated in the text. Her sons' reforming aspirations did not sit easily with conservative opposition to further reforms in the late Republic.[48]

Caecilia Metella's life was an example of how women were used to help aristocratic factions control the political arena through alliances, made or broken as needs required. Caesar's daughter Julia was married to Pompey in 60 BC as a symbolic and practical means of consolidating their political association. Julia's death in 54 BC in childbirth contributed in no small part to the unravelling of the relationship. Caesar also used the tragedy to emphasize his divine lineage. In 46 BC he instituted an unprecedented funeral games in Julia's memory on 26 September, the day of the festival of Venus Genetrix.[49]

Wives had other political uses. When his first wife, Cornelia, Julia's mother, had died in 69 or 68 BC at the age of twenty-eight, the young and ambitious Caesar spotted an opportunity.[50] He made a public speech in her honour at her funeral, something normally reserved for much older women. Caesar must have noticed a change in the perception of women because the gesture only enhanced his popularity, by showing that he was a 'tender-hearted man'.[51] The following year he made another speech, this time for his aunt Julia, widow of Marius, taking care to note her descent from Venus on her mother's side, and from the fourth king of Rome Ancus Marcius (c. 642–617 BC) on her father's, in a respectful but otherwise blatantly self-serving fashion that subtly revealed his ambitions.[52]

From birth a woman, especially in an aristocratic family, was earmarked as a dynastic, political and reproductive commodity. Men determined whom the women married, though 'girls' would be a better word; they were generally betrothed as children and married when they were no older than fourteen or fifteen at most, often to much older men.[53]

Women continued to be under the control of their fathers until they were twenty-five. Even so, women had far greater powers of self-determination in the form of property they owned as of right and their freedom to choose divorce, something that had been unthinkable until the third century BC.[54] Women could also enjoy more freedom after the death of their fathers, which conferred on them a higher degree of legal independence.[55] Cicero's wife Terentia owned both rural and developed property which she brought to the marriage and which they visited and managed together. She was also quite prepared to use creative accounting while her husband was away between 51 and 47 BC in order to siphon off some of the money under her husband's nose. Cicero found out. He discovered that she had helped herself to two thousand sesterces and there had been 'innumerable other incidents'.[56] That this had probably been her own money in the first place illustrated the kind of constraints women were kept under, and the subterfuge they might need to resort to.

By the mid-first century BC marriage had become more of a matter of mutual consent. That consent was theoretically as easily withdrawn as it was granted. For those marriages that had struck a rocky patch there was the opportunity to visit the shrine of the goddess Viriplaca on the Palatine. It functioned as a sort of primeval form of marriage counselling. There a husband and wife could rattle off their grievances and then head home 'in harmony'.[57] Where for whatever reason a marriage had broken down or turned into an inconvenience then divorce had become a relatively simple matter. No sooner had Octavian's wife Scribonia given birth to their daughter Julia in 38 BC than he divorced her to marry Livia. Livia, for her part, divorced her husband with similar ease, even though she had borne him two sons. Since Livia was already cohabiting with Octavian the new marriage was little more than a technicality. The match was as much based on mutual attraction as it was on any political advantage to be had. Octavian's dynastic machinations then, and as Augustus, show that he was determined to use the marriageable women in his circle in whatever ways he needed. This was regardless of their acquiescence or not in his schemes, just as would have applied in any other elite family.

Although Roman society was changing, there are plenty of instances that show established traditions had a long life. Pliny the Younger, writing around the early second century, was invited by his friend Junius Mauricus to recommend a suitable husband for Mauricus' niece. It is clear from the letter Pliny wrote to Mauricus that the request was quite normal. He took great pleasure in recommending a young man, making particular note of his looks and the bonus of his descent from a grandmother called Serrana Procula noted for her exemplarily strict propriety (*severitatis exemplum*).[58] We learn nothing about the young woman, but since she was probably only in her mid-teens it is unlikely that she had either the inclination or the ability to put up a fight.

A woman's role might also include the preservation and honouring of the memory of her father or husband if she outlived them. Cremutius Cordus was a Roman historian during the reign of Tiberius. His misdemeanour was to have praised Brutus and Cassius, a pro-Republican stance Tiberius could not stomach. He was prosecuted in 25 in a case brought by the praetorian prefect Sejanus' stooges. The outcome was a foregone conclusion, so after defending his actions Cordus committed suicide. His books were to be burned on the orders of the Senate. Before that could happen some were squirrelled away by his daughter Marcia and escaped destruction. For this guardianship of her father's legacy she was honoured in later years. Marcia had performed a service to Roman society by enabling people to find out 'what it is to be a Roman hero', said Seneca.[59]

Education was a critically determining factor in an elite woman's prospects, though educated for what mattered even more. The fact that women were married at a younger age than men unavoidably inhibited their education even if they came from high-status backgrounds (plate 4). They were also specifically not normally educated for public life unlike the males in their families. By the early first century BC it was becoming more common for Roman women of upper-class origins to benefit from the type of education once limited to males. Even so, a high-status girl was only likely to benefit from a more sophisticated education if a personal tutor was found for her. Quintus Caecilius Epirota, a celebrated freedman tutor, was hired for Caecilia Attica by her father, Cicero's friend Titus Pomponius Atticus. Unfortunately he was dismissed after being accused of improper conduct towards his pupil.[60] Caecilia Attica was already the wife of Marcus Agrippa (since around 37 BC when she was fourteen), a union that brought this educated young woman directly into the future Augustus' circle. By 28 BC Agrippa had married Octavia's daughter Claudia Marcella Major as part of Augustus' conciliated efforts to build up the Julio-Claudian dynasty, either divorcing Caecilia Attica or because she was already dead. Her fate aside, the experience of being educated at least to be literate appears to have become much more commonplace for aristocratic women by the days of the late Republic.[61]

Hortensia, daughter of the lawyer and orator Quintus Hortensius, was an exceptional example of a woman whose education and abilities enabled her to participate in public life – up to a point. She defended in court the rights of women whose husbands had been penalized by excessive taxation imposed on them by the members of the second triumvirate, Octavian, Antony and Lepidus. Hortensia's speech survived and was admired, not because it was the work of a woman, but because of its quality.[62] She was not entirely alone. Gaia Afrania who died about 48 BC successfully defended her own interests in court, acting before any of her male relatives could do so on her behalf. So too did Maesia, who defended herself so effectively that she was acquitted.

Hortensia, Afrania and Maesia were treading in dangerous territory. An educated woman could so easily be seen as a threat, especially when combined with a powerful personality and sexual allure. Valerius Maximus, our main source for Afrania and Maesia, particularly revelled in his disgust at Afrania's conduct. Afrania acted as she did, he said, because 'her shamelessness abounded' (*impudentia abundabat*) and with her barking (*latratibus*) she wore everyone out. The reduction of her speeches to the equivalent of animal noise was a particularly crude way of dismissing a woman. This attitude remains an issue for some female politicians even in our own time, as Hillary Rodham Clinton has described. In Roman public life it was bad enough if through a lack of physical robustness a man allowed himself to sound like a woman with her 'feeble shrillness'. Afrania's name became a nickname for 'women of shameless habit'. In the early third century the jurist Ulpian said that Afrania was the reason an edict was passed prohibiting a woman from representing anyone else in court and 'performing the functions of men'. Maesia was rewarded with the nickname *androgyne*, an ambiguous term that can be translated as a 'masculine, heroic woman'. The label in her case might have been a compliment. Alternatively it could have insinuated that as a result of her actions Maesia was neither a man nor a woman. Hortensia was forgiven by Valerius Maximus because she was only speaking up for women's interests.[63]

Participating in public life for women therefore, if it was managed at all, came at a price. It was treated as an explicit intrusion into a man's world. Valerius Maximus had commented on how women such as Maesia had been a matter of note precisely because 'their natural condition and the modesty of the matron's robe' had not kept them silent.[64] Sempronia was the wife of Decimus Junius Brutus, consul in 77 BC, and an enigma to her contemporaries. She was highly intelligent, educated, a poet, witty, gifted, charming and acutely conscious of her sexuality.[65] The result was her scandalous career in the limelight, including involvement in the Catiline Conspiracy (or War), which became a template for Roman moral outrage and perhaps conversely also for other women determined to escape the oblivion of compliant obscurity. Sallust's most damning indictment of Sempronia was that she had held nothing more cheaply than her *decus atque pudicitia* ('virtue and chastity'), actively pursuing men. Sempronia's actions were directly compared to the 'boldness of men', which in her case therefore were classified as 'many crimes'. Of course no man who behaved that way would have been judged similarly.[66]

The Romans, especially in the late Republic and early principate, were troubled by what they perceived as increasing immorality and decadence. These involved indulgence at almost any level such as luxurious building projects and were inextricably linked with what the Romans identified as female traits or deficiencies. This sense of unease was paralleled by extolling the fantasy masculine virtues of Rome's bucolic primeval origins where toil, self-sacrifice and honour were imagined to be the building blocks of what made Rome and the Romans great. Livy described the poverty of those good old days as part and parcel of contentment. This had justly brought the Romans great power and wealth but paradoxically simultaneously propelled more and more Romans into preferring excess to exertion, hedonism to honour and decadence to dignity.[67] Sallust identified the growth of *avaritia* (avarice), especially for money, and how 'virtue began to lose its lustre'. In his description *avaritia* is almost a miasma, a poisonous substance in the atmosphere that pervaded a man's body and soul and 'effeminated' him.[68]

Part of Augustus' self-determined remit was to reverse the tide of immorality. By the time he was in power the idea that aristocratic women at least had moved beyond some of the confines of traditional roles had clearly pervaded his own family. The fact that they could not hold office, regardless of their level of education, continued to inhibit their potential when it came to formal powers but paradoxically allowed them remarkable freedom to act as semi-autonomous agents in their own interests. The more astute female members of the Julio-Claudian family were able to exploit their special status by association, whether as wives, daughters or mothers. Actions they undertook or privileges they enjoyed were implicitly made legal by virtue of the fact that the men closest to them could do these things.

This way the Julio-Claudian women shared in and even reinforced what made the imperial family different from the rest of the Roman elite. Augustus allowed this because he knew their profile would strengthen his regime. At the same time he tried to engineer a restoration of what he regarded as a traditional and submissive role for women. Confining women to the uppermost galleries at gladiatorial shows and presumably other venues was just one example of his conservative measures.[69] This policy created conflict within the imperial family throughout the Julio-Claudian period. Augustus' daughter Julia and his sister Octavia both experienced the consequences of his conservative views.[70] Octavia complied, but Julia was not so acquiescent. Her resistance presented Augustus

Augustus' own infidelities were well known, but were excused both by himself and his friends as political opportunism, on the pretext that they allowed him to learn about the women's husbands' scheming.[79] Yet well into the days of the principate conservative values could continue to hold sway and were used to suppress any misdemeanours. In 19 during the reign of Tiberius a scandal broke about how Roman women of status were working as prostitutes in order to evade the legal sanctions imposed on 'normal' women for sexual misconduct. The traditional view, at least in Roman lore, was that a prostitute was sufficiently punished merely by admitting to her vices. This time, after a woman called Vistilia had advertised her availability, the Senate introduced measures to make sure 'the lust of females was curbed'. Women whose fathers, grandfathers or husbands were equestrians were prohibited from profiting by selling their bodies. Vistilia was banished to the island of Seriphos (in the Aegean).[80] Nonetheless, it is clear that a degree of respectability was sometimes attributed to the profession. There was a prostitute in the imperial period called Vibia Calybenis, a *lena* or 'madam', defensively commemorated on a family tombstone for earning her living 'without cheating others', presumably unlike other prostitutes. Even the word for a prostitute, *meretrix*, meant literally 'female wage earner'.[81] Another likely prostitute, Allia Potestas, was memorialized on an epitaph also of indeterminate imperial date. It recorded her respectable virtues as a matron before moving on to some ambiguous compliments that appear to record how much more she cost than other prostitutes and her cleanliness in the Forum.[82]

The supreme irony of the Messalina crisis was that Claudius, oblivious to what was going on, had to be told by a favourite prostitute of his called Calpurnia, she being put up to the job by his freedmen. Remarkably, Claudius, who was initially stunned by the news, had to have the horrible truth confirmed by his other favourite prostitute, Cleopatra.[83] While the occasional dalliance with prostitutes does not necessarily bear comparison with a bigamous marriage as the basis of a coup, the hypocrisy is still quite apparent; at the time it would have been inconceivable to regard it as such.

The brutalization of women was a very real part of Roman society. Women were likely to be venerated, so long as they unquestioningly followed and obeyed their husbands, bore children and performed their duties.[84] Often they were younger than their husbands and in many instances this seems to have amplified the virtual parent–child nature of the marriage.[85] When women were perceived to have stepped outside the constraints of the decorous behaviour expected of them they were all too susceptible to condemnation and even violence. After Nero kicked his empress Poppaea to death in a rage he appears to have escaped any real and sustained degree of moral opprobrium beyond casual jibes other than from himself (plate 26).

The unpalatable truth about Nero's tirade is that he was behaving in a way that was regarded as being largely acceptable under the alleged circumstances. This was especially so given the suggestion by the sources that she had dared to question his behaviour. Tacitus commented that while Poppaea's death was sad it had been welcomed by anyone recalling her 'immorality and savagery'.[86] This sort of attitude was enshrined in Roman lore which was still being circulated in the first century AD with the story of Egnatius Mecenius, a mythical figure attributed to the period of Romulus and Remus. Mecenius reputedly beat his wife to death for having drunk wine. For this he escaped punishment since his wife was regarded as having been at fault. This seems to have become part of a more entrenched tradition that women could not be allowed to drink. Traditionally women had been prohibited from touching wine on the basis that drinking led straight on to 'illicit love-making'.[87] Pliny reported that Cato had described how male relatives kissed women specifically to see if they could taste alcohol. Severely punishing women who misbehaved, for example a group who had 'made impure use of Bacchanalian rites', was considered an asset to society in general. In this case many were executed by their families. As late as the fourth century AD St Augustine was able to recall, with unsettling admiration, his mother's acquiescence as a victim of his father's violent tirades, and also to describe how women routinely bore the scars of their husbands' beatings.[88]

Juvenal's famous line *Quis custodiet ipsos custodes?* ('Who will guard the guardians?') is usually today regarded as a warning to people in supreme power about their bodyguards or security services. In fact the original context of the line could not have been more different. Juvenal was concerned with the intractable problem of keeping women under control. His friends were, so he claimed, constantly advising that a wife should be locked indoors. His riposte was that a woman, whatever her social status, was likely to start by using those placed in charge of her to serve as accomplices and go-betweens who could help her pursue illicit affairs. Moreover, Juvenal went on, a woman regardless of her means, 'never gives a thought to what her delights cost', handing over for example the 'last of the family silver' to an athlete who has taken her fancy. Men by contrast, he claimed, were more likely to prioritize the practicalities of avoiding cold and hunger.[89] Nothing could better sum up the tension between men and women at the heart of Roman culture. It was entirely predicated on one enduring Roman male tradition of seeing women as unreliable, unpredictable and destabilizing.

2

AGE OF THE IMPERATORS
CLEOPATRA, FULVIA AND LIVIA 44–31 BC

In theory women had no part to play in Roman politics or power structures. Caesar's dynastic ambitions were revealed by his adoption of his great-nephew Octavian in his will. This was the first stage in the creation of a Julio-Claudian dynasty. From the outset the role of women became increasingly important. The relationship was transmitted through the female line, establishing the mechanism through which the whole dynasty would be continued. The key moment in the enhanced status of women in the new era was when Octavian (Augustus) married Livia in 38 BC, causing her to divorce her former husband whose dangers and risks she had shared in the civil war. This decisive union contributed greatly to the image of the regime he proceeded to establish. Livia was well placed to have observed the ambitions of Mark Antony's wife Fulvia and the opprobrium heaped on her for her interference in political and military affairs.

Augustus came to power at a time when the role of Roman women was already changing. Whatever the general cultural context in which the women of the Julio-Claudian dynasty had to live, they were also subjected to the intensely complicating and supercharging effect of being members of the imperial family. They were not only very important to the identity of the imperial regime but also to the succession. The stakes were therefore a great deal higher than they were for other elite women. That meant there was more to play for. Like the men involved they were inclined in some cases to take risks and, like some of the men, they were liable to pay a similar or even greater price. It is in the nature of history to focus on the machinations of the great and powerful, regardless of the geographical or social imbalance. The drama that engulfed the Julio-Claudian family was very largely played out within and around Rome, especially insofar as the women were involved. Yet the implications and effects of what happened in Rome were felt across the Roman Empire, and that included the shift in the profile of women at the centre of the state.

Supreme power was one thing. Establishing a dynastic line of rulers was something else entirely. The Julio-Claudians were just another elite Roman family. Women functioned in the way that they would have been expected to in any family of high status. A woman's ability to bear children was generally regarded as the main reason for marrying her, rather than the prospect of enjoying her company. It was also inextricably linked with the quality of her family origins.[1] No wonder then that during the annual festival of the Lupercalia on 15 February women of high rank stood in the streets and held out their hands so that young men from noble families cavorting past naked could strike them with thongs cut from goat hide. The blows were thought to ease delivery for pregnant women and help barren women become pregnant.[2] At the time the occasion might have seemed like a light-hearted romp, though the experience must have been painful, but the challenges and dangers for women were very great. There was no guarantee that they would become pregnant, go to full term and give birth to a healthy baby, or even survive themselves. Pliny the Younger recounted with great sorrow how the Helvidiae sisters both died in childbirth though the babies survived.[3]

In the everyday Roman world, the succession within a family was transmitted from father to son in the role of senior male, the *paterfamilias*. This amounted to something much more than the prosaic and almost vulgar concerns of money and property. The son and heir would usually carry his father's name and in a spiritual and symbolic sense thereby effectively represent the continuity of his father. No wonder then that it was customary for a Roman home to display *imagines* (funerary images) of ancestors, which were also carried in procession at funerals; this was especially important for aristocratic families. Pliny's view was that 'there was no greater happiness than that all people for all time should want to know what kind of a man a person was'. It was treated as a form of immortality.[4]

However, the possession of supreme power in the person of the emperor introduced the challenging concept of how that power could be passed on. Since there was in theory no 'emperor' then in that sense the question clearly did not arise. And yet it did because Augustus' regime depended on maintaining the fiction that the Republic had been restored while simultaneously he wanted to ensure his family retained control of its interests through a man with the prestige, authority and offices commensurate with that level of power. Making arrangements for the succession proved to be one of the most intractable problems of Augustus' reign. It also brought the women an exceptional degree of significance and influence since the circumstances that affected the dynasty magnified their importance, and therefore their power and influence, to a level that could not have been anticipated.

The idea that descent through a bloodline conferred a monarch's qualities and principles on his successors was well understood, and loathed, in Republican Rome. Cicero defined any man who had power of life or death over other men as a tyrant who passed himself off as a king. In 509 BC the last of Rome's early kings had been expelled, leading to the basis of the Republican constitution through which the city was ruled by the Senate and the people. This new system operated as a self-regulating balance between the powerful and the ordinary people.[5] This was in many ways a sham, with the lower orders holding very little real power in practice.

There was therefore something fundamentally incongruous about creating a line of dynastic succession in the Roman imperial family. It was one thing to reject the idea of monarchical succession and quite another to come up with a reliable alternative that would keep hold of power and disqualify anyone outside the bloodline.[6] For all the faults of medieval kingship in later centuries the rule was relatively simple: a king should be succeeded by his son, both being backed by divine right. When a medieval royal male line failed, as it often did, a line was sustained through transmission to a brother or nephew, or at worst a daughter. Blood was everything.

In the Roman world with its ingrained disgust for anything that smacked of kingship, the way lay open to any potential challenger. That helped explain the decades of civil war and disorder which had torn the Republic apart. The regime Augustus established turned out to be the only workable solution but if it could not outlive him then it would have been a complete waste of time. The dilemma that faced Augustus was how to combine the stability of a ruling dynasty with a system that rejected the idea of one. Moreover, the succession strategy he adopted was not one followed by the later Julio-Claudian emperors. Different circumstances in each instance meant different solutions but the reliance on the female line of descent remained a constantly recurring factor.

In Republican Rome the easiest way to destroy a political rival was to accuse him of having ambitions to be king. This was precisely what had happened to the reforming tribune of the plebs Tiberius Gracchus in 133 BC. The allegation that he had sought kingship lasted long after his murder at the hands of a senatorial mob.[7] Caesar wanted supreme power for himself. That did not apparently even have to be in Rome. He famously once said to the inhabitants of a poor Alpine village that he would prefer to be 'the first man here than the second in Rome'.[8] In 44 BC Caesar's 'passion for the royal power' had been what the tyrannicides used to justify his assassination. Caesar had lurched dangerously and recklessly close to posing as sole ruler. When it was deemed necessary during a national crisis to grant one man supreme power the emergency post of dictator was explicitly temporary only. Caesar, however, was made *dictator perpetuus*, 'dictator for life', because by then exceptional measures were considered not only unavoidable but also desirable. That, and his overwhelming dominance of Roman politics, amounted to signing his own death warrant.[9]

It was not until Caesar's will was read that any evidence emerged of dynastic ambitions on his part. Even when these ambitions appeared, they were in a form that was entirely normal for a Roman aristocrat and his family and this brought with it the significant role of women in the Roman *familia*. Under the terms of his will Caesar was effectively transferring to the Roman state the normal process of perpetuating a family. Caesar had no suitable son. His sole legitimate child, Julia, born to his wife Cornelia, had died in childbirth in 54 BC while wife to his then political associate, Pompey. Caesar's third and last wife, Calpurnia, bore him no children, and neither had his second wife Pompeia.

In the absence of a son, either through a failure to produce one or premature death, the Roman world had a practical solution. The process of adoption was routinely employed though it could also take place just as an arrangement between families – a family did not have to be without a son for the adoption of another boy to take place. A male relative could be the beneficiary, or so also could someone else entirely whom fate and circumstance had brought into the family orbit. When the male line failed, the Roman aristocratic family normally resorted to adoption, a procedure that conferred full legal and social status on the adopted son who might have been a relative or not one at all.[10] The celebrated general of the Third Punic War (149–146 BC), Scipio Aemilianus, had been adopted by his cousin Publius Cornelius Scipio, son of Scipio Africanus. The English word 'adoption' does not really carry the full weight of the Roman meaning of the term. It meant that the adopted son was technically in every sense the same as a blood son.

Caesar's son Caesarion, born to Cleopatra in 47 BC, later 'ruled' alongside Cleopatra as Ptolemy XV but in 44 BC the child was far too young and too remote to serve in any meaningful sense as a suitable heir in Rome (plate 3). As the son of a hated oriental monarch, Caesarion could never have enjoyed currency as a Roman aristocrat and even less as a replacement for his father. There was an irony here. Cleopatra's ambition and ruthlessness made her Caesar's equal in many respects yet while she was vilified in later Roman tradition he was deified.[11] Caesar did what any other Roman aristocrat would have done. He looked to his extended family. He adopted the son of his niece Atia Balba Caesonia, the daughter of the praetor Marcus Atius Balbus and his wife Julia, sister of Caesar. Atia's husband was Gaius Octavius, hence her son's name. Gaius Octavius the Younger (now normally called Octavian) was only eighteen when Caesar died. Although both plebeian and an equestrian he had the crucial eligibility conferred on him by his mother's birth into the Julii.

Under the terms of Caesar's will Octavian was adopted as his son, and was given Caesar's name as well as three-quarters of Caesar's estate.[12] Quite what Caesar's intentions were beyond this, we do not know. He had undoubtedly spotted Octavian's potential and had a 'high opinion of his character'.[13] Whether Caesar had anticipated that the possession of his name would propel the young man to the point where he not only matched Caesar's power but also exceeded it will never be known. While adoption could have involved, literally, anyone deemed fit by the adopting father, in the case of the Julio-Claudian family adoption was applied by force of circumstance to eligible men whose line of descent was in the female line, starting with Octavian. Adoption only within the extended family became the basis of the succession policy adopted by Octavian when he ruled as Augustus.

By 44 BC Octavian had done little of note, which was hardly surprising given his youth. What little he had achieved had been by virtue of his family associations. As a sixteen-year-old he had greatly impressed Caesar by following him to war in Spain in 46 BC, even suffering a shipwreck en route as well as still recuperating from a serious illness.[14] When he was adopted by Caesar, Octavian became the next generation in a dynasty. Octavian was renamed Gaius Julius Caesar. He took every opportunity to subsume himself into the identity of Caesar's son and heir. Although it would take him thirteen years of war, alliances and ruthlessness to secure supreme power he did so as the head of the Julii. However, to avoid confusion with the dictator he is today usually referred to as Octavian until 27 BC when he became Augustus.

On 17 January 38 BC, now forging a military and political career that placed him at the centre of Rome's destiny, Octavian married the daughter of a deceased senator called Marcus Livius Drusus Claudianus.[15] How this union, by far and away the most significant political marriage of the whole era, came to be is a remarkable story in its own right. Livia's father had originally been known as Appius Claudius Pulcher, making Livia and her first husband very distant cousins through their shared descent from the sons of Appius Claudius Caecus (c. 340–273 BC).[16] Livia's father had been adopted by the reforming tribune Marcus Livius Drusus and therefore changed his name to Marcus Livius Drusus Claudianus, which Livia automatically inherited in its female form.[17] He had supported the tyrannicides, Brutus and Cassius, fighting with them at Philippi in 42 BC. He escaped ignominy because he took his own life after the catastrophic defeat and did not seek mercy. Such an honourable end only enhanced her father's posthumous reputation for bravery and nobility.[18]

Livia had been born at the end of January in 58 BC. This means that she grew up in a Rome increasingly disrupted by the collapse of the political association between Caesar and Pompey, and Caesar's rise to the position of *dictator perpetuus* prior to his assassination in early 44 BC. Livia was just fourteen when this decisive event took place. It is inconceivable that she could have had the slightest idea of how either the ensuing political and military chaos would be resolved or how her own prospects would turn out. Sometime between 43 and early 42 BC Livia Drusilla was married to Tiberius Claudius Nero, a man noted for his intelligence and honourable character.[19] Tiberius Nero had made his name under Caesar, fighting for him with great success and being rewarded with the job of establishing colonies for Caesar's veterans. Caesar's gradual and reckless lurch ever closer to a monarchical style of rule disturbed a great many Romans and Tiberius Claudius Nero seems to have been one of them. After Caesar's assassination he had openly supported the idea that the tyrannicides be rewarded.

In an age of chronic infant mortality and unpredictable adult lifespan, it was important for a married Roman aristocratic woman to start fulfilling her dynastic responsibilities as soon as possible by proving her fertility. One of the first references to Livia's early life in our sources is that recording the birth of Tiberius in Rome on 16 November 42 BC.[20] She had gone to some trouble to try and make sure she bore a son. The 'method' was for a woman to remove an egg from under a hen and then warm it with her own body heat and that of a nurse. This supposedly resulted in a male chick, a sure sign a woman would have a boy, or so it was said.[21] Livia obviously appreciated the enormous potential significance of bearing a son into a prominent political family. Giving birth so young was dangerous and it is interesting that Livia did not become pregnant again for several years. The marriage and the birth consolidated her membership of an esteemed old patrician Roman family, with a thoroughly mythologized tradition stretching back to the city's earliest days. It was said that the Claudii had been Sabines and that one of their surnames, Nero, was the Sabine word for 'strong and valiant'. Their line of descent through Livia was also to make them one of the two key ancestral families of the Julio-Claudian emperors.

During this early part of Livia's life she must have been aware of the rise to prominence of Mark Antony, a close political and military associate of Caesar. Antony's career had benefited greatly from the efforts of his wife Fulvia, thanks to the loyalty shown her by the *collegia* gangs of supporters of her first husband, Clodius Pulcher.[22] *Collegia* were associations which in their most benign form were legitimate trade associations or guilds. *Collegia* could also be gangs, sometimes consisting of criminals and thugs, who proved useful to politicians interested in having muscle on hand to intimidate rivals during elections. Pulcher's death at the hands of a political rival, Titus Annius Milo, in 52 BC was followed by Fulvia's very public grieving and presence at his murderer's trial, where Cicero spoke for the defence.[23] Fulvia's previous husband, Gaius Scribonius Curio, was a tribune and also fought with Caesar in Africa where he died in 49 BC. On the face of it these were personal catastrophes and ought to have earned Fulvia the undying gratitude of the Roman people for her sacrifice. Instead, because of her evident ambition she was regarded as stepping wildly outside an elite Roman woman's sphere. Fulvia earned the opprobrium of Roman historians or commentators, in her own time and thereafter. The deaths of her first two husbands were treated as evidence of her defective personality. With the benefit of hindsight and traditional Roman suspicion of female ambition, Antony's later career and fate were treated as proof of the effects of Fulvia's portfolio of degenerate characteristics. Naturally there was no need to supply any reliable evidence for making such accusations. Unsubstantiated allegations were quite sufficient to suggest that Antony was subservient to a woman and even sexually passive.[24]

Fulvia's first husband, Publius Clodius Pulcher, involved her in further damaging associations. Pulcher was particularly well known for his outrageous immorality. He was notorious for allegedly dressing as a woman in 62 BC so that he could trick his way into the women-only rites of the Bona Dea. His plan was to seduce Caesar's second wife Pompeia who presided over the cult. He also was accused for good measure of incest with his sister.[25] Clodius Pulcher was caught and sent for trial but Caesar's reaction is particularly interesting. He declined to give evidence because he knew Clodius' friends would ensure his acquittal. Consequently he was asked why instead he had divorced his wife. 'Because,' Caesar replied, 'I thought my wife ought not even to be under suspicion.'[26] Like any man of substance he knew any doubt about his wife's sexual virtue could damage him. An interesting aspect of the story is that Caesar's mother, Aurelia Cotta, a woman of impeccable virtue, presided over the household with an eagle eye. She had done everything she could to impede Pompeia's tryst with a man regarded as one of 'the most notorious evil livers of his time'.[27]

The lax morals of Clodius Pulcher allegedly ran in the family. His sister Clodia's unhappy marriage to Quintus Caecilius Metellus Celer led to her having a number of affairs, including possibly one with the poet Catullus.[28] Her liaison with Marcus Caelius Rufus became the most well known because Clodia accused her lover of an attempted poisoning. Cicero defended Caelius Rufus and used Clodia's infidelity as a stick with which to beat her, as well as referring to the rumours that she had committed incest with Clodius. 'Why had the vices of your brother more weight with you than the virtues of your father, your grandfather, and others in regular descent ever since my own time?' His purpose in criticizing Clodia was just as much to damage Clodius further.[29] These are yet more examples not only of the expectations of an aristocratic Roman woman in her own right but also of her importance as an accessory to a man of power, and indeed to his lineage (plate 2).[30] An honourable woman could enhance a man, and by the same token a dishonourable one could destroy him, just as Fulvia was later blamed for being an integral part of Antony's eventual fall. Cicero castigated Clodia to save Caelius and did so by showing how she had damaged her own family. A woman's moral rectitude was then an integral component of that of the morality of the men of her family as well as her husband.

Fulvia and her affairs offer us an exceptional opportunity to gauge how Roman women of rank were likely to be judged by posterity if they did not behave in the way that was expected of them. She also offered her contemporaries the opportunity to compare her with women who did behave appropriately. These included Livia who was surely able to see the dangers inherent for a woman in overt political activity. Livia was about twelve when Antony married Fulvia in around 46 BC. He was then Caesar's Master of Horse (*Magister Equitum*) and consequently second in Rome. It is quite reasonable to speculate that as Fulvia's political and military adventures became widely known Livia was affected by seeing what happened to her. This must have been especially the case after the assassination of Caesar in 44 BC when Antony, Octavian and Lepidus formed a triumvirate in late November 43 BC. As the triumvirs carved up the Roman world, Fulvia presided over politics in Rome, enjoying unprecedented power and influence for a woman. She was later accused by Dio of actively participating in the proscriptions organized by the triumvirs in Rome in 43 BC in order to pursue personal feuds and money, regardless of whether the victims had been intended targets. Hortensia, who successfully defended in court the financial interests of women damaged by the triumvirs' activities, provided a useful contrast.[31]

After the battle of Philippi in October 42 BC the tyrannicides' faction had been destroyed. The triumvirate ruled the Roman world which they had divided between them. By 41 BC the combined power of Fulvia and Antony was so great that the pair were effectively acting as the consuls in Rome, rather than the legitimately elected incumbents, with Fulvia's wishes determining Senate business.[32] In a remarkable and unprecedented move, even coins depicting her image were issued. They emulated those already being minted with the names and likenesses of the triumvirs. Martial reverse themes such as a soldier attacking a defended compound, or portraying Fulvia as a winged Victory only make the comparison more valid.[33] Nevertheless, her authority remained implicitly derived from her association with Antony. To reinforce the triumvirate Octavian had married Fulvia's daughter Claudia, Antony's stepdaughter, despite being already betrothed to someone else, but the arrangement was soon to break down.[34] Later on, in 37 BC, Fulvia and Antony's son, Antyllus (b. 47 BC) was betrothed to Octavian's infant daughter Julia, though this did not save the boy in the aftermath of Actium in 31 BC.[35] It was very significant that after Octavian married Livia he never issued similar coins of himself and Livia even once he ruled as Augustus, though some such pieces appeared in the provinces after he came to supreme power.

Fulvia then actively involved herself in the war that followed the breakdown of relations between Antony and Octavian, raising an army to support Antony's brother Lucius Antonius who was fighting Antony's cause in Italy while the triumvir was still in the East. She and Lucius claimed to be acting in Antony's interests though from the outset their campaign was disorganized. The basis of the conflict was over the right to allocate lands to veterans, with Octavian determined to take precedence over Italy. Lucius and Fulvia wanted to delay the process until Antony returned, to prevent Octavian taking all the credit. They fell out when Fulvia was advised that if war broke out in Italy then Antony would leave Cleopatra and come back; this was exactly what she wanted.[36]

In the event Fulvia occupied Praeneste (Palestrina), while the hapless Lucius became holed up in Perusia (Perugia) and was besieged by Octavian. Fulvia took charge of the defence of Praeneste, arming herself and giving orders to soldiers.[37] Octavian broke into the city, releasing Lucius unharmed and letting Fulvia go in February 40 BC. She escaped to Greece, but died there, allegedly distressed by Antony's criticisms of her for involvement in the war.[38] Dio suggests that her death might have been the reason that reconciliation was effected between Antony and Octavian, unless it was simply an excuse.[39] Either way, Fulvia's behaviour was presented as both destabilizing and inappropriate for a woman.

Fulvia's career made her a legitimate phenomenon. She had contradicted everything expected of a Roman woman, especially as a woman of quality, even though her conduct after Pulcher's murder ought to have made her widely admired as the embodiment of a dutiful wife. She had had devoted husbands, but she was not regarded as beautiful (she was said to have one swollen cheek). This suggests that she was unusual in the context of how

Roman women were pigeonholed and must have had considerable personal qualities.[40] The acerbic comments of Roman historians were founded in a long-established distrust of a woman who had the temerity to move outside her sphere. They flaunted their satisfaction at her ignominious end and completely ignored the way she stood by her husbands.[41] Such women represented a threat to male power. This invoked a sense of fear easily excited by tales of women who challenged the natural order.

Cicero pursued a campaign of words against Fulvia. It began with his defence of her first husband's killer when he described Fulvia as 'fatal' to her three husbands. He said also that she was in debt to the Roman people for each of them, and accused her of auctioning off provinces and kingdoms. For good measure he implied that Antony had had an affair with her while she was married to Pulcher. Running down Fulvia was an excellent way of damaging Antony.[42] She got her own back. Cicero was one of those assassinated by the triumvirs in 43 BC. Antony ordered the head and right hand to be cut off the corpse and displayed on the rostra where Cicero had so often spoken in public. Before the decapitation took place, in a peculiarly revolting gesture Fulvia allegedly spat on Cicero's head. Next she pulled out the tongue and spiked it with her hairpins while mocking him. The opportunity to depict a dangerous woman like Fulvia abusing what should have been feminine adornments was simply too good a story for Dio to let pass. Velleius Paterculus said Fulvia had 'nothing of the woman in her except her sex', castigating her for being responsible for *tumultus* ('disorder', 'agitation') thanks to her actions. According to Plutarch this was a woman who, incomprehensibly, had shown no interest in spinning or weaving and spurned ordinary men, preferring to seek the domination of a man who ruled or commanded. In their terms she was the perfect example of a woman who had not been contained within the rational and organized framework defined by men. She had therefore by definition become a danger to the state. Livia, who cannot have failed to be aware of Fulvia's public profile and fall, had surely observed that in order to take advantage of her own status she would have to be very much more oblique.[43]

Meanwhile the newly married teenage Livia found herself at the heart of a major political and military drama. In 41 BC with tension mounting between the triumvirs Tiberius Nero had started a war in Campania, leading the protest movement against the appropriation of lands in the aftermath of Philippi, and immediately attracting Octavian's attention.[44] At the same time Antony and Octavian had yet to settle their differences, though they were only to do so temporarily. Tiberius Nero was forced to abandon that position and after a series of movements via Naples in southern Italy and Sicily he eventually joined Mark Antony as a way of escaping from Octavian. He had with him Livia and the infant Tiberius, as well as the boy's nurse.[45] He had no choice if he was to protect them except that their son nearly cost them all their lives by crying. The young Tiberius burst into tears twice when well-wishers tried to relieve first the nurse and then Livia of having to carry the child.

It was, as Dio put it, rather ironic that Livia had been in the process of fleeing from a man with whom she would soon spend the rest of his life and that her son would succeed Octavian as emperor.[46] At some unspecified point during this flight Livia, Nero and the infant Tiberius took refuge in Greece after travelling via Sicily. So precarious was their safety that while in the care of the Spartans they were caught up in a forest fire that burned Livia's robe and hair.[47] Octavian and Antony were reconciled in a treaty drawn up at Brundisium in 40 BC. With Fulvia dead an important ingredient was the marriage of Octavian's widowed older sister Octavia to the widowed Antony. Using Octavia like this was only to be expected. Octavian was head of the Julii family and only acting as his deceased father might have done. His mother Atia had died in 43 BC. It was, however, the first time Octavian used a female relative this way. There would be many more such instances.

The prospect of political advantage was enhanced by the graphic contrast between Fulvia and Octavia. Octavia was and remained until her death in 11 BC a compliant and virtuous member of Octavian's family. The 'most illustrious and blameless' Octavia would turn out to be one of the key ancestors of the Julio-Claudian dynasty.[48] The emperors Caligula, Claudius and Nero were all descended from her through her marriage to Mark Antony, as was the empress Messalina who was also descended from her through Octavia's first marriage to Gaius Claudius Marcellus (see Family Trees 1a and 1b).[49]

A few years earlier Octavia had proved herself not only a woman of moral courage but also of guile and with a willingness to challenge her brother. The triumvirs had named Titus Vinius as one of those to be executed. His wife, Tanusia, hid him in a chest at a house owned by one of their freedmen. As a result it was believed that Vinius had been killed. Tanusia bided her time and asked Octavia to help. It was arranged that during a festival Octavia would make sure that only Octavian would come into the theatre, instead of all three triumvirs. This went according to plan and Tanusia was able to confront Octavian with the chest and her living husband. Octavian was so astonished that he let husband and wife, and the freedman Philopoemen, off.[50] It is obvious that Octavian could simply have ordered Vinius' immediate execution; the involvement of his sister in the ruse was almost certainly the decisive factor in staying his hand.

Octavian knew that arranging Octavia's marriage to Antony in October 40 BC would be of enormous benefit to consolidating the triumvirate, just as Julius Caesar had used his daughter Julia in his political association with Pompey. Antony's new wife was soon being advertised on coins issued by him in the East in 39 and 38 BC. Silver tetradrachms minted at Ephesus showed Antony and Octavia's portraits side by side on the obverse. Others, minted also at Ephesus and Athens, showed Antony on one side and Octavia on the other.[51] She also appeared with him on the bronze coins of the so-called 'fleet series' struck possibly in Greece. One of these used facing and jugate busts of Antony and Octavian to symbolize the political union between the two men.[52] By 37 BC Octavia had been sent back to Italy, allegedly for her safety.[53] This conveniently prevented her from cramping Antony's style as his relationship with Cleopatra became ever more serious. It culminated in their marriage in the winter of 37 BC, Antony explicitly declaring to Octavian that Cleopatra 'is my wife'.[54]

Meanwhile, Livia and Octavian are likely to have met in southern Italy by 39 BC while Octavian and Antony were trying to deal with Sextus Pompey and his pirate fleet. The Treaty of Misenum with Pompey temporarily solved the problem when he agreed to limit his sphere of control to Sicily and Greece.[55] For most of that year Octavian's wife Scribonia was pregnant with Julia ('the Elder') though the fact that she was bearing a daughter was of course not revealed until she was born on 30 October 39 BC. The appearance of a daughter rather than a son may have troubled Octavian. We do not know. Livia was also pregnant again, but some months behind Scribonia. Dio said that Octavian was 'beginning to be enamoured' of Livia and that that was the reason he divorced Scribonia as soon as Julia had been born.[56] It was alleged that Scribonia had had the temerity to object to Octavian having a mistress (Livia) whose influence was becoming too much to bear.[57]

In 38 BC Livia was in a tight corner. Her father's support for the tyrannicides remained a potential liability. Her husband's opposition to Octavian ought in theory to have compromised her further. Octavian was so smitten by Livia that any political issues or even matters of taste, given her condition, were blithely dismissed. There is no good reason to doubt Octavian's motivation. Livia had an excellent pedigree and he was highly attracted to her. She had also demonstrated her fertility and the ability to bear sons. There are other and better attested examples of power marriages which came about for some of these reasons, regardless of and even in spite of political considerations.[58]

Whether the attraction was mutual is less clear. There is no hint of Livia objecting to the summary divorce from Tiberius Nero and transfer to a marriage to her husband's former enemy, but it is unlikely she would have been able to do so. If she had spotted in Octavian a man of remarkable potential and happily acceded, then it was the most astute decision of her life. Physical attraction must have played a part in marrying Octavian. The sort of personality she later exhibited as empress also suggests that she surely decided from the outset that his chances were so great that her interests and those of her children would be best served by the union. It was too easy to see her acquiescence to marrying Octavian as a sign of her malevolent intent and proof that from the outset she was an opportunist and schemer, determined to see one of her sons become emperor. Matthew Dennison amusingly likens the Roman historians' depiction of Livia to that of Louis Mazzini, the fictional serial murderer of the celebrated motion picture *Kind Hearts and Coronets* (1949). Mazzini was determined to succeed to the dukedom of Chalfont. He did so by systematically murdering each of his relatives with a superior claim to his. Dennison has a serious point: the inherent absurdity of Mazzini's story, however entertaining, ought to demonstrate the basic implausibility of the notion that Livia proceeded to sustain an uncompromising programme of assassination to ensure her descendants ruled (as indeed they did). It should be equally easy instead to see that by marrying Octavian Livia was showing that she was a realist and only doing what was natural in the circumstances.[59]

Livia above all else understood that she was engaged in 'the exercise of power'. It was the simple fact that she was a woman behaving thus that troubled Roman historians who at the same time appreciated the storyline potential of portraying Livia as a calculating villain. If Livia was in any way inspired by what she must have known about Fulvia's role in Antony's career she also knew that Fulvia had destroyed her own reputation through her overt ambition. Livia was to demonstrate a far more astute sense of how to play the *pudicitia* card. She kept her reputation intact while becoming one of the most effective female political players in Roman history.

Inevitably the question arose, unanswered then and now, of whether Octavian was responsible for Livia's second pregnancy. If he was, it was never officially claimed. Tiberius Nero agreed to divorce her, perhaps under coercion. Livia and Octavian may already have been cohabiting.[60] The fact that she was six months pregnant was put to priests to ask whether it was legal to be married while carrying an unborn child. The priests concluded that if conception had definitely occurred then there would be no obstacle to the marriage. Under the circumstances, it was also quite clear that obstructing Octavian in his wishes would be a stupid thing to do. So the question of whether or not this was really an arrangement permitted by precedent and ancient laws was quietly buried. It would soon be joined there by other traditions. Octavian and Livia would never have any children, though she was subsequently awarded the honours normally only accorded women who had had three or more children.[61] Livia became pregnant by Octavian once, but the child was premature and either stillborn or died soon after birth. Pliny the Elder later concluded that the infertility they experienced was an example of what he called a 'specific physical incompatibility'.[62]

In the meantime Livia gave birth to her second son Nero Claudius Drusus on 14 January 38 bc. A curiosity of the marriage to Octavian that took place three days later was that her ex-husband Tiberius Nero acted in the place of his deceased father-in-law and gave away his own wife as the bride.[63] This volte-face on his part is so striking it cannot escape comment but defies explanation other than being the result of a timely case of political expediency and survival. For Octavian the acquisition of Livia was an important moment. The benefits were mutual though the risks were considerable. In 38 bc there was absolutely no basis for being able to anticipate the course of future events. He and Livia were gambling on a marriage contract that each expected to be to their individual and mutual advantage. The marriage represented a milestone in Octavian's incorporation into the old established Roman Republican elite and the development of a dynastic context for his march towards supreme power. It would also soon have the gratifying benefit of enhancing his image as a protector of moral standards and tradition.

The renewed war against Sextus Pompey which followed Livia's midwinter marriage had a disastrous start. Pompey soon reneged on his part of the bargain, though he must have also realized the triumvirate would never have left him as he was once they were in a position to remove him. Pompey built up his fleet, meaning that Octavian had to prepare for a major naval confrontation. Octavian's general, Agrippa, who was to play a key dynastic role in Octavian's regime, was given the job of creating a fleet in Italy.[64] The new fleet was laboriously built and its crews trained in Italy, only to be seriously damaged by storms and subsequently defeated by Pompey at Tauromenium (Taormina).

The triumvirate staggered on into 37 BC, shored up by the Treaty of Tarentum (Taranto). Mark Antony then headed out to the East and Egypt in search, as it turned out, of self-destruction. In 36 BC Pompey's luck ran out. He was catastrophically defeated at the Battle of Naulochus off the coast of Sicily and fled to Asia where he was killed on Antony's orders.[65] Antony's involvement with Cleopatra played perfectly into Octavian's hands by gifting him a sensational publicity opportunity. When he cuckolded his co-triumvir's sister for the sake of an oriental monarch, Antony personally destroyed his reputation in the eyes of many Roman people. He made it extremely easy for Octavian to paint him as a treacherous villain who had fallen under the control of a dangerous female enemy of everything Rome stood for.

This was all marvellously handy propaganda for Octavian, who used this chance to damn Antony for his immorality. He milked the opportunity with ill-disguised glee. Antony reciprocated in kind but he had little or no hope of winning over the Roman public, many of whom were easily persuaded that he was rotten to the core. A new war was looming like a vast thundercloud rolling in from the East. Dio later said Antony had become enslaved to the 'passion and witchery' of Cleopatra (plate 3).[66] Of course it was not entirely Antony's fault; blaming Fulvia and Cleopatra was a convenient way for Roman historians to avoid admitting that a man of Antony's status had been solely responsible for destroying himself. Plutarch observed that Cleopatra ought to have paid Fulvia for her success in training Antony, 'so docile and trained to obey a woman's commands was he when she [Cleopatra] took him on'.[67]

Antony's insult to Octavia amounted to a slap in the face for Rome. Cleopatra was about as unsuitable a partner for a Roman of his status as it was possible to be. His war in Armenia in 34 BC was followed by a triumph in Alexandria which included distributing territories, including Roman provinces, amongst Caesarion and Cleopatra's children by Antony, over which they would rule as monarchs. Crucially, this included creating Cleopatra and

Caesarion queen and king respectively of Egypt and Cyprus (plate 3). This implicitly 'legitimized' Caesarion as Caesar's son, not something that Octavian had any intention of accepting. It had the dangerous additional quality of a direct male line descent from Caesar. Since Octavian's entire image had been built round the idea that he was Caesar's 'true' son, he was unlikely to give all that up for the sake of his rival's obsession with Cleopatra. Silver denarii of Roman type were issued at Alexandria, showing Cleopatra on one side and Antony on the other following his well-established tradition of depicting his wives on his coins. The combined legends appear to mean 'the kingdom of Cleopatra, the kingdom of her sons, and of Antony, conqueror of Armenia'.[68] The message was clear, and represented a development from the coins struck in both their names in Syria up to two years earlier in which she was identified as a queen and Antony as a triumvir.[69]

Cleopatra was believed to have 'bewitched' Antony with magic, and the popular view that she wanted to rule in Rome made her a sort of bogey-woman.[70] Compared to Cleopatra, Octavia and Livia had impeccable credentials. Livia was only in her mid-twenties, Octavia her mid-thirties. Octavian commissioned statues of the two women and in a striking move in 34 BC awarded them the same inviolability enjoyed by a tribune of the plebs as well as the legal right to 'administer their own affairs', unfettered by having to defer to a guardian. These privileges augmented their qualities and virtues, and together benefited Octavian's authority, judgement and identity by associa-tion. The statues were a major innovation because they were public statues of women; the only precedent was the statue of Cornelia.[71] All these honours were hugely amplified by being compared to Antony's wretched treatment of Octavia. Octavia and Livia had also both demonstrated their fertility, albeit with other partners, which further enhanced their *pudicitia*. This also helped subtly promote the notion of a first family in the making.[72]

Octavian's triumviral powers had expired at the end of 33 BC. He had not made any arrangements to get them renewed because by definition this would have meant renewing Antony's too. Octavian was also stuck with the fact that he and Antony had previously organized the candidates for the consulship, which for 32 BC did not include him. Unfortunately, the prearranged consuls, Gnaeus Domitius Ahenobarbus and Gaius Sosius, were members of Antony's dwindling faction.[73] In a practical sense, Octavian could have simply ridden roughshod over the agreements – Antony was, after all, in no position to do anything about that – but it would have dented Octavian's need to pose as a man of honour and of his word. It would also have provided Antony with useful ammunition for his own propaganda machine. Fortunately, Octavian's standing was so high that Italy, Sardinia, Sicily, Spain, Gaul and Africa all decided one after another to swear loyalty to him personally rather than to the Roman state.[74]

The febrile mood in Rome together with Antony's actions amply proved that Octavian, naturally, was in no position to offer Livia either security or certainty. He was in the middle of one of the greatest political and military gambles in Roman history: Octavian's progression to supreme power was still far from guaranteed. Although Livia played no overt part in the dramatic politics and posturing, the very fact that Cleopatra was so important a component in denigrating Antony made Livia by contrast an implicit part of Octavian's profile.

The pace quickened on 1 January 32 BC when Antony used his new consul stooges, Ahenobarbus and Sosius, to denounce Octavian in the Senate but a tribune's timely veto saved the day. Octavian, who had kept himself out of the Senate and even Rome, now reconvened the Senate and marched in with a military escort and an armed group of his friends. The Senate and the two consuls were terrified into silence by the allegations he made about Antony and Sosius. Octavian then notified them all to come again on a future day when he would prove Antony's guilt. Ahenobarbus and Sosius made themselves scarce, and headed off to join Antony with some of his other senatorial supporters.

Octavian and Antony now presided over rival 'senates' in Rome and Alexandria. Octavian rattled off his accusations about Antony to what was left of the Senate in Rome. Antony used what passed for a senate made up of those who were still with him or who had joined him to declare that he was formally divorced from Octavia. Some of his senators absconded and went over to Octavian. They provided him with the dynamite intelligence that Antony's will contained the incriminating evidence Octavian so badly needed. Octavian commandeered the will from where it was stored by the Vestal Virgins and then read out its various explosive clauses to the assembled Senate. His actions in this regard were indisputably illegal but the will's provisions were so outrageous that no one cared. The clauses revealed that Antony had plans to leave important bequests to his children by Cleopatra, in addition to the lands given them in 34 BC. It was a colossal further insult to Octavia and therefore also to Rome. This led to speculation that Antony intended to hand Rome over to Cleopatra and rule from Egypt.[75] Even Antony's friends were horrified and swiftly sided with Octavian.

Before long the Senate voted for war, but specifically against Cleopatra rather than Antony. The reason was simple: by not being targeted personally Antony could be depicted as the victim of his own failings and of Cleopatra rather than of the Roman people turning against him. The preparations for the inevitable battle commenced throughout the rest of 32 BC.[76] Appian commented that 'whatever Cleopatra ordered was done, regardless of the laws of man or nature'.[77] That a woman with such power was deemed unnatural was the fundamental issue. Cleopatra's stay in Rome at Caesar's invitation over a decade earlier between 46 and 44 BC had cast a long shadow. She had only left Rome shortly after his assassination, once it became obvious that Caesarion was not to be declared Caesar's heir.

The upshot was that by 31 BC Antony's relationship with Cleopatra had damned him for eternity in many self-respecting Roman people's eyes. His behaviour had manifestly led to drastic political consequences; therefore, it was his immorality that was automatically perceived as the cause, as part of a broader cultural ideology of the negative power of immorality. Antony's fall was so precipitous that it was later regarded as even exceeding the record held up till then by notorious predecessors such as Philip of Macedon and Hagnon of Teos.[78] Be that as it may, it was entirely conceivable that the last act in this drama could have resulted in the defeat of Octavian and the end of Livia's prospects. Antony still had supporters and also had access to substantial resources from a large part of the eastern Roman Empire. Rome began to divide between factional affiliations to either the Antonians or Caesarians. It was a form of political polarization reminiscent, but on a much grander scale, of the political gangs the imperators had funded in the days of Caesar and Pompey.[79] The scene was set for the final showdown.

3

WOMEN IN THE AUGUSTAN STATE
31 BC–AD 14

*O*nce in power after the Battle of Actium in 31 BC Octavian, known as
*Augustus from 27 BC, set about manufacturing an image for his new regime
as the restored Republic but with himself solely in charge. Augustus was committed
to the notion that immorality and degeneracy were integral causes of the chaos of the
civil war period. Female immorality was regarded as particularly dangerous. He
was determined to reform the image of elite Roman women with a clear eye for
tradition. Cleopatra was also depicted as an example of a woman who had stepped
outside her sphere with disastrous consequences, and was used as a template of what
could go wrong. Augustus was assisted by supporters such as the poet Virgil, who
helped create an allegorical myth to celebrate his rule. Livia and Augustus' sister
Octavia became crucial features of the Augustan regime. They served not only as key
dynastic figures but also symbolized and embodied definitions of key female virtues
and personifications in Augustus' programme of moral reform for the Roman Empire.*

In the end, like most wars, Cleopatra and Antony's defeat at Actium on
2 September 31 BC was the result of a chaotic series of circumstances ranging
from Agrippa's superb military and naval leadership to Antony's bad decisions.
Antony had for example made his troops camp in a swampy area where none
of the resident malarial mosquitoes went hungry during his stay. The victory
was more to Agrippa's credit than Octavian's but that did not matter to
Octavian, who 'for the first time . . . held all the power of the state in his

hands', or Livia who had evidently made a very sound decision in 38 BC when she married him.[1] Actium was then and thereafter depicted as a triumph of order over chaos, of good over evil, and the manifest proof of Octavian's supreme *auctoritas* and influence. Accordingly, he proceeded to travel down through Asia and Syria to Egypt in pursuit of Antony and Cleopatra.

Believing that Cleopatra had already taken her own life, Antony committed suicide. Cleopatra sought an audience with Octavian and tried her best to play him. He refused to be drawn on his intentions while trying his best to reassure her. He wanted to discourage her from committing suicide so that she 'might add brilliance to his triumph'. The opportunity to show how his mastery of order had tamed her disorder was too attractive to miss. Cleopatra knew the humiliation would be unbearable. She decided to pretend to be supportive of Octavian and also Livia.[2] Evidently Octavian and Livia could already be perceived as a power couple, even if Cleopatra was only choosing to see them as a counterbalance to her and Antony. Antony's suicide saved Octavian the ignominy of having to execute a triumvir of Rome but Cleopatra's deprived him of the chance to parade her in Rome.

Octavian made sure that Caesarion, officially known as Ptolemy Caesar, was killed as he tried to make his escape into Ethiopia. So also was Antyllus, Antony's eldest son by Fulvia. Octavian was now about to rearrange his dynastic plans. With those two obvious dynastic rivals removed, the remaining three children of Antony and Cleopatra, two boys and a girl, were brought to Rome where it seems they were taken into Octavia's household and brought up.[3] The treatment of Caesarion and Antony's children was a calculated balance of uncompromising brutality and clemency, but at the time Octavian still had no child of his own by Livia. It is very unlikely at this date that he believed that would remain the case since Livia was still only in her late twenties. Cleopatra's sons by Antony, Alexander and Ptolemy, probably died as children because they are never heard of again, but the daughter, Cleopatra Selene, was used by Octavian as a pawn in his political dealings with client kings. In the mid-20s BC she became the wife of Juba II, king of Mauretania from 25 BC to AD 23, and bore him their successor, Ptolemy. Ptolemy was the second and last client king of Mauretania, being killed by Caligula in Rome in AD 40.

After Actium Cleopatra's image as the epitome of just how dysfunctional female ambition could be was immediately enshrined in Roman culture. She was an uncomfortable reminder of the self-inflicted chaos of the late Roman

Republic. Her destruction was also another of the prices paid for Octavian's triumph and the restoration of order. Erstwhile supporters of Antony and Cleopatra disappeared from view and by and large kept their mouths shut. Extolling the virtues of the new regime went hand in hand with venting as much spleen about Cleopatra as possible. As far as Horace, who died in 8 BC, was concerned she was a *regina dementes*, 'a mad queen'. She was so mad in fact that her insanity had driven her to 'crazy ideas' fuelled by Mareotic wine at the head of 'polluted' followers, who included 'shrivelled eunuchs' (*spadonibus rugosis*). The picture Horace painted sounded like an orgy in a freak show presided over by a drug-fuelled harpy who had lost her reason. It was a caricature and must have been recognized as one even at the time. However, the image still both cashed in on and amplified contemporary prejudice as well as serving as a means to help the Romans evade blame for the violence of recent years.

Having enjoyed himself with composing this fusillade of bile Horace conceded that by committing suicide Cleopatra had at least avoided plunging into the abyss. That way she had escaped the humiliating prospect of being part of Octavian's triumph in Rome. What Horace was saying of course was that Cleopatra had in the end found it within herself to do as a man would have. She showed 'no woman's fear' when she made the courageous decision to take her own life.[4] It was a theme Virgil developed for his depiction of Dido, another victim of Rome's supremacy, though he also took care to refer to Cleopatra's role as Antony's wife as a 'horror' or 'shame' (*nefas*). Like Horace he could not bring himself to name Cleopatra.[5] There was an element of ritual about slating Cleopatra's reckless ambitions, but it was an important part of asserting the Roman self-image of a culture built around the steely-eyed determination and restraint of a proper Roman man.

Antony had amply proved just how catastrophic it could be to drop one's guard. He was regarded more with pity than anything else. The vitriol was reserved for the female villain of the piece to avoid openly admitting that a Roman man of Antony's status could have fallen so far. Cleopatra thus served a symbolic and allegorical function. Perhaps the most remarkable aspect of the way Cleopatra was depicted was the incongruous fact that the statue of her Caesar had set up in the Temple of Venus Genetrix survived. It was still on display in Appian's time, and remained so another century later in Dio's. He reported, 'glorified . . . she herself is seen in gold in the shrine of

Venus'.[6] The truth is that Cleopatra was impossibly glamorous and has continued to be so ever since. Cicero, Horace and all those others who professed to be disgusted were also obviously tititlated by her. They simply did not know how to cope with their own reactions and overcompensated as a result. It was another manifestation of the confused way Roman men dealt with women but Cleopatra, by definition, lay outside their control in both life and death.[7]

Almost overnight the Roman world had fallen under the control of one man. Not only did that one man deny that this was the case but also virtually everyone else decided to indulge in the same pretence. Content with this self-delusion the Roman people proceeded seamlessly into being the subjects of a monarch. Caesar had not been an emperor, either explicitly or implicitly, even though by 44 BC he was without question the most powerful man in the Roman world and was clearly toying with what that meant. Octavian, once he assumed supreme power in the Roman world after 31 BC, never explicitly posed as an emperor and even considered restoring the Republic at this stage.[8] In the event he claimed to have restored the Republic but the reality was that he was effectively a monarch, reinventing himself as Augustus from 27 BC on. He had concluded (and convinced himself) that he would expose his person, and the state, to risk if he retired. Therefore it is convenient for us to regard Augustus as an emperor and Livia as an empress, and describe them as such, even though Augustus' official powers and privileges were designed to obscure the reality of his status. He did not, unlike a medieval monarch, rule by divine right or dynastic transmission of inheritable power. Augustus also moved quickly to consolidate his family's hold on power. A dynastic future was clearly part of that, with the women of that family playing now an even more important role than they already had. In this sense Augustus was transferring to centre stage the manner in which a Roman *familia* operated with the *pater-familias* and *materfamilias* at its heart.

However, the need to obfuscate the nature of Augustus' powers and to avoid the establishment of any constitutional monarchy and succession created serious problems with keeping the ruling dynasty in power. This contributed directly to the elevated importance of the female line of descent especially when the male line failed, as it consistently did throughout the period. This meant that Augustus took every opportunity to organize suitable marriages for his sister Octavia and his daughter Julia.[9] Indeed, no reigning emperor would father a son and successor until Marcus Aurelius over 150 years later.

Augustus' ideas about the identity of his regime marked a significant stage in the evolution of Roman culture. It both built on developments in Roman society and introduced new opportunities for the role of women as well as offering them an increasingly high profile. The bedrock was asserting a moral renaissance in the aftermath of an imagined era of moral decline which paralleled the political chaos of the late Republic and was also deemed to have helped cause it. Decline had to represent a comedown from something better. In Roman lore that something better was a myth of a poorer, purer and simpler Roman society which had been soured. Women whose *pudicitia* was beyond reproach would form an integral part of that vision.

Virgil composed his grand epic poem the *Aeneid* partly in order to create a mythological validation of the Augustan regime. For the poet, like so many of his contemporaries, the distressing experience of the civil war had been replaced with stability and a sense that Rome had been somehow reborn. The eponymous Trojan hero, a peripheral character plucked by Virgil from the *Iliad*, had become a voyager charged with the vast and overwhelming responsibility of finding a new home for his people. The analogy was obvious, and verged on the banal. Reluctant, troubled and bewildered in the face of the divinely contrived jeopardy and destiny he gradually came to recognize as his, Virgil's Aeneas was a proto-Augustus figure. Most significantly of all, he was the son of Venus (plate 1). From the outset then, the Julian line was one that began with a divine female progenitor. Virgil could not have anticipated that being a son of a Julio-Claudian 'Venus' would turn out to be the only way Augustus' regime would survive at all.

The two principal divine female protagonists, Juno and Venus, do a great deal to drive the *Aeneid*'s narrative. Indeed, their feud is essential to the plot with Juno in particular attempting to thwart the forces of fate and destiny, while Venus plays the role of maternal protector, intervening on her son's behalf. The very pettiness of their conflict, with its squalid indifference to humanity, was another way of depicting females as destabilizing and dangerous forces which Aeneas had to deal with and stand up to. The *Aeneid*, like all classical heroic myth, is a man's world in which mortal women appear but by contrast are more readily discarded. Aeneas escapes Troy with his son Ascanius and his father Anchises, while his wife Creusa is abandoned to the flames, the victim of fate, the gods and the needs of the grand Roman narrative. Conveniently written out, Creusa is entirely disposable.

The key female character instead is Dido, queen of Carthage, whose susceptibility to the weaknesses of women renders her incapable of living up to the needs of her own people. Dido is 'fickle and ever-changing' in spite of her remarkable achievements as a leader who has brought her people to Africa and begun the dramatic task of building a whole new nation and capital.[10] It is her susceptibility to emotion, depicted as the result of divine interference by Juno and Venus, that epitomizes her inadequacy. Nevertheless, this is never depicted unsympathetically. Dido is subjected to forces beyond her control. In the Roman idiom this exhibited straightforward proof of women's inabilities, when tested, to cope with or manage power. As a woman she is used to symbolize disorder, irrationality and a lack of self-control. Inevitably this reflected the perception of women's weaknesses in the Roman world. Nonetheless, Dido is a more complex and innocent figure, owing much to the model in Greek tragedy.[11] Virgil made it very clear that Dido was a victim of more than just herself. She is manipulated into a passionate love for Aeneas by Juno in an attempt to divert Aeneas from his destiny. Dido is then abandoned by Aeneas, who is reminded of his duty and leaves her. Dido plunges into irreconcilable despair.

Dido's suicide at the end of Book 4 wipes her out of the story, though Aeneas remains disturbed about her fate and his part in that. Dido has been sacrificed for his sake and the future Roman people. In that respect she symbolizes all those who have been pushed aside and destroyed to make way for Rome. Dido's brief and silent reappearance in the Underworld, during Aeneas' visit there in Book 6, is a fleeting jog to his guilty conscience before he returns dutifully to pursue his destiny when he is shown the future. His pity for her enhances his piety and humanizes him.[12] But Aeneas has learned his lesson. The woman he ends up becoming betrothed to, Lavinia, the daughter of Latinus, is no more than a convenient medium for generating offspring with Aeneas through whom the Trojans and Latins will conflate their cultures and traditions to create the basis of the Roman people. Lavinia, 'almost entirely faceless, and certainly speechless', is opaque to the point of virtual invisibility.[13] Lavinia is offered by her father to Aeneas to fulfil a convenient ancient prophecy that a foreigner would arrive and marry into the Latins. This way Aeneas could initiate the union between Trojan and Latin stock and form the basis of the merging of the two peoples in Roman ancestral tradition. Somewhat confusingly, the Julio-Claudians of course traced their mythical descent from Aeneas' son Iulus by his first wife Creusa, who had been left behind in the burning ruins of Troy.

Appropriately for a woman on whose shoulders so many male expectations were hung, Lavinia says nothing in the *Aeneid*. She simply complies with what her father and future husband have organized. Since she was presumably conceived of as being no more than around thirteen to fifteen years old this is hardly surprising. Had it been unnecessary for Aeneas to begin a new race there would have been no need to install Lavinia as a character. As it stands the word 'character' is to suggest a density of dramatic and narrative creativity that would grossly misrepresent the truth. If ever there was a Roman Stepford Wife, then Lavinia was her. In that respect she exemplified a form of Roman ideal. Of course the marriage arrangement was too straightforward. Lavinia was already betrothed to Turnus, prince of the Rutulians. To begin with Turnus is content enough to let her go until he and his mother Amata are wound up into a fury by Allecto, daughter of Pluto, sent by Juno. Amata provokes Turnus into a war with the Latins and therefore also Aeneas and the Trojans. When she believes that Turnus has been killed she too commits suicide. Turnus inevitably is killed in the final moments of the battle, removing the final obstacle. Destiny can now take its course, but only with a long shadow cast by the price paid by so many of the protagonists.

Lavinia was the symbol of a deferential and dutiful nonentity. Dido, who was anything but a nonentity, is the symbol of the woman as titillating source of temptation and a moral warning. It is clear which one Aeneas must choose. His dalliance with Dido was brief and impulsive and he had to be drawn away by the gods who reminded him that his destiny came first. By the time Lavinia materializes Aeneas has wised up and proceeds to accept that she is the key to the future. Ironically, despite Lavinia's innocuous nature and the fact that she is the symbolic prize, her mere existence as the epicentre of the conflict is enough for Virgil to blame her for everything that has gone before. She was 'the cause of all this evil'.[14] Of course the poem ends long before the future happens, but Aeneas has already been shown what is to come so he and we know exactly where this is all heading. The outcome in the *Aeneid* always was a foregone conclusion. Aeneas' line would one day climax in the birth of the brilliant young Caesar, known to us as Octavian and then as Augustus.

This messianic tone was echoed in Virgil's Fourth Eclogue which foretells the return of a Golden Age with a 'new race' sent down from Heaven. The poem includes the line 'the virgin goddess returns', a reference to Vesta who was the divine embodiment of the Roman home and hearth, and a personification of the Earth, embodied in the symbolic circularity of her temple.[15] Her virgin status was permanently commemorated in the operation of her cult by the Vestales (Vestal Virgins), overseen by the *pontifex maximus*, the post of senior priest held by Augustus from 12 BC and by his successors from the dates of their succession or shortly after (plate 17). Vesta and Venus were perhaps the two most important divine figures in the Augustan regime's messianic myth of destiny.

Virgil's women were often stereotypes, but they have much to tell us about the underlying attitudes in Roman culture still prevalent in the Augustan period. Ovid was no less conscious of the ideals of womanhood while avidly enjoying the pursuit of married women into adulterous affairs, prostitutes and casual liaisons. Thus he famously cited the circus as a perfect meeting place where one could be ignored by everyone else and enjoy the titillating possibilities the tight-packed seating afforded.[16] His recommendations on how to pursue an affair involved hints to women on posing as a loyal wife at dinner while at the same time making signs and gestures to their lover. Yet elsewhere he also condemned the mythical Tarpeia for her greedy betrayal of Rome to the Sabines.[17] Ovid's comments show how important it was for a wife to go about in public at least as a woman of unassailable virtue, while at the same time exposing another side to Roman life. Of course, part of his purpose was to create vaguely erotic literature, but he also illustrated the enduringly complex ambivalence about women in Roman society.

Ovid's poetry cut right to the heart of a serious moral issue for Augustus. When Virgil wrote the *Aeneid* the dust of the civil war had barely settled. The new regime was only a few years old. Augustus was already making great efforts to emphasize how he was restoring a sense of the old order based on traditional moral standards. It is no less clear that the image of the Roman state was changing and the prominent role more women began to play was an important part of that. Adulterous activity, and even incest, had already been identified as a defining characteristic of the late Republic's malaise though the line between literal truth and metaphor is difficult to unravel. Obviously it is impossible for us to assess whether adultery had genuinely increased. It is unlikely that the Romans were any better equipped to measure a change. It is possible, for example, now to argue that depictions of 'sexual misbehaviour' amongst the elite of the late Republic were deployed as metaphors for anxiety about the malaise of the period and its impact both on politics and private individuals. It was a depiction of an era that Augustus was keen to exploit because it helped his own image as a moral crusader and as an agent of reform. In this sense his reforms were not only intended to result in practical change but also, and perhaps more so, to serve a symbolic purpose. Restoring the Roman woman as a bastion of morality was a useful symbol of how his regime was repairing the damage done by the tumult of the late Republic. This explains the perception of women as the 'moral agent' in concerns about sexual morality.[18]

Women of the right sort would play a frontline role in the Augustan state, but this itself also gave them unprecedented power and influence.[19] Women like Fulvia and her sister-in-law Clodia were to be part of the past. Augustus was helped by his wife. Livia once chanced upon a group of naked men (we are not told the context). As a result they were instantly condemned to death, despite their quite obvious innocence. With remarkable presence of mind, Livia dealt with the situation in a way that not only showed her clemency but also amplified her moral qualities. She announced that to chaste women of restraint naked men were of no more significance than statues, and thereby saved them.[20]

The lex Julia de Adulteriis Coercendis of 18–17 BC was a law Augustus wanted to use to enforce a traditional form of morality, or at least what he imagined was traditional morality. He was very proud of his initiative, recording in his *Res Gestae* that 'By means of new laws brought in under my censorship I revived many ancestral practices which were by then dying out in our generation, and I myself handed down to later generations exemplary practices for them to imitate.'[21] This law made adultery with a married woman or relations either with an unmarried woman (except prostitutes) or a widow a matter for the attention of public courts.[22] It criminalized unfaithful wives and their lovers and reflected the standards of the times by ignoring unfaithful husbands. The focus was therefore on adultery as a crime against the family, and seeing women as the main route through which that might occur.[23] The guilty were liable to have some of their property seized and to be banished to an island. The law also legalized the killing of an adulterous daughter and her partner by her father. A husband was obliged to divorce his adulterous wife, and could kill her lover.

The new laws, and indeed the whole morality pitch, turned out to be hostages to fortune.[24] The morality laws were followed by the lex Papia

Poppaea of AD 9 which attempted (unsuccessfully) to impose penalties on voluntary celibacy.[25] Augustus was particularly concerned about childbirth or, rather, the lack of, amongst the upper classes. Some men were being betrothed to infant girls, and thus escaping proscriptions for not being married, yet obviously no children could possibly result from such arrangements for ten to fifteen years at the earliest. Augustus decreed that the marriage had to take place within two years of betrothal which meant that only girls of ten years or older should be involved.[26] In between these laws Augustus had taken the title *pater patriae* ('Father of the Nation') in 2 BC. This formalized his role as the equivalent of the *paterfamilias* for the Roman state and the overseeing of moral standards with that authority.

The declining birth rate amongst the upper classes had come about because of some couples choosing not to have children and a drop in the rate of marriages. There may well have been other environmental and cultural factors. An aristocrat fearing that his class was being compromised by a failure to replicate itself was hardly a new idea, and certainly not in Rome, but Augustus went out of his way to act on his concerns.[27] Financial incentives were offered. According to Dio there were now fewer aristocratic women than men (a phenomenon that goes unexplained but which may have been linked to a higher death rate) so Augustus also permitted marriage by equestrians to freedwomen; senators were excluded – he was not prepared to compromise Roman aristocracy to that extent.[28] He regarded himself as exempt from the same standards, but had exiled Ovid in AD 8. Ovid's *Art of Love* poem served as a form of erotic instruction manual, which was not in tune with Augustus' efforts to reform the moral life of Rome. What precisely triggered Ovid's expulsion when it came remains unknown as he was not forced to leave until seven years after publishing the *Art of Love*.[29]

The belief in women's potential association with luxury and corruption, which had become ever more current in the late Republic, endured. In AD 21 during a senatorial debate in the reign of Tiberius a senator called Caecina Severus suggested that because of women's susceptibility to luxury, greed and even the seeking of power, provincial governors should not be accompanied by their wives. He was subscribing to a long-established traditional Roman belief that women should be subservient to their husbands; to be otherwise threatened the stability of the state. Caecina Severus' proposition provoked a virulent argument about whether men were already corrupt or likely to be corrupted or compromised by their corrupt wives. Another point of view was expressed that it was a bad idea to leave women behind and abandon a 'sex which was ineffectual by nature', thereby exposing it to its 'own luxuriousness and the desires of others'.[30]

Caricature was a recognized Roman literary rhetorical device, utilized to emphasize the judgements being made in the form either of panegyrics or denunciation. The debate of AD 21 involved an argument based on stereotypes. This was essential in the oratory of the Roman law court and amounted to 'formal expressions of opinion in the course of debate'.[31] This translated into a wider tradition of forming polarized judgements, and this was no less true of individuals considered to be beyond reproach, especially women believed to exhibit dignified and honourable self-control, and acquiescence in what was expected of them, as well as those who were considered to be the exact opposite. Techniques not only included specific examples of criticism or praise but also being suggestive, oblique and implicit, encouraging the reader or listener to form his or her own opinion. The targets for great praise or castigation were almost invariably the elite; there was little or no interest in what the broader population got up to. They were easily dismissed as generally being beyond contempt unless in some paradoxical context they exhibited the very standards the elite had failed to live up to. In this way Pliny cited how the rebel slave leader Spartacus ordered that none of his followers should possess gold or silver, unlike Antony who was condemned by Pliny for using gold even for his basest requirements.[32] The anecdote about Antony was explicitly used to reinforce his 'effeminacy'.

Augustus' stand on public morality was a posture that fitted perfectly into his broader image as the saviour of the state. Seeking to prohibit and punish immorality was as important a means of protecting the Roman state as destroying his military and political enemies.[33] Roman moral standards, real or imagined, were part of being Roman. Moreover, when referred to as the 'custom of our ancestors' (*mos maiorum*) their force and significance were greatly enhanced as a foundation of Roman identity. To follow their precepts was thus to enhance one's own credibility and entitlement. It was a posture welcomed by Augustus' supporters. Horace, clearly with an eye for the mood of the times, suggested that 'to curb untamed licence' was the duty of any man who wanted to be the 'Father of Cities', that is literally 'Father of Civilization' in terms of the Roman definition of civilization as being founded in the order of a city.[34]

Women of course were as subject, if not more so, as their men folk to these expectations, with empresses and other members of the imperial family necessarily expected to be standard bearers. This was precisely what Virgil had played into in his depiction of the fallen Dido. As we have seen, Antony's fall was equally easily portrayed as that of a man who had let himself and the state down. It therefore followed that maintaining morality was essential to Roman society's success and stability. Octavia thus stood for Rome herself. The image of the Roman woman whose personal standards were beyond reproach was thus a central component in the structure of Augustan Roman values.

The victory at Actium in 31 BC epitomized the masculine and militarized nature of the Roman state. Much of the previous century had been characterized by the professionalizing of the Roman army and emergence of the *imperatores* (imperators), the generals who led parts of the army and increasingly against one another. Octavian, who for the sake of simplicity we will now always call Augustus, was fully aware that although he had achieved peace the principal challenge he faced was to cast a veil over the fact that peace had been won by military force. He also now stood at the head of a gigantic army that was not only no longer necessary but which was also an embarrassing symbol of how he had come to power; the peaceful image he now wanted to project was compromised by the very existence of the means by which he had been able to end the conflict. The late Roman writer Flavius Vegetius Renatus said, 'Let he who desires peace prepare for war.'[35]

Vegetius' words were a maxim Augustus would have understood: he could not possibly disband his army but he had to find a way of creating the impression that he had. This was not a challenge to a man who had already proved himself to be a master of spin. His solution was simple and has long been recognized as a skilful one. He drastically reduced the size of the army, paid off its veterans with donatives and colonies to prevent them turning into lawless and penniless bands of disaffected criminals, and dispersed what was left predominantly around the frontier provinces. The army's power was thus retained but was simultaneously neutralized.

Senatorial politics had long been defined by male posturing, factionalism, confrontation and even violence. The Senate was also the centre of power but in reality that had now drifted away to Augustus, his family and his immediate associates. The women of the imperial family took on a new political identity within that changed dynamic. This included acting as the living embodiments of the new ideals. This was manifest both in the claims to divine origins and also the projection of Roma herself as a female personification and other virtues and qualities such as Victory depicted in female form.

In short, the new world that Augustus offered the Romans was one in which women and symbols of women were a fundamental part of disposing of the memories of violence that had led to its creation, as well as acting as its saviours and protectors. The Temple of the Magna Mater ('Great Mother'), founded in 205 BC, was built in the latter part of the Second Punic War. A Roman deputation went to Phrygia to secure the cult statue at Pessinus and brought it home to save Rome on the advice of the oracular Sibylline Books. The structure was rebuilt several times and one of those occasions was in AD 3, commissioned by Augustus. This helped the cult's development over the next century and contributed to its importance in Roman culture.[36]

The quasi-religious associations of the name Augustus made him especially venerable without taking the fatal leap into becoming a divinity. This way he was converted into the peaceable first citizen by whose authority the stability and security of the Roman state were guaranteed. Where to place Livia and other women of the imperial family within this arrangement was more complicated. The process was accompanied by a series of two constitutional settlements that manufactured – or perhaps contrived would be a better word – a position for Augustus within the framework and mechanisms of the Roman Republic. Anyone who contemplated criticizing Augustus for misleading the Roman people would have had no more luck than someone firing javelins into fog. Augustus emerged as a man with imperium, power of military command, but without that in any sense being on overt public display since the legions and auxiliary forces were all based well away from Rome. His Praetorian Guard was largely dispersed around Italy, with only three cohorts actually stationed in Rome.

Augustus' principal constitutional status was his possession of the annually renewed powers of a tribune of the plebs. This tribunate was a Republican concession to the plebeians which dated back to 494 BC. Like most concessions awarded by elites to the lower orders it turned out more often than not to be a con. Tribunes, elected annually, represented the interests of the plebeians against the patrician Senate. Tribunes were inviolable, and could both propose legislation and veto the Senate's measures. Naturally the Senate did everything possible to ensure that elected tribunes were of senatorial rank. In Augustus' case the sleight of hand was a little more subtle. Instead of being elected (or having himself elected) to the post of tribune itself, he held only the powers of a tribune, which crucially included inviolability of his person. Since these powers were awarded by the Senate, Augustus could pose as the recipient of the privileges rather than as someone who had seized them. After all, any ruler who takes power by force and retains that power by force exposes himself to the same treatment. Since Augustus had initially handed back all the special powers he had been given in the civil war by the Senate there was no means by which he could be accused of seizing power, regardless of the reality.

Augustus also had to operate within the technical limitations these positions were associated with while at the same time sidestepping them and avoiding any appearance of being incorporated as a monarch. He had held the consulship several times as an imperator, ignoring the normal qualifications required. He continued to hold it annually from 27 to 23 BC but he was fully aware that this was not technically legal. He therefore only held it twice more during his reign. The powers of the tribune were annually renewed, emulating the tenure of a tribunate or indeed any Roman magistracy, but Augustus did not actually hold the position of tribune.

In any case, Augustus' constitutional status was peculiar to him. His tribunician powers made his person sacrosanct, a privilege also enjoyed by Livia from 35 BC. It was a short distance from this to his family members sharing that special sense of separateness and unique superiority of status, including the women. Livia was acutely conscious of her own sense of entitlement, and therefore was quick to take offence if it was not acknowledged.[37] There is no question that their behaviour showed that in practice imperial women assumed an equivalence of inviolability. In distancing himself from office Augustus' power and authority were also far less subject to the associated restraints, regardless of how he postured as being subject to them. He had succeeded in moving himself closer to the position of women outside the political system while at the same time pretending that he was operating within it. Women, and at this time particularly Livia, were manifestly not restrained by the nature of office at all. In that respect Augustus and Livia were now in remarkably similar positions. This would afford Livia enormous power in Augustus' lifetime and after his death, and also benefit later empresses.

The constitutional position which Augustus now found himself in amounted effectively to a self-inflicted and necessary emasculation of the civil war imperator he had been. He had created order and brought peace. He claimed to have restored the Republic. In reality he had reinvented it. It was the Republic but not as the Romans knew it. They gaped in fascination at the new order as Augustus proceeded also to develop a new image for the Roman world fashioned out of both tradition and innovation. It was one in which female attributes, qualities and symbols played an essential part. This, however, only started a process that took a considerable period to evolve, lasting well beyond the reign of Augustus.

Roma had been a visual symbol for some time on the Republican silver coinage. Helmeted in the manner of Minerva, Roma was the normal, but not invariable, choice for the obverse of the silver denarius. During the civil war she had retreated into the background. The *imperatores* manufactured coinage that was more likely to depict their own portraits, divine affiliations and political legends and slogans. Caesar's coins associated him with victories, priestly implements to reinforce his religious credentials and also – critically – his lineage. The lineage was a simple, if outright fraudulent, descent from Venus and her son Aeneas, the mythical founder of the Roman people (plate 1). Caesar was far too intelligent to be explicit about this. He merely depicted the standard image of Aeneas leaving Troy while carrying his father Anchises on one side, together with one word: CAESAR. On the other was a portrait of Venus. Caesar's message was clear, just as it was with his Temple of Venus Genetrix in his forum in Rome. Divine female lineage therefore lay at the heart of the Julian family's claim to their destiny. Moreover, even though Augustus was legally Caesar's son by adoption in his will, the reality was that his membership of the Julii came via his mother Atia, Caesar's niece by his sister.

During his time as an imperator Octavian's coins often present him in military garb or with military symbols and frequently with simple abbreviated legends that stated no more or less than that he was 'son of the deified Caesar'. After 27 BC the military associations almost, but not entirely, vanish. He was not usually portrayed in military costume even if he was being greeted by soldiers or presiding over supplicants or other symbols of victory. More often he was described as the 'saviour of the citizens'. The portrait of Augustus is softened compared to the brutal realism of the civil war *imperatores* in which Caesar was depicted as a harsh-faced and austere authority figure and Mark Antony as a thug. Looking like a thug might once have seemed a good way to portray oneself, in the interests of looking forceful and assertive in the machismo world of the late Republic. That time had gone and Augustus knew it. Even as Octavian he had appeared in a more ethereal way than the other *imperatores*, already mindful of the sense of youthful, strangely androgynous promise a gentler portrait might evoke. There is something of the young god in these early portraits of Octavian. So appealing was this notion that Augustus, perhaps with a hint of vanity too, continued to utilize variants on this theme for the rest of his life. Like that of a god, his public image never aged.

The greatest surviving symbol of the peaceful idealism of the Augustan era is the Ara Pacis ('Altar of Peace'), commissioned by the Senate in 13 BC and dedicated on Livia's birthday, 30 January 9 BC (plates 7, 8).[38] It stood in the northern part of the Field of Mars (Campus Martius) by the Via Flaminia not far from Augustus' mausoleum and overlooked Augustus' sundial, the Horologium. The façade that faced the Via Flaminia was flanked by two sculptural panels featuring key female personifications. On the left is a matriarchal female figure accompanied by two infants and two young women who symbolize the benevolent winds of earth and sea. The principal figure and the symbols around her represent divine prosperity, fecundity and peace. Once identified as the earth mother goddess Tellus, other possibilities have been suggested such as Pax Augusta, Ceres or Venus Genetrix.[39] Equally, there may be no special reason why the figure had to be one specific divine figure. If so it may be better to see her as a conflation of personified virtues and divine attributes best collectively defined in female form, and reflected in the women of the Julio-Claudian family.

Opposite this side of the altar façade was the far less equivocal figure of Roma. So little of this panel remains it is impossible to say more than that Roma is shown Minerva-like as a seated and armed female figure.[40] The importance of Venus in showing loyalty to the state is evident in other examples of dedications to her in Augustan Rome, even in small-scale localized contexts. The year the altar was dedicated was a bad one for the imperial family. Livia's second son, Nero Claudius Drusus, died after a fall from his horse in Germany while on campaign. Livia proved more stoical than Octavia had when her husband Gaius Marcellus died in 40 BC. Unlike Octavia, Livia observed the proper forms of grieving, and then 'she laid away her sorrow'. She did, however, preserve his memory by keeping his likeness in public and private places and talking about him whenever she could. This earned her admiration for behaving in the correct manner for a bereaved Roman matron.[41]

In 7 BC, just two years after the Ara Pacis was consecrated, Augustus reorganized the city into fourteen regions and wards, managed by (usually) freedmen *magistri* in charge of administrative and religious duties. The latter included the dedications in wayside shrines in the streets of Rome to the Lares (spirits), which became known as the Lares Augusti, together with other deities associated with Augustus. One of the divine beneficiaries was Venus Augusta. These were a way in which these officials could emphasize their association with a goddess who was so intertwined with the regime. Marcus Lucius Hermeros Aequitas was one such *magister*. He commemorated the fact that he had been elected to the post three times by the local people of the *vicus* he served by erecting a statue with inscribed base to Venus Augusta.[42] Women were also able to participate in these dedications, serving as members of the *collegia* (guilds) responsible, and having themselves depicted on the sides of altars in the act.[43]

On the west façade of the Ara Pacis, which formed the main entrance to the altar enclosure, the sculptures counterbalanced the female imagery of the east side. Aeneas is presented in one panel sacrificing to the Penates, the Trojan household gods, in the company of his son Iulus. In the other the myth of the twins Romulus and Remus suckling from the she-wolf appears. In neither case does the image of heroic warrior appear. Aeneas is portrayed as a priestly elder in whom politics and religion are conflated into a figure of stability and moral rectitude serving as a metaphor for the benefits offered by the Augustan triumph. Compared to Roma and Ceres (or Venus) he looks irremediably dull, as indeed he was.

In the side panels that portray a public procession Augustus is accompanied by priests and all his key family members, among whom the women play a conspicuous part. Military attributes are absent. All the male figures are dressed in togas and the women in the traditional woollen dress (*stola*) and their heads covered, symbolic of their virtue, as befitted a religious ceremony. Julia appears prominently facing out, her son Gaius beside her. Augustus' nieces, the daughters of Octavia, are close by, while other female relatives mingle amongst the male members of the extended family and its associates.

The Ara Pacis sculptures thus featured the Augustan family as the central bastion of the regime's public image. It was an extension of the conventional Roman *familia* now depicted as the focal point of the state. In this context the female figures inevitably played crucial roles even if the lineage had become fictionalized. Livia was Augustus' wife and therefore she was in all legal senses of the role the grandmother of his grandchildren; Scribonia, his previous wife and mother of Julia, was ignored. Statues of Livia promoted a timeless image like those of her husband and her likeness even became a popular decorative icon. Livia's features also became used as a template for sculptures of female divinities such as Ceres (plates 9, 10, 11).[44] In this way the prominence of the Julio-Claudian women as major players in the regime, also evoking useful divine associations, was being widely disseminated. This was something the Severan emperors developed even more.

The equality of enhanced status the imperial women enjoyed had already been clearly publicized through the building projects that formed a major part of the regime's image as a public benefactor. These projects also marked the end of competitive munificence amongst senators vying for popularity, with the emperors and their families monopolizing the provision of prestigious facilities and architectural conceits thereafter. A *porticus Juliae* is attested in the Forum and so also is the *basilica Antoniarum duarum* ('basilica of the two Antoniae').[45] The former is connected with two unnamed female members of the family as the benefactors, and the Antoniae can only be Augustus' nieces, the daughters of his sister Octavia by Mark Antony, her second husband. Neither of these buildings is known any more, but the porch to the Porticus of Octavia is extant though it now includes extensive traces of later repairs and reconstruction in antiquity, mainly of Severan date (plate 6).[46] Its survival is thanks to its conversion into a church porch in the eighth century. The structure replaced an earlier porticus in 27–25 BC and was renamed for the widowed Octavia. The Porticus of Octavia was a substantial architectural complex. It contained temples of Juno Regina and Jupiter Stator, functioned both as a library and an art gallery and, appropriately, contained an 'exceptionally beautiful' statue of Venus believed in Pliny's time to be by the fifth-century BC Greek sculptor Phidias, as well as a statue of Cornelia, mother of the Gracchi.[47]

On the Esquiline Hill, close to the Forum of Augustus, was a palace left to him in his will by a rich freedman called Vedius Pollio. Augustus demolished the palace, allegedly to distance himself from the private wealth it symbolized, and made the site available for Livia's new Porticus. Today the Porticus of Livia is only known from surviving fragments of the ancient marble plan of Rome, a few references in our sources and some patchy archaeological traces. The marble plan shows a large rectangular courtyard surrounded by a double colonnade with a shrine in the middle. Around the edges rectangular rooms and apses opened on to the colonnade (plate 15). The Porticus was built between 15 and 7 BC and was also embellished with fountains, gardens and an art gallery. It provided a refuge from the bustle of Rome for the less affluent and gave them a chance to enjoy an elegant retreat in a style otherwise only enjoyed by the rich, remaining in use at least until the fifth century. The shrine in the middle of the courtyard is perhaps the one known to have been dedicated here to Concordia by Livia and presented to Augustus. Given Livia's central role in Augustan ideology as the embodiment of marital and maternal harmony, Concordia was an obvious association.[48]

Another Temple of Concordia Augusta, this time in the main Forum, was repaired and dedicated by Augustus' successor Tiberius in AD 10 in his name and that of his son Drusus (who had died in 9 BC) close to the foot of the Capitoline Hill. Sculpture was used to depict suitable virtues in female form. Three female statues were installed at the top of the temple's pediment. One must have represented Concordia, but the others may have represented Peace (Pax) and Health (Salus) or Security (Securitas) and Fortune (Fortuna).[49]

One of the most interesting echoes of the presence of Livia within the great Augustan building works at Rome survives at Pompeii, and goes some way to making good their loss. Eumachia was a public priestess in Pompeii in the late Augustan period and into the reign of Tiberius. She seems to have been married to a city magistrate (*duumvir*) called Marcus Numistrius Fronto. By the time she enters the extant record she had been widowed but had a son, also called Marcus Numistrius Fronto, whose political career she was busily, and expensively, promoting. That Eumachia was closely associated with the guild of fullers suggests that the family's wealth was derived from, at least in part, this extremely lucrative and dominant trade in Pompeii. Some of her money was used to construct a large building at the southeast corner of Pompeii's forum.

At about 40 metres (131 feet) wide and over 75 metres (246 feet) in length, the Building of Eumachia was larger than almost all other structures in Pompeii.[50] However, it probably only covered around a quarter to a third of the area of Livia's porticus. Perhaps better described as the Porticus of Eumachia it consisted of a large covered porch, called a chalcidicum, overlooking the forum, which led into a large trapezoidal courtyard surrounded by a cryptoporticus (plate 12). At the rear of the courtyard was an apse where a statue of Livia as Concordia Augusta was displayed. It is obvious that this had been inspired by monuments in Rome, the Porticus of Livia surely being one of them. The Pompeii building was explicitly dedicated to Concordia Augusta and Pietas in both Eumachia's name and that of her son. It had been paid for solely by Eumachia, just as it appears Livia had been personally behind the Concordia shrine in her porticus. Those entering the Building of Eumachia through the chalcidicum were greeted by statues of both Aeneas and Romulus, accompanied by descriptive inscriptions, matching those that flanked the Temple of Mars Ultor in the Forum of Augustus at Rome.[51] In both instances these mythological references were clearly designed to evoke a sense of patriotism and tradition. Eumachia stands for a number of examples of high-status women in other civic communities who found in Livia an inspiration to make a mark on their own cities.[52]

Augustus had done an enormous amount to reinvent the Roman Republic. To anyone who had been out of Rome for years much remained to suggest that the Roman world was being ruled as it had always been. The Senate was still in existence and so were the magistracies that had been elected annually for centuries. It was a sham. Much had changed. In fact, everything had, not least the prominence of women at the heart of the new state. Quite apart from anything else Rome was at peace. The factionalism that had plagued the Republic had gone, or at any rate had been suppressed to the point of virtual annihilation. Everything hung on the person of Augustus, but his contribution to this role was the sum of more than just his own attributes. Octavia and especially Livia had been integrated into the greater image of power as if they and he formed a single political and dynastic entity. Their personal morality and metaphorical roles as the embodiment of Augustan qualities were vital to enhancing the validation of the Augustan state as a bastion of virtue and defence against chaos and licence. The Augustan regime was thereby synonymous with entitlement to the supreme authority (plate 28). The real question now was: how was this to be sustained? Octavia and Livia were to play an equally important practical role in the regime's future and could be relied on to do so. Augustus' daughter Julia, who provided the only opportunity to create a dynasty descended from Augustus personally, could not.

4

FORGING THE FUTURE
LIVIA, OCTAVIA AND JULIA 27 BC–AD 14

In Livia, Augustus had a wife who could not bear him children but who played a major role in the image of his regime. That left him with Julia the Elder, his daughter by Scribonia. She became the key part of the bloodline since only her children were descended from Augustus himself. Other collateral lines of descent in the imperial family went back to Augustus' sister Octavia and his wife Livia. Julia proved to be able to bear healthy children but Julia's real problem was her studied resistance to the image Augustus wanted to project. Augustus claimed to have restored the old morality and wanted to encourage traditional family standards. After the death of Agrippa Julia had been pushed into what turned out to be a loveless union with Livia's son Tiberius. Julia's private life was suddenly thrown into sharp focus when the story broke about her endless affairs and other subversive activities. It created a moral crisis for the Augustan regime and she was sent into exile. Nonetheless, Julia's children were absolutely essential to the continuity of the dynasty.

Augustus had resolved to create a regime in which the imperial family was to represent all the stability and harmony of the Roman state. Within this the roles and contributions of female members of the family were more than just appropriate; they were essential. As key dynastic figures the success and future of the state were invested in their roles and identities. Nothing could alter one crucial fact: Augustus needed to find a way of transmitting his regime to the next generation and he could not do that on his own. Augustus prioritized securing the succession from the outset. This was interesting in its own right since technically there was no need to have an heir. After all, he had posed simply as a *primus inter pares*, 'first among equals'. He was, literally, just the first citizen in a Republic that by definition had no place explicitly or implicitly for a monarchy and certainly not any kind of dynasty. His personal qualities were therefore not transmissible in any straightforward sense for the simple reason that no one else could lay claim to his achievements.

All that could happen was to imply a form of transmission of Augustus' qualities through a bloodline, however incongruous this was within the Roman world. Had he and Livia had children that had lived to adulthood there can be no doubt that they would have taken precedence over all his other relatives, including his daughter Julia and her children. That both Livia and Augustus had had children by others proved that neither was infertile. They must have assumed that they would proceed to have children with each other. When this did not happen they were simply left with the frustrating fact that they could not. This lies behind almost everything we know about Livia and the allegations or suggestions made about her by some ancient historians. Had she borne Augustus a son, or sons, who had lived to adulthood, and fiercely promoted their interests and futures she would have enjoyed the sort of veneration reserved for women like Calpurnia or Agrippina the Elder. Nonetheless, there was a tradition that marital loyalty took precedence over barrenness, which was frowned upon as a reason for divorce.[1] Their childlessness did not dent the importance of their marriage to the Augustan state.

In spite of this, the inability of Augustus and Livia to have a child was also the most significant factor behind his dynastic policy. Regardless of the cause Augustus was left with no alternative, once he had developed dynastic ambitions, other than to seek the direct route via his daughter Julia. The less direct routes via his sister Octavia or Livia were inevitably secondary. It was clear that his bloodline through Julia was automatically his first choice when it came to earmarking his successor. By the same token he marginalized Livia and her own dynastic ambitions in making that choice. The eventual outcome, in the form of Livia's son Tiberius succeeding Augustus, demonstrated that the Julio-Claudian family relied wholly on women of the bloodline (as opposed to those who were married into it) for that continuity to have any prospect of happening. It also left Tacitus in no doubt that this had been

Livia's intention all along. The role of fortune seemed hardly credible to him even though he pondered elsewhere in the *Annals* on how important chance usually was in the way it rewarded the undeserving and cheated the deserving.[2]

Livia was described by Tacitus as having a traditional form of domestic virtue. He qualified this by adding that her *comis*, a word that denotes elegance, courtesy and friendliness, went beyond that of Roman women of former ages.[3] By 27 BC she was around thirty-one years old. Her first son, Tiberius, was fourteen, and her second, Nero Claudius Drusus, was eleven. Her stepdaughter Julia was the same age. By the time of Augustus' death in AD 14 Livia was in her seventies. Her younger son Drusus had been dead since 9 BC. Perhaps it was just as well. He was not in favour of the way Augustus ruled and his reactionary sympathies had led him even to contemplate forcing Augustus to restore the Republic.[4] Tiberius was in his mid-fifties, a highly experienced politician and soldier, but embittered and frustrated. By both her sons Livia had grandchildren. Drusus' children included the general Germanicus, beloved of the Roman people, the future emperor Claudius, and Livilla. Claudius was handicapped in some way that in those unsympathetic times labelled him as mentally defective and crippled. It was a gross miscalculation as circumstances would later show. Livilla ('little Livia'), or in full Claudia Livia Julia, had already been fielded as a dynastic pawn. In 13 BC Vipsania Agrippina had borne Tiberius a son called Drusus, usually known now as Drusus the Younger to distinguish him from his uncle. In AD 4 he was married to his cousin Livilla.[5]

Livia herself was not to die until 28 September 29 when she was eighty-six. It was a remarkable age and meant her life had spanned the fall of the Republic, the reign of Augustus and two-thirds of that of Tiberius. Her sixty years as wife of an emperor and mother of an emperor amounted to nearly two-thirds of the whole Julio-Claudian imperial era, making her by far and away the most dominant female figure. She had played a full and active role at Augustus' side, though it is not entirely clear quite to what extent she travelled with him during his peregrinations. Since she was not encumbered either with pregnancies or small children she may have accompanied him to Spain and Gaul between 27 and 24 BC, and into the East from 22 to 19 BC, though this is not emphatically clear from the sources.

The only real basis we have for assuming that Livia probably did travel with Augustus on both these occasions and other trips that have gone unrecorded in the sources available to us is a reference in Tacitus. This concerned the senatorial debate over forty years later in AD 21 about whether wives should accompany their provincial governor husbands. One of the decisive observations that settled the debate in favour of wives accompanying their husbands came from Tiberius' son, Drusus the Younger. He pointed out that *principes* (literally 'first citizens' and in this context a euphemism for 'emperors') had to make all sorts of frequent journeys around their possessions. Drusus observed that Livia had on numerous occasions accompanied Augustus. He could hardly have been lying since Livia was still alive, and we should assume that Tacitus had read the official records of the debate. He was certainly in a position to.[6] Finding independent confirmation of Livia's presence on these trips is, however, extremely difficult.

Dio describes Augustus setting out for Britain in 27 BC but abandoning this in favour of staying longer in Gaul to oversee provincial government and hold a census before moving on to do the same in Spain, where he fell ill. Livia's presence or otherwise goes unmentioned even though had she been available she would have taken care of him while he was indisposed. We cannot assume that her modesty is the only reason she is absent from Dio. The more obvious one is that she was not there.[7] Given the evolving partnership Livia and Augustus were developing it would also have made good sense sometimes to leave her in Rome to represent his presence. This would also fit his preference for military commanding officers not returning home to visit their wives, demonstrating that it was normal for them to be left behind.[8] The evidence from Horace serves amply to show how complicated it is trying to reconcile the scattered evidence available to us. In one of his *Odes* Horace describes Augustus' 'victorious return' to Rome from Spain in 24 BC. Here he was greeted by 'his wife . . . and sister of our illustrious leader' who participated in a thanksgiving sacrifice.[9] On the face of it, the picture is a vivid one of the triumphant Augustus being received back into the welcoming arms of the two most important women then in his life and regime. Either Livia was already in Rome or simply switched roles to act as the homebound wife welcoming back her husband in accordance with tradition, which seems ludicrously unlikely. Alternatively, we might speculate that Livia did not travel with Augustus on a continuous basis, only venturing out in summer or at other convenient points during his absence. Perhaps Augustus did not even want Livia along. Not many years later the gossips would suggest that Augustus had travelled to Gaul only so that he could continue an affair with Maecenas' wife Terentia.[10]

Dio also recounts how Augustus' journey of 22 BC began in Sicily and continued to Syria via Greece. Augustus left Agrippa in charge of Rome. He also forced Agrippa to divorce his wife and marry Julia in order to elevate him to the right level of dignity.[11] Some of the limited evidence for Livia's possible presence cannot even be tied to the time of the journey. At Thermae Himereae (Termini Imerese), on the north coast of Sicily, an altar was dedicated to the 'Imperator Caesar (Augustus), Livia, mother of Tiberius Caesar, son of the Imperator Caesar'.[12] Since this explicitly refers to Tiberius as Caesar, as heir apparent, and no one else it must in fact belong to when Tiberius was adopted in AD 4 or later, and not before. There is no reason to assume that any of the three were there when the altar was made. Other inscriptions recording dedications to Livia are demonstrably not from the time of the journey. Livia was bequeathed several cities in Judaea in the will of Salome, sister of the client king Herod I. Salome died in AD 10, an event that also took place long after Augustus' visit.[13]

By 21 BC Augustus was awarding honours to the Lacedaemonians (Spartans) because of the time Livia, Nero and Tiberius had spent there after escaping from Italy. Dio, however, makes no mention of Livia being present. We can certainly assume it was a possibility, but not a certainty.[14] Livia was the recipient of a number of honours though the inscriptions that refer to her are not precisely dated and in some cases must belong to after this trip. The city of Haluntium (San Marco d'Alunzio) in northeastern Sicily is a case in point. The simple text of an inscription describes the town as 'The Municipium of the Goddess Livia, (wife of) Augustus'.[15] There is no date to substantiate associating the dedication to the journey of 22–19 BC and nor is there any indication that Livia was present. That she had been named as a goddess was a great honour and a subtle way in the Western Empire of attributing divine qualities to the imperial family while avoiding giving them to Augustus, which would have been completely unacceptable. Even if this inscription belongs to that journey, Augustus' presence would have been quite sufficient.

Livia accompanying Augustus to Samos for a second winter in 20–19 BC is presented as fact by some historians, though the evidence available refers to Augustus alone; others are more circumspect. Another inscription from the island refers to Samian independence being refused by Augustus in 21–20 BC, despite Livia's efforts to convince him. She may have done this in person in

Samos but nothing from Samos verifies her presence (despite some modern historians assuming that she was there as a fact); however, her influence is beyond doubt because Augustus specifically refers to his desire to do her a favour in a letter in this regard which was reproduced in an inscription at Aphrodisias in Asia Minor, even though he had turned Samian independence down.[16] Dio, who also refers to the award of independence being given the next year, makes no mention of her presence, or indeed even her efforts, wherever she was. Given that in fact we do know Livia was involved, presumably succeeding in convincing Augustus to grant the Samians independence by the second winter, and that the inscription was a chance find, this shows just how hard it is to draw any firm conclusions about where she was.[17] Augustus returned to Italy in 19 BC, sneaking into Rome by night to avoid a welcoming deputation; again, no reference to Livia is made but, remarkably, one modern historian still states it as a fact that Livia was with Augustus.[18]

Whether Livia was with her husband or not it is clear that Augustus' unique personal status was shared in some degree by Livia though not in any formally recognized manner. Augustus' moral reforms had also made it essential that the women in his circle lived up to the exacting standards he felt so strongly about. If they fell short, then they would compromise his entitlement to rule since acting as the state's moral guardian equated to legitimating his position and power. It must have been the case to begin with that Augustus assumed at some point Livia would bear him a child who would grow to be his successor. However, by 17 BC or thereabouts it must have become obvious that that was not going to happen. This was a serious problem for Augustus since one of the defining aspects of his moral crusade was to replace sexual licence and elective childlessness with marriages that were focused on producing children. The purpose was to increase the production of legitimate children from high-status backgrounds who would then serve the state, the men in administrative and political roles and the women as mothers of the next generation.

When it became evident that the first lady of Rome was not able to produce children for Augustus the image of the state was dented. The absence of children left Augustus with a very real problem if he was to avoid the state collapsing back into the very moral crisis he claimed to have rescued it from. Crucially though, Livia already had her own children and they were both sons. Livia's dynastic ambitions were not therefore necessarily the same as those of Augustus. Moreover, she had potential rivals in the form of Julia and

Octavia, both of whom were Augustus' blood relations. We now need to look back a little earlier in the story to see how both of these other women took on such importance in the reign.

Octavia's son Marcus Marcellus was about fifteen when Octavian became Augustus in 27 BC. The boy seems rapidly to have been identified by his uncle as a potential successor. He had already been introduced in public after Actium when he and Tiberius rode flanking escort horses in the triumph held in Rome, Marcellus taking the preferred right-hand one.[19] In 25 BC Marcellus was married to Augustus' daughter Julia, his first cousin.

Julia's life was both privileged and unenviable. As Augustus' only child a huge amount was invested in her. She was burdened with expectations that were impossible to live up to. Augustus saw to it that his daughter had a very traditional upbringing. Julia was taught spinning and weaving, which included making his clothes. He also insisted that she was only to say things that were beyond reproach, could be spoken in public and could be safely recorded in a diary. It was a style of upbringing he also later used for his granddaughters.[20] By attributing Julia's education to Augustus alone the role either of Scribonia or Livia was simply ignored. It is therefore impossible now to know what part they played, or to what extent. Roman men and women shared their houses so it should be no great surprise that Augustus expected his female relatives to be around him. The Augustan architect Vitruvius was at pains to point out the contrast with Greek houses, where separate areas were provided for the 'mothers of the family' to do their spinning.[21]

Julia was said to have been very well read, this being a pleasure for her rather than an imposition; it should not automatically be assumed that her childhood was an intolerable experience.[22] However, even this raises the interesting question of how her reading was managed, especially as the evidence for women's ownership and use of books or libraries is very limited. It seems there is not a single instance in any ancient source that refers to a woman using a public library, even though women were known to act as patrons of such institutions. Octavia, for example, had included a library in her Porticus in memory of her son. The lack of evidence for women using such facilities must reflect their function as a venue for political and commercial business from which women were habitually excluded.[23]

The likelihood is that Julia, and other women in the imperial family, if they read books at all did so in personal libraries within the palace or other houses owned by the family, as well as those acquired by or brought to them. Octavia's daughter Antonia Minor is known to have been given a book, a trivial occurrence no doubt and recorded only in the incidental survival of an epigram. She also seems to have employed the services of a female librarian called Onomaste, who was presumably a slave, though this is not conclusive proof Antonia had a library.[24] In truth, though, neither of these pieces of evidence demonstrates that Antonia or other women in the Julio-Claudian family were enthusiastic bibliophiles as some scholars imply. Owning books is not the same as reading them. Gatsby's library was purchased wholesale, greatly impressing one 'stout, middle-aged' guest for consisting of real books rather than 'durable cardboard', even though the pages had not been cut, demonstrating that they had never been read and had been acquired purely for the purposes of display. The same guest feared that if one was removed from the shelf the 'whole library was liable to collapse'.[25] Of course Antonia and others as well as Julia may have been avid book owners *and* readers but we simply do not have the evidence to argue it either way, though in an era of constraints on female freedom a library may have proved an appealing refuge.[26] If they did indulge in reading, women were well advised to keep quiet about it. A woman who advertised her education in company by expressing opinions about what she had read was treated with the same sort of disdain shown for those would-be female advocates in the late Republic, Hortensia, Afrania and Maesia. There was even a special word for an over-talkative woman – a *lingulaca*.[27] If women chose therefore to keep their education to themselves for the sake of an easier life we would have even less chance of hearing about it.

Julia, like all the other women of the imperial household, was constrained within a framework defined by Augustus and according to tradition. Julia was to act as, and be, a showcase example of the moral strictures Augustus wanted to impose on wider Roman society. This was reflected in some of the legal restrictions he placed on women. Women were, for example, not allowed to attend athletic contests until after the fifth hour and could only watch gladiatorial fights from the uppermost tier of seating.[28] This prevented women of status from sharing the best seats in the lower rows, even though these were reserved for the elite. Only the Vestal Virgins were exempt. Augustus also had conservative views when it came to female dress which he thought husbands as a matter of routine should impose on their wives.[29] Julia therefore was expected to have no say in anything. Instead she was supposed to conduct herself in a manner that placed her beyond criticism and suspicion, and to acquiesce in any marital arrangements her father organized for her. This would dramatically backfire twenty-three years later as Julia emerged as the leading malcontent in Augustus' programme of moral reform.

In the meantime Augustus was ill at the time of the wedding of Julia to Marcus Marcellus in 25 BC and unable to attend. Indeed, the illness may have been the reason the marriage was arranged at that point, though Marcellus would have been far too young to replace Augustus.[30] His career was fast-tracked. He was given propraetorian rank and allowed to stand for the consulship ten years early.[31] Inevitably this also enhanced the thirteen-year-old Julia's potential dynastic importance. It was clear that the general assumption was that Marcellus would be the successor. Augustus knocked that into the long grass when at the height of his illness he handed his ring to his general Agrippa. How this would have played out had Augustus died will remain forever unknown because he recovered, thanks, or so it was believed, to the treatment arranged by a man called Antonius Musa.

Whatever Musa's skills were they failed to work for Marcellus who became ill himself soon afterwards and died in 23 BC. Not surprisingly he and Julia had not yet had children. If they had done so, their mutual Julian descent would have resulted in offspring with unbeatable dynastic credentials. That must have been the plan. Marcellus' remains were placed in the mausoleum Augustus was building for the imperial family.[32] He had already been honoured by the reassignment of a theatre begun by Caesar shortly before his assassination. The project had been reinstated by Augustus in the name of Marcellus. The work continued after Marcellus' death as a monument to his memory, and was not completed before 13 BC (plate 5).[33] Today it is one of the most important Augustan buildings still standing in Rome.

The death of Marcellus was the first in a series of dynastic disasters caused by the remarkably poor health of the men and boys of Augustus' family. Augustus went on to insist that he had not intended Marcellus to be his successor because he had not named anyone. He even wanted to read his own will out in public to prove this but was prevented from doing so, though why or by whom is not clear. He seems to have acknowledged that Agrippa was more popular and that Marcellus was too young, but realized he could not go as far as actually specifying that Agrippa should succeed him.[34] This was odd because Agrippa had removed himself from Rome when Marcellus embarked on his public career specifically to avoid overshadowing the young man.[35] Moreover, in the *Aeneid* Virgil quite explicitly described the young Marcellus as 'a youth of wondrous beauty and brilliant in his arms'. Marcellus had raised the 'hopes of his Latin ancestors' more than anyone else. The implication was clear: in Virgil's view, at least, Marcellus was the intended heir.[36] In reality then, Augustus must have been seriously worried about what to do next.

The death of Marcellus left his mother Octavia devastated. She seems to have entered a phase of inconsolable despair that lasted the rest of her life. She was said to have lost any sense of optimism or joy thereafter, rejecting any consolation she was offered. Worse, she allegedly took against other mothers and especially Livia because it seemed that the happiness she had once enjoyed had been transferred to her sister-in-law.[37] Livia had given birth to Tiberius in 42 BC at around the same time that Marcellus was born.

The rumour began to circulate that Livia had arranged the death of Marcellus on the simple grounds that he had been preferred over her own sons. Dio, our source for the allegation, balances it by noting that some sort of plague had caused an unusual number of deaths that year or the next.[38] That was nothing like as good a story as the idea that Livia had had Marcellus killed, so the rumour persisted. Today we would call those responsible for the rumours conspiracy theorists, and Livia's guilt would be the subject of countless websites and trashy 'revelatory' paperbacks. In essence it was no different in Rome twenty centuries ago. Livia's involvement is possible, but premature death was so common there is no good reason not to believe that Marcellus died of natural causes, especially if there was a serious disease circulating in Rome at the time.

Livia would also have had to work hard to see her own sons preferred as replacements for Marcellus. This was not an implausible prospect since Julia was now, by definition, available once more for marriage. Either way, the death of Marcellus caused Octavia enormous grief. Decades later Seneca wrote about Octavia's loss, describing Marcellus as someone whom Augustus 'had begun to depend upon, and to place upon his shoulders the weight of the empire'.[39] No doubt much of Octavia's distress was the normal consequence of bereavement that any parent might feel, but she had also lost the chance of seeing her own descendant take supreme power one day now that her 'happiness had passed' instead to Livia's son Tiberius.[40] There is more than an element of hindsight here. Seneca knew that Tiberius would later become emperor. Moreover, far from turning to Tiberius as a prospective successor,

Augustus pursued a number of other opportunities first, beginning with Agrippa. The idea that Octavia was acting out of spite to damage Livia's chances of being the progenitor of Augustus' heirs is not very convincing.

Octavia might very well have been more resentful of Julia. Had Marcellus lived then Julia's children would have been descended from Octavia and Augustus. With Marcellus gone Julia was now free to have children by another man. They would still be Augustus' grandchildren but Octavia would have been out of the picture. The strange case of Gaius Proculeius occurred around this time. He was 'highly honoured by Augustus', and had even acted as his envoy to Antony and Cleopatra after Actium. He was, however, later crippled by stomach pains, eventually leading him to consume gypsum in desperation, which killed him – doubtless after giving him even worse stomach pains.

Proculeius, surprisingly, was the brother of the alleged anti-Augustus conspirator Lucius Licinius Varro Murena, and had even spoken up for him in the trial of 22 BC. Murena had the previous year been involved in defending a provincial governor of Macedonia; the case had inadvertently exposed the possibility that Augustus had breached senatorial protocol by intervening in the affairs of a senatorial province, and even that he might have acted through Marcellus. This seemed to raise the possibility that Augustus had indeed earmarked Marcellus as his heir, revealing that he was trying to create a monarchy and a hereditary one at that. Murena's alleged involvement in a conspiracy led by Fannius Caepio may have been a ruse to get rid of him, and he was duly executed.[41] Proculeius' potential marriage to Julia goes unmentioned in the records of Augustus' reign. Instead it comes up during the reign of Tiberius. Tacitus recorded a letter from Tiberius to his praetorian prefect Sejanus who had had the temerity to suggest that he might marry Tiberius' widowed daughter-in-law and niece Livilla, on the basis that Augustus had considered marrying Julia to an equestrian. Tiberius expressed his concerns on the grounds that this would put an equestrian above his station. He added that Augustus himself had hesitated on the same basis, even though an equestrian candidate for Julia's husband such as Gaius Proculeius would not have had any complicated involvement in affairs of state.[42] Whether this was in reality a scheme of Livia's to ensure Tiberius ended up as Augustus' heir goes completely unsubstantiated; it relies on the complicated and implausible notion that if Julia was married to Proculeius then she would have been unable to marry Agrippa, thereby preventing Agrippa from being promoted to heir apparent.

Then, as Proculeius was sure to die soon anyway from his stomach problems, Julia would be freed up before too long to marry Tiberius at a later date.[43]

Proculeius may well have been a potential husband for Julia but the evidence we have to hand suggests it was his track record and loyalty that made him eligible, not his stomach pains which if anything must have diminished his appeal. In any case a much more likely-looking candidate was already on hand. Suetonius implied that it was Augustus' idea to marry the widowed Julia to Agrippa, though the notion was hardly a surprising one. Unfortunately, Agrippa was already married to Octavia's daughter, Marcella the Elder, but this was just a technical inconvenience. Augustus had therefore to lean on Octavia to accept the two being divorced.[44] Octavia acquiesced though even if she had objected she would have been overruled. She organized Agrippa and Marcella's divorce so that the forty-two-year-old veteran could marry the teenage Julia in 21 BC. If what Dio had suggested was true, that Augustus had considered making Agrippa his heir, then Octavia had facilitated just that. In fact Dio describes Augustus as being the prime mover behind the marriage arrangements so that Agrippa's status would be sufficiently exalted to match his new job: overseeing Rome while Augustus travelled for several years to the East (see above, p. 80). Augustus was also removing a threat. His other chief friend and confidant Maecenas had warned him that Agrippa had now become so great he would either have to become Augustus' son-in-law or be killed.[45] The machinations of trying to manufacture a pseudo male line of descent while in reality relying on the female line were becoming ever more involved and complicated.

Agrippa was now restored to centre stage, suddenly promoted to being Augustus' heir through his marriage to Julia. It was an incongruous arrangement since he was neither a blood relation to Augustus nor Livia. Agrippa was not even originally of senatorial rank, though nor had Augustus' father been, the first of his line to become a senator. However, Agrippa was not only alive but also not suffering from stomach pains which, under the circumstances, were useful assets. He had already also fathered a child, a crucial practical qualification. Vipsania Agrippina had been born in 36 BC to his first wife, Pomponia Caecilia Attica, and was betrothed to Tiberius while still a baby. This might have been a sensible precaution but there was no possibility that Augustus or Livia could have seen this as a serious dynastic option in the mid-30s BC. Augustus, then Octavian, was still far from power and the chances of both children living to adulthood were not worth relying on. It was a gesture of confidence in Agrippa; in that political sense it was valuable. As things turned out Tiberius and Vipsania did live to marriageable age and were joined in 19 BC. Their son Drusus the Younger would play an unexpected part in Augustus' revised succession plans towards the end of his reign.[46]

Meanwhile, the marriage to Julia in 21 BC changed everything for Agrippa. That Agrippa was not a blood relation of the imperial house was neither here nor there. If anything, it helped water down the impression of a monarchical dynasty being manufactured. After all, his personal reputation was beyond reproach. In any case the real purpose was that he would father Augustus' grandchildren by Julia. By 20 BC Julia had started successfully bearing Agrippa's children. The death of Marcellus three years earlier had been a tragedy but now hardly mattered. Gaius was born in 20 BC and was promptly celebrated with an annual sacrifice to be celebrated on his birthday; Julia the Younger followed in 19 BC.[47] As the children started to appear Augustus must have been delighted that everything at last was beginning to fall into place. Agrippa and Julia went on to produce three more children who survived infancy. Lucius followed in 17 BC, Agrippina the Elder in 14 BC and Agrippa Postumus in 12 BC.

Augustus now constructed a complicated hierarchy of potential successors. Agrippa was clearly and publicly marked out as one by 18 BC when he was awarded some of the quasi-constitutional powers that formed Augustus' unique personal portfolio, including the tribunician power and also proconsular imperium. Even so, it must have been obvious to Augustus after Marcellus' death, if it had not been already, that he could take nothing for granted. It would be some time before he would know if Agrippa and Julia's children would survive. On his return from the East in 19 BC Augustus had given Tiberius propraetorian rank and allowed Drusus to stand for office five years earlier than normal. In 16 BC his two stepsons represented Augustus at gladiatorial bouts and fulfilled other duties, Tiberius for example serving as a praetor even though he already held propraetorian rank (someone who had been a praetor). A campaign in Raetia followed, with both men serving as leaders, and further campaigns ensued.[48] Livia's sons were in exceptionally prominent positions. While they were not in any sense yet designated as potential successors, it was clear that they might also easily be included. If so, that would not necessarily have been a sop to Livia. It was quite clear that both Tiberius and Drusus were men of high ability. Moreover, in 16 BC Drusus had married Antonia Minor, Octavia's younger daughter by Mark Antony. This reinforced Octavia's bloodline (see below).

Agrippa's marriage to Julia was an essential ingredient in positioning him as a potential successor but he was only a stopgap. Augustus quite obviously intended that Julia's role as the mother of his grandchildren was the key element in the arrangement. Of those grandchildren, the boys Gaius and Lucius were the closest Augustus would ever have to his own sons. They were rapidly propelled to centre stage, their doting grandfather's greatest hopes. The bloodline had had to pass through a female but this latest scheme meant at least it would revert to the male line when one of the boys succeeded Augustus. In the event this turned out to be a complete miscalculation. Far from the boys fulfilling Augustus' dreams, the key dynastic individual in fact was to be their sister Agrippina ('the Elder'). Agrippina's children included Caligula (37–41) and via her daughter Agrippina the Younger her only grandchild to grow to adulthood was her grandson Nero (54–68).[49] Caligula and Nero were the only two subsequent Julio-Claudian emperors descended from Augustus.

Obviously, Augustus had no idea this would turn out to be the case. Before Agrippina was born he had in 17 BC already accelerated the reversion to the male line by adopting Gaius and Lucius, convinced he could control the future. They became Gaius Julius Caesar and Lucius Julius Caesar respectively. By adopting them 'immediately' after Lucius' birth Augustus was legally bypassing Julia's role to prepare for the succession. He was also, incidentally, beginning the process of bypassing Agrippa's role too. The boys were now Augustus' sons, just as he had been Caesar's, and he took an active role in their upbringing and education.[50] Moreover, Dio says that they were actually appointed as his successors even though they were still underage. A fire damaged the Temple of Castor and Pollux in the Roman Forum in either 14 or 9 BC. This provided Augustus with an opportunity not only to rebuild the temple but also to associate the cult with Gaius and Lucius as living symbols of the heavenly twin cavalry heroes (plate 18).[51] Augustus was weaving the boys into his own myth, embellishing the semi-divine allusions of his name and descent.

Augustus had issued coinage from the outset of his career which made considerable use of his portrait. It reflected a wider policy of disseminating his appearance throughout the Roman world. More remarkably, Augustus was the first Roman who appeared on Roman coinage who also routinely incorporated his family members into the repertoire of designs. These did not usually include Livia, whose evolution into the symbol of Roman female sanctity was still developing, though she did appear on provincial issues in the Greek-speaking East where the idea of emperors and empresses was more familiar. Augustus may also have wanted to avoid any memories of Fulvia or Cleopatra in order to protect Livia and her reputation.

Even though Augustus had adopted Gaius and Lucius this did not entirely involve erasing Julia and Agrippa from the record as their parents. The dynasty and implied line of descent was promoted in coin issues. Julia appeared in the guise of Diana on the reverse of a denarius issued in 13 BC, a time by which Julia's growing family had validated her role as the route through which Augustus' line could continue. Like her sons and the rest of the imperial family Julia became the subject of obsequious cults in cities across the Empire. To amplify her importance Julia also appeared on another denarius produced in 13 BC, but this time flanked by her sons Gaius and Lucius. The design was part of a mechanism by which the boys were associated with Julia's qualities as a wife and mother. Local coinage in some of the Greek cities of the East, such as Magnesia in Asia, featured both Augustus and Livia, together with their grandsons Gaius and Lucius.[52] Augustus and Livia's busts are conjoined, a clear statement of their common dynastic identity, and imbuing Augustus and his grandsons with Livia's virtues by association. This was in spite of the fact that the boys could claim no descent from Livia. Indeed, a coin minted at Pergamum in Mysia depicted Livia on one side and Julia as Aphrodite on the other.[53]

The coin designs strengthened the identities of Gaius and Lucius as suitable successors. Agrippa was marginalized on the coinage. This was hardly surprising since he had been sidelined, despite his offices and privileges, from the dynastic fiction created by Augustus' adoption of the boys. Instead, he appeared, unnamed, on a silver denarius of the same year, side by side with Augustus on the reverse and seated on a platform; there is no explanatory legend but the issue probably records his renewed tribunician power.[54] Agrippa only ever appeared in his own right on commemorative coins issued by Caligula fifty years after his death.[55] However, Gaius and Lucius also appeared as children on the Ara Pacis, executed between 13 and 9 BC at the Senate's behest, Gaius being depicted clutching Agrippa's toga (plate 8).[56] Quite why Agrippa appeared here and not on the coinage is a mystery, unless it reflects uncertainty about exactly what Augustus was trying to create, especially as he had not personally commissioned the altar. Since Agrippa died in 12 BC his appearance on the finished monument turned out to be posthumous anyway. Until then there was plenty of other evidence to suggest that Agrippa was intended to be the successor until Gaius and Lucius had come of age.

One of the purposes of manufacturing the promise of a succession was to discourage further plots against Augustus. This made some sense. His serious illnesses were recent enough to have caused disquiet about his chances of surviving in power. If there was no designated successor then it was far more likely that a political opponent could see his chance to challenge Augustus. What is not so clear is just how important a component in this complicated plan Tiberius and Vipsania were. It is possible that their marriage, even though the betrothal had taken place some sixteen years earlier, was intended as a way to avoid marginalizing Livia. Yet it must have been obvious to Livia that that was precisely what had happened. Gaius and Lucius were now earmarked as potential successors, but very definitely not Tiberius. Tiberius' son by Vipsania, Drusus, was never accorded the portfolio of privileges that the benevolent Augustus organized for Gaius and Lucius.

If Augustus thought he had constructed some sort of happy family out of the various arrangements, he was entirely wrong. The remarkable history of the Julio-Claudians veered from ruthless violence to outright farce. It was also plagued by illness and death, unexpected or otherwise, which constantly intervened to destroy the best-laid plans and divert the narrative down a different path. It was not so much an attempt by Augustus to designate a successor as to find a designated survivor who had more than a cat in hell's chance of outliving him. That no one was safe was never truer than it was for the male Julio-Claudians and their male associates who sometimes seemed to die like flies. By 12 BC Agrippa had had his tribunician power renewed for five years. Renewal of the award was essential to avoid the idea of entitlement or presumption and it added to earlier renewals and privileges that had raised Agrippa to such heights that he almost equalled Augustus in having 'supreme power'. Agrippa was, however, smart enough to avoid overstepping the mark. Two years earlier, in 14 BC, he declined the honour of a triumph even though he had been voted one.[57]

Nevertheless, there was no doubt now how important Agrippa was to the regime. He was shortly to become an irrelevance but his genetic legacy would echo down the decades to come. Agrippa was sent out on campaign to Pannonia, where a rebellion was simmering. He set off, no doubt after fond farewells, even though it was late in the year. Leaving so late ought not to have been a good idea if fighting was going to follow. Agrippa's stellar military reputation, however, preceded him and the Pannonians promptly abandoned their rebellion when they heard he was on his way. Unexpectedly presented with nothing to do, Agrippa headed home. All seemed well but he fell ill soon after landing in Campania. News was rushed to Augustus who was then in Greece where he was presiding over contests of armed warriors in the names of Gaius and Lucius. This was part of the process of publicizing them to the wider population as his successors. Augustus immediately set out for Italy, only to discover to his horror that he was too late and Agrippa was already dead. A funeral modelled on the one he had already planned for himself followed, with Agrippa's remains being buried in Augustus' mausoleum instead of the one Agrippa had already prepared for himself.[58] It was a way of reinforcing Agrippa's membership of the dynasty for the sake of Gaius and Lucius' prospects as intended heirs.

Agrippa's death would have been something of a convenience, had he died a decade later when his sons by Julia were grown up. Dying when he did was distinctly inconvenient because neither Gaius nor Lucius was old enough to fill the void. Whatever opportunity Agrippa had once offered as a prospective successor now abruptly turned out to have been a mirage. If Agrippa was the threat to Augustus that Maecenas suggested he might be, he no longer was because he was no longer anything at all. All that was left of Agrippa, apart from his various children, were the public buildings and facilities he had provided for the people of Rome, an act of philanthropy that had also enhanced his image and reputation.[59] They now stood round the city like cenotaphs. Ironically, seventy-six years later the Baths of Agrippa would be the venue for an outrageous banquet held in honour of his great grandson Nero, last of the Julio-Claudians, descended from his daughter Agrippina. Agrippa also left a widow. How to solve the problem of Julia would become a major issue for Augustus. For the moment the rumours about her promiscuity and other disreputable behaviour remained no more than quiet simmering. If Augustus heard the rumours, and he may well not have, he ignored them.

Regardless of Agrippa's fate, Gaius and Lucius were the real focus of Augustus' dynastic plans. All they had to do now was survive to adulthood and beyond after Augustus' death. Both inconsiderately let their indulgent adoptive father down in this respect but for the moment the prospects looked good even though they were far too young yet to serve in any useful official capacity. There was at least another decade to wait before then. Augustus felt a need to share his load but had no alternative to choosing Livia's son Tiberius, which he did, according to Dio, 'reluctantly'. Not that Augustus necessarily disliked Tiberius. Augustus wrote to him around this period to tell him in a convivial and informal way about gambling with Drusus while playing a board game.[60] It suggests there was a degree of relaxed familiarity between them. If Tiberius thought for a moment things could stay that way he would have been wrong. Tiberius had to fill Agrippa's shoes in more ways than one. In 11 BC Tiberius was married to the widowed Julia, who was still pregnant by Agrippa, under coercion from Augustus. Tiberius was forced to divorce Vipsania for the purpose.[61] It was an intriguing twist in the tortuous family relationships caused by Augustus' dynastic tinkering. Tiberius was divorcing his father-in-law's daughter in order to marry his father-in-law's widow who was also his stepfather's daughter. Tiberius was furious but acquiesced since he had no real choice. Neither his, Vipsania's, nor Julia's feelings were of any concern whatsoever to Augustus, though as it happens Julia appears to have been amenable. Indeed, she was positively interested in the prospect. Tiberius was not. Like an aqueduct snaking across the Roman campagna, Augustus took whichever route he believed would achieve his goal, regardless of any natural obstacles in his way.

That same year, 11 BC, Octavia died, aged about fifty-eight. She had been a bastion of the Augustan state by complying with the marriages her brother arranged for her and facilitating the enlargement and continuity of the dynasty. She had also symbolized some of the personified virtues that Augustus wanted to associate with his regime. Her endless grieving for Marcellus was a sign of someone unable to come to terms with loss.[62] It also helped her image as an honourable Roman matron. In short, she had been a vital component in Augustus' consolidation of power. It was therefore only fitting that she was commemorated properly, though her presence was still visible in monuments such as her Porticus. Her legacy would live on. Her marriages had resulted in a number of children, some of whom would serve as crucial dynastic links. Her eldest daughter by Mark Antony was Antonia Major. This Antonia's descendants included Messalina, the third wife of Claudius, and Gnaeus Domitius Ahenobarbus, the father of the emperor Nero. The descendants of her younger daughter, Antonia Minor, by her husband Drusus would turn out to include the emperors Caligula, Claudius and Nero. Octavia was publicly honoured in what amounted to a state funeral, as befitted the mother of Marcellus. Orations were read by Augustus and Drusus. Her body lay in state in the Temple of the Deified Julius Caesar, ironically close to the golden statue of Cleopatra VII, her polar opposite in Roman moral judgements. Her remains were subsequently carried in a procession by Drusus and Lucius Domitius Ahenobarbus, her sons-in-law. A number of honours were voted her, presumably by the Senate, but Augustus vetoed some of these.[63] Since we do not know what the honours were, it is difficult to judge why he did this but a possible reason is that he wished the main focus now to be on Julia and the late Agrippa's children.

Octavia's contribution to the imperial family was great but Julia remained the essential dynastic link to the future. Marrying the widowed Julia to Tiberius was a method of increasing the possible outcomes in a way that invariably linked the dynasty back to Augustus. This latest marriage also had the potential to tie Augustus and Livia together through their children. The nuptials were described by Suetonius as 'rushed', which fits with Dio's description of how Augustus acted 'reluctantly'.[64] Having just achieved a degree of stability Augustus moved quickly to recover some semblance of continuity in the aftermath of Agrippa's death, despite the fact that Julia gave birth to her last child, Agrippa Postumus, shortly after Agrippa's death (hence the name). It seems that Julia found Tiberius an appealing prospect; given the later allegations about her adulteries, this may be a reference to her soliciting an affair with him while she was still married to Agrippa, though there is no suggestion that this was ever reciprocated. Julia was certainly unfaithful to Agrippa. She had already embarked on an affair with a senator called Sempronius Gracchus, an articulate man known for his intelligence. Agrippa had been aware apparently of what she was up to.[65]

If Julia had ever needed inspiration for indulging in infidelity she did not have to look very far. In 16 BC when she was about twenty-three and had been married to Agrippa for five years Augustus went away to Gaul. On the face of it the trip was to deal with wars that had broken out. Augustus had other fish to fry. He had issued so many decrees that he was now having to impose a large number of punishments, while at the same time letting some people off. Naturally enough the unfairness and hypocrisy did him no favours. Wagging tongues put about another story: Augustus had gone off to Gaul with Maecenas' wife Terentia so that they could continue their affair in peace and quiet away from Rome. Little is known about this liaison but Antony referred to Augustus' earlier interest in Terentia, along with several other mistresses, in a letter written some twenty years before. There were rumours that Augustus slept with the wives of men whose political ambitions and schemes he wished to know about. As an elderly man he was alleged to have developed a taste for virgins, sometimes even provided for him by Livia.[66] Augustus was a hypocrite but then he could afford to be.

If it was true that Julia was attracted to Tiberius this might have helped the marriage. Suetonius said Tiberius 'disapproved' of her feelings for him and was bitterly upset about being parted from Vipsania. To begin with the new marriage was a moderately happy one, briefly reinforced by the birth of a boy whose name is lost to us. The child's death in infancy ended any prospects of the Julio-Claudian line continuing through this route. Just to make things worse, the ill-starred marriage fell apart too. Tiberius and Julia ceased to live together. Tacitus says that Julia regarded Tiberius as her 'inferior'. This is particularly interesting because it implies there was an existing perception of precedence when it came to descent. If Julia regarded herself and her children as a superior bloodline to Livia's and if she openly expressed this view, then her comments must have created tension between her and Tiberius.[67]

In a Roman social context Tiberius was not inferior to Julia at all, especially as in a technical sense Augustus did not pose as being superior to anyone else from the senatorial class. In any case, Tiberius' pedigree from both his father and mother was patrician, unlike that of Augustus whose real father Gaius Octavius had been plebeian. The only discernible difference was that Augustus had routinely described himself as the son of the deified Julius Caesar and indeed continued to do so. Julia was therefore legally the granddaughter of a god and a descendant of Venus, though crucially she was not yet the daughter of a god.[68] While this divine association was a political stance adopted by Augustus, in Julia's eyes this may have been more easily translated into a literal belief that it conferred on her a special status. It was certainly a trump card that no other member of the imperial family was able to play; no one could dispute the fact that she enjoyed the unique privilege of being Augustus' only child. In a day-to-day sense this may well have converted itself into continual pressure from her for her sons, rather than Tiberius, to be promoted. She may have been encouraged in this by her lover Gracchus with whom she had continued to have an affair. Tacitus claimed that Gracchus, a 'persistent adulterer', had whipped up her hatred of Tiberius. She had written about her loathing for Tiberius in a letter to Augustus, possibly penned for her by Gracchus.[69] The women of the Julio-Claudians had a very clear sense of what counted for female precedence. Half a century later Agrippina the Younger was equally certain that her descent from Augustus made her son Nero a superior candidate for the succession after Claudius to his previous wife Messalina's son Britannicus, who could only claim descent from Octavia, Antony and Livia.

In the meantime, the death of Tiberius' brother Drusus, while on campaign against the Chatti in Germany in 9 BC, only made things worse in Tiberius' life. Drusus had fallen from his horse and was seriously injured. This resulted in a fatal infection that carried him off. A mark of how hard this hit Tiberius was that on Augustus' orders he went to Drusus, arriving just before his death, collected the body and accompanied it on foot the whole way back to Rome for burial.[70] Drusus was treated with great honour, Augustus and Tiberius reading orations, before he was cremated and buried in the Mausoleum of Augustus. He was not only awarded the title Germanicus but this title was also conferred on his sons Germanicus and Claudius (the future emperor). In an additional gesture statues of Livia were voted for, the second such grant of this innovatory practice that we know of.[71] She was also awarded the honour of being a mother of three children, her third being premature and dying at birth. It was a special privilege to compensate parents who had been unable to have three or more children and exempted them from any of the legal sanctions designated for childlessness.[72] These honours were all offered for the express purpose of 'consoling her'. They were bolstered by a funeral lament written for Drusus by an equestrian who had participated in the ceremony. He expressed his hope that Rome's search for a model of virtue would be fulfilled when Livia became *Romana princeps*, 'first lady of Rome'.[73]

Livia's bloodline was starting to look more important. Tiberius seemed ever more a better prospect to succeed his stepfather than anyone else, in spite of Augustus' fondness for Gaius and Lucius, who were still too young. Tiberius' loyal supporter, the historian Velleius Paterculus, insisted that his early promise had been very clear.[74] His military career had been peerless. Most famously he had travelled to the East in a campaign led by Agrippa in 20 BC to Armenia. Within a year Tiberius had taken a force into Armenia, restored its king Tigranes III and recovered the standards lost to the Parthians by Crassus at the Battle of Carrhae in 53 BC. It was a major achievement and reversed one of the most humiliating episodes in the history of the late Republic. He had also campaigned in Raetia, Pannonia and Germany.[75] By 7 BC, the same year that Augustus' powers were renewed for ten years, Tiberius had served as consul for a second time, convening the Senate in the Curia Octaviae (probably part of the Porticus of Octavia). He committed himself to restoring the Temple of Concordia in the Forum and to doing so in his name and that of Drusus. He also dedicated the Porticus of Livia, carrying this out with his mother. They then gave banquets, that in Tiberius' name for the Senate and Livia's for the women.[76] If it was the case that Tiberius was now in prime position to succeed Augustus (though this was not publicly acknowledged by Augustus), then in 6 BC the tables turned once more. Tiberius was given tribunician power for five more years, and imperium in the eastern provinces. He had been consul twice and had two triumphs. He was, apparently, 'the equal of Augustus'. Despite surfing 'the flood tide of success', he promptly mysteriously decided to disappear from public life and retired to Rhodes, an 'insolent withdrawal' according to Pliny the Elder.[77] The burning question of the day was why he had done this. It seemed irrational, inexplicable and insulting.

Tiberius subsequently claimed that going to Rhodes was really to avoid any suspicion of rivalry with Gaius and Lucius. He could just as easily have been infuriated by the elevation of two patently inexperienced boys, though Tacitus says it was Julia's attitude to him.[78] He may also have discovered some of Julia's extra-marital activities. Dio says there was a rumour that he could 'no longer endure her' but does not specify why. The result was that Julia was left behind in Rome.[79] Nothing was more attractive to Roman historians than the possibility of seeing underhand motives and malicious intent lying behind actions and events. It is just as possible that Tiberius had simply had enough of public life for the moment, demoralized by his forced marriage to Julia and the prospect of an enervating return to public life when Augustus died.[80] Julia's infidelities damaged Tiberius by association, partly because they had happened at all (and must therefore have somehow been his fault, or so it would have been perceived at the time), and because rather than dealing with the fallout he had just walked away.[81]

Either way, Tiberius' self-imposed exile meant Augustus had no one on hand to take over because Gaius and Lucius were still far too young. If that left Augustus with a sense of betrayal there was worse to come. If Agrippa knew about Julia's infidelity, then by this date Tiberius must have been fully aware of it too even if he also felt unable to tell Augustus about what was going on.

Dio presents a slightly more complicated context. According to him, Tiberius' renewed tribunician power, and commission to deal with Armenia, had annoyed Gaius and Lucius. Tiberius was worried about what might happen to him if they resented anything that made it look as if he was threatening their supposed birthright. We can be sure that the person responsible for encouraging Gaius and Lucius to believe they were specially privileged was Julia, the woman who had so pointedly tried to put Tiberius in his place as her inferior. In the event Tiberius went off to Rhodes leaving many of his staff and most or all of his friends behind. Dio's most useful comment is where he says that 'all possible conjectures' were made to explain Tiberius' disappearance, which at least exonerates him from blatantly interpreting Tiberius' actions to show him in the worst possible light.[82] In short, all, some or none of the reasons speculated about at the time or since might have been the cause. Given his subsequent withdrawal to Capri while emperor himself, we might simply have to content ourselves with accepting that for Tiberius his personality alone made him inclined to absent himself from circumstances that he found, for whatever reason, uncomfortable or distasteful.

Tiberius' absence from Rome was obviously going to raise eyebrows, and indeed it did. A cover story was drummed up by Livia and Tiberius who persuaded Augustus to allow him to act in Rhodes with the title *legatus Augusti*. The term meant that anyone who held it, such as governors and commanders of legions, was acting in the name of Augustus.[83] He was thus literally Augustus' delegate and personal representative. It made it look as if Tiberius was there on Augustus' authority and thus saved face. Even leaving Julia behind was not untoward; a prevailing school of thought held that senators acting on official business in the provinces should leave their wives at home.[84]

With Tiberius' departure to Rhodes, the evident failure of his marriage to Julia, and the lack of any child, Livia's prospects of being the mother of an emperor began to diminish. Gaius and Lucius seemed to be managing the remarkable achievement of surviving towards adulthood. Augustus gambled on promoting them further. By 8–7 BC Gaius was presented to the troops on the Rhine, depicted as an action-man warrior on horseback with a backdrop of legionary standards on gold and silver coins issued about then.[85] By 6 BC Gaius had been awarded the toga of manhood, the *toga virilis*, normally adopted when a boy reached puberty. Lucius was not far behind. Others joined in to welcome their impending manhood, with a keen eye on the possibilities for future imperial favours. Cities around the Empire took steps to celebrate their coming of age. In or around April 5 BC Sardis, in Asia Minor, made the occasion of Gaius' manhood a matter of public religious celebration and sent an embassy to Rome.[86] Honours for Drusus and Livia aside, the fact remained that Julia's children by Agrippa were still very definitely the preferred dynastic line. At Ephesus a pair of wealthy freedmen called Mazaeus and Mithridates dedicated a new arch leading into the agora to Augustus, Livia and, with clear acknowledgment of the line of descent, also to Julia, and the deceased Agrippa.[87]

Julia's misdemeanours did not erupt publicly until 2 BC. The revelations, when they came, were the subject of an epic crisis that threatened to undermine Augustus' entire programme of moral legislation, in particular the lex Julia de Adulteris Coercendis of 18–17 BC concerning adultery.[88] Quite how the story broke is unclear but Velleius Paterculus described the scandal as a 'calamity in the emperor's own household', brought about by a daughter who comprehensively disregarded her father's achievements and reputation. Julia had had affairs with a number of men, senators and equestrians, including Antony's son (and Octavia's son-in-law) Iullus Antonius, Appius Claudius, Sempronius Gracchus and Scipio, as well as various unnamed others. Augustus' own hypocrisy went without mention, naturally.

Julia and, as it would turn out a number of years later, her daughter Julia the Younger seem to have shared a mutual interest in 'every form of vice'.[89] Velleius Paterculus, a diehard supporter of Augustus, said Julia 'left untried no disgraceful deed', and Dio that her 'conduct was so dissolute' that she had been participating in drunken revels in the Forum and on the speakers' rostra.[90] Julia though was a woman whose life had been defined by being subject to the total control of her father and the men to whom she had been married. For a Roman woman there was nothing especially unusual about that, but Augustus was a father like no other and with an agenda like nobody else's. While Octavia seems to have been content enough to live within the framework set out by Augustus it is clear that Julia was not. It is much easier in our own time to understand that for some people, especially women, being contained to that extent and being denied any personal autonomy left no choice other than mute compliance or frustrated rebelliousness. After Agrippa's death Julia chose the latter.

Augustus was beside himself with rage and disbelief. 'Perhaps too strict' is one judgement of Augustus' upbringing of Julia.[91] In truth Augustus probably behaved as strictly as other fathers of his class and society. Julia was unlikely to have found herself less subject to a regimen of spinning and weaving, decorous conversation and compliance than any other young woman of her status. Augustus was quite capable of indulging her from time to time, as might have been expected. He once wrote to Julia to say he was sending her 250 silver denarii, to match the amount he had given each of his dinner guests so that they could gamble during the evening.[92] It was a lot of money – more than a legionary's annual pay. The fact that there was only Julia must, however, have concentrated Augustus' attention on her. Meanwhile his very particular political interests and needs made his requirements and expectations of Julia not only urgent but overbearing. He had chosen his position and path through life, but she had not. That it was a 'lifelong hardship' for Julia to be born the Roman equivalent of a princess, as it is for any other princess, is surely a reasonable judgement, not least because she had no siblings and was therefore, in her father's terms, 'the wrong sex'.[93]

Roman historians were usually completely unforgiving. Velleius Paterculus' description and that of Dio depict Julia as the wilful epicentre of licentiousness. In that sense their portrayal of her must be seen in part as based on the stereotype of fallen women that they believed in. The literal truth is harder to unravel as it so often is when the record is so one-sided. Julia was clearly being portrayed as belonging to a 'tradition' of immoral women. She had not just been allegedly promiscuous but also supposedly engaged in drunken partying in the Forum and acted as a political dissident. In Roman terms, especially at this time, to be 'immoral' was synonymous with being politically suspect. Many years later Seneca indulged himself with a salacious description of how Julia had enjoyed the attention of 'a whole crowd of adulterers', had engaged in 'nocturnal revels' and had even publicly advertised her availability by posting herself by the statue of Marsyas and dressing it with her hair garland.[94] This seems to have been the climactic moment in her scandalous behaviour because the gesture could not possibly have escaped her father's notice. The choice of statue was allegedly no coincidence. Marsyas had become associated with free speech and therefore also a symbol of opposition to the Augustan regime. Augustus regarded Apollo as a key divine patron of his reform programme. He had built a Temple of Apollo on the Palatine and used it, amongst other functions, as a meeting place for the Senate and also 'to revise the list of jurors'. There was even a Julian family myth that his mother Atia had been impregnated by Apollo who was, therefore, his father.[95] In legend Marsyas had challenged Apollo and lost, being flayed alive as his punishment, so Julia's actions were clearly designed to insult Apollo and therefore her father.[96]

Augustus was particularly disgusted by Julia's behaviour and said so in a letter, if the reading of the Latin is correct.[97] This could in one sense mark him out as a self-righteous prig and a hypocrite, and there was some truth in that. However, Julia's behaviour was potentially extremely damaging to him and was no doubt in part intended to be. It undermined his attempts to restore moral standards but far worse was the possibility of compromising his authority, which was so essential to the stability of the new regime. That Julia had had an affair with Iullus Antonius was particularly humiliating. His family origins only exacerbated the sense of outrage by tapping into Antony's reputation as the epitome of decadence and moral degeneracy. It was almost as if Antony had been revived to challenge Augustus once again.[98] Iullus' actions only seemed the worse precisely because he had been the beneficiary of Augustus' clemency, though exactly what Iullus was up to is not at all clear. Dio says he had 'designs upon the monarchy' which at the very least implies planning a coup and therefore also the killing of Augustus.[99] Such an extreme scheme is not referred to by any other historian; it seems unlikely that Julia could have become embroiled in something so audacious, reckless and unlikely to succeed. Even so, Messalina's better-attested conspiracy with her lover to topple Claudius half a century later shows that such things could happen, however insane they might appear. A number of other men, drawn from both the senatorial and equestrian orders, had been members of Julia's circle. Although they were to be severely punished too, it was Julia who was the most publicly vilified for wilfully presiding over the eye of the storm.

Augustus had eventually suspected something was going on but had refused to believe the rumours. His daughter had played him for a fool. He could hardly have wanted to admit it either to himself or anyone else. That rage was not only based on frustration and shame; it was also based on the fact that he knew only too well how he personally would be judged for having let Julia, through his own negligence, behave as she did. In a Roman context it would automatically be perceived as being his fault. Augustus knew that it could be extremely damaging to him to the extent that it might threaten his whole position if a critic used Julia's scandalous conduct against him and challenged his rule.

Julia had used the best possible form of subterfuge: she had hidden in plain sight and Augustus had failed to notice. Agrippa, who had died ten years earlier, had already suffered the shame of Julia's adulteries, which had only added to his 'irksome subjection to . . . Augustus'.[100] One of the named guilty, Sempronius Gracchus, seems to have been carrying on with Julia for at least ten years and possibly longer since Tacitus says that affair had begun during her marriage to Agrippa.[101] Evidently Agrippa had not told Augustus; after all, it would have reflected badly on him for failing to control his wayward wife.

Shouting too loudly about Julia's misdemeanours carried a risk for Augustus. It might have caused people to speculate on whether some or all of her children were illegitimate, though at least they were said to resemble Agrippa, or so she was keen to point out. Julia was said to have snapped at anyone who commented on her conduct with, 'I carry a passenger under no circumstances unless the ship is full.' In other words she took the simple precaution of only having affairs when she was already pregnant, thereby saving her from having to rely on the limited and cumbersome methods of contraception available.[102] This fact alone suggests that many of her infidelities were conducted before Agrippa died. Augustus for his part decided that since the children looked like Agrippa then it must be the case that Julia's 'extrovert character' just created a false impression that she was lustful. Therefore, he had to put up with two spoiled children: Rome and his daughter. He was fooling himself and he probably knew it, but it was the best way of saving face.

The source for these observations is a collection of sayings about Julia gathered in the early fifth century by a writer called Macrobius in a work called the *Saturnalia*.[103] They portray a bon viveur of wit and guile, both in love with the idea of being Augustus' daughter and repelled, frustrated and embittered by the way her unique status trapped her. She was determined to act as she pleased, rejecting advice from her father to emulate her stepmother Livia's conduct and choose older, wiser and more respectable friends and associates. She also dressed to kill, utilizing a wardrobe made up of showy clothes. Ever equal to the occasion, Julia pointed out tartly that she and her fast-set friends would all be old one day too, so she might as well enjoy herself while she could.[104] Perhaps Postumia, the errant Vestal Virgin of 420 BC known for her ostentatious dress habits and witty repartee, had experienced a similar form of frustration.[105] Julia was genuinely liked for her kindness, education and empathy, but she also provoked bewilderment at her 'depraved inclinations'. She was irritated that her father was able to indulge himself with the ridiculous pretence that he was an ordinary man, while she was never able to forget that she was 'Caesar's daughter'.

Macrobius' anecdotes about Julia are treated sometimes as a reliable portrait of the woman but in truth it is now impossible to know; the separation in time between Julia and Macrobius' lives was so great that with no intermediate source to substantiate any of his claims it is entirely possible that confusion, conflation, exaggeration and invention have all intervened along the way. This is invariably a problem with ancient sources to some degree but in this case the connection is even more tenuous than usual. The gap in time is equivalent to that between us and the early 1600s. Samuel Johnson's wit in the mid-eighteenth century was recorded in Johnson's lifetime by the lawyer James Boswell whom we know to have been Johnson's constant companion and admirer. The ever-vigilant Boswell also troubled himself to write Johnson's sayings down as they were uttered. He subsequently published them personally in his biography of Johnson. We have no basis whatsoever for knowing that anyone was present to write down Julia's observations about herself, Augustus or life in general (or those of Augustus about her). Nor do we know of them being retained in any form which allowed them to survive until Macrobius compiled his account. It is just as possible – perhaps more so – that even if there was some basis in truth, Julia's reputation was such that it became convenient to attribute established or anonymous witticisms to her, as well as to adapt or embellish them, generating an apocryphal element to the collection that we cannot now distinguish from the authentic elements.[106] Cicero had exactly this problem even in his own lifetime, finding to his annoyance that jokes were attributed to him that he had never made.[107] Nevertheless, it must have taken a personality of considerable strength to behave as Julia undoubtedly did; examples from other periods show that aspects of Julia's personality and some of her behaviour were not unique to her. Allegations of her promiscuity also raise the real possibility that Julia exposed herself to the risk of venereal disease, known to the Romans but not understood, especially if she believed her pregnancies absolved her of the need to use contraception. We know nothing about this in her case or any other female (or male) member of the imperial family, but it would be remarkable if the behaviour attributed to some of the Julio-Claudian men and women had not resulted in some incriminating evidence of infidelity, saved only by ignorance of the cause of some of the symptoms.[108]

When he was finally forced to accept that Julia really had been up to what the Roman gossip machine was saying, Augustus knew only too well that he had locked himself into a corner. His laws and stance on morality had earned praise from useful supporters. He had also already been given earlier that year the title *pater patriae*, 'Father of the Nation', the very epithet that Horace had said was synonymous with overseeing moral reform.[109] Augustus regarded the title as the crowning glory of his achievements, especially his moral reforms, and it would be one routinely adopted by his successors. Suetonius suggested it was an impulsive initiative offered by ordinary citizens which Augustus turned down to begin with. Finally, a senator called Valerius Messalla addressed him on behalf of the whole Senate, saying that giving him the title was part of praying for lasting prosperity and happiness for Rome. On 5 February 2 BC Augustus had accepted, tearfully, and said he hoped he would retain the title for life.[110]

In short, Augustus had stitched himself up. Having set himself up as the supreme moral guardian while his daughter ran amok under his nose meant he risked looking like an exceptionally bad case of humbug. Much more dangerous than any prospect of being called a humbug or a hypocrite was the possibility that one of Julia's lovers could have used an adulterous affair as a route to toppling the Father of the Nation, adding to fears of actual and potential conspiracies. Augustus had no choice but to let the law take its course, subsequently calling his daughter's crimes 'infringed obligations and violated sovereignty'.[111]

Whether Augustus liked it or not, Julia, not him, had through her actions determined the agenda. She would not be the last female member of the ruling house to do so. Had Augustus dealt with her behaviour in any other way he would have compromised his entire regime, his credibility destroyed. Julia was forcibly divorced from Tiberius and was banished to the island of Pandateria (Ventotene), off the coast of Campania, accompanied by her mother Scribonia, who went with her troublesome daughter on a voluntary basis.[112] Julia was to remain in exile for the rest of her life though after five years she was allowed to return to mainland Italy and live in the city of Rhegium (Reggio Calabria). This seems only to have come about because in around the year AD 3 there were popular protests that focused on Julia's banishment, even if it was only symbolic of wider dissent, and demands were made that she be allowed to come home.[113] Augustus said that he would see fire mixed with water before that would ever happen. The truculent mob responded with wit and audacity. They threw firebrands into the Tiber, blatantly insulting and defying Augustus. Confronted with what was obviously a dangerous and deteriorating uprising Augustus decided on a compromise and let her return to Italy.[114] There is no suggestion that Julia had any personal involvement with this episode but it illustrated how easy it would be for her to become a potent rallying point for anyone or any faction bent on toppling the regime.

Augustus remained closely involved with the everyday management of Julia's exile. She was banned from wine and any other luxury, which were so closely involved in the Roman mindset with immorality. She was permitted to be visited by men only with Augustus' permission, and then only after he had been supplied with an exact description of each visitor, including any blemishes.[115] This must surely have reflected the way in which Julia had been brought up, representing continuity in the control Augustus had exerted over Julia from her childhood that she had so determinedly resisted. Whatever Julia's culpability and responsibility for her behaviour, her final downfall was just as much Augustus' fault. In reality though there was little alternative. Julia was getting on and the end of her fertility was approaching. There was no obvious route down which she could have been sent to rehabilitate her. With Gaius and Lucius available, she had done her dynastic work. Julia was, unfortunately for her, becoming surplus to requirements. Had she found it within her to reinvent herself on the lines of her aunt Octavia then Julia could have found a lasting place at court. The spotlight, however, had moved away to Gaius and Lucius, and Tiberius.

Sempronius Gracchus was also exiled. He was dispatched to an island called Cercina (Kerkennah, off the southeast coast of modern Tunisia) where he was to remain for fourteen years until he was killed by soldiers sent to execute him. He died well, expiating to some degree the dissolute nature of his life.[116] Iullus Antonius was executed precisely because he was suspected of having ambitions to rule. This added to the revelation that even Julia might have been plotting to kill Augustus though another source says Iullus took his own life.[117] Since other women were implicated in Julia's activities Augustus had to impose a time limit on hearing other cases or else the scandal would have dragged on indefinitely, providing endless bad publicity. Augustus expressed his admiration for one of Julia's freedwomen, Phoebe, who had been involved also but taken her life before she could be prosecuted. He went as far as saying he would have preferred to be Phoebe's father than Julia's.[118] In other words, had Julia committed suicide then she would at least have earned her father's respect. It was not the only time he expressed such a sentiment. His former wife Scribonia had also been married before. Her daughter from that previous marriage, Cornelia Scipio, was exactly what Julia had not been. The poet Propertius recorded that Augustus had wept while saying that Julia had had a worthy [half-] sister in Cornelia and thus 'we saw that even a god may weep'.[119] Cornelia had died in 16 BC, fourteen years before Augustus found out what Julia had been up to, and doubtless Cornelia had become even more idealized by comparison in the interim.

Augustus blamed his bad luck on the deaths of Maecenas and Agrippa, believing that had they not died none of this would have occurred, even though it is quite obvious it had been happening before Agrippa died. Augustus' anger eventually gave way to shame but Julia remained in exile.[120] Julia was not to die until after Tiberius came to power, allegedly because Tiberius had her starved to death. Since Tacitus usually painted Tiberius in the worst possible light we should not automatically accept this at face value.[121] Julia was by then in her fifties, had borne a number of children and had been excluded from the life she had known for sixteen years; death from a variety of any number of possible other causes is as likely.

In the immediate aftermath of Julia's fall in 2 BC Tiberius seems to have made some effort to reconcile Augustus and his daughter, albeit from a distance in Rhodes.[122] He was pleased to have been divorced from Julia, but why he should have felt the need to intervene on her and her father's behalf is hard to discern. Perhaps he felt that, like himself, Julia had been the victim of circumstances and Augustus' diktats. Tiberius also felt relief at the fact that in 2 BC Gaius and Lucius were ever closer to adulthood, having evaded the chronically high levels of infant mortality so prevalent in pre-modern societies. It was beginning to look as if he was off the hook. Gaius was eighteen, and Lucius was not far behind at fifteen. In 1 BC Tiberius asked Augustus if he could return to Rome to visit relatives. Augustus denied the request on the grounds that since Tiberius had abandoned his family in the first place he might as well concentrate his efforts on forgetting them.[123] Under the circumstances Tiberius probably treated this as good news.

Before this time Gaius and Lucius had already been made into consuls-elect as they each reached the age of fifteen, 'as an honour to me' by the Senate and people of Rome, said Augustus. They were sent to visit the provinces and provincial armies.[124] The freedom, independence and indulgence they were allowed contrasted graphically with the way Julia had been brought up. One of the largest issues of silver and gold coins issued by Augustus showed him on one side and Gaius and Lucius on the other standing on either side of a pair of shields and holding spears. The legend described them as consuls elect and as the *principes iuventutis* ('the first amongst youth'). It was a novel title that suggested they were junior versions of himself as *princeps*, 'first among equals', commemorating how they had been acclaimed by the equestrian body. The coins appeared by 4 BC and continued to be struck for several years. The coins omitted any reference to the boys' true parentage. Some cities in the East were less politically sophisticated and had made dedications specifying the parental detail that must have been common knowledge, whatever the dynastic fiction Augustus' adoption of Gaius and Lucius was supposed to create. An inscription from Ephesus was in the names of Augustus, Livia and Lucius Caesar, who is identified as the son of Agrippa and Julia, and provides details of Augustus' titles which fix it to 4–3 BC.[125] There are other instances of Julia's dynastic role being openly acknowledged, especially in a military context where loyalty to the ruling family was of prime importance. An Augustan-era scabbard shows busts of Gaius and Lucius on either side of their mother's, commemorating their presentation to the troops on the Rhine.[126]

In 1 BC Augustus went a step further to consolidate the dynasty. Before going out to Syria Gaius was married to Claudia Livia Julia (also known as Livilla), the deceased Drusus the Elder's daughter by Antonia Minor, and thus the granddaughter of Livia, and sister both of Germanicus and the future emperor Claudius. She was about twelve years old. The idea was that by being married Gaius' authority and status would be enhanced, thereby compensating for his lack of experience. En route the places he visited were only too well aware of Gaius' importance and paid court to him; even Tiberius travelled to the island of Chios in order to pay homage to Gaius, in the hope that a public display of grovelling would make it look as if he was above suspicion.[127]

Julia's shame might have been a notorious episode in Augustus' rule, but Gaius and Lucius were unaffected. Augustus delighted in their prospects. On 23 September in the year AD 1, the occasion of his sixty-fourth birthday, he wrote to Gaius, calling him 'most beloved little donkey' (an absurd description of someone by then aged around twenty-one, but surely how he had referred to the boy as a child). He looked forward to seeing 'you and your brother proving your mettle and preparing to succeed to my position'.[128] The statement was unequivocal. Obviously Gaius and Lucius were the designated successors, while Tiberius remained in now enforced exile. Unfortunately, Augustus' optimism about his grandsons was about to be wiped out with dramatic consequences for Livia and her descendants.

Lucius Caesar had been betrothed to Aemilia Lepida, granddaughter of Augustus' former fellow triumvir, Marcus Aemilius Lepidus, great-grand-daughter of Pompey the Great, and great-niece of Caesar's assassin Brutus.[129] But before the marriage could take place the would-be groom inconsiderately expired on 20 August in AD 2 at Massilia (Marseilles) in Gaul. Within a month Pisa, of which he was patron, had commemorated his passing with plans for mourning that showed the Italian city's loyalty to the regime.[130] As if that was not bad enough, just eighteen months later Gaius died at Limyra in Lycia after the siege of Artagira in the campaign to recover Armenia. Gaius had been wounded on 9 September AD 3, which seems to have afflicted him both physically and mentally. In a curious echo of his father Agrippa's fate he finally succumbed on 21 February the following year while trying to make his way back to Italy.[131] At Rome all legal proceedings were put on hold until his remains had arrived back in the city to be deposited in the Mausoleum of Augustus.[132] Pisa's civic worthies also commemorated Gaius' passing, but amplified their fulsome praise this time round because it was obvious that Gaius had been the primary successor. Gaius had been 'snatched away from the Roman people by the cruel Fates' in an 'unexpected calamity' that had compounded the grief the city was still suffering for Lucius. Gaius' 'virtues' had matched those of Augustus, or so it was claimed. Various rituals and memorials were voted for by the council, including two equestrian statues of the deceased brothers.[133] In Rome the rebuilding of the Temple of Castor and Pollux after the fire of 14 or 9 BC was still under way; the plans to associate the cult with Julia's sons as the living embodiment of the mythical heroes had to be abandoned. The temple was subsequently dedicated in AD 6 by Tiberius for himself and his deceased brother Drusus.[134]

Augustus was, not surprisingly, devastated by the loss of his grandsons, in whom he had invested so much. Tacitus later cryptically suggested that Livia was somehow implicated in their deaths, subscribing to the Roman tradition of refusing to believe that such misfortune could possibly be down to something as banal as bad luck.[135] There was obviously no chance now that Julia would have more children, by Tiberius or anyone else. In the *Res Gestae* Augustus bemoaned the fact that fortune had snatched the young men away from him. In a private letter at the time he had been perplexed that one of his best friends had insensitively still accepted a dinner invitation.[136] All that was left of Augustus' hopes were the monuments erected in the boys' names that, just like those of Agrippa, stood like ghostly cenotaphs amongst the monuments of Augustan Rome. These included a porticus attached to the Basilica Paulli in the Forum. The basilica was rebuilt by Augustus well after it burned down around 35 BC, with an extravagant porticus in the names of Gaius and Lucius. Part of the inscription naming Lucius is still visible on the site today (plate 16). The text describes Lucius as Augustus' son and grandson 'of the deified [Julius Caesar]'.[137] Naturally, no reference to Julia or Agrippa was made.

Augustus knew he had to act quickly. Gaius and Lucius were immediately replaced as his adoptive sons by Agrippa's last child, Agrippa Postumus, born after his death, and Tiberius.[138] Tiberius also adopted, by or around this date, his nephew Germanicus. This meant that along with his own son Drusus the Younger, a grandson of Agrippa through his mother Vipsania, Tiberius now had two possible successors himself. The arrangement was strengthened by marrying his son Drusus the Younger to Germanicus' sister Livilla later in AD 4. The potential line of dynastic descent was now equally shared by the children of Julia and Livia, though it rapidly became apparent that Agrippa Postumus was entirely devoid of any of the necessary attributes apart from the unusual fact that he was still alive. That, unfortunately, was not all. Suetonius said that he had 'low tastes' and a 'violent temper' so Augustus rejected his last grandson as a potential heir and sent him to Surrentum (Sorrento). Of all the places to be exiled to Surrentum, with its elegant coastal villas overlooking the Bay of Naples, hardly counted as a Roman gulag. Augustus was still trying to be an indulgent grandfather of sorts.

Exile to Surrentum did nothing to make good Agrippa Postumus' personality defects. Instead, the young man only became more and more difficult to handle. Under the circumstances he could be forgiven for being annoyed at not having the privileges afforded his deceased elder brothers. Augustus finally resorted to having Agrippa sent to the island of Planasia (Pianosa, off the coast of Tuscany) and placed under a military guard.[139] The boy and his mother Julia remained potential focuses of dissent. A bizarre plot was concocted by an old man called Apicadus and a slave named Telephus to spring them from the islands where they were imprisoned. Their idiotic scheme involved kidnapping Julia and Agrippa Postumus and taking them to the army while Telephus pursued his absurd notion that he was to become emperor. It is not clear what part Julia and her son were intended to play.[140] Needless to say this ludicrous conspiracy came to nothing but the fact that it was uncovered at all showed that a more organized plot to use Julia and Agrippa Postumus in a more imaginative way might turn out to be a very real danger.

In terms of potential heirs, the only senior one left now was Tiberius, though choosing him as an heir meant accepting someone who was Livia's son rather than Augustus'. Tiberius did not even have the compromise qualification of at least being descended from Octavia. However, Augustus could see a way through this for the long term. He had already been turning over in his mind the alternative option of choosing Livia's grandson Germanicus, perhaps encouraged by her.[141] Germanicus enjoyed enormous popularity for his looks and youthful military vigour, and was also descended from Octavia through his mother Antonia Minor. He was now adding to this the attractive qualities of being a successful and happy Roman husband and father, guaranteeing a line of descent from Augustus through his marriage to Agrippina the Elder. His marital faithfulness was a matter of public note and admiration, clearly because it was considered exceptional.[142]

Agrippina the Elder had a reputation for volatility and being headstrong, both essentially 'masculine' characteristics that might have severely damaged her reputation as a Roman matron, but this was more than made up for by her devotion to her husband and her chastity. She remained defined in Roman history as his wife, *Agrippina Germanici*, 'Agrippina [the wife] of Germanicus'.[143] Her spirited personality was therefore directed in a way that helped Germanicus rather than hindered him. At any rate, Roman historians, especially Tacitus, were more understanding than they might have been no doubt precisely because she was married to the beloved Germanicus. She was also educated.[144] Their reputation as the golden couple of the imperial family was to become a significant factor in political developments. As the years rolled on, Germanicus seemed ever more the obvious option as successor. He was also twenty-seven years younger than Tiberius. It was, according to some of the sources, only because Livia interceded that Germanicus was pushed into second place through the process of adoption: Tiberius had adopted Germanicus, and Augustus had adopted Tiberius. As far as Livia was concerned she had done Tiberius an enormous favour in this respect and never failed to remind him of it.

The arrangements involving Tiberius and Germanicus seemed at last to have resulted in a workable plan for the succession. But some of the other problems had not gone away. Instead, they inconveniently turned into new problems. One of these was Augustus' granddaughter Julia the Younger who, like her mother, seemed irritatingly to have no sense of respect or duty. Born in 19 BC she had been married to a cousin of hers through their common descent from Augustus' first wife Scribonia. He was called Lucius Aemilius Paullus. She had at least one daughter by him called Aemilia Lepida (not to be confused with the earlier intended wife of Lucius Caesar mentioned above) whose marriage to Marcus Junius Silanus Torquatus led to a direct descendant of Augustus named Lucius Junius Silanus. This man was later betrothed to the emperor Claudius' daughter Claudia Octavia.[145] Julia the Younger annoyed Augustus because she had built herself an extravagant showcase house. This was in vulgar contrast with his own attempts to live as a 'modest' citizen in what he liked to think was an ordinary house on the Palatine.[146] It also conflicted with the respectful and compliant behaviour she had been taught by her grandfather to display.[147] Worse, her husband turned out to be suspect too. Aemilius Paullus was executed some time during the latter part of Augustus' reign for allegedly being a member of a conspiracy.[148]

Accused of adultery (though this was perhaps a trumped-up charge as a result of her husband's conspiracy) with Decimus Junius Silanus, Julia the Younger was also banished to the islands of Trimerus (Isole Tremiti) to the east of Rome in the Adriatic. She was prevented from bringing up a child she gave birth to after her sentence in around the year AD 8.[149] So ashamed was Augustus that he bemoaned the existence of both his daughter and granddaughter. In a vindictive gesture he gave orders that when they died they were not to be buried in his mausoleum.[150] Julia the Younger lingered in exile for twenty years, helped and supported only by Livia.[151] Oddly, Julia's lover Silanus was treated a good deal more leniently than her mother's adulterous associates. He was told that he could no longer enjoy Augustus' friendship and it was suggested that he exile himself, rather than it being imposed on him. Under

Tiberius he was allowed to come back on the basis that, legally, he had never been obliged to go into exile in the first place. He did so, but was effectively excluded permanently from public life.[152]

By the latter part of his reign Augustus had been through a number of complicated manoeuvres in his efforts to ensure a succession. From the outset he had found himself completely dependent on the female lines of descent available to him. As later generations came into being so he found himself trying to create alternative options through the tactical use of arranged marriages while at the same time being confounded by the unexpected deaths of, first, Marcellus and then Lucius and Gaius. Although he did have living descendants, these were the children of Agrippina and Germanicus, whose own origins were variously tied back collectively to Octavia, Livia and Julia. Whatever happened now, it was quite clear that the female line of descent in some form was to play the principal decisive role in what happened next to the Julio-Claudians. Livia's time had come and she was going to make the most of it.

5

THE DOWAGER EMPRESS AND MATRIARCH
LIVIA 14–29

After the death of Augustus in 14 two women dominated the imperial family. First and foremost was Augustus' empress Livia from whom all the later Julio-Claudian emperors were descended. Her son Tiberius had succeeded Augustus, but had no empress of his own. This gave Livia an unmatched opportunity to exert enormous power and influence over him, to his endless frustration. He denied her titles but could do nothing about the authority she had acquired as the wife of Augustus. She used this prestige to great effect. Agrippina the Elder, Augustus' granddaughter, was her only rival and represented the crucial bloodline. Agrippina was venerated as a Roman matron but she was famously 'impatient of equality'. She was married to Livia's grandson Germanicus, widely regarded as the most brilliant Roman general of his time. Both were loved by the mob. Agrippina was to bear him six children who grew to adulthood, one of whom would succeed as the emperor Caligula. After the sudden death of Germanicus in 19 a distraught Agrippina did all she could to promote the interests of her family but became the victim of a systematic campaign of persecution by Tiberius and Livia.

After the death of Augustus in 14 few people could remember what living under the Republic had been like. Anyone able to had to be in their late fifties at the very least and those with any political experience considerably older. In the intervening six decades since the Battle of Actium the Roman world had been transformed. Livia had experienced life as a privileged aristocrat, a fugitive and then as the most influential woman in the Empire. Although she bore her husband no children, every one of the four Julio-Claudian emperors who followed Augustus was descended from her. She had also outlived Octavia, from whom three were descended and Augustus' daughter Julia from whom only two could claim descent and thus from Augustus himself. Had Julia left a son fit to succeed Augustus then despite her damaged reputation she might have enjoyed restoration to the court. Instead, Julia was to die in shame in the first year of Tiberius' rule after sixteen years of exile. It was Livia alone who had survived as the grand matriarch of the imperial family.

Livia's power as Augustus' wife was complex, founded in the partnership they had operated, and expressed through her ability to influence him. She had reached what Dio called 'a very exalted station', far above women of former days. In this position she had no need to try and enter the Senate, public assemblies or military encampments, but was able to operate as if she was the one exclusively in charge of the Empire. She simply summoned anyone she wanted to her house. Whether this was deliberate on her part or simply a consequence of the way Augustus had arranged the manner in which he and Livia ruled is an academic point. What mattered was what happened in practice. As such Livia, the head of Roman upper-class womanhood, served as a force within the Roman body politic; she did so openly and not just as a manifestation of 'boudoir or bedroom politics'.[1] Since her power had even less constitutional basis than Augustus' then hers was founded even more on the nebulous concept of her personal authority, but it was no less a genuine force. Livia's general conduct and influence increased her fame to the extent that she was eventually being openly called what Dio described in Greek as *mētera patridos*, 'Mother of the Nation', though this title did not officially exist (in Latin it would have been *mater patriae*). It showed that by some of the public at least she was perceived as the other half of Augustan power, which she certainly believed herself, as we have seen.[2] The title was among the honours vetoed by Tiberius but it was informally revived after her death in 29.[3] Oddly, bronze coins of Livia were issued in Egypt between AD 1 and 5 bearing the legend *Liouia sebastou patros patridos*, 'Livia Augusta [empress] of the father of the nation [i.e. Augustus]'. The Roman administration of Egypt was evidently more convinced of Livia's entitlement but had found a circumspect solution. This was a neat way of associating Livia with the title *pater patriae* but which avoided creating a non-existent female version.[4]

Livia did not even have to give up her influence after the death of Augustus. Tiberius had no empress. Livia therefore lived on into his reign, determining and asserting her power while he, frustrated by her constant interference, tried to contain her and struggled to develop his own influence and pre-eminence. It was almost a dress rehearsal for Agrippina the Younger and her son Nero nearly half a century later. Livia was promoted and renamed Julia Augusta in Augustus' will. This made Livia into a symbolic continuation of his principate and reduced Tiberius to a support act. As far as Livia was concerned, she was the real thing and Tiberius only had his power because of her – she never stopped reminding him of that. Getting to that point was a remarkable convergence of circumstance, opportunism, guile and chance. This image of Livia is likely to have had its origins just as much in the desire to show Tiberius in a bad light. Merely depicting him as impotent in the face of his mother's dominance was an effective way of diminishing him. Perhaps he took some small consolation from the extraordinary fact that the best-quality papyrus (hieratica) paper had been renamed after Augustus, while the second grade was labelled 'Livia paper'.[5]

Although Livia had no other younger empress poised to steal her thunder, Augustus' granddaughter Agrippina the Elder soon emerged as a very real challenge to Livia's authority. Agrippina deliberately cultivated a following amongst the troops. Since she was married to Livia's grandson Germanicus, a man whose reputation for greatness grew by the year, the prospects looked good, but less so for Livia or Tiberius. Germanicus' Achilles' heel was, however, his long-dead father Drusus' reputation as a Republican. It was a stick to beat Germanicus – and Agrippina – with. And beaten they would be.

Julia's disappearance into exile, the deaths of Gaius and Lucius, the banishment of Agrippa Postumus, and then the shame of Julia the Younger had been a run of exceptional bad luck for Augustus. Worse, they effectively ended any immediate prospect of a dynastic descent from Augustus through Julia. From Livia's perspective the dynastic disasters looked more like remarkable good luck. The only reliable opportunity left for a successor was Tiberius whom Augustus had adopted only a few months after Gaius' death in AD 4. While others had fallen by the wayside, Tiberius had survived. To Tacitus, obsessed with the idea that villainy was afoot in the imperial palace, it seemed impossible that this was merely down to chance. He could not resist taking advantage of rumours that had circulated at the time that Livia had been behind all the untimely deaths, beginning with Marcellus. So he depicted Livia as the supreme architect of the downfall of Julia and her children, and as working constantly to see her own descendants rule the Roman world.

Tacitus was not alone. It was Pliny who recorded the mysterious portent that took place at Livia's villa known as Prima Porta on the Via Flaminia. In his version an eagle dropped a white hen carrying a sprig of laurel into her lap. Livia kept both on the instructions of the augurs, the chicken proving to be the progenitor of a vast brood. The laurel flourished so that it provided the wreaths for all those celebrating triumphs thereafter. Suetonius' version is fairly innocuous. Over a century later Dio repeated the story, though he did not bother with mentioning the hen's fertility. For good measure though he added that the phenomenon showed Livia was destined to 'hold in her lap even Caesar's power and dominate him in everything'. In an unsubstantiated conclusion he threw in an extra detail that while Livia might have been delighted, the story had caused widespread alarm. He was following Tacitus' lead by using the anecdote to suggest malice aforethought.[6] It was also a classic example of working backwards and 'finding' a series of pieces of evidence that explained what had happened as being deliberate and preordained rather than the product of chance.

Tacitus was typically oblique, throwing in various insidious suggestions here and there and allowing the reader to draw his or her own conclusion. Gaius and Lucius, for example, were carried off according to him by 'fatefully early deaths or by their stepmother Livia's guile'.[7] It was little more than an aside, beginning with the obvious explanation that their deaths were just bad luck, and then adding in a vague allusion to skulduggery on Livia's part without supplying any evidence. When describing Livia's compassion for her step-granddaughter Julia the Younger, exiled to an island in the Adriatic, Tacitus supplied another of his incriminating hints. He said that when Agrippa and Julia the Elder's children had been in trouble Livia had shown pity for them, but that when they flourished Livia had secretly undermined them.[8] By the time Julia had been exiled Augustus was in his sixties, and therefore by the standards of the day an old man. Tacitus believed this had also made him susceptible to Livia's force of personality, manipulating him into banishing Agrippa Postumus even though, despite his deficiencies, the young man had committed no crime.[9]

Livia was only a few years younger than her husband and therefore advancing years herself. If it was true that she had been involved in seeing off any of Augustus' earlier designated heirs then she had played a very long game. By the time Augustus was dead her own family's future was also vested in her grandchildren by Tiberius and Drusus. The deceased Drusus had left his widow Antonia Minor, whom he had married in 16 BC, with several children. The eldest, Germanicus, came to be regarded as the greatest hope of the Julio-Claudians. He was loved by the army and mob alike. His marriage to Agrippina was a match made in Augustan heaven. All they had to do was survive to adulthood and have children who did too. They achieved both, which in the circumstances was no mean feat. The offspring they started producing from AD 6 had the enormous advantage that through Agrippina they were descended from Augustus via Julia. In the event they had nine, six of whom made it through childhood.[10] Through the combined genetic forces of their parents these children were descended from all the great luminaries of the dynasty. As well as Augustus their forbears included Octavia, Agrippa, Livia and even Mark Antony. They were also bathed in their father's glory: Germanicus' military career, bearing and sheer charisma made them the golden family of the era.

Germanicus' sister Livilla (born 13 BC) had already been married to Augustus' grandson Gaius. His death in AD 4 wiped out that route to combining Augustus and Livia's descendants. Livilla was subsequently married to her first cousin Drusus the Younger, Tiberius' son by Vipsania. They had two children, Julia Livia and Tiberius Gemellus. Julia Livia was to marry a Gaius Rubellius Blandus. One of their possible children, Rubellia Bassa, may have had a descendant who was a consul under Hadrian. This is far from certain, but if it is correct the line is a rare instance of the Julio-Claudian descent reaching into the second century but it was not one that played any other part in imperial history.[11] Tiberius Gemellus would fall foul of Caligula's determination to be Tiberius' sole successor and was murdered, wiping out what might have been a rare instance of succession through the male line, albeit only from Tiberius rather than Augustus. Germanicus and Livilla's younger brother Claudius followed in 10 BC. He suffered either from cerebral palsy or some other handicap that resulted in his being dismissed as any serious dynastic prospect, though ironically he was the one who became emperor in 41.

A rumour circulated that Augustus also had played a part in the deaths of Lucius and Gaius, perhaps to ensure that the experienced Tiberius succeeded in their stead.[12] Velleius Paterculus suggested that Gaius was not, as a result of his wounds in AD 3, even mentally capable of fulfilling Augustus' ambitions for him. The story is another excellent example of how Roman historians were prone to invent motives and circumstances to explain events as they had turned out. Velleius Paterculus was a loyal supporter of Tiberius and it suited his purpose to write a story in which the 'best' man won out in the end. Whatever the explanation, true or invented, it did not alter the fact that Julia's line of descent in the space of a very few years almost evaporated. When it revived, as it soon did, it did so through an unexpected route.

Julia had been included on coinage produced by Augustus for obvious dynastic reasons, and always as a subordinate feature. Conversely, Livia never appeared on coins made at Rome during Augustus' lifetime. Her absence was an interesting omission, and difficult to explain unless she was simply not seen as part of the bloodline of descent from Augustus. She was, however, featured on a number of issues produced by cities in the Greek-speaking East where the tradition of monarchy was far better established, and so also was the idea of female monarchs. For example, some time between 11 BC and AD 12 Livia and Augustus appeared side by side as conjoined busts on bronze coins produced in Thrace. On the other side were the similarly conjoined busts of the client king of Thrace, Rhoemetalkes I, and his queen, Pythodoris.[13] Livia goes unnamed as does Pythodoris but there is no question about their identities. Both women appear at the same size as their husbands, but behind them. Augustus and Livia were being shown as joint monarchs in Thrace, as in some other places, because that was an image of power that was understood locally and must have been officially approved for this reason. It is no less significant that Livia was not depicted like this in Rome. No other empress of the Julio-Claudians would be portrayed this way until Agrippina the Younger. The combining of their busts on the eastern coins may simply have been symbolic, but if it is true that Livia routinely accompanied Augustus on his tours abroad it may also have been a literal depiction of how they were seen in public in the provinces.[14]

The coins show that the public image of Livia's role was adapted according to circumstances in different parts of the Empire. The question is whether the image on coins like the one produced in Thrace was closer to the reality in Rome than Livia's omission from issues there might have suggested. The coinage parallels the rest of the record in other ways. Under Tiberius Livia became the subject of a number of coins, reflecting her prominence in Tacitus' account of the reign, whereas under Augustus Livia only features occasionally in Velleius Paterculus, Suetonius and Dio, who are our main sources.[15]

The easiest way of analysing Livia's role is to look at the obvious difference between Livia as the embodiment of Augustan matronly virtue and Julia's flagrant disregard for her father's programme of moral reforms. Livia must have been fully aware of her husband's mistresses and so must Julia. At one point Augustus, enraptured by Maecenas' wife Terentia, had insisted on Livia and Terentia competing in a beauty contest.[16] We do not know who won but we can be sure that Livia bore the outcome with stoicism. The story about Livia and the unclothed men was a useful way of promoting an image of Livia as a bastion of moral rectitude.[17] Her influence over Augustus was a matter of some widespread interest. Here was a man who had battled his way through the ugly world of late Republic war and politics and ruthlessly seized supreme power over the Roman Empire. Yet Livia was clearly able to control and direct him to some degree. Her explanation was that she had made sure her own behaviour was beyond reproach, keeping out of Augustus' business and turning a blind eye to his infidelities.[18] He, for his part, indulged the belief that he was in a position to 'admonish and command' Livia as he wished, and confidently instructed senators that they should do the same since 'that is what I do'. They pressed him for examples of how he dealt with Livia but all he was able to come up with were some feeble comments about telling off women for how they dressed or adorned themselves.[19] Augustus, it seems, was a husband who had altogether too easily fooled himself about the level of control he exerted over his wife.

That Livia was able to manipulate Augustus is beyond doubt. He trusted her and sought her advice. Tacitus suggests she shared her husband's cunning, and her son's hypocrisy.[20] It was not so much a criticism as an acknowledgement of her ability to control affairs behind the scenes. After all, as a woman and as Augustus' wife she had in theory no agenda of her own and no rivals to pursue. When the conspiracy of Cornelius Cinna emerged in or around AD 4 he sought her guidance. We know little about the plot itself, but Dio invented a conversation between Augustus and Livia concerning it, perhaps borrowed from an earlier reference by Seneca. The discussion was manufactured as a vehicle for Dio to present points of view, but his choice of Livia as the medium through which Augustus considered an alternative option must reflect something that had become generally accepted as having some basis in truth. It provided a context in which Dio could pursue what he knew or understood about the relationship between the couple. In the course of their 'discussion' Livia assured Augustus that he was bound to be the subject of plots because 'all men covet the office of ruler' and told him to protect his person and sovereignty with a retinue and the 'soldiers who guard us', 'that we may hold the throne securely'.[21] She also assured him that they had an 'equal share' in the good and bad side of rule, but was aware that his safety was the only way in which she could hope to participate in ruling. She urged him to understand that ruling by fear was a great deal less effective than persuading people to love him.[22] Livia's final advice was to start with this conspiracy and choose clemency over terror. It was a variation on 'keep your friends close and your enemies closer'.

Augustus thanked her for her advice, which he followed. Cinna was even made a consul. Dio credits Livia with resolving the crisis in such a successful way that none of the conspirators ever tried anything like it again or were even suspected of doing so. He was, however, writing in the context of the more overtly despotic imperial monarchy of Septimius Severus and Julia Domna two centuries later. Nevertheless, the attributed plural 'we may hold the throne' is surely significant when considering how Livia saw herself by this point in the reign of Augustus, thirty-five years after he had come to power. If Dio's account here is accurate in spirit, Livia was not depicted like this in public in Rome. Around the year 10 Augustus was portrayed seated in the guise of Jupiter with other deities on the Gemma Augustea; he looks towards Tiberius, by then his intended (and only) heir, and his grandson Germanicus. Alongside Augustus is Roma rather than Livia, and Roma is not in the likeness of Livia.[23]

Livia was nobody's fool, and certainly not Augustus'. Her image was as carefully cultivated as her husband's and perhaps more so since it is quite clear that she was complicit in its construction (plates 9, 10, 11). She knew that her chastity and purity (*pudicitia*) were crucial to the credibility of the Augustan regime, so it is no great surprise that she restored the ancient temple of the women's healing cult of Bona Dea Subsaxana ('The Good Goddess beneath the Saxum Rock'), and probably also the plebeian and patrician shrines to Pudicitia.[24] Another beneficiary was the ancient temple of Fortuna Muliebris, literally 'Fortuna of Women's Lives', restored by Livia (and, much later, again by Julia Domna).[25] In this way Livia paralleled her husband's building programme and restoration of old virtues. She associated herself with other women, and it seems these must have been women who had been compromised by losing their husbands or suffering some other calamity. Livia brought up the children of some and also provided financial assistance to pay their daughters' dowries, as well as other acts of generosity and philanthropy.[26] One of the beneficiaries may have been the future emperor Galba, who was born in 3 BC. His mother died soon after his birth and so he was adopted by his stepmother. Augustus had been impressed by the boy and suggested he might one day have imperial power, though it is more likely to have been a teasing compliment to an impressionable child or plain invention.[27] Livia seems to have taken a great interest in his upbringing, so much so that he was the principal intended beneficiary of her will.[28]

Livia also enjoyed particular privileges though she was up to interpreting them her own way. She shared Augustus' inviolability of the person through the incongruous award of tribunician privileges to a woman.[29] Livia's presumption that she could protect her friends from due legal process merely by virtue of the fact that their prosecution would be an assault on her own inviolability was an inevitable consequence. It first surfaced under Tiberius in the year 16 with the case of Urgulania, Livia's friend. Urgulania's son Marcus Plautius Silvanus had served as consul with Augustus and also under Tiberius in Illyricum. Evidently Urgulania assumed this proximity entitled her to special privileges. Exactly what had happened is unclear (as so often) but it seems that Urgulania had acted unlawfully, assuming that Livia's friendship would protect her, and was being prosecuted by Lucius Calpurnius Piso, an independent-minded and bad-tempered senator 'who mistook inflexibility for firmness'.[30] To Piso's fury Urgulania moved into the imperial palace for protection. Piso refused to back off. Livia complained that she had been violated by his continued interference. Even more significantly, Livia also complained that she had been *imminui* ('humiliated', 'diminished'). In other words, Livia was asserting that by virtue of one of her friends being pursued she had now been reduced in the standing she regarded as her right. Piso's actions may have been a faux pas by the standards the imperial family regarded as their right; the fact that he behaved this way at all suggests that even two years after the death of Augustus the high profile and status of the Julio-Claudian women was something some members of the male senatorial diehards were still struggling to come to terms with.[31]

For all his protestations about his overbearing mother, Tiberius promptly set out to attend the court to support Urgulania. He went with a praetorian escort to add muscle. As the tension mounted Livia defused it by ordering the money Piso was seeking in redress for whatever misdemeanour Urgulania had committed to be handed over, but presumably without any admission of guilt. In other words the affair was 'settled out of court'. Nevertheless, Urgulania continued to flout the law when it suited her. She refused for example to appear before the Senate as a witness. Instead she had to be heard at home by a praetor who visited her to record her statement in private. Once a friend of Livia's, always a friend of Livia's. Piso was fighting a losing battle. By AD 16 several decades had passed and Livia had had plenty of practice at defining and applying her privileges.[32]

Livia was also given immunity from some of the legal restrictions imposed on women, such as the law that confined them to the upper seating at gladiatorial shows. This was achieved by allowing her a form of honorary membership of the Vestal Virgins. It was another inspired example of Augustus' ability to break the rules in a way that made it appear that he had done no such thing. The Vestal Virgins were allowed to sit opposite the praetor's tribunal in the theatre and Augustus deemed that Livia should sit with them.[33] The Vestal Virgins had formed just as important a part of Augustus' moral programme as Livia's image. It therefore made perfect sense to manufacture the completely contradictory notion of a married woman and mother, who was patently not a virgin, as being somehow entitled to the privileges of one. At this distance in time it seems faintly churlish to question Livia's personal qualities when there is no evidence to suggest that she did not largely deserve the pedestal she had been placed on; in the Roman world this convenient blurring was commonplace. After all, Augustus enjoyed the privileges of a tribune without actually being one, with Livia also benefiting to some degree. He had all the powers of a monarch yet never acknowledged that he was. Giving Livia the privileges of the Vestals elevated her in a quasi-divine way as if she was imbued with the metaphysical qualities of virginity and purity rather than the mundane reality of the fact that she was obviously not a virgin. Perhaps in some bizarre way Livia's unimpeachable morality was being fielded to redress the balance caused by Augustus' philandering and his daughter's.

Livia avoided any suggestion that she sought power in her own right. Our sources, ancient and modern, were and are only too aware of the parts played earlier by Fulvia and later by Agrippina the Younger. Both these women attempted to assert themselves as if they were equivalents of their husbands, exercising power and influence to a large extent in the same way they would have done had they been men. Livia understood that she had absorbed some of the power and privilege awarded to Augustus; the inviolability of tribunician status had seen to that. She seems to have otherwise perceived her power to lie in her role very specifically as a kind of first lady of Rome and therefore within the context of what a woman could do. Her posturing as the embodiment of traditional chastity, the implicit *mater patriae*, was the basis of her influence rather than any attempt to stride on to the stage and direct the course of history as her husband had. Livia operated in the background as an influence on Augustus. That was a cloaking device which meant that her influence was channelled and therefore largely hidden, rather than openly asserted. It cannot be coincidence that as a result Livia survived not only Augustus' reign but also well into her son's to die a natural death at an advanced age, unlike both Fulvia and Agrippina.

As for Julia the Elder, she had of course experienced at first hand life in an imperial household with a stepmother of such impeccable credentials that she could not possibly compete at any level. And she did not try to. She smugly dismissed Livia and her staid friends as oldies and stuck to the party girl lifestyle that would bring her down. Julia and Livia appear as such polar opposites because of the Roman sources and also the way that Augustan propaganda presented Livia. There is not even a hint that Livia compromised herself in any way. If there is anything incongruous about Livia it is that whereas other members of the Augustan family died off with alarming regularity and inconvenience, she and her son Tiberius seemed to be armour-plated and immune to any danger. It was this of course that lay behind the hints and suggestions made about her possible implication in the various family deaths.

We know nothing about how Livia reacted to Julia's fall from grace but she is unlikely to have dwelled long on her stepdaughter's fate. It is possible that Livia helped that along but under the circumstances it is improbable that Julia's position could have been any worse than she had made it herself. Livia's mere existence and profile were enough in their own right because they provided such a graphic contrast. All Livia had to do was sit back and wait while Julia hung herself. Julia's behaviour may have angered her, but it also inevitably helped make Livia look better than she already did. Julia, after all, was not her daughter and could not, therefore, reflect badly on her.

Instead Livia confined herself to making sympathetic noises about the tragedies that had befallen some of Julia's children. Three remained alive for the moment. By the year 8 two were in exile: Agrippa Postumus and Julia the Younger. The reasons for their removal were quite different but they came to the same thing; their behaviour precluded them from being allowed to dent further the image of the Augustan state so primly presided over by Augustus and Livia. Only Agrippina the Elder remained. Since she was married to Livia's grandson Germanicus she was an essential dynastic component and was soon fulfilling exactly what she was expected to by providing children descended from both Augustus and Livia. As they started to appear, beginning with Nero in AD 6, Augustus used them shamelessly to justify his laws encouraging childbirth. One of these obliged a widower or widow to remarry more or less immediately. Under public pressure Augustus allowed a three-year exemption. This was not enough for the equestrians who demanded persistently that the law be repealed. Augustus responded by displaying Germanicus' children, along with their father, in public and told the equestrians they should not decline to follow Germanicus' example.[34]

Livia's life changed completely when Augustus died on 19 August 14 at the age of seventy-five. She went from being the wife of an emperor to being the widow of a god and the mother of the new emperor. Of the Julio-Claudians only Agrippina the Younger would match this achievement. No other empress would manage the same until Julia Domna, wife of Septimius Severus, saw her sons Caracalla and Geta succeed their father in 211. The role of mother of the emperor involved a completely different dynamic and in Livia's case was unprecedented.

Prior to his death Augustus had shown distinct signs of failing health. Given his age this was hardly surprising but his life had been far from usual and his passing had the potential to cause the biggest political crisis for over forty years. Foul play was instantly suspected by cynics. They only had to look back a decade or more to the deaths of Gaius and Lucius, and before that Agrippa and Marcellus, to wonder if an impatient and ageing Livia had had enough of waiting and was actively helping Augustus along his way to the River Styx. A story was put about that Augustus had secretly gone to visit his last remaining, but exiled, grandson Agrippa Postumus. Augustus had gone with a friend called Fabius Maximus. On his return Fabius told his wife that it looked as if the two might be reconciled. Fabius' wife Marcia passed on this information to Livia who told Augustus. Fabius paid for his indiscretion either by dying shortly afterwards or being murdered, with Marcia blaming herself for the outcome.[35] The story is impossible to verify. If it was the case that Augustus was to be reconciled with Agrippa Postumus then there was a possibility that Tiberius was about to be bypassed in favour of the unreliable, but bloodline, grandson who was to be Augustus' heir. That seems unlikely.

Augustus had made errors of judgement in the past but he surely did not think that Agrippa Postumus, who had been isolated from public life for years, could now supplant Tiberius. This did not stop rumours circulating that that was precisely what Augustus had indeed decided.[36] Tacitus was scathing about Agrippa Postumus. He was 'callous' and 'unequal' to the task in every possible respect. Tacitus was no less derogatory about Augustus' stepson who had the 'old endemic haughtiness' of the Claudians to add to his inherent 'savagery', and despite the privileges heaped on him he always resorted to 'anger, deception and secret lusts'. To make things worse Tiberius was allegedly enslaved to his mother and her 'unruliness' and beholden to his son Drusus and nephew Germanicus, the latter having been adopted by him by around the year 4.[37]

Tacitus made no effort to pin on Livia the outcome of the secret visit to Agrippa Postumus other than to say that she told Augustus about Fabius Maximus blurting out the story to his wife. It was a subtle way of allowing the reader to see this as more evidence of Livia working to make sure Tiberius succeeded Augustus, especially as it followed on immediately from his character assassination of both Livia and Tiberius. Tacitus subscribed to the general view that the principate was a corrupting influence both on the individuals involved and the state. As such it therefore exacerbated the moral and political degeneration of the Roman world. Tiberius' defects and Livia's cynical self-interest were themes he developed to maximize the impact of his story. He knew they provided a compelling narrative strand and had sufficient basis in the gossip and rumour of the times he was writing about to be plausible. It helped inspire later historians. Dio repeated the rumour that Livia had fed Augustus poisoned figs once she heard about the visit to Agrippa Postumus.[38]

Tiberius had not been long with Augustus during a stay in the ailing emperor's villa on Capri from where they headed back to the mainland. Augustus was hit with serious bouts of diarrhoea so they started for Nola, a town to the east of Naples, but Tiberius left for Illyricum. Hot on his heels followed a letter from Livia telling him to pack his bags and come back at once. He went straight to Nola where Augustus had taken to his bed. Suetonius describes the two discussing business but Tacitus says it was not clear whether Tiberius arrived in time or not to see the prostrate Augustus before he died. It made no difference since death came soon.[39]

Neither Livia nor Tiberius seems to have been distraught at Augustus' demise. Livia's reaction was instantaneous and organized. Realizing the danger to the state should a power vacuum become common knowledge she cordoned off the house and even the nearby streets with armed guards. She then proceeded to release a fusillade of fraudulent optimistic updates on Augustus' health. Meanwhile, behind the scenes, preparations for the transfer of power to Tiberius were in full swing. In Dio's version this was because she was still waiting for Tiberius to arrive; he had clearly considered the records available to him. Dio concluded that not only was this what most writers had said but also that these were the more trustworthy ones. With that settled only then did Livia announce that Augustus had expired.[40]

Agrippa Postumus was immediately killed. Tacitus, who ominously describes it as the 'first act of the new principate', says Tiberius and Livia suspected and detested the young man. The story was out that Augustus had left instructions for his ignoble grandson to be murdered. Tacitus said this was mere pretence on Tiberius' part, not least because it would have been beyond Augustus to murder any of his own relatives. There was the added possibility that Livia had written the letter ordering the execution in Augustus' name. The story is not entirely implausible.[41] If Augustus was intending to have Tiberius succeed him then he must also have realized that Agrippa Postumus was a potentially dangerous focus for any malcontents who might see in him a chance to set up an alternative emperor. The strange Apicadus and Telephus plot a few years earlier certainly made that possible.[42] Augustus' visit then could be seen simply as a tearful farewell, conducted in the full knowledge that Agrippa Postumus' death warrant had already been signed. Tacitus was incapable of accepting such a possibility. He could not see beyond the notion that Tiberius and Livia were behind the killing. It is precisely this sort of issue in the sources that makes it so difficult to unravel what was going on. If Livia was as ruthless as Tacitus says, she would still have struggled to be as uncompromising and brutal as Augustus had been decades before. Moreover, Augustus had not killed Julia but he had still subordinated her interests to those of the state. Tiberius followed suit and unhesitatingly made Julia's conditions of exile even worse. Instead of being restricted to one town she was now held under house arrest. Her income was suspended on the pretext that she had gone unmentioned in Augustus' will.[43]

After Tiberius, Livia was the second heir of her husband's will, receiving one-third of the estate to her son's two-thirds share, though this did include secondary bequests to other members of the imperial family (not including

Julia) and tertiary bequests to civic dignitaries. The will, read out in the Senate, began with a tone of grudging reluctance that did Tiberius no favours. Augustus' opening clause was to refer to the cruelty of fate that had deprived him of Gaius and Lucius, so he was therefore leaving two-thirds of his estate to Tiberius. Tiberius could not have been made to sound more of a last resort option. Perhaps this was why one of his first moves was to make sure he had a Praetorian Guard escort.[44]

Augustus had made a special request of the Senate to allow Livia to be awarded rather more than the law allowed for, which was only a tenth.[45] It was another of his law-bending tactics that placed the imperial family, and especially Livia, above others. Augustus incorporated an important dynastic feature: Livia was classified as being of the Julian family. It was the equivalent of an adoption that made her in legal terms the daughter of himself as the deified Augustus, just as he had been the adopted son of the deified Caesar. This was the way she became Julia Augusta, just as he had become Gaius Julius Caesar. Since she was Tiberius' mother this was another legal way of establishing her son's credibility as a dynastic heir.[46] Fate had completely fallen into Livia's lap. It could of course have been, and probably was, purely a product of circumstances but in the Roman world such a convenient development was automatically seen by some as evidence of underhand dealings; whoever had succeeded Augustus would have been under suspicion. It happened to be Tiberius, so Livia – who had presided, apparently without the slightest harm to her person, over the death of one alternative heir to her son after another – was a prime candidate for the rumour mill.

As Julia Augusta Livia was a living version of some of the special qualities that Augustus had so proudly proclaimed in his *Res Gestae*, for example how his *auctoritas* exceeded that of everyone else. Augustus was a title he had taken in 27 BC which endowed him with quasi-religious enhanced qualities; now Livia had acquired some of the same elevated attributes. The deification of Augustus established a cult in his name, complete with temple, college of priests and its own rites, to which Livia was appointed priestess and allowed the privilege of a lictor when she performed her duties (plate 28).[47] She was evidently mindful of not only publicizing the cult but also her dedication to it. She awarded a million sesterces to a senator called Numerius Atticus who had the wit and presence of mind to swear blind he had personally witnessed the apotheosis of Augustus.[48]

Livia could now bask in the notion that her own special qualities had taken on a semi-divine status. Across the Empire she was also the subject of dedications by private individuals who wanted to show off their affiliation to the regime. Identifying Livia with a goddess made it possible to worship her in that guise. This tactic skilfully avoided making her into a goddess in her own right even if the difference on close examination was splitting hairs. It was far too early in the principate for a living member, whether male or female, of the imperial family to be explicitly promoted as a deity. Later emperors who tried that, and Caligula (37–41) was the most obvious example, tended to be murdered, making the unfortunate discovery that they were not divine after all.[49] On the island of Gaulos (Gozo, close to Malta) a woman called Lutatia commissioned a statue of Livia as Ceres and dedicated it along with her five children to 'Ceres Julia Augusta, (wife of) the Deified Augustus, mother of Tiberius Caesar Augustus'. She and her husband, Marcus Livius Optatus, served the cult as priestess and priest, *sacerdos* and *flamen Augustae*, for life.[50] His name inevitably links him with Livia's family and he therefore may have been attached to her household. At this time Livia's relative importance was amplified by the fact that she had no rival in Tiberius' empress since he did not have one, and also that there was no precedent for her role. The only possible rival was Agrippina the Elder and her significance had yet to emerge though she never became an empress. Livia was therefore the only female manifestation of Roman imperial power at this time and would remain so until her death. It was as if she was posing as both Augustus' and Tiberius' empress at the same time.

On the Palatine Hill are the remains of a traditional type of Roman *domus* now called, in an excellent example of wishful thinking, the 'House of Livia'. This type of house is much better known at Pompeii and Herculaneum where dozens have survived partially intact. Each has some or all the features of this type of building, but no two are identical. The 'House of Livia' is no exception. The house, which was originally built around 175–150 BC, was extensively redecorated with wall paintings of the highest quality during the time of Augustus. The design is an irregular rectangle, with an atrium (hall), triclinium (dining room), cubicula ('bedrooms'), peristyle (internal garden) and other rooms. Its remains are located between the ruins of the Temple of Victory and the Temple of the Magna Mater. Of relatively modest size, the building was a good match for the so-called 'House of Augustus' next door. It avoided being pretentious and the blatant flaunting of wealth. The house has only been identified as Livia's on the basis of a lead pipe inscribed IVLIAE.AVG(VSTAE), '(the property of) Julia Augusta', although there are several possible other candidates who used this name. Lead pipes could easily be reused – indeed the Julia pipe was physically connected to others of late first century and early third century dates, demonstrating that it had indeed been recycled.[51] Today the building is called the 'House of Livia' purely as a convention and no special significance should be attached to it, or conclusions drawn about Livia's lifestyle.[52]

Livia certainly did own other houses, the best known being the Prima Porta villa that lay close to the Via Flaminia, a short distance north of Rome.[53] The house is generally assumed to have been her principal residence once widowed. It was the source of the famous statue of Augustus, found in 1863. The statue shows Augustus in full military garb in his prime and at the height of his powers though the fact that it is barefoot makes it possible it was created posthumously from a bronze original made during Augustus' lifetime. Livia's property also included other estates in Italy and abroad, including Egypt.[54] Some of these she had inherited from Augustus. After he died she was wealthier than she had ever been.[55] The remarkable discovery in 1726 of a columbarium, known as the Monumentum Liviae, used for burials of her slaves and freedmen produced inscriptions that show how Livia's personal staff consisted of as many as forty-one slaves and forty-three freedmen, with the number of slaves probably being greater.[56] Her household as early as 39 BC had also included the decorative menagerie of naked 'prattling boys' who seem to have been treated like entertaining pets by older Roman women, alongside other performers, and dwarfs including a freedwoman called Andromeda.[57] Livia also owned further estates in Italy which included a brickworks in the Bay of Naples area, in Sicily and in other provinces including Gaul and Judaea.[58] The dowager empress Livia was, in every sense of the word, truly a *domina*.

Within five years of Augustus' death Livia began to appear on coins issued at Rome for mainstream Roman coinage rather than just on local provincial issues in the cities of the East. A series of brass dupondii minted under Tiberius depicted her on the obverse respectively as Justitia (Justice), Salus Augusta (Augustan Health) and Pietas (Piety). The first two carried on their reverses Tiberius' imperial titles and the third the titles of Drusus as heir apparent, which makes it possible to date them.[59] Given her apparent dominance over Tiberius it is possible she played a significant part in the coinage programme. At that date the dupondius was one of the commonest coins serving as small change. This, and the fact that the Livia types are not especially rare today, suggests that they were produced in significant numbers at Rome. They would have soon become a familiar sight in everyday commerce in the streets and markets of Rome and the Western Empire. The portraits are idealized and do not portray a woman in her late seventies. There is more than a hint here of the same perpetual youth used to portray Augustus in his own coinage and in sculpture, with Livia surely participating in the development of the image of an empress.[60]

Livia's status was further amplified by the issue of a sestertius, worth two dupondii, of the same date. Instead of a portrait of Livia it carried the abbreviated title of the realm SPQR ('the Senate and the People of Rome') and a two-wheeled carriage called a carpentum with the words IVLIAE AVGVST(AE), '(the carriage) of Julia Augusta'.[61] The significance was considerable. Carriages had been banned for generations in Rome and only under the rarest circumstances were people even of the highest status allowed to use one.[62] It was as if wheeled traffic was banned in London and only the monarch and a few other people were permitted to go about in limousines, forcing pedestrians out of their way. The coin was therefore an advertisement of elitist privilege, flaunted on an ordinary unit of currency. A law passed by Caesar in 45 BC, the lex Julia Municipalis, increased the restrictions on wheeled traffic in Rome but made an exception for some priests and, crucially, the Vestal Virgins. The coin's allusion was therefore obvious at the time. It was a public display of Livia's continued equivalence in terms of privilege to the Vestal Virgins, reinforcing her image as the collective embodiment of all prestigious female virtues. The carriage on the coin is probably a literal depiction of the actual vehicle in which Livia moved around Rome. Whether the use of a carpentum at this date was a new award that Tiberius had granted her or simply a reminder of a privilege she had already enjoyed for years is unknown.

Some of the provincial cities also paid homage to Livia in a way that confirmed her exalted status. Colonia Romula (Seville), formerly known as Hispalis, in Spain, issued a sestertius-sized bronze coin for local use with the deified Augustus on one side. On the other is a bust of Livia set on a globe and with a crescent above. The legend read IVLIA AVGVSTA GENETRIX ORBIS, 'Julia Augusta Mother of the World'.[63] It was a remarkable acknowledgement of the position Livia had reached. The word *genetrix* was clearly linked directly to the Julian descent from Venus, commemorated by Caesar's Temple of Venus

Genetrix in the Forum at Rome, even though Livia of course did not share that line. Her adoption by Augustus into the family had neatly dealt with that technicality. The coin evoked a semi-divine identity for Livia, enhanced by the presence of her deified husband on the other side. At Aphrodisias in Caria in Asia Minor the conflation of Livia with a divine identity was more explicit. Here a coin depicted Livia on one side, named simply as Augusta, and on the other a cult statue of Aphrodite-Venus in a temple. At Aezani (Aizanoi) in Asia she was paired with the great eastern mother goddess Cybele, known locally as the Anatolian earth goddess Meter Steunene.[64] In the East the blurring of rulers into living divinities was much better established.

None of these coin issues had a precedent either in the Republic or under Augustus. They belong to a new class of dynastic coinage which became more and more a characteristic of the Julio-Claudian period. Augustus, apart from the coins showing the mollycoddled Gaius and Lucius, had been very restrained in this respect. From now on the principal female members of the dynasty were much more likely to have a visible presence on the coinage whether as mothers, empresses or wives.

Livia seems to have been greatly pleased with herself that her son was now emperor; after all (so the sources allege), this was what she had wanted all along. She certainly believed that Tiberius was in her debt. Some years before she had seen to it that instead of giving up on Tiberius in favour of Germanicus, the golden boy of the Julio-Claudians, Augustus had adopted Tiberius and Tiberius had adopted Germanicus. In short, what Tacitus called Tiberius' despotism had been Livia's gift. Livia never stopped reminding Tiberius of where his power had come from and even demanded something back in return.[65] What form that recompense was supposed to take is not specified but it must have meant the privilege of sharing the power and influence, increasing the role she had filled under Augustus. Tiberius, for his part, constantly insisted that he was only emperor because the Senate had forced it on him; anything rather than admit his mother was responsible.

In public Tiberius' authority was shown as having been inherited from Augustus. It was constantly flaunted in coins and inscriptions that reminded everyone he was 'son of the deified Augustus'. Despite his professed reluctance to be emperor, Tiberius was not a man disposed to put up with any sort of half-baked compromise version of imperial power. He limited or denied Livia's honours as a result, though to be fair it should be noted that he sometimes limited his own. For example, he refused to allow September and October to be named after himself and his mother respectively. He was also appalled by a suggestion in the Senate that he style himself as 'Son of Julia' as well as 'Son of Augustus'. The latter, though, was quite acceptable, perpetuating the fiction of a male line of descent despite the obvious evidence to the contrary. There was a need to suggest that he now was a manifestation of Augustus in the manner of 'Augustus is dead, long live Augustus'. Depicting himself in public as 'Son of Julia' would not confer on him the same advantage, not least because she was so conspicuously still alive. To have allowed the 'Son of Julia' title to go ahead would have been an open acknowledgement that descent from his mother was his main qualification for being where he now was.[66]

Much more serious was Livia's idea that she was indeed entitled to equal power with Tiberius, which the title Julia Augusta seems to have suggested to her. Dio was quite certain that the reality was that Livia was taking a more or less equal part in ruling alongside Tiberius 'as if she possessed full powers'; the pair of them were passing decrees in the name of the Senate, as if the technical authority that came from the Senate could be transmitted via either of them.[67] Tiberius did not explicitly disabuse her of the notion; instead he avoided meetings with her whenever possible, thereby dodging the prospect of the long and detailed consultations she had been accustomed to having with Augustus, and told her to keep out of public affairs. He could not, however, ignore her experience and was obliged sometimes begrudgingly to seek her counsel. But Tiberius firmly denied her the title *mater patriae* ('Mother of the Nation') which was now proposed in the Senate, some of the senators coming up with the tactfully oblique 'Parent of the Nation', a title once used on posthumous coins of Julius Caesar. It was a way of keeping Livia in check.[68] Tiberius was emphatic that titles for women should be limited and he would show similar restraint with any voted to him. Part of his reasoning, Tacitus said, was the shamelessly traditional perspective that elevating a woman by definition would diminish his own standing.

With Tiberius seeking to restrict Livia's profile, she had to take advantage of any publicity opportunities that came her way. One day the Temple of Vesta in the Roman Forum went up in flames, no doubt assisted by the presence of a perpetual hearth burning inside it (plate 17). Livia raced down to egg on soldiers and civilians who were fighting the fire. It was the perfect gesture for the woman Ovid had called 'the Vesta of chaste mothers', a goddess she and the Augustan regime had actively identified her with.[69] This infuriated Tiberius who chose to see her actions as straightforward interference by a woman in public affairs where she had no business. By intervening she had publicly undermined him.[70] None of this friction went unnoticed by a wider audience who mocked Tiberius' character and his dysfunctional relationship with Livia.[71] Suetonius reproduced a collection of verses whose author castigated Tiberius for being 'cruel and merciless' and asked to be hanged if 'even your mother can feel affection for you'.[72]

Of course all these stories were very convenient to Roman historians. They provided ample evidence, as if more were needed, for Tiberius being a thoroughly embittered middle-aged man, humiliated by the presence of his domineering mother and trying to assert an authority that had been handed down to him rather than earned. It was an easy way to belittle Tiberius. Tiberius' efforts to restrict Livia provided an opportunity to show that she was rather too keen on authority and status for her own good; in other words, she would have assiduously pursued anything and everything that might turn her into a ruler in her own right. She had never attempted this under Augustus, at least not openly. The conclusion was obvious: she had decided that with Augustus' death her moment had come.

Meanwhile, another sub-plot in the story of the Julio-Claudians was taking shape. Livia had, to date, enjoyed the great privilege of having as few challenges to her status as possible. Julia had done Livia an enormous favour by turning out to be the worst daughter Augustus could possibly have had, and had been conveniently shamed and exiled, as had Julia the Younger. Octavia had had the decency to die years before, her reputation completely unsullied. Livia's daughter-in-law, Antonia Minor, had remained in the background, never remarrying after Drusus' death in 9 BC and had acquiesced in Tiberius' adoption of her son Germanicus. She had behaved exactly as required though she would have a dramatic part to play in later life.[73] That left Livia's step-granddaughter Agrippina the Elder. As she grew into adulthood as the wife of Germanicus she emerged as the key rival not only for popular affection but also as the supreme Julio-Claudian *domina* who was descended from Augustus and had borne his great-grandchildren. This became of crucial importance as the question of who would succeed Tiberius began to come into focus.

Livia did not get on with Agrippina, just as Tiberius did not get on with his own son Drusus or his nephew and adoptive son Germanicus. Nor indeed as it happens did Tiberius get on with Agrippina. Agrippina turned out to be quite a shock to Livia who had presumably never seen anything quite like her before. Agrippina was said to be volatile, apparently deliberately provoked by Livia. When describing Agrippina's death (which occurred in 33), Tacitus was moderately acerbic about her. She was, he said, 'impatient of equality and greedy for mastery' and as a result had let her masculine-style ambition take over the normal female frailties.[74] In short her only real crime was to be a woman in a world of men, run by men for the benefit of men. The phrase 'impatient for equality' (*aequi impatiens*) is one that seems entirely reasonable today. In Tacitus' world it had a more pejorative undertone because it meant a desire for open equality of power that was improper for a woman. However, because Agrippina managed to combine her ambitions with the proper wifely virtues of chastity and love for her husband she was regarded as a force for the good.[75] As far as Tacitus was concerned she and Germanicus, who in his eyes could do no wrong, had been destined for greatness.

Agrippina the Elder was born in 14 BC. Two years earlier in 16 BC Agrippa had been sent to the East, remaining there for much of the next few years.[76] Julia had presumably travelled with him, unless he had returned episodically, so it is possible that Agrippina was born abroad. An inscription recording Agrippa, Julia and their children, as well as Livia, was fixed to the base of a statue group commemorating the family at Thespiae in Boeotia in Greece after Agrippina's birth but before Agrippa's death in 12 BC. It may have been set up in honour of the family during a personal visit.[77] However, there had been a three-year gap since Julia's previous child, Julia the Younger, so it is no less likely that Agrippina was born in Rome. Not enough is known about the exact personal movements of Agrippa and his family to pin her birthplace down.

After her father's death the rest of Agrippina's childhood in the orbit of the imperial palace went on to be darkened by a series of unfortunate events. Her mother Julia's fall came when Agrippina was about twelve, not long before she came of marriageable age. When the story broke Julia's disgrace was a matter of such public notoriety that Agrippina can hardly have avoided feeling she was in the eye of the storm. We know little of her childhood but we can be sure that she was brought up as her mother had been, Augustus personally overseeing training in spinning and weaving, infusing her with a sense of decorous behaviour, and auditioning anyone whom she might see so that any undesirables could be kept away.[78]

The picture this paints is of a benevolent and overbearing autocratic man who clearly believed absolutely in his traditional entitlement to control the upbringing and behaviour of females in his family. Augustus had not ignored his grandsons; far from it. They were brought up in an equally traditional way appropriate to boys, in order that they had the skills suitable to embark on public life. That was precisely how Gaius and Lucius had been prepared for the futures stolen from them by fate. The girls, however, were supposed to grow up to be respectful, chaste, compliant and dutiful wives. That plan had gone badly wrong with Julia the Elder, and it was also to go badly wrong with Julia the Younger. Agrippina was a different prospect. She had been brought up in close proximity to her cousin Germanicus, his brother Claudius, and their sister Livilla. Their mother Antonia Minor, after being widowed when Drusus the Elder died in 9 BC, had moved in with Livia. Agrippina was therefore brought up in the centre of affairs. Her awareness of the importance of her position would affect much of her behaviour and judgement as an adult. As the empress who never was, Agrippina would still turn out to be one of the most important female figures of the whole Julio-Claudian era.

By the time of Augustus' death in 14 Agrippina the Elder was about twenty-eight years old and in her prime as a wife, mother and woman of high status. She had been married to Germanicus for almost ten years. Germanicus was 'the hero of the early years of Tiberius' reign', expiring mysteriously in Syria in 19 and leaving a widowed Agrippina then with six children.[79] His unexpected death magnified his reputation and that of Agrippina because of what happened to her later and because she and her children were direct descendants of Augustus. Tiberius was constantly judged by comparison to Germanicus; Roman historians treated Germanicus with quasi-religious awe, firmly depicting him as having been the lost emperor of the Rome-That-Might-Have-Been. Agrippina was seen as in every respect his soul mate, and a victim of the scheming Livia, the foetid malevolence of Tiberius and the devastating consequences of fate. Everything that was written down about Agrippina's life before and after the death of Germanicus was therefore done so with the benefit of hindsight. It was also done so in the comfortable refuge of the promise of Germanicus and Agrippina that was never tested.

The impact of Agrippa Postumus' murder was not altered by the motives behind his death. It effectively limited the biological Julian bloodline from Augustus to the children of Agrippina. In 14 Agrippina and Germanicus had already had three sons: Nero Julius Caesar, Drusus Julius Caesar and the future emperor Caligula (37–41) whose birth name was Gaius Julius Caesar.[80] Within the next four years they had three daughters: Agrippina the Younger, Drusilla and Livilla. Agrippina the Younger would turn out to be the most remarkable of all the Julio-Claudian women. Through Germanicus the children were also descended from Livia and Octavia. There seem to have been at least three more children who must have died in infancy, about whom nothing is known. Collectively it was a remarkable pedigree which would remain unmatched for the remainder of the dynasty's existence. Tiberius' own son Drusus the Younger could only boast of descent from Livia, but since Tiberius was emperor the potential for a serious problem of succession existed when weighing up the pros and cons of Drusus against his first cousin Germanicus. As so often, fate would step in to resolve the problem and lead to an outcome that no one could have predicted.

In 14 Germanicus was overseeing the administration of a census throughout the Gaulish provinces. Tacitus insists that Germanicus was *anxius* ('tormented') by the knowledge of the *occultis odiis* ('secret loathing') Tiberius and Livia had for him. Evidently the secret loathing was not secret enough. Tacitus was setting the scene for forthcoming events. Since Germanicus was Livia's grandson and his children her great-grandchildren on the face of it is hard to see why this exceptionally popular young man should have been singled out by his grandmother to be hated. The only real possibility is that his long-dead father, Drusus the Elder, was reputed to have sympathized with restoring the Republic.[81]

In Livia's mind this political betrayal on the part of her younger son could have, had he lived and carried through his wishes, denied her the very position she now held. But since Drusus the Elder was long dead the prospect was not only entirely academic but had also manifestly not happened. Perhaps Livia believed that if Germanicus succeeded one day he would seek to end the principate. Tacitus suggested that Drusus' Republican views were still very popular and that therefore Germanicus' fame was largely based on the notion that he would fulfil his father's dream.[82] If Tiberius was also anxious about Germanicus' intentions he had some reason to be. Germanicus was made governor of Germania Inferior shortly after Augustus' death.[83] He embarked on a campaign in the latter part of the year 14 which was designed to be punitive and also to settle the mutinous frontier legions by giving them an opportunity to win a little more heartwarming glory. The fighting went on into 15 with Germanicus doing remarkably well, attacking the Chatti and restoring a pro-Roman chieftain called Segestes.

He also came across the bone field of the Varian disaster of AD 9 and buried the Roman dead of the three massacred legions from that ignominious day.

Germanicus had travelled to Germany with Agrippina whose presence enhanced his popularity even further. Nevertheless at the beginning he had been severely criticized for putting his 'tiny little son and pregnant spouse' into danger caused by mutinous Roman soldiers. A huge drama followed with Agrippina as the epic centrepiece. Germanicus sent his family, and other women, off to the unreliable prospect of the Treviri tribe, the only chance of safety. Agrippina protested volubly. She pointed out that since she was descended from Augustus she was not going to do anything as degenerate as running away from danger. But Germanicus sent her off just the same. The sight of the women leaving was so shameful to the soldiers that they blocked the way and insisted the pregnant Agrippina lead them back. With her was Caligula, aged then about two, and already a great favourite with the troops because he wore miniature military sandals (*caligae*) on his feet. He was an invaluable public-relations accessory for Agrippina. Caligula's footwear is an interesting case in its own right. He was far too young to have understood the significance of his shoes but Agrippina, whose presence as a woman on campaign was an unusual arrangement, especially considering her condition, obviously did. It would later be put about once he was emperor that he had actually been born in the camp, though it seems in reality he had been born in Italy.[84] Her elder sons, Nero and Drusus, who go unmentioned, had presumably remained in Rome. The child in her womb was possibly one of those she miscarried or lost in infancy since Agrippina the Younger, her next child, was not born until November 15.

Germanicus confronted the soldiers. He told them he would gladly sacrifice even his own family for their glory, but he would not do so for the sake of 'their madness'. He would put only himself up for sacrifice to save them from the additional guilt of being responsible for the death of Agrippina and Caligula. The soldiers capitulated. Germanicus agreed to Caligula staying, but not Agrippina since her confinement was so imminent. This, at any rate, was Tacitus' version of events and from it Agrippina emerges as a remarkable figure who was clearly very aware of her lineage and its significance.[85] Dio's version differs in some degree. In his account Agrippina and Caligula were seized by the mutinous troops, furious at discovering that a letter from Tiberius offering them twice the bequest left them by Augustus was a fake manufactured by

Germanicus to calm them down. At his request they released Agrippina but held on to Caligula, soon capitulating by killing or punishing mutineers.[86]

Agrippina's profile in the context of the campaign was quite remarkable. Her conduct had echoes of Fulvia's activities decades before. She was not done yet. The following year, by which time she was definitely pregnant with Agrippina the Younger, she intervened forcefully in the actual fighting. A report emerged that a German force had surrounded Roman forces and was bent on heading over the Rhine and making for the Gaulish provinces. The obvious thing to do would have been to destroy the bridge and prevent the German advance. In Tacitus' view dismantling the bridge would have been an 'outrage', a straightforward act of cowardice. By adopting that position he could go on to celebrate Agrippina for acting as a *femina ingens animi* ('a woman of great spirit'). In action-heroine mode she stood at the head of the bridge, handed out fresh clothing and wound dressings to the troops as they fell back, and praised and thanked them. Agrippina was conducting herself in a way that undermined Tiberius and the male military leadership and probably deliberately; therefore one might have expected Tacitus to criticize her, just as Fulvia had been castigated by others for her interference in military affairs. Paradoxically, whereas Tacitus had been contemptuous of what he said were Livia's designs on having Tiberius succeed Augustus he was rather more supportive of Agrippina. This was based on his disdain for Tiberius even though he also intimates that Agrippina's purpose was to promote Caligula as a future emperor, presumably at Tiberius' expense.

Tiberius inevitably took a dim view of her actions for the obvious reason that by acting this way Agrippina was effectively marginalizing the soldiers' own commanders, as if she had not already gone too far by carrying the mascot Caligula around. That was Tacitus' suggestion but Tiberius could have been forgiven for feeling frustrated at an adoptive daughter-in-law who seemed to be operating a personal publicity campaign at the expense of everyone else. If Agrippina offered soldiers this sort of support and encouragement then there was nothing left for the generals to do. In any case Tiberius' real fear must have been that, rather than his commanding officers, it was he who was really under threat from Agrippina's actions. The loyalty of the army had, since Augustus' time, explicitly been focused on the person of the leader to whom the soldiers swore an oath. Had Agrippina been a man the threat she was posing would have been more obvious; as it was, the situation was so unusual it is clear Tiberius did not know what to do. It did seem plain enough that Agrippina's popularity now outweighed that of the commanding officers of the legions.[87]

Statues or busts of Agrippina the Elder show a steely-eyed woman with an elegant oval face. There is more than a hint of Augustus' expression and looks but that would have been deliberate. Given Agrippina's evident and understandable pride in her lineage she must have been keen to see any resemblance amplified. She did not appear on any coins until the reign of Caligula, by which time she had been dead for several years. These coins show a similarly firm profile with coiffured hair tied back and a loose ringlet on either side behind her ears.[88] The coin dies must have been engraved from surviving busts of Agrippina in the imperial palace or in public monuments. However, some of these may also have been posthumously carved once Caligula came to power, adding to the idealism. The impassive expressions on the coins and the sculptures are difficult to reconcile with the image of an imperial woman on campaign shouting out her right to stay with the army or refusing to allow a bridge to be demolished. There is, however, a consistency in the impression of a woman who knew her own mind and would not hesitate to assert it.

The complicating factor at this time was the gradual rise of the praetorian prefect Lucius Aelius Sejanus, though he had yet to show his true colours. Not long after Tiberius' accession Sejanus was appointed co-prefect with his father Lucius Seius Strabo. Some years hence Sejanus would be exposed as having conspired with Tiberius' daughter-in-law Livilla (by then the widow of his son Drusus the Younger), to try and wheedle his way into the imperial family with designs either of becoming emperor himself or of fathering one. That lay in the future, but it was convenient for Tacitus to suggest that Sejanus was responsible even at this point for sowing in Tiberius' mind the notion that Agrippina was trying to undermine him in the interests of her husband and sons.[89] This way Tacitus prepared the ground for exposing the destruction of Agrippina by Tiberius.

There was also the question of Tiberius' son Drusus the Younger born to Vipsania, the wife he was forced to divorce by Augustus in order to marry Julia. Drusus was on the face of it the most obvious prospective successor to Tiberius. At the time of Tiberius' accession in 14 Drusus was about twenty-seven years old, a similar age to Germanicus. He was descended from Livia through his father, and through his mother from Agrippa. Vipsania was Agrippa's daughter by his first wife Pomponia Caecilia Attica. Drusus could not claim descent from Octavia, unlike his cousin Germanicus. He had, therefore, no Julian blood.

Theoretically Drusus' Julian dynastic links were cast-iron because Tiberius was Augustus' adoptive son and Livia had been made Julia Augusta. Nevertheless, he could not compete with Germanicus and Agrippina. This perhaps meant little either to Tiberius or Livia but the lack of any connection to Augustus or Octavia was a serious disadvantage when it came to considering his potential popularity. At least his wife Livilla was Germanicus' sister and therefore obviously shared his descent through their mother Antonia Minor, the daughter of Antony and Octavia. Their children would therefore have some Julian blood in their veins. It was better than nothing. For the moment Livilla was a nonentity compared to Agrippina. Eventually she would pose a far more serious threat to the state. Drusus was certainly presented as a potential heir. At Augustus' funeral Tiberius had given Augustus' eulogy in front of the Temple of the Deified Julius Caesar, an impeccable 'Julian' setting. Drusus also delivered it in the Forum by the old rostrum. Drusus and Germanicus, along with the latter's three sons, were to share the bequests made by Augustus to his secondary heirs.[90]

Tiberius trusted Drusus up to a point but does not seem to have had any real fondness for him. Drusus had, allegedly, led a 'loose and dissolute life'. He also had a notoriously bad temper. Even so, in 14 when Tiberius was unable to finish his first address to the Senate after Augustus' death, apparently overcome by grief, he had asked Drusus to finish it for him.[91] He also sent Drusus later that year to quash a mutiny in the Pannonian legions, along with a deputation of senators and two praetorian cohorts.[92] The soldiers, who were protesting about conditions of service being ignored, were not impressed. They were frustrated by being sent, yet again, a 'son of Caesar' to fob them off. Drusus ordered the summary execution of some of the ringleaders and dispatched a posse to hunt for others. This soon encouraged other troops to show their loyalty by joining in the chase which, added to the onset of winter, saw the mutiny evaporate. Drusus returned to Rome, mission accomplished. When Tiberius commended the actions of both his son and Germanicus he implied that Drusus had resolved the problem without having to indulge the soldiers to the same extent as Germanicus.[93] The occasion helped highlight the contrast in popularity between Drusus and Germanicus and, by extension, Agrippina. That at least was the narrative Tacitus was so keen to drive. It was a way of reinforcing the idea that Germanicus and Agrippina were to be the victims of a conspiracy led by Tiberius and Livia.

Drusus was quite capable of damaging his interests by himself. The following year he blotted his copybook by choosing to put on a gladiatorial show in his name and that of Germanicus. It was a public-relations fiasco. No one could understand why he was bothering to celebrate with unnecessary bloodshed, including Tiberius who stayed away.[94] Even so, by 16 Tiberius was becoming anxious that Germanicus' activities were making Drusus' chances of winning glory ever harder. So he recalled Germanicus to Rome, telling him that if the war really needed to carry on then Drusus should have a crack at the whip.[95] Drusus' lack of maturity was becoming an ever more serious problem. Tiberius knew age was catching up with him. Travelling round the Empire to assert imperial power was a young man's job. Drusus was sent to Illyricum for a military command to get him away from the temptations of Rome and give him an opportunity to earn the army's loyalty and respect. Germanicus was left to deal with the much more serious problems festering in the East. That meant Agrippina being involved too.[96]

Armenia had become a problem once more for Rome. Under Augustus the region had been unreliably ruled by a series of client kings. At the start of Tiberius' reign Quintus Creticus Silanus, governor of Syria, had imprisoned Vocones for failing to rule properly. In 17 Germanicus was sent out to dismantle the client king system, turn the kingdoms into provinces and deal with the inhabitants' grievances. By then Agrippina had two daughters, Agrippina the Younger and Drusilla, as well as her three sons. During that year she fell pregnant again. Germanicus was dispatched to the eastern provinces late the same year and, as was their custom, Agrippina and two of their children went with him. Caligula was one of them.[97]

Germanicus and Agrippina travelled via Illyricum to visit Drusus. They carried on next to Greece by sea. It was a dangerous voyage that damaged the fleet and forced a delay for repairs. En route to Athens they visited the location of the Battle of Actium, Germanicus musing on how he was descended from Antony but also that Augustus had been his great-uncle. It was quite clear that the journey was becoming a symbolic progress through the imperial posses-sions of the East. The couple and their retinue sailed across to Lesbos where they delayed while Agrippina gave birth to her last child and third daughter, Julia Livilla. Agrippina's remarkable forbearance was illustrated by the fact that they were soon off into Asia Minor, paying a tourist visit to the site of Troy and the mythical origins of the Roman people. Germanicus also consulted an oracle of Apollo at Colophon who told him that he would experience a *maturum exitum/exitium* ('timely departure' or 'timely extermination').[98] The prophecy was a little wide of the mark. Germanicus' 'departure' turned out to be anything but timely – depending of course on one's point of view.

Germanicus' arrival in the East coincided with the installation of a new governor of Syria, Gnaeus Calpurnius Piso. Their relationship immediately collapsed, beginning with Piso slating Germanicus for favouring Rome's traditional Greek enemies over the 'dignity of the Roman name'. As an enemy of Germanicus, Piso was automatically depicted as a pantomime villain by Tacitus. The two met up in Rhodes but not before Germanicus had heard about the insults; even so he still magnanimously sent out a rescue party to help Piso's flotilla, which had been caught up in a storm. Piso then set out to start his governorship in Syria, his tenure being noteworthy only for rampant corruption.[99] He was assisted by his wife Munatia Plancina who joined in with her husband in the mud-slinging at Germanicus and Agrippina, conveniently supplying Tacitus with a 'bad' woman who was everything his beloved heroine was not.[100]

Tacitus, inevitably, assumed that Piso was entirely responsible for all the problems and depicted Germanicus and Agrippina as the innocent victims. Germanicus proceeded to get on with the job he had been sent out to do, arriving in Egypt in 19. We do not know if Agrippina accompanied him. She would have known it was not a good idea. Germanicus committed a serious transgression just by visiting Egypt. Augustus had prohibited senators and the higher equestrians from going there in case anyone decided to use the wealth of the Nile Valley to mount a challenge to Rome, as Antony had.[101]

Catastrophe followed. Germanicus returned to Syria only to discover that Piso had reversed his reforms in the leadership of the garrison and government of the cities. A fusillade of accusations flew between the two and Piso decided to leave. At that moment Germanicus fell seriously ill. Piso postponed his departure so that he could prevent any religious ceremonies for Germanicus' recovery taking place. Quite what he expected to achieve from a display of such puerile vindictiveness is impossible to unravel, especially given Germanicus and Agrippina's popularity. The story then becomes truly bizarre, or at any rate more bizarre than it already was. As Germanicus sank deeper into his sickness various pieces of evidence that black magic was afoot were uncovered. An allegation also materialized that Piso was arranging for him to be poisoned. Germanicus was worried about what would happen to Agrippina and the children, as well he might, but some respite followed when Piso left once more.[102] It was clear that Germanicus was dying. Referring to the crime committed by 'Piso and Plancina', describing how he had been the victim of 'womanly foul play', Germanicus asked his friends to protect Agrippina, 'granddaughter of the Divine Augustus' as he reminded them, and their children. He asked Agrippina to show restraint, begging her not to challenge those in power when she got back to Rome.[103] If true this is interesting evidence that he must have found her behaviour in Germany frustratingly difficult to keep under control, and realized how dangerous what she was doing might turn out to be.

Germanicus gave up the fight for life soon afterwards. He was cremated in Antioch after an inconclusive post-mortem had taken place.[104] Agrippina found the entire experience completely shattering and was ill herself, no doubt from stress and total incomprehension at the collapse of her world. She was determined to pursue her interests. She also had an eye for the moment. Even though she could not possibly have wanted this turn of events, she could make something of it by putting on a peerless performance of the grieving Roman matron. So Agrippina set out for Rome with her husband's ashes conspicuously accompanied by the two children she had with her, Caligula, aged about seven, and the infant Julia Livilla. Her position was potentially very vulnerable so she had good reason for making a drama out of her return journey. As Germanicus' wife she had been lined up as the spouse of a future emperor. That had evaporated in an instant. The only immediate prospect of an heir was automatically going to be Tiberius' son Drusus and his wife Livilla.

When the news of Germanicus' death reached Rome the conspiracy theorists set to work immediately. It was obvious to them that Germanicus had been sent to the furthest reaches of the Roman world along with Piso precisely so that he and Plancina could destroy Germanicus. Worse, Plancina was 'clearly' in cahoots with Livia because they had been involved in 'secret conversations', plotting because of Germanicus' father Drusus the Elder's Republican sympathies. Dio claimed that while everyone else was plunged into grief, only Tiberius and Livia were 'thoroughly pleased'. Tacitus was clear about the rationale: 'rulers were prone to be displeased about citizen-like [i.e. republican] sympathies in their sons'.[105] Rome was said to be sunk in gloom, only fleetingly to be restored when merchants, who had left Syria when Germanicus briefly rallied, brought news that he was on the mend. The hopes were quickly dashed with worse to come when the news broke that Drusus' wife Livilla had produced twin sons: Tiberius Gemellus and Germanicus the Younger. This was seen as pressure on Germanicus' own family. Tiberius, however, was delighted and bragged about the news.

Meanwhile Agrippina was still en route to Rome. She had continued to travel even though it was the winter of 19–20. She paused for a few days at Corcyra (Corfu) before braving the Adriatic. News had already reached Italy so supporters, who included soldiers, began to gather at Brundisium to greet her when she arrived with her husband's remains. The disembarkation was theatrical and clearly carefully planned for maximum effect. Agrippina walked off the ship with the children and holding the urn containing Germanicus' ashes herself. She handed the urn over to the tribunes and centurions of two praetorian cohorts sent to greet her. The whole entourage set out for a very public funerary journey to Rome across Italy through various cities, every place suitably out in mourning, while others off the route sent deputations. They were met along the way at Tarracina (Terracina) 47 miles (76 km) southeast of Rome by Drusus and Germanicus' brother Claudius, together with the rest of the couple's children.[106] The procession across Italy had been brilliantly choreographed to bring the Roman people together in shared mourning for their hero. It also amplified Agrippina's popularity so that she and her children presented a very real political threat to an increasingly unpopular emperor. Defining what the threat amounted to is less clear since Agrippina clearly could not be emperor and none of her sons could hope yet to rule either. The one realistic possibility was trying to position herself and her sons as the only succession option Tiberius could choose without incurring the wrath of the mob. That was what would happen many years later but Agrippina would be made to pay a terrible price along the way.

On arrival in Rome Germanicus' ashes were interred in the Mausoleum of Augustus. Neither Tiberius nor Livia made a public appearance. Nor did Germanicus' mother Antonia. Tacitus naturally had his own theory: if Tiberius and Livia had been seen openly mourning it would have been obvious they were only pretending. Also, they had ordered Antonia not to be seen mourning in public so that it would look as if they were following her example. They could not win. As far as Tacitus was concerned, they could do nothing right. Public mourning would have been hypocritical. Not showing up proved their underhand motives. Tacitus described an entire community in mourning as if a paroxysm of public grief had gripped the whole population, to the extent that some regarded the state as being on the point of collapse.[107]

In 19 just five years had passed since the death of Augustus. His death had symbolized the end of an era of epic change and renewal. It is easy to see how another prominent death, particularly of someone in whom so much hope had been vested, could be too much. Tiberius' subsequent treatment of Agrippina and the children heightened suspicions.[108] The situation risked getting completely out of control. What mattered was not the truth but the public perception that they had been cheated out of Germanicus and his family by the emperor himself. The occasion of Germanicus' burial was remarkable for the lack of honours but Tiberius said that a time had come to draw a line and move on. There was to be nothing on the scale of the funeral of Drusus the Elder. Tiberius urged people to get back to work.[109]

Not surprisingly, all eyes were on Agrippina. She stood as the sole grandchild of Augustus (Julia the Younger being ignored as she was in exile), a symbol of the state and also the mother of children whom people hoped would be the future of Rome. This was a dangerous development for Tiberius, though it was also one he might have anticipated when he heard about Germanicus' death. Around the Empire communities decided to commemorate Germanicus. At Siarum in Baetica (Saractin, Ultrera in Spain), plans were made to erect a marble arch in his honour with his female relatives as prominently depicted as the male. Although the main focus would be a statue of Germanicus on the top, it would be flanked by statues of his deceased father Drusus, his mother Antonia Minor, his sister Livilla, Agrippina and of all their children, including the daughters. An honorary tomb for Germanicus was suggested too, which would be the focus of an annual commemoration ceremony. No doubt mindful that that might have looked dishonourable to Tiberius, other arches were proposed for him and Drusus.[110]

Piso and Plancina were even sent for trial by the Senate on Tiberius' orders. Tacitus of course saw the whole process as a sham though Tiberius undoubtedly presented the case to the public as a genuine attempt to seek justice for the children of Germanicus.[111] Once proceedings were under way Plancina quickly put self-interest first and abandoned her husband when Livia interceded to have her pardoned. Plancina also had more friends in high places than her husband. With crowds outside ready to lynch him, and symbolically smashing up statues of him on the Gemonian Stairs, Piso realized he was finished. It was about now that posters were being put up all over Rome demanding 'Give us back Germanicus'.[112] Piso had only one option left and he took it, cutting his own throat. A rumour went around that Piso was about to produce instructions he had received from Tiberius to kill Germanicus but had been persuaded not to by Sejanus, only then to be killed by an assassin. The story about the secret instructions may or may not have been true (no other source supplies it). Tacitus included it to help reinforce a narrative in which Germanicus and Agrippina were the victims of a plot by Tiberius. He also insisted he had heard it from people he had known when young and who had been around at the time.[113]

Plancina managed to escape justice thanks to Livia. According to Tacitus Livia had persuaded Tiberius to speak up for Plancina in court. This provoked even more popular outrage. Then ironically the scale of accusations being levelled at Plancina on Agrippina's behalf began to inspire sympathy for Plancina because her children did not defend her. As a result, and helped by Livia's contribution, Plancina was acquitted. Tiberius also reduced the penalties imposed by the court on Piso's memory and allowed Piso's son to inherit his father's estate. Tacitus dismissed the event as an *imagine cognitionis*, literally a 'phantom investigation'. As far as he was concerned it was another disgusting example of Tiberius and Livia's persecution of Agrippina.[114]

Despite the acquittal of Plancina, Agrippina had good reason to be optimistic. Her eldest son Nero Caesar was on the cusp of manhood. He was fourteen in the year 20 and ready to be introduced to public life. As Germanicus' son he could be seen as either a great hope or a threat. Tiberius presented the youth to the Senate and asked that he be exempted from the normal preliminary vigintivirate magistracy so he could enter the quaestorship five years early.[115] The vigintivirate (twenty men) magistracies were posts of minor importance allocated to young men to kick-start their political and public careers. Tiberius pointed out that both he and his brother Drusus had been given the same opportunities by Augustus so there was a precedent. Nero's first public appearance was greeted with great excitement in Rome, largely because he was Germanicus' son and was also soon to be married to Drusus the Younger's daughter Julia Livia. Three years later Nero's brother Drusus Caesar followed in his footsteps.[116]

Meanwhile, lurking in the background was the praetorian prefect Sejanus who was scheming to see either himself or his own descendants on the throne.[117] In 21 Tiberius and his son Drusus the Younger served as joint consuls. This, and giving him the tribunician power in 22, marked out this Drusus formally as the successor because it seemed that with a young family and suitable experience behind him he was now up to the job.[118] Livia herself fell ill, relieving the pressure on Agrippina and, no doubt, Tiberius though he had to come back to Rome to see to her. Tension remained between them because she had recently placed her name before his on a dedication of a statue of Augustus, something he found most offensive.[119]

If Agrippina thought the worst was over and that she could look forward to a brighter future for herself and her children she was soon to have a rude awakening. The crisis appeared to have passed but, as so often, the reality was that this was only a lull before the next one. Drusus the Younger died in 23. Another potential successor had been vaporized by fate. Tiberius appeared to be genuinely devastated, as it behoved him to be. He instructed the Senate not to make the traditional vows for the safety of his great-nephews Nero and Drusus Caesar on the grounds that this was normally only done for men of experience and maturity.[120] Dio said the death of the boys' father Germanicus, a man of 'striking physical beauty' and 'the noblest spirit', had deprived Tiberius of someone whose very existence had kept him in check. Tiberius was now free to degenerate into cruelty and the use of accusations of treason (*maiestas*) against anyone he thought was an enemy.[121] Sejanus also spotted his chance to pursue his own ambitions, and that meant removing Agrippina and her children.[122] Quite prepared to be patient, he had started by seducing Livilla, Drusus' wife, before Drusus' death in 23.[123]

Drusus' death was subsequently blamed on Sejanus and Livilla. On this occasion the suspicions of murderous intent seem to have had more basis than those associated with Livia. They had allegedly poisoned him.[124] Sejanus and Drusus had fallen out and on one occasion ended up fighting. Sejanus realized that he would have a much better chance of manipulating Tiberius if he could remove Drusus. With Livilla's help and the use of willing servants poison was given to Drusus. With Drusus gone, along with Germanicus, Tiberius was suddenly presented with no eligible male heir to succeed him. Nero and Drusus Caesar were not yet old enough to fill the empty shoes but Tiberius entrusted them to the Senate's care and had Nero read out the funerary eulogy for Drusus.[125] It may have been around this time that the Grand Camée de France was created. This cameo depicts Tiberius surrounded by Agrippina the Elder and her children, and Livia. Above them in a celestial zone float the deified Augustus and the deceased Germanicus. Clearly intended to promote the interests of the children of Germanicus and Agrippina the Elder, there is a reasonable possibility that it was commissioned by Agrippina herself to advertise her sons to Tiberius as suitable successors. So few of these items survive that it is impossible to know for certain why they were made and for whom, but it is quite clear that emphasizing the women's role in dynastic and regime propaganda was a priority.[126] The design certainly marked a new stage in the image of the imperial family where both Augustus and Livia were portrayed as the key progenitors rather than just Augustus (plate 28). This was to become an enduring idea.

There were already signs that Nero and Drusus Caesar were being marginalized as part of the campaign against Agrippina and her descendants. Tiberius' twin grandsons, Tiberius Gemellus and Germanicus the Younger, were only four years old. A commemorative sestertius had been issued by the mint of Rome in 23 before Drusus' death. It bore his titles on one side and on the other a bust of each of his sons in a pair of crossed cornucopiae, symbolic horns of plenty.[127] Unfortunately, by the end of the year Germanicus the Younger had joined the ranks of deceased Julio-Claudians. No such offering was made by the Rome mint to commemorate Germanicus and Agrippina's sons, though coins in their honour were produced by some city mints in Spain. Since Claudius, Germanicus' brother, was universally regarded as hopelessly unsuited to rule, the only person left seemed to be the praetorian prefect Sejanus, a man whose status and influence equated in some ways to those of Agrippa under Augustus. The difference was that whereas Agrippa seems studiedly to have avoided overtly seeking office, Sejanus was rather more proactive in advancing his interests. He was also very well aware that his master plan had one rather glaringly obvious flaw. So long as Agrippina and her sons were around he had no more chance than a palace freedman of becoming either an emperor or a father of one. It was inevitable that, if they lived, Nero and Drusus Caesar would be promoted publicly as heirs apparent; he would be sidelined while Agrippina preened over her sons.

If that was equally obvious to Agrippina she soon found that her prospects and those of her sons were nothing like as straightforward as she might have hoped. To begin with Sejanus blew his own cover. He wrote to Tiberius to ask to let him marry the widowed Livilla who was just as keen on the plan. It was a reckless gamble and based on the argument that long before Augustus had considered marrying Julia the Elder to an equestrian called Gaius Proculeius (p. 88).[128] It was clear what Sejanus wanted, but he also suggested that it was a way of protecting himself against 'the unfounded animosities of Agrippina'.[129] Sejanus had decided to depict himself as a victim. That was a ludicrous suggestion but remarkably it seemed to take root, at least for a while. Technically speaking Tiberius did not turn Sejanus down; instead he pointed out how such a marriage would be inappropriate because Sejanus was an equestrian. Tiberius encouraged him to wait because high office would come at the right time. Nevertheless, the prospect of an alternative line of succession had come into play.

Agrippina was ever more certain that the only person who would look after her interests was herself. The net began to tighten. In 24, under pressure from Sejanus, Tiberius became suspicious that Agrippina was pushing the dynastic interests of her sons Nero and Drusus Caesar. Priests had been offering vows for their safety in the same breath as those for Tiberius. They denied that Agrippina was behind the additional vows but Tiberius still spoke to the Senate to warn them off from giving the young men the idea they were more important than they were. Sejanus used his colourful imagination to terrify Tiberius into believing the Roman state was becoming divided on partisan lines and threatening civil war. He told Tiberius that a ('faction of Agrippina') had become the rallying cry of opponents to the regime, and that the only solution was if 'one or two of the most active were brought down'.[130] There was a great deal of advantage to be had by suggesting there was some sort of coherent and subversive opposition coalescing around an identity that gave it form. If the term *partes Agrippinae* really was the one cited by Sejanus then the praetorian prefect was using it because he knew precisely what its impact would be. It would hardly have been surprising if Agrippina was the focal point for opposition – there was no one else, but whether it amounted to any more than a nebulous aspiration is impossible to say. Sejanus would not have cared one way or the other. Creating the impression was far more important than any substance. As a device it provided the perfect pretext for bringing in other more oppressive measures on the grounds that the state needed to protect itself.[131]

In 24 Tiberius started attacking Agrippina's circle. He ordered the arrest of Gaius Silius and his wife Sosia Galla. Silius' mistake had been to be a friend of Germanicus, Sosia's that she was very close to Agrippina. The friendship must have been formed in Germany where Silius had been a general in the earlier part of Tiberius' reign. His crime was to boast that his soldiers had been the only ones amongst the Roman forces in Germany not to mutiny, and that had they done so then Tiberius would have been toppled.[132] It was a stupid thing to say, even if there had been some truth in it. Silius ended up committing suicide while Sosia went into exile.[133] In 26 Octavia's granddaughter Claudia Pulchra was charged with committing adultery by a senator called Domitius Afer.[134] She was also accused of plotting against Tiberius. Claudia Pulchra was Agrippina's cousin, as well as being especially fond of her just as Sosia had been. As far as Tacitus was concerned the whole case was brought with the express purpose of tainting Agrippina by association. It is impossible to know whether Agrippina was guilty in any way of conspiring either with Claudia Pulchra or with Silius and Sosia; there is no evidence to confirm her involvement and nor is it worth speculating.[135] What mattered was the guilt by association – Agrippina was badly damaged by both affairs, and that must have been the intention.

To substantiate that storyline there is really only Tacitus' selective use of the evidence to go on. Agrippina would have agreed with his interpretation. She was only too aware that she was in serious trouble. After the Claudia Pulchra affair broke she stormed round to Tiberius only to find him sacrificing to Augustus. She exploded with rage at the sheer hypocrisy, considering that he was apparently going to so much trouble to persecute Augustus' descendants, especially as – and here we have an insight into how Agrippina allegedly saw herself – she was the 'true image' of Augustus. Tiberius dismissed her, suggesting that she was only aggrieved because she was not an empress, in this case using the word *domina* in its most exalted context.[136] It was a powerful and damaging allegation.

Realizing just how exposed she was Agrippina pleaded with Tiberius to allow her to marry again. She was, she pointed out, still of marriageable age (she was about thirty-nine years old by this time, so in Roman terms she was pushing the point), and marriage was the most suitable route for a woman of her virtue. The episode illustrated perfectly just how little power a woman could have in the system; she was entirely dependent on Tiberius as the senior male of the family and she could do nothing at all to secure her future other than on his say-so. It also illustrates the mounting stress she was under. The story had only come down to Tacitus in the personal archives of Agrippina the Younger who had kept evidence of the various problems her family had been through. It had otherwise gone unrecorded. We can therefore assume that Agrippina the Elder had told her daughter herself what had happened. Tiberius seems to have understood what she was saying but decided not to commit himself either way. In short, Agrippina was left hanging in limbo. She had pleaded and she had been ignored.[137]

The murk descended further when Sejanus decided to use people he knew Agrippina trusted to tell her that Tiberius was planning to poison her at a banquet. Armed with this 'intelligence' Agrippina refused to eat any of the food on offer. Tiberius, who may have had his attention drawn to her mysterious behaviour, personally offered her fruit which she also turned down. That gave him an excuse to justify his strictness with her, leaning over to Livia to comment on Agrippina.[138] Tacitus' version of events is strung out over several years. Suetonius collected abbreviated versions of these anecdotes and packed them into a single section. Both served to help create the impression of an ever more paranoid and cruel emperor.

Sejanus kept up the pressure. He was helped by the fact that later in 26 Tiberius decided to do another of his disappearing acts. Instead of Rhodes this time he took himself off more or less permanently to Capri. Tacitus refuted the idea that it was part of Sejanus' scheming and claimed that it had more to do with Tiberius' perverse personality and shame at his degenerating experience, as well as frustration at his mother's controlling influence. However, the withdrawal to Rhodes almost thirty years earlier suggests that Tiberius was someone who disliked public life to such an extent that self-imposed exile was his way of dealing with the pressure.[139]

Sejanus had been handed on a plate the freedom to pursue his duplicitous activities as he pleased. He also had a chance to act the hero and seized it with zeal. During a party in a villa at Spelunca Tiberius was nearly killed but Sejanus famously saved his life. The dining room was in a cave and the roof suffered a sudden and partial collapse. Sejanus sprung to his feet and leaned over the emperor to protect him. His actions might have been genuine, spontaneous and courageous but they had the added benefit of making him look completely selfless. Tiberius trusted him all the more, or so it seemed.[140]

Sejanus was left in charge of everyday government. No wonder Tiberius called him 'partner in my labours'.[141] By 27 and with the resources of the Praetorian Guard at his disposal he was sending praetorians out to spy on Agrippina and her son Nero and write down everything they did or said. The pretext was, naturally, that he was protecting the person of the emperor. This, after all, was the job praetorians were supposed to do though it is unlikely Augustus had ever envisaged them being used for covert surveillance of his own granddaughter. Other agents of Sejanus encouraged Agrippina and Nero to flee to the army in Germany or openly plead with the spirit of Augustus in the Forum for help. They refused, but the story was put about that they had thought about saving themselves like that anyway.[142] The destruction in 28 of another friend of Germanicus, an equestrian called Titius Sabinus, was achieved by a tawdry set-up organized by Sejanus. A casual acquaintance of Sabinus called Latiaris was primed to strike up a conversation with Sabinus, praising Germanicus and expressing sympathy for Agrippina. As with so many of Sejanus' victims Sabinus walked straight into the trap set for him. He joined in, adding his accusations about Sejanus and even Tiberius.[143] The outcome was inevitable once Tiberius had been told. Sabinus was killed. The climate of fear in Rome became even more febrile. Tiberius wrote a letter, presumably to the Senate, thanking them for dealing with Sabinus and referring to the various threats he felt existed to his life and the state. This was taken to be an obvious, if unspoken, reference to Nero and Agrippina.[144]

The praetorian prefect had always been prepared to take his time. Agrippina had been increasingly isolated for a decade in a war of attrition. In 28 the supine Senate was packed with men who were terrified of Sejanus. These syco-phants blithely voted for altars that would commemorate the relationship between Tiberius and Sejanus, who were currently both in Capri. It was a nauseating and obsequious display. Just in case an innocent passer-by wondered what the altars of Clementia and Amicitia (Clemency and Friendship) were supposed to be for, statues of Tiberius and Sejanus were set up to make their purpose clear.[145]

Tiberius had withdrawn from public life to such an extent that rumours abounded about his perverted, scandalous and sadistic behaviour. By disap-pearing into isolation, and leaving Sejanus at the helm, Tiberius had set himself up. Becoming the subject of scurrilous rumour and titillating scandal was more or less inevitable. It was a gift to Roman historians. Suetonius in particular delighted in tales of Tiberius' perversion.[146] Rome's former action man had turned into an ageing, filthy-minded and malevolent sloth lurking on Capri like a vindictive cave troll. It was around this time, in mysterious circumstances, that Julia the Younger was killed, still exiled on the island of Trimerus (Isole Tremiti). She had been festering there for two decades, appar-ently provided for by Livia. Augustus had accused her of having had an affair with Decimus Silanus but Seneca, who says she was executed with a sword, later claimed that 'no man called her guilty'.[147] If Tiberius gave the order, it has gone unrecorded, as has the reason for her death.

Tiberius still had his eye on the ball though. In 28 Agrippina the Younger, Germanicus and Agrippina's fourth child and eldest daughter, then aged about thirteen, was married on his orders to a descendant of Octavia. Her husband, Gnaeus Domitius Ahenobarbus, a brutal and unpleasant man, was the son of Antony's elder daughter by Octavia, Antonia Major. His family was old and esteemed, and his blood relationship to the Julio-Claudians only made him more suitable. Antonia Major's younger sister was Antonia Minor, the mother of Germanicus. Gnaeus Domitius was therefore Agrippina the Younger's first cousin once removed through her father. The relationship had other Julio-Claudian ties. Agrippina the Younger's great-grandfather was Augustus, Gnaeus Domitius' great uncle. Should Gnaeus Domitius and Agrippina the Younger have a child then that child would be descended from Augustus, Agrippa, Octavia, Livia, Germanicus and Agrippina the Elder.[148] They did, and one day he would succeed as the emperor Nero. But in the meantime, just as Tiberius was playing the dynastic game of thrones, death, the most effective catalyst of change in the days of the Julio-Claudians, weighed in again.

6

IMPATIENT FOR EQUALITY
AGRIPPINA THE ELDER 29–41

The death of Livia removed one threat to Agrippina but Sejanus, the ambitious and scheming praetorian prefect, maintained his attack on her, as did Tiberius. With designs on becoming emperor himself, or at least fathering one, Sejanus identified Agrippina and her children as his greatest obstacle and determined to remove them. His fall in 31 did nothing to end the campaign of persecution and she died in 33. However, her remaining son Caligula was so popular it was impossible for Tiberius to set him aside as a successor. Caligula rehabilitated his mother's memory and reputation when he became emperor in 37, along with some of his other female relatives. In the end, although she never became an empress, Agrippina the Elder's legacy was a remarkable one. She was depicted as an ideal of Roman womanhood, widely admired thereafter and going down in Roman lore as someone to be respected and emulated.

By 29 Tiberius had been emperor for fifteen years. His mother Livia had been an empress for approaching sixty years. She had exerted an enormously powerful influence over Augustus behind the scenes. Since the accession of Tiberius she had been a more publicly vocal and influential presence, asserting her control over Tiberius and being publicly presented in a way that made her as close to a *princeps* as it was possible for a woman to be. Her sole rival was Agrippina the Elder whose challenging circumstances since the death of Germanicus had completely marginalized her from public life. Agrippina's sons, the only dynastic prospect of male successors descended from Augustus, were also openly under threat from a praetorian prefect who was increasingly out of control, and plotting with Tiberius' own daughter-in-law, the scheming and ambitious Livilla, to seize power.

It was in late September 29 that Livia died after an illness that started earlier in the year. She was around eighty-six, by the standards of the day a remarkable age. Of 'brilliant nobility', she had been born during the convulsions of the late Republic, known or seen many of the main protagonists and fled for her life. Despite all that she had become the wife of the man who triumphed against all odds to take supreme power.[1] If Livia had an exalted sense of her own destiny and entitlement it was hardly surprising, and even justified. Rome had become a monument to the Augustan regime and Livia had become the symbol of the feminized image of the state. She had also become the female manifestation of the power of the emperor. Unfettered by a new younger empress to supplant her, Livia had been all but unchallenged. Even her son, Tiberius, had given up trying to defy her and exiled himself to Capri. Velleius Paterculus called her *eminentissima*, 'pre-eminent among women', and closer to the gods than human beings. He also claimed that her death was Tiberius' crowning sorrow, which is at odds with how Tacitus described her son's reaction.[2]

There is an important difference between Livia and the later empresses of the Julio-Claudians. She had not been born into a family that ruled the Roman state, but when she died she was one of the most important members of one that did. In later life Livia appears to have become increasingly frustrated by Tiberius, her only surviving child, and he by her. In the mid-20s Livia had used her influence to obtain citizenship for a man (whose identity is unknown to us). She followed that up by demanding that Tiberius appoint him to be one of a panel of ten judges known as the *decuriae*. She kept asking and he kept refusing. Eventually Tiberius said he would only do so if it could be on record that she had forced him. Furious, Livia looked out letters that Augustus had written rubbishing Tiberius' character and inclination to austerity, and read them to him. Baffled and irritated that the letters had been written and preserved in the first place, he exiled himself from Rome and only saw her one more time before she died; at any rate, it was believed by some that the letters were the main reason he disappeared from public life.[3]

Dying was straightforward enough for Livia but her affairs proved harder to resolve. Recalled to Rome from Capri for her funeral in the autumn of 29,

Tiberius refused to visit her. He dithered long enough to make sure that putrefaction forced Livia's burial before he arrived. Tacitus, typically, put all this down to Tiberius wishing to carry on his lifestyle, even though Tiberius claimed to have too much work to do. The Senate, ever more reduced to the state of an acquiescent and obsequious claque for the principate, voted Livia honours which Tiberius mostly turned down, including vetoing the idea of her deification. He claimed he was following her instructions.[4] She was buried in the Mausoleum of Augustus, and was voted an arch which was never built because Tiberius insisted that he would pay for it. He did not dare actually cancel the commission but by removing it from a potential charge on the public purse he could simply quietly forget about it.[5] He then overturned her will, and instigated a purge of her friends and associates.[6] It was not until the reign of Claudius, who authorized her deification, that she was posthumously rehabilitated.

Livia's death removed a threat to Agrippina, but at least Livia had had the wit to realize that Agrippina's children were also her great-grandchildren, and had sought to protect them from a greater danger. Sejanus was far more of a threat because he had 'greatly incensed Tiberius against' Agrippina.[7] Tacitus described the nature of Tiberius' rule from that point on as a *praerupta . . . et urguens dominatio*.[8] *Dominatio* is easy enough; it means 'despotism'. *Urguens* is a word that suggests an 'oppressive grinding'. *Praerupta* is harder. The word can mean either 'precipitous' or 'rash'. The implication is that a grinding despotism followed so quickly that it felt like a plunge into an abyss. It is a typical example of Tacitus' ability to use a very few words to create a damning judgement. The reason the plunge into the abyss seemed so fast is because a letter from Tiberius and Sejanus denouncing Agrippina and her son Nero Caesar was produced almost instantly. The letter was read out to the Senate, leading to the widespread belief that Tiberius had written it some time before, only for Livia to intercept and suppress it. Livia was now in no position to present any further obstacles.

In the letter Tiberius resorted to a well-tried Roman method of discrediting somebody. Nero Caesar was accused, not of political manoeuvring or of being a traitor, but of obscenity and homosexuality. Moral degeneracy, so closely linked to effeminacy, was the easiest accusation of all to make and the hardest to refute. He and later his brother Drusus were accused of being *hostes* ('public enemies'). Agrippina now found herself faced with memories of the ignominious fall of her mother Julia, and her son now being accused of depravity on a similar scale. Making such allegations against Agrippina would have been a step too far. She had too many friends in the army. Instead, Tiberius contented himself with a more casual form of character assassination by simply criticizing her arrogance and her insubordinate behaviour (*adrogantia et contumax*).[9]

The letter left most of the senators uncertain of what to do next. Normally self-interest would have told them whose side to back. This time they were not so sure. A senator called Junius Rusticus pointed out that pursuing a motion against Agrippina, as another senator called Cotta Messalinus was proposing, might backfire if Tiberius ended up regretting what had happened to Germanicus.[10] Junius Rusticus had, presumably, spotted what was going on outside. A crowd had gathered near the Senate house with effigies of Agrippina and Nero, chanting that the letter was a forgery and that it was impossible to believe Tiberius wanted members of his family wiped out. Tiberius was enraged and refused to back down. He sent out edicts that repeated the allegations against Agrippina and Nero, demonstrating that the letter was no forgery, and expressed his fury that one senator had obstructed his power.[11]

As the mood in Rome grew more febrile, opportunists and sycophants spotted their chance. Aulus Avilius Flaccus was one of those who had joined in with those making accusations against Agrippina, even though he had been a childhood companion of Agrippina and her sister Julia the Younger and shared in their education. His behaviour shows how personal affiliations could play so decisive a part in events, and also result in demeaning betrayals. Flaccus had later been chosen as a friend of Tiberius; this flattering elevation appears to have coloured his judgement. Flaccus presumably therefore participated in Agrippina's trial, about which we know nothing. In return for his efforts he was made the prefect of Egypt in 32, evidently the price of his soul.[12]

Agrippina was removed to a 'very beautiful villa near Herculaneum' for the moment.[13] Nero Caesar was eventually exiled to the island of Pontia (Ponza), dying of starvation or being executed in 31.[14] By 30 Sejanus had drummed up spurious allegations against Nero's brother Drusus Caesar, thanks to information supplied by his wife Aemilia Lepida. She was a thoroughly unpleasant and unfaithful woman who had spent her time making all sorts of accusations about her husband.[15] Drusus was thrown into a room on one of the lower levels of the imperial palace and locked away. There he would die in 33. That left the only viable prospects as dynastic successors Nero and Drusus Caesar's younger brother Caligula (Gaius) and Tiberius' grandson Tiberius Gemellus.

Sejanus had been working on the basis that by helping to remove Germanicus and Agrippina's children he was laying the way open for himself. Suetonius suggests that in reality Tiberius was using Sejanus to get rid of Germanicus and Agrippina's sons so that the way would be open for his grandson Tiberius Gemellus.[16] In fact Tiberius had either finally realized what Sejanus was up to or had decided that the prefect was no longer useful. Either way, bringing down Sejanus, and later destroying Agrippina, would be convenient ways to show that Tiberius' power was ultimately the supreme arbiter. Sejanus was put off his guard by being granted proconsular power. He and his son were also given priesthoods, serving alongside Caligula, only to discover that Tiberius had suggested to Caligula he might be his successor.[17]

The prospect of Caligula, son of Agrippina and Germanicus, as the next emperor was so popular that Sejanus realized he could not now possibly organize a coup. For his part, Tiberius began to register that Sejanus was so feared by the Senate and ordinary people that he could bring him down, using Macro, a former commander of the night watch as his agent. Sejanus' fall was engineered by letting him believe he was to be awarded the tribunician power, which was how Tiberius' status as successor to Augustus had been indicated. Sejanus went to the Senate rubbing his hands with glee where a letter from Tiberius was read out that started out well but slowly and surely began to raise concerns about his behaviour. Eventually it became obvious that there was no tribunician power to come. Senators who had previously acted as Sejanus' friends and associates made themselves scarce by darting out of the chamber. Sejanus was taken out by Macro and imprisoned by the night watch. He was executed the next day (18 October 31) and his children murdered. His wife Apicata committed suicide and left a note that implicated Livilla in Sejanus' plot.[18]

Meanwhile Tiberius was waiting outside Rome to see what happened. He had a fleet ready in case Sejanus had taken the city and he needed to escape. However, there was a rumour that Tiberius had also arranged for Macro to declare Drusus Caesar as emperor in the event of a rising.[19] It was the closest Agrippina came to being the mother of an emperor in her lifetime. When Tiberius learned that Sejanus was dead the plan was abandoned. Macro was made praetorian prefect, his reward. A purge of all Sejanus' relatives, friends and associates followed, lasting well into the following year. An interesting aspect of this was the way any implicated women were treated. Since women could not be prosecuted for attempting to take over the state, any women who showed grief at the execution of male relatives for being involved in any way with Sejanus were instead 'indicted for their tears'.[20] The investigation ordered by Tiberius also confirmed Livilla's involvement. She was either executed or starved to death by her disgusted mother Antonia Minor.[21] The latter possibility was clearly borrowed from the traditional sanctions imposed on an unchaste Vestal Virgin. Any monument connected with Sejanus was destroyed but plans were also made to subject monuments of Livilla to the same treatment. She was the first of the Julio-Claudian women to be subjected to *damnatio memoriae* (Messalina was to be the second). Livilla was literally erased. There was no funeral and the uncertainty about the nature of her death shows how successfully she had been deleted from the record.[22]

A bizarre twist followed with the case of the pseudo-Drusus. Agrippina's second son Drusus Caesar was still incarcerated in the imperial palace. A story broke in Greece and Asia Minor that he had escaped and had been seen in the Cyclades and then on mainland Greece. This rapidly became elaborated into the notion that 'Drusus' was bent on heading towards Germanicus' former soldiers in the East in order to mount an invasion of Egypt and Syria. The story collapsed when it turned out that the pseudo-Drusus had declared himself to be the son of a senator called Marcus Junius Silanus.[23] In reality Drusus Caesar finally expired in his cell in the imperial palace, allegedly having resorted to eating his own mattress in an attempt to stay alive. Tiberius had ordered food to be withheld but it took him nine days to die. What proved particularly disturbing to onlookers, including the Senate, is that Drusus' imprisonment and attendant abuse and beatings had been so brazen. Tiberius also castigated the young man after he had died, hurling the same allegations of immorality that had been levelled against Nero a few years before.[24]

Agrippina's death came after a short interlude on 18 October 33. She had been moved to the island of Pandateria (Ventotene) where she maintained a defiant fusillade of protests about her treatment. Suetonius described her exile as being on a 'flimsy pretext', which of course it was though at the time there was nothing unusual about flimsy pretexts being used to imprison or execute anyone. He was presumably referring to the trial at which Aulus Avilius Flaccus had been one of her accusers (see above, p. 159). In revenge for her daring to complain, Tiberius allegedly had a centurion beat her till one of her eyes was destroyed. Agrippina then resolved to starve herself to death. Tiberius ordered that food be forced into her mouth, but she managed to kill herself anyway. How much of this detail was true as ever remains a matter for an inconclusive debate – apart from the fact that Agrippina, granddaughter of Augustus, was dead.

Tiberius resorted to spreading stories about Agrippina's all-round awfulness. He congratulated himself for his clemency in not having her executed by strangulation and having her body thrown down the Gemonian Stairs. This was an allusion to Sejanus who had been killed exactly two years earlier on the same day. Tiberius chose to publicize both deaths as deliverances to the state, which was ironic since Sejanus had done everything possible to destroy Agrippina himself. He ordered an annual sacrifice to Jupiter be made in commemoration.[25] The measures matched those meted out to the wives and female relatives of Sejanus' associates and friends. Since, as a woman, Agrippina could not be formally described in law as having sought to take charge of public affairs, she was damned by every other mechanism available.[26] The propaganda failed. Agrippina was venerated in the decades to come. She was 'a Caesar's wife, whose name shone bright throughout the world, whose teeming womb brought forth so many hostages of peace', trilled the chorus in Seneca's *Octavia*, written in the early 60s.[27]

It is possible that we might know more about how Agrippina and her sons were treated had it not been for the fact that Caligula, soon after his accession in 37, destroyed any surviving papers. He did, so he is said to have claimed, because he could thus prevent himself from pursuing people for treason as Tiberius had.[28] Although Agrippina had gone and her two eldest sons were dead, the other four of her children who had lived to adulthood had so far survived. Two of them, first Caligula and then Agrippina the Younger, would be the key dynastic figures in the years to come. Their existence also helped create a completely new aspect to the principate. Regardless of Augustus' dynastic plans, circumstances had forced him to choose Tiberius to succeed him. In any case Tiberius, for all his shortcomings, had unmatched political and military experience. Had he not been a relative at all, he could very justifiably have been adopted as the best man available for the job, just as Trajan was by Nerva in 98. That he was Livia's son was a bonus but with Germanicus' children waiting in the wings Augustus must have felt at the time that eventually his biological descendants would rule Rome.

Augustus turned out to be right. Agrippina's fertility, and fate, had seen to that. A new problem was created though. It must have been clear to Tiberius as the years passed and he entered old age that his own grandson Tiberius

Gemellus and his great-nephew Caligula had no qualifications whatsoever to serve as emperors other than their birth. They had fought no wars, had no political careers, and had served in no useful capacity whatsoever. It was scarcely their fault – they were too young – but that did not alter the fact that they had nothing to offer apart from their dynastic credentials and even those were not equal. It must have been obvious that Caligula's descent from Augustus via Agrippina made him a stronger dynastic candidate than Tiberius Gemellus, who could only claim descent from Octavia. There were no alternatives left. There were, however, another four years of Tiberius' rule to run.

One of the next moves Tiberius made was in 33 to marry off Germanicus and Agrippina's remaining daughters, Drusilla and Julia Livilla, and his own granddaughter Julia (Drusus the Younger's daughter). None of these marriages was dynastically significant in the sense that none of the husbands had any blood connection either to Augustus, Livia or Octavia.[29] This may have been deliberate. The marriages took care of all three by providing them with husbands of the correct status without incurring undue risk of a potential challenger who could claim a connection with the imperial family by blood. Aemilia Lepida, the widow of Drusus Caesar who had made his life a misery with endless gratuitous accusations, was accused of committing adultery with a slave and committed suicide.[30]

There was a raven in the Forum that had a more optimistic take on the imperial family's prospects. The bird had hatched on the Temple of Castor and Pollux, of which three columns remain standing today, and moved into a cobbler's shop nearby. Here the bird had the opportunity to listen to people talking and soon learned to mimic what it heard. Each morning it flew the short distance to the rostra that overlooked the central piazza. Here it called out the names of Tiberius, Drusus and Germanicus, as well as hailing the public, and then returned to the cobbler's. The raven continued this morning salutation for many years throughout Tiberius' reign, long after both Drusus and Germanicus were dead. Unfortunately in the year 36 the bird's popularity, or toilet habits, caused a neighbouring cobbler to kill it. This caused a riot and the bird-killing cobbler was forced out. A major funeral for the raven followed with a procession that led two miles down the Via Appia to a chosen burial spot. Pliny mused on the irony that many Roman men of note had been awarded nothing like the same degree of honour at their deaths. If it was an omen of Tiberius' death the following year, no one seems to have noticed.[31]

The last part of Tiberius' reign did not see an end to treason trials. Tiberius proved to have a worrying capacity to bear grudges about any matter, even those from years before.[32] The picture painted by Tacitus of Tiberius is so compellingly bleak that it is difficult to find the evidence to refute it. Even when Tiberius did something decent Tacitus could not help himself from painting it as a cynical gesture. In 36 a serious fire took hold in Rome with the Aventine being the most badly damaged. Tiberius compensated homeowners and tenants to the tune of 100 million sesterces; Tacitus virtually dismissed this as a pretext to turn a disaster into glory-seeking publicity. One wonders what Tacitus would have said had Tiberius done nothing, though he was able to acknowledge that Tiberius had once had a good side to him when Livia was alive. Livia had also been in the habit of showing generosity to the victims of other fires, setting her son an example that he was only following.[33]

The main issue of course remained the succession. By 37 Tiberius was seventy-eight years old. A handover of power was inevitable, and soon. Unlike Augustus at least he had a choice – his grandson Tiberius Gemellus or his great nephew Caligula. Unfortunately, having a choice also provided an opportunity for factions to grow around each of them. Caligula had been married in 33 to Junia Claudilla, the daughter of Marcus Junius Silanus. She had died by 37 when giving birth to their first child, who also did not survive.[34] This provided an opportunity for the ambitious praetorian prefect Macro to offer his own wife, Ennia Naevia, as Caligula's mistress. Caligula promised to marry Ennia if he became emperor. This remarkable contract was considered advantageous by Macro, and by Caligula who therefore felt he had secured Macro's backing.[35]

Tiberius knew about Macro's machinations. He also knew that Caligula was, as Germanicus and Agrippina's son, extremely popular. Furthermore, he was around twenty-five years old which gave him all the advantages of 'youthful vigour'. Tiberius Gemellus was Tiberius' own grandson but at around eighteen years old had not quite formally entered manhood. There was also the worrying possibility that Gemellus was really the product of one of Livilla's infidelities. The third option was Claudius, Germanicus' brother, by then in his late forties. Claudius was discounted immediately because of what was regarded as his mental impairment. There was another option: to seek someone outside the imperial family. Tiberius decided that this would be to subject Augustus' memory and that of the imperial family to posthumous ignominy.[36] That left him with Caligula and Gemellus but Tiberius could see that only one would survive and that it was inevitable Caligula would kill his younger cousin.[37] It was a cynical point of view, but an accurate one.

Old he might have been, but Tiberius' death had not come soon enough for Caligula. Tiberius' death was notoriously thought to have been caused or at least hastened by Caligula, either by poison or by starvation.[38] However, it was also clear that Tiberius was ailing anyway, though just when it was thought he had expired news was brought that he had rallied. Caligula, at that moment priming himself to become emperor, was stunned into silence but Macro thoughtfully suffocated Tiberius, thereby clearing up any doubt about whether the emperor had died or not.[39]

Caligula's accession was welcomed with gales of enthusiasm from the Roman people; after all, a child of Agrippina and Germanicus, and descended from Augustus (via Julia and Agrippina) had come to rule them. To that he could add descent from Octavia and Livia. It was a magnificent lineage. One could forgive Caligula for making the most of it, and the people for believing in him because of it. At the time there was no hint in sight of the deranged behaviour that lay ahead. Agrippina's choice of costume for her youngest son while they were with Germanicus on the German frontier now paid huge dividends. The army and its veterans remembered little Caligula fondly and they were equally delighted by his becoming emperor. This role as a small child was celebrated as he accompanied Tiberius' body up from Misenum. He was their 'baby', their 'nursling'. It seemed propitious but it was also ominous.[40] Caligula oversaw the dedication of the Temple of the Divine Augustus soon after his accession, organizing major celebrations to commemorate the event. Its construction had been commissioned by Tiberius and Livia back in 14, and was echoed in a number of provincial communities across the Empire.[41] For the moment the shrine remained in Augustus' name only. Under Claudius it was dedicated jointly to Augustus and Livia (plate 28).

Caligula's reign was so notorious, particularly the latter part as it degenerated into an autocratic tyranny, that it has become almost mythologized. Caligula spent most of his time compensating for the unwelcome reality that he had little to offer the people of Rome other than the fact that he was young, he was descended from Augustus and he was not Tiberius. Apart from wearing miniature military boots and being toted as an army mascot as a child he had no military experience whatsoever. His political experience was also virtually non-existent. Unlike his parents he had no imperial family of his own to offer apart from his cousin Gemellus and his sisters. Just as Tiberius had predicted, Gemellus was removed within a year, despite being formally entered by then into manhood with the *toga virilis* and being named *princeps iuventutis*. He had, allegedly, been expressing hopes that Caligula would die after he fell ill in his first year as emperor.[42] Killing Gemellus by early 38 at the latest was almost inevitable under the circumstances, but it reflected Caligula's prime focus on his own immediate family which he was far more interested in.

Caligula desperately tried to find ways of demonstrating his superiority over everybody else, which explains much of his later behaviour. This was in spite of the fact that at the time of his accession his popularity was so great that his possession of the throne was secure. But as a weak man who found himself with enormous power, he was destroyed by it. One method Caligula picked on early in his reign was to revive and develop the memory of his family, amongst whom his female forbears were accorded some of the greatest honours. His grandmother Antonia Minor and his mother Agrippina were singled out for special attention, the latter largely because of the brutal way she had been treated and the ignominy of her death. Antonia Minor was still alive when Caligula became emperor. He immediately tried to give her the same sort of standing that Livia had enjoyed during Tiberius' reign. Since Antonia had done a great deal to bring him up after Livia's death this is not so surprising.[43] Caligula declared that Antonia would be known as Augusta, making her a priestess of Augustus, though she turned it down (Claudius gave her the title posthumously after his accession). However, she was named Augusta on a few provincial coins struck under Caligula, such as those minted at Tomis in Moesia Inferior.[44] He also awarded her the equivalency of privileges enjoyed by Vestal Virgins, just as Livia had during Augustus' lifetime.[45]

The honours for Antonia were just that. They conferred no actual power. Caligula did not take kindly to advice from his grandmother though he could be wary about how he dealt with her. Tiberius had imprisoned Agrippa, the grandson of the client king Herod Agrippa. On his accession Caligula was keen to release Agrippa immediately, but Antonia stepped in. She told him that it would look as if he was welcoming Tiberius' death. In fact Caligula did release Agrippa but not immediately, and made him king of territories formerly ruled by his uncle Philip.[46] On another occasion, or perhaps it was the same one, Caligula snapped back at his grandmother to remind her that he had the 'right to do anything to anybody', clearly thoroughly enjoying the moment.

It was a portent of things to come. He did not trust Antonia. He insisted once on only seeing her, at her request, in Macro's presence. It was a crude way of reminding her of his power, and compensated for his youth compared to her experience. She died on 1 May 37 in unknown circumstances. She was seventy-three which meant that a natural death was entirely possible. However, both Suetonius and Dio suggest that she took her own life. Had she lived she might have exercised some restraint over her grandson's behaviour, but she was an isolated member of an older generation. Caligula was clearly not disposed to listen to her easily or acknowledge her guidance any more than Elagabalus would listen to his grandmother Julia Maesa nearly two hundred years later. Antonia must have recognized that her influence was minimal. Antonia had lived for decades as a widow and experienced the shame of her daughter Livilla's extraordinary and demeaning conduct with Sejanus as well as the loss of Germanicus. She could be forgiven for having had enough.[47]

Caligula criticized Livia for having low birth, based on a completely false claim about her grandfather, and dismissed her as a 'Ulysses in a *stola*'. This scathing comment clearly suggested that Livia had all the qualities of a scheming male. It was made worse by equating it with the traditional distrust of the Greeks who had of course destroyed Troy, the mythical origin of the Roman people and Caligula's own fabled progenitor, Aeneas, son of Venus. Despite this disparaging attitude he overturned Tiberius' failure to deal with Livia's will and paid out the legacies due.[48] The most common coin issued by Caligula with his own portrait was a copper as with a seated figure of Vesta on the reverse, possibly inspired by the statue of a seated Vesta by a sculptor called Scopas which was displayed in the Gardens of Servilius in Rome by the road to Ostia. Given Livia's very close association with the cult of Vesta the choice of design is an intriguing one. Considering the series of other dynastic coins minted under Caligula (see below) it must surely have been intended as a representation of Livia as Vesta. The fact that the Severan women used Vesta on their coins as part of an array of associations borrowed from Julio-Claudian empresses makes this even more likely.[49]

Caligula's attitude to his deceased mother Agrippina was oddly ambivalent. With his stellar lineage he could afford to be dismissive about Agrippa's less than exalted origins. Allegedly he did not like to be reminded that he was his grandson. Agrippina's name of course was a constant reminder of that so in a bizarre twist of fantasy lineage he put it about that she was really Augustus' daughter by Julia and therefore a product of incest.[50] This ludicrous and unnecessary claim, however, showed how far an increasing obsession with a bloodline could go. On the other hand, given the emphasis already placed on the fertility of Livia, Julia and Agrippina the Elder, there was a certain amount of logical symmetry in trying to restrict the scope of descent to within the Julio-Claudian line. This was, after all, a family that traced its origins to a divine progenitor.[51]

One piece of primary evidence is at odds with the idea that Caligula was ashamed of being descended from Agrippa through his mother. A huge issue of copper asses, believed on the basis of style to belong to Caligula's reign (there is certainly no other easy context for the type), was minted in the name of Agrippa. Agrippa appears on the obverse and his favoured god, Neptune, on the reverse. Nothing in the legend associates the issue with Caligula. Agrippa had not appeared on any coinage since the reign of Augustus. The coin, which is easily found today because of the vast number made, circulated widely with Caligula's other issues and on into the early years of Nero's reign. It was also reissued by Titus and Domitian as part of their programme of reviving selected Julio-Claudian types. Its existence remains a genuine conundrum.[52]

Caligula was effectively trying to depict himself as principally a descendant of the Augustan line. He emulated Tiberius in issuing coins that identified his descent from Augustus, the only difference being that in Caligula's case it was true. Caligula could hardly excise Agrippina from that line and in the event he did not attempt to do so. Caligula personally set out to recover the bones of his mother, and his brothers Nero and Drusus. They were brought back to Rome and buried in the Mausoleum of Augustus (plate 13).[53] Agrippina's tombstone has survived and its inscription shows how desperately important it was to Caligula to demonstrate his descent from Augustus and her part in that. The full text, referring to Caligula by his official name, reads:

OSSA
AGRIPPINAE.M.AGRIPPA.[F]
DIVI.AVG.NEPTIS.VXORIS
GERMANICI.CAESARIS
MATRIS.G.CAESARIS.AVG
GERMANICI.PRINCIPIS
[S.P.Q.R.A]

The bones of Agrippina, daughter of Marcus Agrippa, granddaughter of the Deified Augustus, wife of Germanicus Caesar, mother of the princeps Gaius Caesar Augustus Germanicus. (Set up) by the authority of the Senate and the People of Rome [plate 19].[54]

Caligula decided to recreate an image of Agrippina as a Roman matron of such exalted status that she would outshine Livia. His mother's rehabilitation was such that in death she became even more famous than she had been in life.[55] He pursued anyone who had come close to damaging his mother's reputation. Domitius Afer was detested by Caligula because during Tiberius' reign Afer had made an accusation against a female relative of Agrippina's (the identity of this woman is unknown). In 39 Afer had set up an image of Caligula and attached an inscription drawing attention to the fact that Caligula was now holding his second consulship even though he was still only twenty-seven. Caligula had Afer dragged to the Senate to listen to him deliver a speech excoriating him.[56]

The rehabilitation of Agrippina went hand in hand with commemorating her children, including those who were dead. An important small series of coins publicized her portrait and her status (plate 20). Antonia's turn would have to wait until the reign of Claudius. Agrippina's coins struck under Caligula included a sestertius in her own right, with a reverse depicting a carpentum and the legend SPQR MEMORIAE AGRIPPINAE ('The Senate and the People of Rome [in honour] of the Memory of Agrippina'). Her image was also used as the reverse on some of Caligula's gold and silver coins. On all the coins she was specifically identified as 'Mother of Gaius Caesar Augustus Germanicus'.[57] A similar series for Germanicus was produced, but instead of the sestertius for the base metal coins, several different types were issued in the commoner smaller denominations of the dupondius and as. However, the legends did not identify Germanicus as the 'father' of Caligula, while those for Agrippina had specified Caligula as her son. Instead on the asses Germanicus is labelled as Tiberius' 'son', with Caligula's titles on the reverse, whereas the dupondius commemorated Germanicus' military exploits.[58] Caligula also produced a single dupondius type that commemorated his murdered brothers. The two are shown on horseback on the obverse, described simply as 'Nero and Drusus Caesars', with Caligula's titles for 40–1 on the reverse. Stylistically one of the most creative Roman imperial coins produced by that date, its obverse design would be copied by the emperor Nero for one of his magnificent issues of sestertii in the period 64–8.[59] The image of Agrippina the Elder as the idealized Roman matron proved to be remarkably durable. Over four hundred years later, in *c.* 474, Gaius Sidonius Apollinaris, bishop of Auvergne, commended Agrippine, wife of Childeric II of Burgundy, as the 'present Agrippina' for guiding her husband, 'our and her Germanicus', and thus protecting the territory.[60]

Caligula also awarded his sisters, Agrippina the Younger, Drusilla and Livilla, equivalent privileges to those enjoyed by Vestal Virgins, just as Livia had had during Augustus' lifetime. In his sisters' case the honour was even more inaccurate. He also incorporated a compulsory reference to them into oaths. These were now worded, 'And I will not hold myself and my children dearer than I do Gaius and his sisters', with a similar affirmation for consuls.[61] However, the rest of what we know about Caligula's relationship with his sisters is limited to salacious and titillating references that cannot be substantiated. Both Suetonius and Dio assert as fact that all three had incestuous relations with their brother and it is clear that if true these had started during Tiberius' reign. Suetonius makes the claim. He adds that this even extended to a public display at a banquet while his wife looked on, and that Caligula first slept with Drusilla, his favourite, while they were underage. Caligula was allegedly caught in the act by his grandmother Antonia but given that he told her he could do as he pleased, her disapproval would have mattered little to him. The relationship with Drusilla supposedly continued even after her marriage to Longinus. Dio states that he 'ravished all three', and then banished two to an island, Drusilla having died by June 38.[62] Conversely, Josephus says that Caligula slept with only one of his sisters.[63] The number is obviously a technicality.

Depicting Caligula as incestuous was a convenient claim that added weight to his image as a moral degenerate. It also amplified his role as a despotic and crazed tyrant. This was an image that Roman historians were enthusiastic about constructing, not least because he came so close to posing as a king.[64] As a bonus it helped damage the reputation of Agrippina the Younger, which Roman historians also enjoyed slating at every opportunity. Caligula, or at any rate the gossip which surrounded him, provided them with more material that embellished, as if it were necessary, his image as the nerve centre of immorality at court, exceeding even that of Tiberius in Capri.[65] At a banquet one day Caligula allegedly decided to taunt his friend Valerius Asiaticus. He described how Asiaticus' wife Lollia Saturnina behaved while committing adultery with him and how dissatisfying the experience was. Caligula spoke deliberately loudly enough for all the other guests to hear. It was clearly an exercise in publicly displaying his power, expressed through humiliation not only of Asiaticus but also of his wife who happened to be Caligula's sister-in-law.[66] Not surprisingly, Asiaticus loathed Caligula as a result and proceeded to be a co-conspirator in his assassination in 41.

Caligula was a man dedicated to venerating his mother but seemed to treat other women, including his sisters, as little more than sexual accessories. Caligula understood that he could easily assert his absolute power over men of rank. In order to do so, he invited them to dinner with their wives, blatantly scrutinizing each woman as a potential sexual partner. He then left the dining room and sent instructions for the one who pleased him the most to be brought to him for sex. Caligula afterwards returned to the dinner, loudly extolling or criticizing the woman's performance and appeal. His purpose was to humiliate the senators concerned by demonstrating their loss of power under the principate.[67] In the traditional Roman family the husband's power and prerogative over his wife were total. By showing that an emperor's claim completely superseded this entitlement Caligula used sex as a crude means of advertising the power he had but had not earned through ability. Promiscuity and presumption of entitlement are well attested amongst rulers at all sorts of different times and places. Caligula, however, may have believed that he was emulating Augustus and the rumours that circulated about him, but did so in a blatant and derogatory way that undermined, rather than enhanced, his power.[68] In Augustus' case there at least appeared to be some sort of political rationale, assuming the stories were true.

Roman historians were so successful at depicting Caligula as a monster that it is almost impossible to unravel the truth now, even in popular myth.[69] There are two reasons for considering at least a significant basis for believing the stories about incest. Firstly, Caligula was manifestly keen on publicizing his bloodline and keeping it 'within the family'. It is conceivable that he toyed with the idea of impregnating at least one of his sisters. Secondly, he issued a remarkable sestertius with a reverse showing his three sisters, named, and in the guise of the Three Graces. This coin type, perhaps one of the most famous of the entire imperial series, had no stylistic precedent and was never repeated. It is well designed with considerable artistic merit and could be seen at that level and no more. It is equally possible that the design was commissioned by Caligula as a suggestive and mischievous allusion to something he was actually quite proud of. It must have been produced soon after his accession and before Drusilla's death.[70]

Drusilla's unexpected death was not treated by Caligula as a disaster even though he had apparently until then still been having a sexual relationship with her. He showed remarkable presence of mind and promptly turned the funeral into a publicity opportunity. Drusilla's second husband (and cousin), Marcus Aemilius Lepidus, read the eulogy, which might have been expected as a matter of course. The rest was pure showmanship, including cancelling any other festivals due at that time.[71] The Praetorian Guard paraded round Drusilla's funeral pyre along with members of the equestrian order, while high-born boys put on a display of horsemanship in an exercise known as 'Troy'. That was not all. Drusilla was awarded all of Livia's honours but even more importantly she was deified, the first Julio-Claudian woman to be so. Livia would have to wait until the reign of Claudius. This was a significant moment in the changing status of women in the imperial house though of course the gesture was obviously intended by implication to reflect Caligula's growing sense of his own divinity. Drusilla was to be commemorated with statues, including a golden one in the Senate house, and given a college of her own twenty priests to manage her cult. She was to be worshipped in all cities, and given the name Panthea, a divinity that encompassed all goddesses. Provincial cities also commemorated her. Cyzicus in Mysia, Asia Minor, made a dedication to Caligula and included a reference to Drusilla, identified now as the 'New Aphrodite'.[72]

Caligula was not the only one who had spotted an opportunity to make the most of his sister's death. Livius Geminius, a senator, decided to swear on oath that he had witnessed Drusilla's apotheosis. Geminius, no doubt, remembered the vast reward given to Numerius Atticus by Livia for swearing he had seen Augustus' journey to heaven.[73] Geminius had gambled, correctly, on this being exactly what Caligula would want to hear because it confirmed Drusilla's divinity, and therefore the prospects of his own. Geminius was promptly awarded a million sesterces, just like Numerius Atticus well over twenty years earlier. It was a sum of money sufficient to fulfil the property qualification for his being a senator, had he not already presumably been in possession of the necessary funds.[74]

Caligula also tried to establish his own nuclear imperial family. There was little point in having a dynastic past without being able to offer a dynastic future. Characteristically, this was conducted in such a way that it ought to have sounded an alarm about his instability. Caligula decided that he should show his prerogative by taking a wife from someone else; since he was already accustomed to sex with other men's wives on a casual basis this was just a minor modification. For this dubious privilege he chose a woman called Cornelia or Livia Orestilla who was in the process of marrying Gaius Calpurnius Piso. Caligula requisitioned the unfortunate Orestilla and married her. Next he ungallantly abandoned her, though how quickly is uncertain. Dio says the marriage lasted two months, Suetonius that it lasted two years, but both suggest that Orestilla returned to Piso. Either way the marriage produced no issue for Caligula.[75]

Within a relatively short time of his reign starting Caligula had restored his mother Agrippina to being a central figure in the Julio-Claudian regime. She was presented to the public as a Roman matron of the highest possible esteem and, specifically, as the descendant of Augustus and mother of the emperor. By depositing her remains in the Mausoleum of Augustus Caligula gave her that role in perpetuity. It was nearly twenty years since Germanicus' death, and nearly five since she had died. Caligula had also honoured his paternal grandmother Antonia and his sisters, but noticeably (and obviously) not his maternal grandmother Julia. Although he commemorated his deceased male relatives, with particular focus on Augustus, it was the female members of the Julio-Claudians who were the dominant characters in the broader imperial family Caligula presented to the Roman people.

7

SELF-DESTRUCTION
MESSALINA 41–8

Messalina's time as empress was short but notorious. Caligula's excesses almost destroyed the principate. His assassination in 41, however, resulted in his uncle Claudius being made emperor by the Praetorian Guard. Descended from Octavia and married to her cousin Claudius during the reign of Caligula, Messalina cannot have expected to become empress. Her lack of maturity and experience, coupled with a reckless indifference to common sense, led her as empress deeper into corruption and duplicity. This climaxed in an absurd plan to form a bigamous marriage and then with her lover overthrow Claudius. The uncovering of the plot and its revelation to Claudius is one of the great set pieces of Tacitus' Annals *but itself raises questions about the truth of his account. Messalina apparently came close to toppling the regime. Vilified by Roman historians as a harlot and degenerate, her notoriety has echoed down the centuries ever since. Her affairs placed doubt on the legitimacy of her son Britannicus, Claudius' heir, and her fall opened the way for Agrippina the Younger.*

The prominent celebration of Agrippina and Caligula's efforts to use the developed image of the imperial family with all its divine and exalted associations was not enough to counter his increasingly fractious relationship with the ordinary people. Their hopes were so great it is no surprise that they ended up being disappointed. Caligula's image of the imperial family soon started to vaporize. After early efforts, such as recalling those who had been banished,

Caligula did a great deal to make their disappointment worse. He increasingly used his unlimited power to enforce unpopular edicts that ranged from the pointlessly insensitive, such as refusing to have arena awnings drawn to protect the crowd from the sun, to more serious issues like arbitrary arrests and murders. Caligula went out of his way to do the opposite of what the people wanted and the result was an increasingly confrontational relationship.[1]

Caligula also acted quite logically for someone descended from a divinity, in this case Augustus, however preposterous that might seem now. In styling himself as 'son of the deified Augustus', Tiberius had made a political statement, rather than a truly dynastic one. Descent from a deified predecessor was an early instance of a convention that would prove to be an enduring feature of the principate. It was the prime example of how the emperors constructed a fictional conflation of political reality of their supreme power with the qualities of Augustus which they claimed to have inherited. Caligula knew that his descent from the divine Augustus was a literal truth. He was acutely conscious that this above all set him, his sisters and his daughter apart from almost everyone else. He took every opportunity to publicize the fact. Descent from Augustus was also the only real 'qualification' he had. No wonder Agrippina was such a conspicuous part of his publicity campaign. She was his link back to Augustus.

The term *princeps* has no modern equivalent. To the Romans the word meant a man with pre-eminent political stature and experience and whose qualifications and authority were beyond doubt. A *princeps* had to be exceptional. Caligula was manifestly not someone with any of the relevant qualifications to be a *princeps*, whereas both Augustus and Tiberius had been.[2] Caligula's treatment of Domitius Afer (see above, p. 169), who had had the cheek to make an issue of him being consul for the second time while still only twenty-seven, is an instance of how fractious he could become at any reminder of his relative inferiority. It also might help explain his sensitivity about the descent from Agrippa.[3]

Caligula also developed an ideology that he was above the conventional idea of a king because of his divine descent. He claimed to be a god in his own right and established a cult in his own name with its own temple. Being a priest in the cult rapidly became a highly desirable occupation for the elite though this must largely have been provoked by a desire for self-protection. Caligula decided that he was able to talk confidentially to Jupiter Capitolinus and had a connecting bridge built between the Palatine and the Capitoline hills to facilitate the dialogue between fellow divinities.[4] By raising himself to this level

Caligula also freed himself from the normal limits of propriety and behaviour. He could, literally, do as he pleased (as he had pointed out to Antonia Minor). The practice of that prerogative was thus the manifestation and proof of his status and power.[5] It was the simplest and best way of sidestepping his lack of conventional experience and *auctoritas*, that quasi-spiritual form of authority which Augustus had acquired through his unique experience and achievements.

It would not have done, in this context, to have any member of the imperial family incorporated into the broader web of honour and status if they presented a threat. That was why Tiberius Gemellus had been murdered. That left the knotty issue of Claudius. Claudius was Caligula's uncle and the brother of Germanicus. He was the only living member of Caligula's father's family. He was also conspicuously not Germanicus' equal in any respect whatsoever since his stammer and physical ailments had excluded him from public and military life. In short he was something of a family embarrassment, though this had in fact allowed him not only the freedom to pursue his arcane academic studies but also to remain alive, a fact that would soon become a politically decisive element of the principate's continuity.

Caligula could not ignore the fact that Claudius was one of his closest relatives. They shared descent from both Livia and Octavia. He therefore decided to make Claudius his joint consul in 37, elevating his uncle from equestrian status for that purpose. Far from being a generous gesture of familial loyalty, promoting Claudius was Caligula's idea of a joke. Caligula was said to have kept Claudius around simply as a 'laughing stock'. There may have been another reason. Claudius could not possibly have served either as a rival or as a focus for dissent and by being Germanicus' brother there was an implicit homage to Caligula's father in the move.[6]

Claudius had been betrothed twice under Augustus. The first betrothal was to Aemilia Lepida, Julia the Younger's daughter by her first husband Lucius Aemilius Paullus. Had this marriage gone ahead and children resulted then Claudius' offspring would have been descended from Augustus as well as Livia. In this sense they would therefore also have been obvious dynastic rivals to Agrippina the Elder's children.[7] The betrothal was clearly one of Augustus' numerous efforts to maximize potential lines of descent from himself. The marriage to Aemilia Lepida never came off. Augustus cancelled the betrothal because Aemilia's parents had caused some offence to him. The insult is not known but is likely to have been something to do with either his laws on morality or republican sympathies. In an interesting twist her cousin Marcus Aemilius Lepidus had become the husband of Caligula's sister Drusilla and was executed by him in 39. Claudius was betrothed next to Livia Medullina who unfortunately fell ill and expired on the date set for the wedding.[8]

Claudius was finally married to Plautia Urgulanilla some time around AD 9 when he was about nineteen. She had come into contact with the imperial circle through her grandmother Urgulania, Livia's friend and beneficiary of Livia's legal privileges by association. They had a son called Drusus who died as an adolescent when he choked on a pear that he had thrown in the air to catch in his mouth. Urgulanilla was accused of immoral behaviour and was also mysteriously implicated in a murder. Claudius divorced her, and five months later she gave birth to a daughter called Claudia by her husband's freedman Boter. The child was disowned by Claudius, who proceeded to marry Aelia Paetina by 28.[9] Aelia had been brought up by the prefect of the Praetorian Guard at the beginning of Tiberius' reign, Lucius Seius Strabo, and was therefore probably the adoptive sister of his son Lucius Aelius Sejanus, the notorious prefect of the Guard under Tiberius after his father. Claudius divorced Aelia Paetina in 31. Suetonius called the grounds 'slight offences' but after the fall of Sejanus it would have been impossible and unwise for him to remain married to her. Guilt by association in Roman politics could have very long and insidious tentacles. In any case Claudius' prospects had improved under Caligula so it was time to find a more advantageous wife. This would explain the casual description by Suetonius of Aelia Paetina's failings.[10] Their daughter Claudia Antonia survived on through Claudius' reign only to be murdered by Nero.

By 38 or 39 Claudius had married his cousin Valeria Messalina in a union that must have been approved, and was probably arranged, by Caligula. Messalina came with excellent credentials, both dynastic and political. She was directly descended from Octavia through both her parents, which brought to the marriage more Julian blood. The only alternative source of Julian blood would have been Caligula's sisters. Since they were Claudius' nieces such a marriage was an unthinkable prospect, at least for the moment. Messalina's mother Domitia Lepida was the daughter of Antonia Major, Octavia's elder daughter by Antony, Claudius himself being descended from Octavia through his mother Antonia Minor. Messalina's father Marcus Valerius Messalla Barbatus was the son of Marcella the Younger, Octavia's younger daughter by Gaius Marcellus. She was thus the product of a cousin marriage but was also a cousin to Claudius.

177

The Julio-Claudians were becoming ever more inbred in an effort to keep power within the bloodline. All this would have recommended Messalina to the dynasty-conscious Caligula. However, Messalina had another credential. Her paternal aunt was Claudia Pulchra, a woman who had been prosecuted under Tiberius simply for her friendship with Agrippina the Elder.[11]

The marriage of Claudius to Messalina had considerably more to recommend it in dynastic terms than Caligula's marriage to Caesonia had. It was also self-evident that unless Caligula fathered a son and lived long enough to see such a boy grow to manhood there was another succession crisis brewing. This may have been the reason for Claudius' marriage. However undesirable Claudius was as a prospective emperor he was the only other eligible male left. No one considered him to be a suitable emperor; years before, his own sister Livilla had openly expressed her hopes that the Roman people would escape such an invidious prospect.[12] At least there was the possibility that Claudius also would father a son, supplying another potential line of descent. Within a year or two Messalina had borne Claudius a daughter, Claudia Octavia. A brother, Tiberius Claudius Germanicus (later renamed Britannicus after the conquest of Britain) followed in February 41.

In the meantime, Caligula's immediate family was reducing in size, or at least availability. Drusilla's death in 38 had left him with two sisters, Agrippina the Younger and Julia Livilla, whom he routinely prostituted out to his favourites.[13] He was also becoming concerned about conspiracies. By late 39 Caligula was leading what he tried to pass off as a military campaign in Gaul. It was a desperate attempt to provide himself with the pretext to claim military glory. It is not clear whether Agrippina and Julia Livilla were with him. As the campaign progressed a plot was uncovered, allegedly led by Gnaeus Lentulus Gaetulicus, governor of Germany and appointed to the post under Tiberius. Gaetulicus was executed, the main reason being that his soldiers were particularly fond of him. Also killed was Drusilla's husband, Marcus Aemilius Lepidus, son of Julia the Younger and thus great-grandson of Augustus. He was therefore obviously a potential rival. Lepidus was believed to have had a sexual relationship with Caligula, as well as with the emperor's other two sisters. The latter may explain why Caligula later ordered Lepidus' murder. The offence (if even true) was believed somehow to implicate Lepidus either in Gaetulicus' 'conspiracy' or another plot.[14] Killing Lepidus was not enough for Caligula. He ordered his sister Agrippina to collect Gaetulicus' remains and bring them back to Rome in an urn. He then exiled both Agrippina and Julia Livilla to the Pontian Islands, an archipelago including Ponza just off the central west coast of Italy in the Tyrrhenian Sea. He subsequently sold off their possessions. Caligula had caught himself in a trap. By honouring his sisters in the past he had threatened his own pre-eminence. Now he banned any honours being awarded to his family members, and dismissed the ones he had been given as not up to what he deserved. The curious logic was that any honours he had been awarded only drew attention to what he had not been awarded.[15]

For the moment the Julio-Claudian women were out of the loop. As the wife of Claudius, a member of the imperial family regarded as an irrelevance, Messalina was of no importance either. Caligula now turned his attention to his own matrimonial prospects. At the time of the German campaign he was married to Lollia Paulina, former wife of Gaius Memmius Regulus, whose grandmother Caligula had heard was remarkably beautiful. Memmius was then serving as governor of Achaea (Greece). In the aftermath of Drusilla's death Caligula forced Memmius to hand over Lollia and send her back to Rome so he could marry her in late 38. This new liaison went nowhere either, Caligula accusing her of being infertile. He abandoned her during 39, throwing in an instruction that she was never to sleep with anyone else.[16] That did not remove Lollia entirely from the attentions of an emperor. Claudius subsequently considered her as a potential wife.[17]

It was not until Caligula selected a fourth wife, Milonia Caesonia, that any serious prospect of continuing the dynasty appeared. Indeed, it already had. Caesonia was Caligula's mistress and she was pregnant by him. She had borne a previous husband three daughters. She was also said to be promiscuous, as well as being past her youth and plain to look at. Caligula seemed particularly taken with her, and exhibited her nude to his friends and in military costume to his praetorian escort. Even so, he took the precaution of delaying the wedding until the baby was born. She was named Julia Drusilla, after his favourite sister, and became notorious as a toddler in her own right for having a violent temper.[18] The vicious child was not the first great-great-grandchild of Augustus. That honour went to Lucius Domitius Ahenobarbus, later the emperor Nero (54–68), who had been born at the end of the year 37 to Agrippina the Younger and her husband Gnaeus Domitius Ahenobarbus. Gnaeus Domitius was lucky to be alive. Early that year he had been one of a number of men caught out for having affairs with a notorious adulterer called

Albucilla. Albucilla, another of the 'bad' women recounted by Tacitus, had herself been accused of disrespect to Tiberius. Gnaeus Domitius and the other men therefore also found themselves caught up in that allegation. He had, however, escaped on a technicality involving reliability of the evidence.[19]

Milonia Caesonia never had any chance of being venerated as a Roman matron either in her own time or afterwards. Compared to the other female figures in Caligula's family she is relatively opaque. By the early second century Juvenal blamed her for having fed her husband a poison that drove him insane and led to his terrible actions.[20] It was an interesting slant on the customary Roman misogyny that a man's perceived insanity must have been caused by his wife's inherent evil. Caesonia was never able to compensate for her husband's increasingly erratic and arbitrary rule. In the event she had very little opportunity to influence Caligula at all. This was in spite of his reverence for her. He combined this with threats to torture her in order to find out how much she loved him. He also pointed out that he could have her decapitated whenever he wanted.[21]

Plots to assassinate Caligula were almost inevitable given how he was ruling. The conspiracy of January 41 was led by Marcus Arrecinus Clemens, prefect of the Guard, and tribunes of the Guard, including Cassius Chaerea. They worked together in association with a freedman called Kallistos and a friend of the murdered Lepidus, as well as others such as Valerius Asiaticus. They were bent on the notion that the principate could be overthrown and the Republic restored. Caligula's death by stabbing at their hands in a covered passageway at the theatre, where he had been lured to watch a rehearsal, was not enough to destroy a dynasty. Killing Caesonia and her daughter Julia Drusilla was also an inevitable part of the plan, at least for some of the plotters. Suetonius provided a brief but horrifying notice of the brutal murders. Caesonia was stabbed by a centurion and her daughter killed by smashing her head against a wall.[22]

The aftermath was, briefly, total chaos. It also made permanently irrelevant whatever plans Caligula had for the succession. Since he had not anticipated even dying at all it is difficult to know for certain what he had in mind, or whether he had even given the succession any consideration. His despotic dynastic inclinations make it likely that he would have limited himself to blood relatives had he ever nominated anyone. Since he regarded himself as both pre-eminent and divine it is unlikely he would have been able to countenance the idea of an heir whom he would have instantly identified as a threat and rival. In the event, regardless of the conspirators' plans, the fact remained that they had played their hand but failed to eliminate the remaining members of the imperial family. The conspirators had forgotten to think through carefully what they would do next. Claudius and Messalina were still alive and so were Agrippina the Younger and her son Lucius Domitius. Fate had played its hand and once again the succession defaulted to a candidate whose eligibility was conferred by descent through the female Julio-Claudian line.

The failure to organize the simultaneous murder of Claudius was a disastrous mistake, for the plotters at least. That oversight annihilated their plans to restore the Republic because events moved far too fast to find another way of achieving their goal. With angry praetorians and Caligula's German bodyguard on the loose in the streets of Rome the mood was terrifying. More to the point the praetorians were on the brink of losing their jobs and their elite status; they were determined to prevent that from happening. Famously, a band of them roaming the corridors of the imperial palace found Claudius cowering behind a curtain and declared him emperor. The story of his reluctant acceptance of the position of emperor may have been one Claudius had already prepared, especially if he had had prior news of the plot – we do not know this, but his overt and very public gratitude for the Guard suggests there is a possibility Claudius knew what was going to happen to Caligula.[23]

Claudius' accession ensured the praetorians kept their jobs. It also ensured that he and his family kept their lives, and made Messalina empress, though Claudius did not allow her the title Augusta.[24] The praetorians' support ensured their safety; its withdrawal their doom. This was a succession that Augustus could not possibly have anticipated and it owed nothing at all to the various solutions he tried during his reign. However, like Tiberius, Claudius was descended from Livia and this was his principal dynastic qualification as well as his descent from Octavia. A relief found in Ravenna created later in his reign illustrated Claudius' dynastic credentials and reflects some of the intentions behind imperial dynastic cameos (plates 23, 32).[25] These were reinforced by Messalina's descent from Octavia. This lineage validated Claudius in the eyes of the praetorians and helped also keep at bay any opposition amongst the wider Roman aristocracy.

For the foreseeable future, Claudius, his daughter Claudia Antonia (then aged about eleven), Messalina and their daughter Claudia Octavia (aged just a little over a year old) were secure. In the new mood of freedom he was able to recall Caligula's exiled sisters Agrippina and Julia Livilla and return their property to them.[26] However, as it turned out Claudius was by no means safe from further plots and Messalina would turn out to be one of his greatest threats.

In this curious fashion Messalina became empress of Rome by late January 41 in the aftermath of Caligula's assassination. She played little part in the public face of Claudius' early reign but she was very aware of her position. Unlike previous empresses she had been born into the most powerful family in the Roman world. She might have grown up only on the periphery of that family but the experience must have had a considerable effect on her. Until Caligula was assassinated she had probably never considered the serious possibility that the marriage would bring her closer to the inner nucleus of power. Since her husband was the man widely considered to be the one person least likely ever to become emperor, the chances of her being anything other than the wife of an ageing and eccentric academic must have seemed rather small. Instead, fate had abruptly played Messalina a remarkable hand. She was also at that point very nearly nine months' pregnant. When she gave birth to Claudius' son, Tiberius Claudius Germanicus (afterwards Britannicus), her importance was immediately ratcheted up by another notch because she was now the mother of a potential emperor. So also was the threat she and her new child posed to Agrippina the Younger.

As it happened, by a strange coincidence Agrippina's husband, Gnaeus Domitius Ahenobarbus, had also died in January 41, shortly before Caligula's assassination, but of natural causes. This had given Caligula time to steal Lucius Domitius' one-third share of his father's estate, though after his accession Claudius gave it back. Shortly afterwards, and by now restored to the court, the merry widow Agrippina remarried, this time to a friend of Claudius', Gaius Sallustius Passienus Crispus, an extremely wealthy man and renowned orator. He was also her former brother-in-law (Crispus had been married to Agrippina's first husband's sister Domitia). Passienus Crispus was not Agrippina's first choice. She had begun by trying to lure Servius Sulpicius Galba (the future emperor of 68–9) into marriage, and did so in a shamelessly blatant way. He was already married to a woman called Lepida and had two sons. Lepida's mother was so disgusted by Agrippina's behaviour that she publicly castigated her in front of other matrons and allegedly slapped her.[27] Agrippina was completely undeterred by being rejected and moved on to Passienus Crispus. The incident showed what sort of woman Agrippina was though of course Roman historians were inclined to recount stories in such a way as to reinforce a negative image of her. In the event Lepida died not long after anyway. Galba never remarried. It is hardly surprising that Messalina was not pleased by Agrippina's return to the imperial circle. Agrippina's son Lucius Domitius represented a very real threat to her own children because of his cast-iron descent from Julia (and thus Augustus), as well as Octavia and Livia.[28] A story circulated that Messalina had sent assassins to suffocate Lucius Domitius, then aged about three, but they were scared off when a snake appeared from under the child's pillow. The evidence of a snakeskin found on the bed appeared to support the story. Thereafter Lucius Domitius allegedly wore the skin in a gold bracelet until he grew to hate his own mother.[29]

Meanwhile, Claudius was spending his time demonstrating his abilities. He wanted to show that he could not only match his predecessors' achievements but also surpass them. For a man recently treated with universal disdain for being an idiot he showed remarkable presence of mind. Like Caesar he invaded Britain, in 43, but, unlike Caesar, Claudius held on to the new province and trumpeted his victory with a triumph in Rome. Like Caesar and Augustus he considered the mounting problem of the mouth of the Tiber at Ostia silting up but commissioned the design and execution of a vast new harbour to facilitate the offloading of grain for the corn dole. Coins and statues portrayed Claudius as a godlike figure and were augmented by representations of his family. One of the most memorable images of all is that found at Aphrodisias where the conquering Claudius is seen smiting the humiliated figure of Britannia, realized for the first time as a female personification, this time as a broken and defeated woman. It was an ironic scene, given Claudius' experiences at the hands of his empresses, Messalina and then Agrippina. The inspiration for the composition was a Hellenistic sculpture of the killing of Penthesilea, the Amazonian queen, by Achilles.[30]

Claudius produced very little coinage from two years or so into his reign, but began with a considerable range of issues shortly after his accession. However, it was his mother who received the most attention apart from himself. Antonia Minor was prominently commemorated on gold, silver and bronze coins, with the title Augusta that Caligula seems to have been responsible for giving her, but which she had declined to use in her lifetime. She was thus rehabilitated in the grand tradition of a Roman matron, her reputation for being 'supreme in beauty and mind' set on a permanent footing.[31] Antonia was credited with having feminine virtues so great that they outdid the exalted masculine distinction of her family. In later years it was reported that she never spat. The implication was that she was too refined to do something otherwise commonplace for women, even those of status.[32] In promoting Antonia's reputation Claudius enhanced his own as the son of such a mother. Claudius also inherited Antonia's freedmen, including Pallas and his brother Antonius Felix. Other coins commemorated his father Drusus, his brother Germanicus and sister-in-law Agrippina the Elder. At this date bullion coin was apparently still being struck at the safer remote location of Lugdunum (Lyon) in Gaul while the base metal coin was minted at Rome. Neither facility was instructed to produce anything in Messalina's name, even as a reverse type with her husband. This must be because she had not been named Augusta. Any coinage depicting Messalina would therefore have encroached on Antonia Minor's posthumous rank. The mint at Alexandria, which manufactured coin purely for use in the province of Egypt, did produce coins with Claudius' and Messalina's busts, one on either side, and also with Messalina as a standing figure (Demeter?) on the reverse holding Claudia Octavia and Britannicus in her hand with the legend 'Messalina (empress) of Caesar Augustus'. Caesarea in Cappadocia issued a type in Messalina's own right, though not until later in the reign. Some coins from Aegae in Aeolis (Greece) give Messalina the title CEBACTH, the Greek equivalent of Augusta, but this must have been in error because the issue is exceptional (plate 21).[33] The issues depicting Claudius with his fourth, and last, wife Agrippina the Younger are of immeasurably greater significance because they were produced in far greater numbers for mainstream circulation. They are dealt with later in this book.

The family coins reflected Claudius' wider policy of using his immediate relatives, especially the women and including those deceased, as part of the principate's image. For example, by 42 he had deified his grandmother Livia and ordered equestrian games in her honour. He also decreed that women should cite her name in oaths.[34] It was a complete reversal of how Tiberius had treated the memory of his mother. The apotheosis of Livia was an essential part in the manufacture of the Julio-Claudian dynastic myth. Now all its blood members could claim descent from the divine couple of Augustus and Livia, even if in many cases it was only one or the other. Livia's cult was integrated with that of Augustus, Claudius ordering that a statue to her be set up in Augustus' temple as well. The Vestal Virgins were to offer sacrifices in her favour. Livia and her husband were both worshipped in the Temple of the Deified Augustus for long afterwards. In 158–9 Antoninus Pius issued coins depicting the octastyle temple's façade, complete with figures of Augustus and Livia in the middle, which commemorated its restoration. The building is now lost but probably stood in the valley between the Capitoline and Palatine Hills on the basis of one epigraphic reference. It became known simply as the templum Divorum, 'Temple of the Divines' (plate 28).[35]

Claudius instituted games in honour of his parents Drusus and Antonia which were to be held on their birthdays. He made sure that any other festivals already scheduled for those days were moved to alternative dates. A carriage was organized to display an image of Antonia in the circus as Augusta to make up for the fact that she had refused the title when alive. Other honours were paid to Germanicus and even Mark Antony, his grandfather.[36]

Claudius substantially expanded the range of coins in his own name, extending the female side to the Roman state image begun under Augustus with new types. This set the tone for a trend that remained a permanent feature of the coinage, even if many of the types produced for Claudius are unique to the reign. The female deity Spes (Hope) was one of his commonest sestertius issues. It commemorated his birthday, 1 August, which was the Feast of Spes, but also conveniently alluded to the 'new hope' his accession had brought.[37] Claudius was keen to show that the principate brought real benefits to the ordinary people, hence coins with Constantia (Constancy), Libertas (Liberty), and also Ceres, a mother goddess evoking fertility and agricultural plenty.[38] These ideas were clearly the product of careful consideration and represent a thematic programme intended to evoke a collective image of the state. While it is easy to dismiss the significance of coinage in the twenty-first century when so many other sources of information are available, the use of Roman coinage as a propaganda medium should not be underestimated. Coinage was the only available mechanism for disseminating ideas easily and fast. The prominent use of female personifications was also closely connected with the emphasis placed on female members of the Roman imperial family.

It must have been obvious when he became emperor, not only to Claudius but also to everyone else, that in terms of his living relatives suitable males were in short supply. He also became emperor at a time when it was still possible for many people to have remembered the importance of Livia and Agrippina the Elder. Livia had died twelve years earlier, Agrippina only eight. With Agrippina the Younger and Julia Livilla restored, and with his wife Messalina, Claudius now found himself at the centre of an imperial court surrounded by women. This led easily to the allegation that he was himself dominated by those women, and also by his freedmen, preferring their influence to that of the Senate.

Messalina's comparative absence from the coinage series, including provincial coins, is therefore a matter of some interest. Her fall came at a later point in the reign when Claudius was no longer striking many coins. Only a few locations apart from Alexandria featured her, such as Tralles in Lydia, but collectively these coins are so obscure and localized that Messalina had very little presence on coins at all.[39] There was, however, still very little precedent for portraying a living empress on the coinage. Livia was not depicted on coins made at Rome during her lifetime and Tiberius had no empress of his own to feature on his issues, though he did produce a series of coins for Livia. Caligula had also made little of his wives on his coins, preferring his female relatives. However, Claudius' last wife, Agrippina the Younger, is so prominent a feature of his coinage both at Rome and elsewhere that the lack of any mainstream issues depicting Messalina must have some relevance for understanding the real level of her influence and perhaps even her relationship with her husband.

Unlike her predecessors Messalina must have been fully aware that her dynastic entitlement approached her husband's. Her dual descent from Octavia made her more closely related to Augustus than Claudius. Her maternal uncle was Agrippina the Younger's husband, Gnaeus Domitius Ahenobarbus, making Messalina first cousin to Agrippina's son, the future emperor Nero. Claudius of course could also claim descent from Livia, but Messalina still had a lineage no previous empress had enjoyed. It is possible therefore that Messalina's virtual exclusion from the coinage was to avoid suggesting any parity between her and Claudius, or even any precedence. If she was marginalized in terms of rank this may explain some of her later behaviour.

Within a year of Julia Livilla's restoration to court Messalina had seen to it that she was removed again. Julia Livilla was of course descended from Augustus through her mother Agrippina the Elder and this may have been why she refused to pay Messalina the honour she thought she deserved, infuriating the new empress. Livilla's beauty and close relationship with her uncle Claudius also seem to have contributed to Messalina's anger. Messalina employed the usual tactic. She accused Livilla of immoral behaviour by committing adultery, apparently with the philosopher Lucius Annaeus Seneca.

They were both exiled, Livilla being killed not long after while Seneca survived to become her nephew's tutor when he was emperor.[40] While in exile Seneca decided to write a book filled with fulsome praise of Messalina and Claudius' freedmen, no doubt inspired by a hope that it would save his skin. It might have done but the hypocrisy (he was noted for criticizing flatterers) did his reputation no good in later years.[41] The obsequious gesture showed how significant a part fear played in helping Messalina become as powerful as she did. Tiberius' granddaughter Julia, the daughter of Drusus, had taken her life too by 43 thanks to what seems to have been a baseless accusation made by Publius Suillius; this was not exposed until the reign of Nero when he claimed he had been acting under orders from Messalina both in this instance and with others.[42] The birth of Messalina's son Britannicus, an heir for Claudius, may have enhanced her sense of importance and inviolability.

Messalina took against her new stepfather, Appius Junius Silanus, or so the story went. Claudius had summoned Silanus, governor of Hispania Tarraconensis, and married him to Messalina's mother, Domitia Lepida, who had been widowed some twenty years earlier when Messalina's father, Messalla Barbatus, had died. For a while Appius Silanus became a close member of the inner imperial circle. However, the first sign of Messalina's alleged promiscuity became apparent when she tried to seduce him but was rejected. Claudius' freedman Narcissus shared his mistress' anger at being refused. Having no crime to pin on Silanus, Narcissus did the next best thing and invented an oneiric felony, declaring that he had had a dream in which he had seen Silanus murdering the emperor. Narcissus announced his nocturnal omen to Claudius, helped by Messalina who encouraged Claudius to believe it was a dangerous portent. Silanus was executed. Messalina had learned how easily she could manipulate Claudius.[43] That is one way of looking at it. The other is that Claudius had found a way of getting rid of people he had taken against or developed a paranoid fear of, without having to act like a despot. He perhaps either put Narcissus and Messalina up to it, or he took advantage of her fears for her own son's future and let them bring Silanus down.[44] Silanus was certainly not the only senator to fall in those years, albeit at different times and in different ways. Either way, Messalina soon headed down a disastrous path of unprecedented female ambition in the history of the principate.

The death of Silanus badly damaged Claudius' image. Dissatisfaction grew, especially amongst those who had hoped for an alternative outcome to the assassination of Caligula. Annius Vinicianus was a senator whose name had been mooted as a possible successor to Caligula, an ambition thwarted by the fast-moving events at the time. In 42 Vinicianus decided that he might now act once again in an attempt to restore the Republic. He brought the governor of Dalmatia, Camillus Scribonianus, on side with his huge legionary and auxiliary garrison. Unfortunately, the soldiers were less amenable. They refused to participate in a coup that might not only restore the Republic but also the civil war and chaos of those days. Camillus promptly gave up his ill-conceived involvement and committed suicide. Claudius moved fast to crush the plot. Vinicianus was one of those quick enough to take his own life while others were executed. The imperial freedmen also organized their intelligence gathering activities by building up a network of informants, leading to further oppressive measures. In an interesting twist some of those who were guilty of treasonous activities found in Messalina and Narcissus useful friends. By offering bribes or calling in favours the two could be persuaded to save certain people.[45]

Nothing could have been more helpful to Messalina at this point than if Claudius had been away from Rome. Of course she might have accompanied him but since his impending absence in 43 was the military campaign in Britain her involvement was less desirable. Messalina had spotted an opportunity. She was already colluding in a corruption ring operated by the imperial freedmen. Anyone who wanted Roman citizenship and all the associated privileges could make a private appeal to the emperor. Messalina and the freedmen sold citizenship for large sums of money. In practice this probably meant that in return for a payment they would pass on the application to Claudius with their recommendation that it be awarded. The practice became so prolific that the cost was brought down to a trivial level. This damaged Claudius, not least because many of the successful applicants were not bothering to amend their names by adding Claudius to them or modifying their wills to leave him part of their estates. Messalina and her henchmen decided to increase the range of products on offer, adding positions such as governorships, military commands and procuratorships, as well as monopolies on commodities. As she cheapened the principate and all it stood for, so Messalina increased the cost of goods because the monopolies she was busy selling resulted in shortages.[46] As ever the extent of the truth is impossible to ascertain. Accusing her of financial greed was an easy way for Roman historians to mark her out as a degenerate.

1. Temple of Venus Genetrix, Rome
The Temple of Venus Genetrix (the 'universal mother') in the Forum of Julius Caesar. The present remains date to the reign of Trajan (AD 98–117) but the original structure was dedicated by Caesar in 46 BC in thanks for his victory at Thessaly two years earlier. The building commemorated the Julian family's claimed descent from Venus through her son Aeneas. It also contained a statue of Cleopatra VII, installed by Caesar.

2. Tomb of Caecilia Metella, Via Appia
The drum-shaped late Republican tomb of Caecilia Metella on the Via Appia bears this inscription which clearly indicates her role as a dynastic commodity. It states, in conventionally abbreviated form, '(The tomb of) Caecilia Metella, daughter of Quintus (Caecilius Metellus) Creticus, (wife of Marcus Licinius) Crassus'. It was thus primarily a monument to the family's status and association placed in an appropriately commanding position where it still stands. Rome, *c.* 25–1 BC.

3. Cleopatra VII and Caesarion
Cleopatra VII (reigned 51–30 BC) and her son by Julius Caesar, Caesarion (Ptolemy XV, reigned 36–30 BC), shown here as an adult. Flaunted in Rome by Caesar to aristocratic disgust in 46 BC, later Roman sources routinely depicted Cleopatra as a dangerous and destabilizing woman whose influence had effeminated Mark Antony and led to his destruction. She provided a useful contrast for the Augustan state and its image of idealized women in the form of Livia and Octavia. Temple of Hathor, Dendera, Egypt, 30s BC.

4. Pompeii lovers
A fresco panel from Pompeii depicting a man and woman in a chair. The woman plays a *kithara* (lyre) while her lover gazes upon and holds her. The woman's lighter skin was a convention that indicated her status, partaking in suitably refined pastimes. *c.* AD 50–79.

5. Theatre of Marcellus, Rome
Originally a project of Caesar's, the theatre was finished by Augustus in the name of Octavia's son Marcus Marcellus, his (likely) intended heir, but who died in 23 BC. It remains one of Rome's most prominent ancient buildings from the Julio-Claudian period. Marcellus' death forced Augustus to look to his daughter Julia to provide an heir.

6. Porticus of Octavia
The Porticus of Octavia replaced the earlier Porticus of Metellus (an ancestor of Caecilia Metella, see plate 2) in 27–25 BC, dedicated to Octavia, Augustus' sister and the mother of Marcellus, in whose name a theatre was dedicated very close by (see plate 5). Essentially a complex of art galleries, temples, colonnades, a library and schools, only its monumental gateway survives today and even that is a Severan reconstruction.

7. Ara Pacis, Rome
Panel from the Ara Pacis ('Altar of Peace') probably depicting Venus Genetrix, though other suggestions include Pax and Tellus (Mother Earth). Such female personifications were an essential part of the Augustan myth. Commissioned in 13 BC, dedicated in 9 BC.

8. Agrippa and Julia, Ara Pacis, Rome
Panel from the north processional frieze showing Agrippa (left) with, probably, Julia (right) and between them their son, Augustus' grandson Gaius. Commissioned in 13 BC, dedicated in 9 BC.

9. Bust of Livia
A life-size marble bust of Livia made during her lifetime. Nevertheless, the features are clearly both idealized and implausibly youthful, just as statues of Augustus were. From Italy, *c.* 25–1 BC.

10. Posthumous bust of Livia as the goddess Ceres
The image shows how Livia remained the embodiment of idealized virtues and a useful model for realizing female deities or personifications. Probably made in Sicily, *c.* AD 30–50.

11. Clay oil lamp with a bust of Livia
A mid-first-century AD clay oil lamp decorated with a stylized female bust usually identified as Livia. Livia was treated as a kind of template for depicting an idealized representation of a Roman matron, though these images became increasingly distanced from reality. Probably from Pozzuoli, *c.* AD 40–80.

12. Building of Eumachia, Pompeii
Eumachia, public priestess of Pompeii and wealthy businesswoman, used this building to promote the political career of her son, Marcus Numistrius Fronto, in the Augustan period. Appropriately, it paid homage to the Forum of Augustus and the Porticus of Livia and contained a shrine with a statue of Livia as Concordia Augusta. Built late in the reign of Augustus (27 BC–AD 14) or under Tiberius (AD 14–37).

13. The Mausoleum of Augustus
Now a shadow of its former self, this vast drum-shaped mausoleum in the Field of Mars (Campus Martius) once contained the cremated remains of the Julio-Claudians, each grave marked by a marble tablet (see plate 19). It was the symbolic centre of the dynasty where the key individuals through which the succession passed were laid to rest.

14. Dedication to the Deified Augusta (Livia), Herculaneum
Dedication to Livia by Lucius Mammius Maximus 'with his own money' – a successful freedman. From the Porticus at Herculaneum. Mammius Maximus also funded monuments of other members of the imperial family which dates the series, probably *c.* AD 50–4.

15. Porticus of Livia, Marble Plan of Rome
The Marble Plan of Rome was created during the reign of Septimius Severus and was displayed in the Flavian Temple of Peace. This section preserves the plan of the now lost Porticus of Livia dedicated in 7 BC, showing that there was a temple in the centre of a piazza surrounded by a colonnade on three sides with apses. This structure was probably the inspiration for the Building of Eumachia at Pompeii (plate 12). It lay just north of the later site of the Baths of Trajan. *c.* AD 203–11.

16. Inscription of Lucius Caesar, Porticus of Gaius and Lucius
Honorific inscription from the Porticus of Gaius and Lucius, Julia's sons by Agrippa, in the Forum at Rome. The text describes Lucius as the son of Augustus, and grandson of Caesar. Julia and Agrippa are unmentioned. The Porticus, which contained shops and was attached to the Basilica Paulli, was rebuilt and dedicated by Augustus. Rome, 3 BC.

17. Temple of Vesta, Roman Forum
Livia attended a fire here during the reign of Tiberius and urged on soldiers and others to douse the flames. The present structure is heavily restored from what remained of a rebuilding by Julia Domna two centuries later.

18. The Roman Forum
At lower left is the Temple of Vesta, and on the right the three remaining columns of the Temple of Castor and Pollux. Dedicated in AD 6 by Tiberius in his name and that of his brother Drusus, this Augustan temple was originally conceived as being associated with Gaius and Lucius, Julia's sons, but their premature deaths rendered that plan obsolete. Behind at ground level is the House of the Vestal Virgins.

19. Tombstone of Agrippina the Elder
Originally deposited in the Mausoleum of Augustus by Caligula who recovered his mother's remains and brought them to Rome. The inscription makes Agrippina's dynastic role as daughter of Agrippa, granddaughter of Augustus, wife of Germanicus and mother of Caligula crystal clear. Rome, c. 37–41.

20. Sestertius of Agrippina the Elder
A sestertius of Agrippina the Elder struck posthumously under Claudius, her brother-in-law. The portrait is a study in evoking her image as a heroic Roman matron of the old school and implicitly as a victim of Tiberius. Diameter 32mm. Rome, AD 42.

21. Bronze coin of Messalina

Bronze coin (18mm) from Aeolis, Aegae, in the name of Messalina, Claudius' third wife and first empress. The coin unofficially gives her the Greek equivalent title of Augusta (CEBACTH), a title she never received. The reverse shows Zeus Aëtophorus standing left. Struck AD 41–8.

22. Cistophoric tetradrachm (silver) of Claudius and Agrippina

Jugate busts of the emperor and Agrippina the Younger. The issue is an exceptional instance of an emperor and empress depicted in the manner of joint rulers. Diameter 26mm. Ephesus, AD 51.

23. The Gemma Claudia
Sardonyx five-layered cameo depicting
(left) Claudius and Agrippina the
Younger and (right) Germanicus and
Agrippina the Elder. The busts emerge
from cornucopiae resting on captured
military equipment with Jupiter (the eagle)
in the middle. The design symbolizes
the integrity of the dynasty through the
combined descent from Augustus and
Livia. Height 12cm. *c.* AD 49.

24. Agrippina crowns Nero
Sculpture from Aphrodisias showing
Agrippina symbolically crowning her son
Nero. Created *c.* AD 54–9.

25. Nero's Golden House, Rome
One of the now subterranean chambers beneath the Baths of Trajan. Poppaea probably spent her last months in this remarkable complex. Rome, AD 64–8.

26. Tetradrachm of Nero and Poppaea
Nero and Poppaea depicted on an Egyptian tetradrachm. Diameter 24mm. Alexandria, AD 64–5.

27. View of Oplontis
A view across one of the colonnaded courts of the palatial villa of Oplontis near Pompeii, probably owned by Nero and used by Poppaea. The house was extensively repaired and remodelled after the earthquake of AD 62, but was destroyed and buried in the eruption of Vesuvius in August 79.

28. Sestertius of the Temple of the Deified Augustus and Livia
Antoninus restored the Temple of the Deified Augustus and Livia and recorded the fact on this sestertius. Their cult statues are shown inside the temple between the two central columns in a stylistic convention. There was no such gap in reality. The temple is long lost but probably lay between the Capitoline and Palatine Hills in Rome. Diameter 32mm. Rome, AD 158–9.

29. The Severan Women
From left to right: Julia Domna (d. AD 217), Septimius Severus' empress; her sister Julia Maesa (d. *c.* AD 225); and Maesa's daughters, Julia Soaemias (d. AD 222), mother of Elagabalus, and Julia Mamaea (d. AD 235), mother of Severus Alexander. Although the quality of coin portraiture was poor by this date the physical resemblance between the women is noticeable. The hairstyles are largely attributable to the habitual use of wigs by eastern women of high status at this time. From silver denarii struck at Rome. Diameter of each approximately 17–18mm.

30. Julia Domna and Septimius Severus on the Arch of the Moneychangers (Porta Argentarii), Rome
Domna holds a *caduceus* (staff of a herald) to symbolize her title 'Mother of the Army'. The blank space to the right is where a figure of her younger son Geta was erased after his murder by Caracalla in 212, requiring her left arm to be recarved. Meanwhile Severus as *pontifex maximus* (chief priest) pours a libation over an altar. Dedicated AD 204.

31. Sestertius of Julia Mamaea
A brass sestertius in the extensive series of coins issued in the name of Severus Alexander's mother Julia Mamaea, the last of the Severan empresses. The reverse depicts Felicitas ('Happiness'), a stock theme in the repertoire used by the women of the dynasty. Mamaea's death, along with that of Severus in AD 235, marked the end of the dynasty. Diameter *c.* 30mm. Rome, *c.* AD 228.

32. Julio-Claudian dynastic relief, Ravenna
This relief found at Ravenna close to the so-called Tomb of Galla Placidia was designed to advertise Claudius' dynastic credentials in which Livia played a central role. From left to right: seated female figure, perhaps Antonia Minor (mother of Claudius); a male cuirassed figure, perhaps Nero Claudius Drusus; Germanicus; Livia as Venus with Eros on her shoulder; and the deified Augustus as Mars. Height 104cm. Created during the reign of Claudius, AD 41–54.

Selling citizenship and offices was one thing for Messalina, selling herself was something else altogether. By the late summer of 43 Claudius was getting ready to go to Britain. By the autumn he was in Britain and leading his triumphal entry into Colchester, the British tribal capital. With Claudius away Messalina may have felt that the opportunity had arrived to take her very liberal interpretation of her prerogative a stage further. Her exalted origins are likely to have helped spur her on. With a dynastic pedigree as great as her husband's Messalina could be forgiven for deciding she was entitled to more than being just an imperial wife.

The stories about Messalina are so extraordinary, and her behaviour so reckless, that at first reading they are difficult to believe. It was claimed that by 43 she was already openly engaging in promiscuous behaviour and enticing other women to join in with her. These allegedly involved the women exhibiting themselves having sex in the imperial palace while their husbands watched. The orgies seem to have formed a logical extension of Messalina's ideas about the power of her patronage. Husbands who made their wives available were rewarded with honours and position; those who denied Messalina the services of their wives were deliberately damaged by her. She found other ways to experiment with power. In *c.* 43 Messalina secured the death of Julia Livia, Tiberius' granddaughter, after becoming jealous of her. It seems that Claudius acquiesced to his young wife's demand without a murmur.[47] If these stories were true they are best seen as another manifestation of exploring how far the impunity afforded by absolute power could be pushed. Caligula had experimented with ways of advertising and proving his complete and unchallengeable autonomy. He did this with not only deliberate acts of cultivated brutality but also by telling people what he could do if he wished. Both routes reinforced one another. He was, however, the emperor and in a political sense it was clear that there was no way of dealing with such a ruler other than by assassination.

Messalina was in a different position. Despite her Julian ancestry through her great-grandmother Octavia she had only been brought directly into the imperial circle by being married to Claudius and then unexpectedly propelled to centre stage when he became emperor. This meant that she found herself abruptly with access to a remarkable amount of power and influence by association. When she began to act on that she soon found that Claudius did not obstruct her; quite the opposite in fact – he seems to have acquiesced, and disarmingly easily. Consequently, Messalina's experimentation extended in search of how far she could go. Her use of sex is perhaps best seen as an expression of power in its own right, rather than the pursuit of carnal pleasure. It was also unlikely to have been for the same reasons that Julia the Elder had become caught up in undermining Augustus' moral programme. In Julia's case the reasons were more likely to do with a sense of incarceration and suffocating expectation. Julia had also been somewhat older, perhaps in her mid-twenties before stories began to circulate about her behaviour and she was in her late thirties before Augustus found out. She also quite clearly understood what she was doing. By 43 Messalina was little more than in her mid-twenties. She was extremely young and since her late teens had been locked into a marriage with a very much older man. It is therefore unlikely that she had any idea of the enormous implications of her conduct.

Messalina had created a transactional relationship with compliant men in which their wives were the currency they used for personal advancement. This means they were cornered by Messalina. Either they accepted positions provided by her in return for their wives' services or they would see their careers destroyed by Messalina. Whether there was any degree of culpability on the part of the wives is neither here nor there and is in any case impossible to assess. Messalina was the one with the power and she had contrived a trap into which a number of ambitious men had fallen. Even so, the remarkable carrying-on must at the same time have provided a titillating frisson of excitement for the sheer daring. If Messalina was in part pursuing a reckless path for the thrill of it, she was by no means the first. Nor would she be the last.

Like Julia, Messalina hid in plain sight. What must have been common knowledge, especially as the venue for her events was the imperial palace, seems to have escaped Claudius' notice. One of the more audacious public manifestations of this was when the Senate ordered that coinage showing Caligula's portrait be melted down. Messalina had some of the bronze recycled into a statue of a very good-looking actor called Mnester with whom she had become obsessed. Mnester declined her advances so she persuaded Claudius to tell Mnester that he was obliged to do whatever Messalina wanted, Claudius presumably not suspecting what his wife meant. Mnester then gave in, believing he was acting on Claudius' express instructions. It was a useful threat. Messalina claimed to other conquests that she was acting with Claudius' approval.[48]

Messalina took advantage of Claudius' enjoyment of female company by providing him with young girls from the palace staff. The invasion of Britain was probably a much more significant distraction to him. She used threats and intimidation to terrorize anyone who might have let on to Claudius about what she was up to. A prefect of the Praetorian Guard, Catonius Justus, was on the point of telling Claudius but Messalina saw to it that he was removed.[49] Messalina's star apparently continued to rise. Her son by Claudius was renamed Britannicus in honour of the successful campaign in Britain in 43. She participated in the triumph celebrating the war but rode behind Claudius.[50] Her status was advanced closer to that of Livia by allowing her to ride in a carpentum in Rome and to be seated in the front row in the theatre.[51]

Messalina appears not to have become pregnant again after 41. It is impossible now to know whether their sexual relationship had ended (though Suetonius implies Claudius' interest in her did not cool until later), if they used such methods of contraception as were available, or whether either of them had become infertile.[52] Preventing pregnancy for a sexually active woman was not easy, though coitus interruptus was an obvious means. One recommended technique involved attempting to obstruct the ingress of sperm by applying to the vagina a compound of white lead mixed with olive oil, honey, or cedar or balsam sap. Another even more bizarre procedure was to tie on to a woman with a strip of deer hide a couple of worms found inside a 'hairy spider' with a notoriously large head.[53] Neither sounds especially reliable or realistic. After 41 Julia's solution of only sleeping with lovers while pregnant was not open to Messalina. The affairs she was said to have had did not apparently result in any other pregnancies but there is no evidence to suggest she used contraceptive techniques or anything else to achieve that. One remaining possibility is that she had become unable to bear more children for medical reasons.

We do not know the extent to which Messalina continued to behave as she had been but it appears that little had changed several years later. There was an omen in 45. Claudius worried that it might be a bad one. There was an eclipse of the sun predicted for his birthday that year (1 August). Claudius decided to publicize the impending phenomenon adding an astronomical explanation to show that it was a purely natural event and offset any superstitious rumblings. There was indeed an eclipse that day. The path of totality passed over central Africa, so the eclipse was only partial in Italy. In Rome about 21 per cent of the solar disc was obscured by about 0828 hours in the early morning but that would have been enough to excite popular attention into considering its significance.[54]

Unfortunately for Claudius the rational explanation for the eclipse of 1 August 45 was not enough to stop the occasion being an ominous portent. Messalina's persecution of her 'enemies', real or imagined, proceeded without let-up. Marcus Vinicius, a consul in 45 and former husband of Claudius' niece Julia Livilla who had been exiled on a charge of adultery with Seneca, was killed at Messalina's pleasure the following year, despite his best efforts to stay out of any controversies. Since he was also the brother of the Vinicianus who had led a conspiracy against Claudius in 42 keeping a low profile seemed like a good plan. It wasn't. Not becoming involved turned out to be his undoing. The story was that Messalina had had him murdered out of fury that he had refused to sleep with her, and also because she believed Vinicius had killed his wife Julia Livilla perhaps to save her from the ignominy of being re-exiled at Messalina's behest (see above, pp. 186–7).[55] Messalina operated on the basis that those who were not with her were, by definition, against her. This could benefit some people. A former commanding officer of Caligula's beloved German bodyguard, Sabinus, was saved from dying in a gladiatorial contest by Messalina. Claudius was widely supported in his plans to see Sabinus die this way but because Sabinus had had the foresight to take the precaution of sleeping with Messalina she stepped in to prevent this happening.[56] One of her other lovers, allegedly, was a famous doctor called Vettius Valens. His fame, already considerable on account of his eloquence, was enhanced by his affair with Messalina. He did well out of the arrangement because he gained adherents which enabled him to found a new religious-medical sect.[57]

Mnester, now well and truly caught up in Messalina's honey trap, was obliged to miss his theatrical dancing performances and stay with her. Since he was extremely popular his absence from the stage could not go unnoticed. Claudius personally assured agitated crowds that Mnester was very definitely not in the palace. Since the frustrated theatregoers knew very well that Mnester was in the palace with Messalina they were bewildered by Claudius' evident ignorance of what was going on under his nose. They felt unable to do anything: they were terrified of Messalina and were also desperate not to incriminate Mnester.[58]

Being cuckolded, and apparently knowing nothing about it, did not help Claudius' reputation. That he was under the control of his freedmen was becoming a source of general amusement. One of them, Polybius, was able openly to refer to the role reversal while bantering with the audience in the theatre by quoting Menander with the line, 'those who were once goatherds now have royal power'. That Claudius did nothing to punish Polybius made him look negligent or so arrogant that he need not trouble himself.[59]

In the middle of this remarkable series of events Messalina made a rare appearance in the coinage of Claudius' reign, but not at Rome. A very scarce silver didrachm was issued at Caesarea in Cappadocia some time between 46 and 48. Messalina appears on the obverse, presented with a very similar hair-style to Agrippina the Elder's on the coins minted in her honour by Caligula and Claudius. She is named as MESSALLINA AVGVSTI (sic), 'Messalina (wife of) Augustus'. On the reverse all three of Claudius' children, Claudia Antonia (by his second wife Aelia Paetina), Claudia Octavia and Britannicus are shown standing side-by-side with the boy in the middle and as the smallest.[60] The coin was a way of showing Messalina as a central dynastic figure in the Claudian regime. That it came at a time when her behaviour was becoming more notorious is all the more remarkable, though as a product of an eastern mint it is possible that the rumours emanating from Rome were treated as just that and no more. It must, however, have been approved by Claudius or his staff. Another coin in the same series had Claudius on the obverse with Messalina's portrait relocated to the reverse.[61]

In 47 came the mysterious case of Decimus Valerius Asiaticus, a rich senator from Gallia Narbonensis who held land in Italy and Egypt. He was by then aged about fifty-two years old.[62] Asiaticus had been the first Gaulish senator and had risen to prominence, amongst other reasons, for being a friend of Caligula's though they had fallen out when Asiaticus' wife became one of Caligula's mistresses. That led him to join the plot to kill Caligula. He had become a friend of Claudius' too and accompanied the emperor on his visit to Britain during the invasion of 43. Messalina had two reasons to dislike Asiaticus. Firstly, she believed that Asiaticus had been sleeping with Poppaea (the mother of the later emperor Nero's wife of the same name). Secondly, some of Asiaticus' wealth had been invested in the Gardens of Lucullus in Rome, located about 600 metres east of the Mausoleum of Augustus (close to where the Spanish Steps are now), which he was developing. Messalina had taken a fancy to the Gardens. She commissioned a notorious prosecutor called Publius Suillius Rufus to bring a case against Asiaticus. She also brought Britannicus' tutor, Sosibius, in on the pursuit. Sosibius was to use the fact that Asiaticus had been involved in the killing of Caligula as proof of how dangerous he could be to a *princeps*. Asiaticus' wealth helped provide convincing proof of the threat he posed, as well as his provincial connections which meant that with the help of the garrison in Germany he could incite the Gauls into some sort of insurrection.[63]

Asiaticus was in a tight corner, but remarkably he came within a whisker of being acquitted, something that Claudius favoured. He refused to acknowledge even the slightest connection with any of those implicated in the allegations. In a dramatic and hilarious moment a soldier witness identified another man in the court as the man he had been in association with (both the man and Asiaticus were bald). This provoked an outburst of laughter in the court and Claudius decided to let Asiaticus go. Before he could do so Messalina intervened again. This time she persuaded Lucius Vitellius, co-consul with Claudius for 47, to claim that Asiaticus had sought his advice on choosing the manner of his death. It was a fatal moment, literally. It now suddenly looked as though Asiaticus had a guilty conscience. Asiaticus had missed his chance and was rapidly executed.[64]

Messalina had had her way yet again. The same year she even sought, by similarly successful methods, to have Claudius' son-in-law executed too. In 43 Claudia Antonia had been married to Gnaeus Pompeius Magnus, a descendant of Pompey the Great. There was an obvious reason. Although his exact age is unknown he was somewhat older than Britannicus, who was still only a small child, and therefore a better prospect for succeeding Claudius. He had been restored by Claudius to his famous forebear's full name so the auspices for his future were good. Moreover, Claudia Antonia was not Messalina's daughter and Claudius himself was in his late fifties. In short, Messalina could easily have calculated that there was a very good chance that fate would wreck her chances of seeing her own son become emperor. The pretext was that Pompeius had been caught in an embrace with a favourite catamite.[65] Given Messalina's own behaviour the accusation was remarkably brazen but it worked. Unfortunately, Claudia Antonia was already pregnant so the execution of Pompeius did nothing immediately to cut off his line of descent. She was remarried on Claudius' orders to Messalina's half-brother, Faustus Cornelius Sulla Felix, which ensured that any further children would share Messalina's own bloodline. The birth of Claudia Antonia's child by Pompeius, a boy, in 48 was kept quiet. Claudius, presumably at Messalina's behest, ordered that there were to be no decrees honouring the birth of his first grandchild.[66]

194

Messalina was reaching the climax of her powers though; in 47 the first signs of cracks in her circle had already begun to show. Suillius started to overstep the mark, probably assuming that his association with Messalina guaranteed that he could act with impunity. He seems to have been taking bribes either to collude with his own clients' opponents or accepted bungs to drop prosecutions and then gone ahead with the case anyway. As a result Suillius was attacked in the Senate by Gaius Silius, being unfavourably compared to the advocates of old who had been satisfied with fame and the future as rewards enough. Suillius survived, but Claudius placed a ceiling on advocacy fees of ten thousand sesterces, declaring anything more would amount to extortion.[67] We do not know whether this was the sum Suillius had taken or was considerably less. Therefore we cannot judge what Claudius thought personally of Suillius and by extension his relationship with Messalina.

Messalina also made another serious mistake. She fell out with Agrippina the Younger, now her nemesis. The reason may have been dynastic jealousy. Agrippina's son, Lucius Domitius Ahenobarbus, was the grandson of Germanicus and Agrippina the Elder and their only living male descendant. Through his parents and grandparents Lucius Domitius shared a similar level of blue-blooded descent to that enjoyed by Caligula.[68] He was starting to be regarded with the same sort of promise that Caligula had been when he was made emperor. Messalina allegedly engaged in a campaign of persecution against Agrippina. It was an own goal. Since Agrippina was Germanicus' daughter popular feeling immediately went in her favour and that of her son's. She was pitied and Lucius Domitius' popularity increased, enhanced by his reception at the Saecular Games of 47 where he was welcomed more enthusiastically than Britannicus. A story circulated that Messalina had even sent agents to try and strangle the boy in bed while he was taking his siesta. Messalina only backed off because she had found another distraction in the form of Gaius Silius.[69]

In the year 48 Messalina was still only about thirty. According to Dio, Messalina and Claudius' freedmen were extremely pleased with themselves. Callistus, Narcissus and Pallas were effectively ruling Rome. Messalina was prostituting herself and other noblewomen in the palace. This reached its eccentric climax with Messalina's decision to compete with a courtesan of about the same age as herself. It was a bizarre way for her to experiment with the Roman world's fixation with stereotyping women either as matrons or prostitutes.

Messalina, if Pliny's story can be believed, won with a score of twenty-five men in twenty-four hours.[70] Messalina's major error, at least compared to all her others, was to make a false accusation against another imperial freedman, Polybius. He had been executed as a result. Callistus, Narcissus and Pallas now realized what a very dangerous and precarious position they were in. The bubble was about to burst.[71] The main source for what came next is Tacitus. His account is graphic as it describes the mounting crisis and its outcome. Messalina's descent is depicted as the consequence of her feminine and fatal lack of self-control. It was just as much a rhetorical image of women as agents of chaos which provided Roman historians like Pliny and Tacitus an opportunity to show Messalina descending from being an empress to acting as a prostitute, the exact opposite.[72] The image of her self-inflicted degradation thus neutralized her as a threat to the Roman world and the forces of order. Moreover, prostitutes were considered to be experts in contraception.[73] Messalina's lack of pregnancies after 41 would therefore only have served to reinforce suspicion about her activities.

Guilty or innocent, Messalina would not see out the year. The whole saga is a curious one though the behaviour of Julia more than half a century earlier means Messalina's reputation does not stand alone. Augustus had been protected from finding out about his daughter's behaviour for years; there is no good reason to doubt the basic truth of Julia's story and his reaction to it. Claudius had also been kept in the dark about Messalina. By 48 her alleged scandalous behaviour can hardly have been going on for more than about five to six years at most though even that seems astonishing given the enclosed and intense world of the imperial palace. Claudius was, however, a very different person to Augustus. His susceptibility to being manipulated by women and freedmen is such a consistent theme that it would be surprising if there was no truth to it.

The story had to break eventually. Claudius' freedmen knew that blowing Messalina's cover was the best way to save their own skins. They must have been delighted when Messalina handed them an opportunity on a plate. She embarked on an affair with Gaius Silius, even forcing his wife Junia Silana to leave her husband's house.[74] We do not know how or why, though the altercation in the Senate may have been somehow linked. Messalina and Silius' actions were suicidal. That she behaved as she did can only be because she believed Claudius was so foolish and gullible that they could get away with it.

In Silius' case he knew that to have refused Messalina would lead to his certain death. We have no idea what Silius had especially to recommend him over all Messalina's other lovers or obsessions, though he was supposed to be especially good looking. Perhaps that was enough, or maybe he had other talents. Suetonius claims that the most extraordinary aspect of the whole affair was that Claudius actually knew Messalina and Silius were planning a bigamous marriage; he adds that Claudius had even signed a dowry contract in the full knowledge that their wedding was a pretend one. Suetonius' explanation was that various unspecified omens had occurred which suggested Claudius was in danger; therefore the idea of a sham wedding had been dreamed up to divert the effects of the omens onto someone else. Although this seems completely unbelievable it does have the advantage of explaining why the 'wedding' took place so openly and why Claudius absented himself from the vicinity.[75]

Messalina seems to have repeatedly visited Silius' house along with her personal entourage and done so quite openly. Meanwhile Claudius busied himself with routine legislation, as well as bringing in a new aqueduct to Rome.[76] Messalina, according to Tacitus, gradually became bored and amused herself with even more decadent behaviour.[77] She was pushing everything to the limit, simply because she could. For his part Silius became worried and wanted to drop the pretence. This time Messalina went the whole way and organized a bigamous form of marriage with Silius, following this up with a party. One oddity in all this is that Dio claims Messalina had polygamous tastes and would, had she been able to, have married many of her lovers on the basis that she liked the idea of having numerous husbands. However, her other actions make it much more likely that the two of them planned to kill Claudius rather than that Messalina was initiating a game she planned to follow up with other lovers. They may even have felt that Agrippina was such a potential threat now that even this risky course of action was worth taking. Given her previous behaviour Messalina must have already begun to realize how dangerous her position was. Perhaps it had been Silius who had explained it to her.

A coup would have saved Messalina and Silius from having to sit out Claudius sliding into his dotage. It would also minimize the chances of being found out later and being executed. Messalina proceeded to give Silius his own imperial residence and even handed over some of Claudius' prized family heirlooms to him. Silius had also promised to adopt Britannicus, thereby preserving the boy's birthright while Messalina, he assured her, would retain all the power she already had. Perhaps ensuring Britannicus' eventual succession had been the plan all along. Put like that, the plan sounds less reckless and under the circumstances was perhaps the only chance Messalina had of saving her own skin. Even so, she was uncertain whether she could rely on Silius to keep his word.[78]

The opportunity for the wedding came when Claudius headed out to the port at Ostia to inspect the grain supply and make a sacrifice for its protection.[79] The celebrations Messalina organized sent a shockwave through the imperial palace. She had engaged the services of a consul-designate to lend the occasion legitimacy. The whole affair was conducted in front of witnesses who were probably far too scared to say no. The wedding night followed. Whatever had led to this it would now be impossible to keep it quiet. Punishment was inevitable.[80] What worried the freedmen the most was that they might be dragged down along with Messalina.[81] Since there are suggestions that they had already been implicated in the office and honours-selling ring their fears were probably well founded. Turning against Messalina was an easy way out: she was young and foolish, her behaviour had been outrageous, and she had deceived her husband. Fortunately, whatever sort of coup had been planned, neither Messalina nor anyone else had had the wit to secure the support of the Praetorian Guard while Claudius was away.

What the freedmen wanted – the fall of Messalina – was obvious, at least to them. The problem was how to bring it about and on this they were not agreed. They speculated on warning Messalina off but abandoned that idea. It was Narcissus who used lateral thought and suggested that they engage the services of two of Claudius' favourite prostitutes, Calpurnia and Cleopatra, to tell him the terrible news while he was at Ostia. They were bribed with the promise of gifts and how much power they would gain if Messalina fell.[82]

The downfall of Messalina was carefully choreographed. Calpurnia told Claudius what had happened. She immediately asked her colleague, Cleopatra, if she also knew (which she obviously did). Calpurnia then asked that Narcissus be called in to clarify the situation. Narcissus duly presented himself and dropped the bombshell, asking Claudius if he knew about his divorce and explaining that if he did nothing then he had lost Rome to Silius.[83] It was a masterstroke. Claudius immediately consulted his inner circle and discovered that Narcissus' revelations were true. Apparently devastated, Claudius was uncertain if he was even still emperor. He was urged to make sure the Praetorian Guard was on side before taking any further action.

Messalina and Silius carried on their revels, oblivious to the fact that the game was up.[84] Panic only set in when messengers arrived to tell them that Claudius knew. Messalina fled to the Gardens of Lucullus which she had stolen from Asiaticus. Silius decided to play it cool and went to the Forum to go about the normal daily business of a senator. In the meantime soldiers arrived at what was left of the party and started rounding up the remaining guests. Having had time to consider her options Messalina decided to tell both her children to greet their father as soon as they saw him. She also asked Vibidia, the chief Vestal Virgin, to plead for mercy with Claudius in his capacity as *pontifex maximus*. She set out with Vibidia and the children to meet Claudius as he approached up the road from Ostia. In her haste she took a cart used for clearing garden rubbish. It was the only vehicle available but had helped her look like a woman in distress rather than a spoiled empress perambulating round in Rome in a carpentum. On the other hand, the picture of Messalina leaving the Gardens of Lucullus in a gardener's waste cart provided Tacitus with a gratifyingly ironic image of her fall. The journey was far from straightforward. The Gardens lay on the north side of the city, whereas the road to Ostia exited Rome to the south. Messalina would have had to make her way right through the city first. Had she used an official vehicle she would have been able to enjoy automatic rights of passage.[85]

Claudius was also on his way back from the coast. One of the praetorian prefects, Lusius Geta, who had been amongst those who told Claudius about Messalina, was not considered reliable. An emergency, and totally incongruous, one-day promotion was provided for Narcissus who, thoughtfully offering himself, temporarily became praetorian prefect in Geta's stead. He rode with Claudius to Rome, the emperor veering between cursing his wife's antics and indulging in fond memories of happy family life.[86] They were accompanied by Lucius Vitellius, father of the future emperor, a friend of both Claudius and Messalina. He was stunned into silence by events.[87]

Claudius was lost for words when the party met up with Messalina, the children and Vibidia. Narcissus dealt with the confrontation. He had Claudia Octavia and Britannicus removed, but said that Vibidia would be allowed to plead on Messalina's behalf. They headed on to Silius' house where the evidence of Claudius' possessions made it clear that the stories about Messalina were true.

A statue of Silius' father, in direct contravention of a senatorial decree issued in 24, was on display.[88] Only then did Claudius erupt into rage and had to be escorted to the Castra Praetoria (a 'cowardly' thing to do, according to Suetonius) to be greeted by the praetorians who demanded that Messalina and her cronies be punished. That was vitally important. For all Claudius and Narcissus knew, Silius might have prearranged the Guard to be on side though his and Messalina's failure to seize the initiative with the praetorians was a key error. The loyalist praetorians were joined by the body of equestrians. Silius had the good grace to offer no defence and simply asked that he be dispatched quickly. Others, like the successful and eloquent doctor Vettius Valens, confessed and Messalina's remaining associates started being rounded up. They even included the prefect of the night watch, Decrius Calpurnianus, and the commander of the gladiatorial training school, Sulpicius Rufus. It was clear how close Claudius had come to being completely destroyed; the identity of some of the guilty is good evidence to suggest that the coup had been carefully planned.[89]

The actor Mnester tried a different tack which was nearly a much more successful one. Inviting Claudius to look at the evidence of his beatings he said that he simply had had no choice and that had Silius taken power then he would have been the first to die. Claudius was convinced and might have let him go but changed his mind, probably on Narcissus' advice. Mnester was killed, along with others including an equestrian called Traulus Montanus who had been invited in by Messalina for a one-night stand and then promptly discarded. Others escaped for various individual reasons. Plautius Lateranus escaped death because his uncle was Aulus Plautius, the general who had led the successful invasion of Britain, and may have been a relative of Claudius' first wife, Plautia Urgulanilla. Suillius Caesoninus was the son of Suillius Rufus, whom Silius had attacked in the Senate, but the decisive factor in his favour was that in the orgies his sexual role had been the passive one.

While this was going on Messalina was skulking in the Gardens of Lucullus. She was furious but also trying to come up with a sort of plea for clemency. It was even beginning to look as if Claudius, slipping into a comfortable haze over dinner and wine, might find it in his heart to let Messalina off. Narcissus realized that if that happened he was finished because he was the one who had made the accusations. So he instructed soldiers, presumably praetorians, to go with another of the freedmen, Euodus, and kill Messalina; that, at least, is Tacitus' version. Dio is more perfunctory, saying simply that Messalina was killed on Claudius' orders. When they arrived her mother Domitia Lepida was trying unsuccessfully to persuade Messalina to do the honourable thing and take her own life. She seems to have been reconciled to her daughter, in spite of what Messalina had done to her husband Appius Silanus.[90]

Only when Euodus and the soldiers burst in, Euodus winding up the drama by berating Messalina, did she try and stab herself with a sword. She was executed before she could commit suicide. The execution squad left Lepida to deal with the body. If Claudius was mortified he did an excellent job of hiding it. He appears to have reacted without emotion to the news that Messalina had perished. The emperor simply carried on his normal routines while the Senate busied itself by ordering the removal of any monument or statue referring to or depicting Messalina.[91] As such she was the first empress to suffer *damnatio memoriae*.[92]

The following day Claudius unnervingly even asked where Messalina was. This became even more bizarre when he asked for the whereabouts of people he was expecting to dine or game with, even though he had condemned them to death the day before.[93] To the survivors standing shell-shocked in the vicinity it must have seemed as though Claudius was losing his mind. Even though dozens of prominent individuals must have been executed, there seems to have been no fallout and no hint of any dissent either in the palace or the Senate. This has even led to the suggestion that the astonishing series of events had been dreamed up simply to justify a purge.[94] This does not wash. Had it been invented, the story of the Messalina showdown would have been necessarily vague. Instead, what we know about it is remarkably precise and consistent. The problem is not what happened, but why it happened.

Messalina's behaviour had been far more dangerous to the state than Julia's. Julia had undermined Augustus' programme of moral reforms but never threatened the fundamental basis of the principate. Messalina is depicted in a way that linked her to the fictional Dido whose obsession for Aeneas was her undoing; so Messalina's for Silius was hers. Virgil used *furor* to describe Dido's frenzy, and Tacitus employed the same word, surely deliberately, for Messalina.[95] Juvenal called her *meretrix Augusta*, 'the whore empress', in a deliberate echo of Propertius' *meretrix regina*, 'the whore queen' for Cleopatra.[96] Julia had been an enormous embarrassment but she had been contained. None of her lovers turned into, or were fielded as, potential rivals to Augustus. Messalina's antics were more reckless and she eventually descended to a point of no return with Silius. She used and abused her power to such an extent that she risked destabilizing the whole regime. Worse, her enthusiastic associates showed how far self-interest and self-preservation can go in a regime characterized by absolute power. Messalina had conducted herself in a way that was oblivious to common decency. Her behaviour resembled Caligula's, which she must have witnessed in person. Messalina's actions had the effect of advertising and enforcing her superiority and power. They may have been her direct response to the way she had been treated as a political pawn in her teens. It also helped her create a faction that was tied together through sexual liaisons. She would have had little opportunity to achieve that any other way and had seen how male factions were assembled with the use of women as sexual partners to create political bonds.[97] If she was presiding over, rather than necessarily participating in, the various orgies and affairs she is accused of being associated with that would explain how she managed to avoid pregnancies.

Messalina's fatal misjudgement was not to recognize how much more highly charged her position was as an empress, unlike Julia who was merely the embarrassing daughter of an emperor. If Britannicus' prospects were a motivation, the idea that he would be better off as the result of a coup was foolhardy. His age alone would have required Silius to have been emperor for at least another ten years or more. Her followers were not reliable anyway. Fear played a very large part in the compliance of those who went along with Messalina, though the reckless belief that honour and position could be obtained that way too showed how indifferent they were to the potential consequences. Some of those who survived went on to support Claudius' marriage to Agrippina. A case in point was Lucius Vitellius. Claudius of course cannot escape censure, regardless of the extent to which the truth was hidden from him. Knowingly, or unknowingly, he let Messalina act without restraint. Had she and Silius been able to seize power and kill him an era of civil insurrection and possibly civil war would have immediately followed. Messalina and Silius would have been obliged to murder Agrippina and her son to secure their own possession of the throne, exciting enormous popular fury. The power of descent from Augustus, and Agrippina and Germanicus, would have been too great.

The Messalina saga with its calamitous outcome defies rational explanation. It is all but impossible to imagine how she and Silius could ever have pulled it off, or have believed that they might. As schemers they were hopelessly incompetent. Seneca generously suggested in his tragedy *Octavia* some years later that Messalina had been driven mad by Venus, rather than it being her own fault. It was an obvious nod to mechanisms of divine interference in the *Aeneid*.[98] In modern times she has been called 'a woman of unbridled licentiousness and cruelty', but this overlooks her youth, inexperience and unexpected propulsion to the centre of power where she attracted opportunists and hangers-on who willingly cooperated.[99] This takes us back to Tacitus who argued that it all came about because Messalina's boredom drove her on to find new thrills.[100] If so, then the disastrous 'marriage' was simply another stage in her incremental self-destruction. Having got away with one reckless misdemeanour after another perhaps it really was the case that the plan to marry Silius seemed to Messalina like a logical step in her pursuit of amusement.

In the event Messalina's death brought the danger to an abrupt end and also provided Claudius with someone else to blame for what had gone wrong in recent years. Far from obliging Claudius to have to search in a fog for the culprits and dream up imaginary accusations to purge his court of all the usual and any other suspects, the villains had been considerate enough to provide enough incriminating evidence to satisfy even the most vindictive despot for a lifetime. Cases like that of Valerius Asiaticus could now be conveniently pinned on Messalina alone. Messalina and Silius had also provided the portal to another twist in the saga of the Julio-Claudian women.

By dying Messalina had opened the way now for Agrippina.[101] What is not clear is whether Claudius had already been considering his niece as an option. The only obstacles Agrippina faced were Claudius himself, and his children. She would prove herself more than equal to that challenge. The dismal sequence of events that was to follow established for her an unrivalled reputation for opportunism, a shameless greed for power, and murderous intent. Agrippina also turned out to be the cleverest Julio-Claudian since Augustus with an unmatched political sense and exceptional abilities. By the same token she also made some of the gravest errors of judgement.

8

THE REIGN OF AGRIPPINA THE YOUNGER
PART 1 49–54

Agrippina's reign as empress lasted from her marriage to her uncle, the emperor Claudius, in 49 to her death on the orders of her son, the emperor Nero, in 59. She was Augustus' great-granddaughter, descended through Julia the Elder and Agrippina the Elder, and sister of the emperor Caligula. Her determination not only to see her son become emperor, but also to wield unprecedented power and influence led to her acting in a way no previous female member of the Julio-Claudian family had. She was extraordinarily creative, manipulative and ruthless, destroying her enemies and building up a power base of acolytes and supporters in the imperial palace and the Senate. She came closest of all the Julio-Claudian women to ruling in her own right. By 54 she was routinely appearing alongside Claudius in the manner of a co-ruler and had engineered Claudius' adoption of her son Nero as his successor, displacing his own son Britannicus.

Agrippina the Younger exploited the opportunities her position afforded her more assiduously and creatively than any of her predecessors. Her career was bound to end in tears and of course it did, but in 49 the end for her still lay ten remarkable years in the future. Livia and Messalina had both tried to manipulate imperial affairs, but nothing like to the extent Agrippina did. Perhaps she was motivated by an omen, reported by Pliny the Elder. She was said to have two upper right canine teeth, an indication, he assured his readers, of a woman destined to be favoured by fortune.[1] Livia may have played a part

204

in making sure that Tiberius succeeded Augustus, but it is far from certain that she had that much influence, regardless of what was believed at the time. Chance and circumstance were more likely to have been responsible. Messalina's efforts to topple Claudius, if indeed that was even the plan, were phenomenally ill conceived and lacked the sophistication and focus of a carefully considered strategy. Agrippina, on the other hand, seems to have intervened rather more successfully in the course of history and with a piercing determination and focus.

Agrippina was a hand-picked empress, hand-picked by herself as it turned out. Agrippina had a far better grip on reality than Messalina. She had the measure of most of those around her, and she also understood how a woman needed to operate, at least up to a point. Following her mother's 'impatience for equality', she very nearly pulled off a brilliant coup by working steadily towards the point where she was more equal than anyone else. She was ruthless and ambitious but she was also accomplished and effective. She proceeded to build up her position in a way that both corrupted and enhanced her. It is very easy to see Agrippina as a pantomime villain; that was, after all, how Roman historians regarded her because of the way she had broken out of a woman's traditional role. They were also outraged by the irredeemable allegations of incest that surrounded Agrippina. The mud stuck. Her reputation for using her 'unscrupulous skill' to destroy anyone she saw as a rival, and seizing wealth she could use to pursue her dynastic ambitions through her son, has survived effortlessly into our own era.[2]

This sort of image has had a very long tradition and it must be considered in the broader context of male historians writing about assertive female figures at the centre of power. Margaret of Anjou, queen of England's inadequate and incompetent Henry VI (1422–61, 1470–1) and who took over day to day ruling in his stead during the Wars of the Roses, was described by contemporary historians and chroniclers who supported her as having the attributes of a man. Those who opposed her accused her of adultery, greed for riches, presiding over corruption and using any means to try and see her son succeed as king. These allegations served the same purpose of drawing attention to the inadequacy of her husband, just as Agrippina's reckless pursuit of her own interests was a way of illustrating Claudius' shortcomings. It is clear from some of the language employed that some medieval historians self-consciously used allusion to classical texts to reinforce their points, knowing full well that their readers would recognize the references.[3] These medieval accounts indirectly helped further cement Agrippina's reputation in popular tradition.

Agrippina also suffered by association with her once-loved and later reviled son Nero. She appeared to be deficient in the crucially vindicating characteristics her assertive mother had possessed of chastity, fertility and loyalty to her celebrated husband. But it is no more accurate to see Agrippina the Younger as a heroic female figure in a man's world than in a banal modern revisionist feminist rehabilitation. Agrippina in every respect was a product of both circumstances and her own abilities. She took advantage of her position, well aware also of the unmatched prestige she enjoyed as the daughter of Germanicus, the best-loved member of all the Julio-Claudians and as great-granddaughter of Augustus. Whether she was really any more unscrupulous than many others in the court circle or who have been at the centre of power since then is a moot point. Her weapons were false accusations or poison but she was not unique in making use of either though she was perhaps more successful than some.

Agrippina was intelligent – highly intelligent in fact. Intelligence alone was not enough in the Roman world for a woman to rise as high as Agrippina did. She also had to be in the right place at the right time and use an exceptional level of ruthlessness and guile. When Messalina was executed Agrippina was in a very strong position, in spite of the fact that she was Claudius' niece (and therefore theoretically unable to marry him). That is not the same as her having already planned to become his empress. What she certainly had been planning was that her mollycoddled son Lucius Domitius would be emperor. Her own dynastic credentials were cast iron and her son's father was also descended from Octavia. In those respects, even if Claudius had been Lucius Domitius' father the boy would have been no more of a Julio-Claudian than he already was. As a bonus Lucius Domitius was older than Britannicus. All of that was true, and would have remained true, even if Messalina had not behaved as she did. Meanwhile, until Messalina was out of the picture Agrippina could only sit by and wait like a spider.

There is no suggestion that Agrippina played any part in Messalina's downfall, even if there was considerable tension between them. Messalina had proved to be quite able to destroy herself without any help. Agrippina must have found it difficult to believe her extraordinary good fortune though it is easy to imagine that she might very well have found a way to destroy Messalina herself eventually, had the need arisen. With Messalina gone, the unthinkable now not only became possible but also turned out to be the only serious remaining option that preserved dynastic integrity. Agrippina used every asset in her arsenal to thwart the full weight of the male Roman establishment bearing down on her. Within a short time she had swanned triumphantly into a marriage with Claudius, the succession had been rearranged in her son's favour, and she had become, in fact if not in name, joint ruler with Claudius. She was certainly presented to the public as such. After his death she managed to continue in precisely that role, but this time with her son. The years 49 to 59 might just as easily be seen as the reign of the Empress Agrippina as the last five years of Claudius and the first five of Nero.

Agrippina knew that flattering Claudius' vanity would draw him closer to her. She had also been widowed again. Her second husband Gaius Sallustius Passienus Crispus had conveniently expired by 47.[4] Agrippina did not trouble herself with even a casual expression of grief. Instead she focused on making sure her interests were served as well as possible. It was a reaction she was already practised at, given the way she had tried to entice Galba into marriage after her first husband died.[5] She would show the same self-serving contempt in 54 when Claudius died. In the meantime she inherited Passienus Crispus' substantial estate. Her son Lucius Domitius also did well out of his stepfather. Perhaps Agrippina had helped her husband on his way. Suetonius said her 'treachery' was responsible for his death; the term is vague but the only reasonable interpretation is that she had had him murdered, perhaps by poison (a method she would use on her next husband).[6] On the other hand, it was almost inevitable that a self-respecting Roman historian like Suetonius would regard Agrippina as rotten from birth and therefore someone who had spent her life plotting evil deeds. Ipso facto, she *must* have killed him. Since Passienus Crispus' death must have occurred when Messalina was still alive, Agrippina was not necessarily preparing the ground to replace her. Agrippina may simply have been interested in the prospect of inheriting Crispus' estate, though she was soon beginning to play Claudius just as she once had the rather less compliant Galba. Even so, it is no less likely that Crispus expired from natural causes and Agrippina struck lucky once again.

Agrippina developed the habit of seeking Claudius' advice constantly and was often alone with him.[7] After the death of Messalina, however, there was by no means any guarantee that Agrippina's relationship with Claudius would change. Finding him a wife was important. He disliked celibacy and was more compliant when there was a woman around; the freedmen found it easier to govern the state while Claudius was distracted. The question was – who would be his wife? Agrippina could be discounted immediately by anyone with good sense. As Claudius' blood niece any such union was legally and morally impossible. That did not stop Pallas deciding she was the best prospect. Callistus preferred Caligula's former wife Lollia Paulina, while Narcissus favoured Claudius' original second wife Aelia Paetina. Each badgered Claudius to accept his choice, confusing Claudius who ended up preferring the idea of each one as she was mooted.[8]

Since Aelia Paetina had already been married to Claudius and was the mother of Claudia Antonia, her remarriage to the emperor would be convenient and represent continuity. Callistus chose Lollia Paulina because she had never been a mother and so therefore the question of a different relationship with Messalina's children, as opposed to her own, could not occur. Pallas argued from a straightforward dynastic angle. Agrippina's lineage was of the first rank and a marriage would bring the Julian and Claudian lines together once more. Agrippina used the relationship she had established already with Claudius to encourage the emperor to choose her, but she was helped by the fact that it would get the freedmen out of a tight corner. Agrippina's son, Lucius Domitius, looked like a safer bet. The freedmen were worried that if Britannicus succeeded he would have his revenge on them for bringing down his mother.[9] There was also the problem that Messalina's conduct made it technically possible Claudius was not Britannicus' father.[10]

Tacitus and Suetonius both said Agrippina used her wiles to ensnare Claudius. The main problem was that a marriage would break the law. In the Roman world the rule of law was a flexible one. Claudius simply leaned on some senators to propose the marriage in the interests of the state and to allow such marriages in future, even though the idea had always been considered incestuous until then. To make things even more distasteful, Claudius routinely described her as his 'daughter and nursling'. Naturally, the Senate obliged, legalizing such marriages thereafter so that Claudius and Agrippina's union could be presented as the new norm. This was, after all, the chance to set things right, given the terrible treatment meted out to Agrippina the Elder. Within a day of the marriage being approved in early 49 the wedding took place.[11]

Although Agrippina was a wealthy woman in her own right already, she still did well out of the day. One of her presents was a white nightingale costing 600,000 sesterces, an astronomical sum of money. Agrippina added it to a collection of birds that went on to include, if it did not already, a thrush that supposedly mimicked people.[12] The stories about the birds could of course just be more gratifyingly outrageous anecdotes about certain profligate super-rich Julio-Claudians, especially as her son went on to become the most outrageous of them all. Exaggeration and embellishment had surely played their part by the time Pliny recorded these stories, but must have had some basis in truth or else they would never have started circulating in the first place.

On a more serious point, the marriage served two important other purposes. Claudius' descent only from Livia and Octavia was not as solid as Caligula's had been. Agrippina's descent from Julia the Elder and therefore Augustus was of course passed on to her own son Lucius Domitius. The new nuclear imperial family had now a rather more convincing dynastic base and it strengthened Claudius' position. Agrippina was now better protected herself. It was some years since she had been publicly humiliated in 40 by Galba's irate mother-in-law for attempting to lure him away from his wife Lepida. No one could do anything like that again to her without risking their life. Galba was safely away in a provincial governorship. Titus Flavius Vespasianus, who had participated in the invasion of Britain in a legionary command, was a friend of Narcissus. Consequently he was frightened of Agrippina, knowing how much she hated anyone associated with the freedman (in 52 they were to fall out spectacularly when a naval battle show Narcissus put on went disastrously wrong). Vespasian wisely absented himself into semi-retirement to keep out of her way.[13]

One of the most remarkable relics surviving from the occasion is the so-called Gemma Claudia (plate 23). An onyx cameo carved out of sardonyx around 12 cm high in *c.* 49, it depicts on one side the jugate busts of Claudius and Agrippina the Younger facing on the other the jugate busts of Germanicus and Agrippina the Elder, the parents of Agrippina the Younger. The busts are shown emerging from cornucopiae sitting in stacks of captured military equipment. In the middle is an imperial Roman eagle representing Jupiter looking up at Claudius. Claudius and Germanicus are thus shown as successful military leaders, their wars providing the plenty symbolized by the cornucopiae that nourished the Empire. Their wives, a mother and daughter descended from Augustus and like their husbands descended also from Livia, embodied the dynastic integrity and credibility of the imperial family despite the bizarre incestuous undertones to the design. The quality of the piece is so high that there can be no serious doubt it was created for the imperial court, perhaps at Agrippina's behest as a gift to Claudius to emphasize the primacy of descent through her own line rather than Messalina's. It certainly resonates with Agrippina's prominent appearances on Claudius' coinage in a similar style (plate 22). At Aezani in Phrygia a provincial bronze coin was struck about this time with Agrippina depicted as Augusta and on the reverse her mother as Persephone. Persephone was queen of the Underworld and connected to concepts of immortality and regeneration. It seems to have been designed to evoke a sense that the new empress was a regenerated version of her esteemed mother.[14]

There had been a serious potential dynastic complication for Agrippina by marrying Claudius. She took care to deal with it before the marriage. This is the only evidence that she might already have been preparing her way for the aftermath of Messalina's fall beforehand. Messalina's daughter by Claudius, Claudia Octavia, obviously shared her mother's descent from Augustus' sister Octavia and was therefore an invaluable dynastic pawn. Claudia Octavia had already been betrothed to Lucius Junius Silanus Torquatus. This Silanus was the grandson of Julia the Younger, daughter of Agrippa and Julia the Elder, and therefore the great-great-grandson of Augustus.[15] If this marriage proceeded to take place and then produce children, it was patently obvious that they might present serious competition to Agrippina and her son Lucius Domitius. Worse, Silanus was favoured by Claudius because he was a thoroughly decent individual. He had been welcomed into the fold with a gladiatorial show in his name and had also been awarded triumphal regalia, an honorific privilege.[16] At the very least there was a possibility that some years down the line a son of Claudia Octavia and Silanus would become a rival and Agrippina would find herself outmanoeuvred.

Agrippina, ever equal to the occasion, decided that Lucius Domitius would be a far more suitable husband for Claudia Octavia. Undeterred by Silanus' excellent reputation Agrippina came up with a simple plan: she would simply put it about that Silanus was not what he seemed. Using the pliable Vitellius, then serving as censor, as her go-between, Agrippina managed to get the message through to Claudius that Silanus was a traitor and a degenerate.

Vitellius suggested to Claudius that Silanus was involved in some sort of conspiracy with his sister, Junia Calvina (who had been until shortly beforehand Vitellius' daughter-in-law). The two were already known to be rather too fond of each other for comfort. If they were not already in an incestuous relationship it was heading that way, or at least it was possible to believe it. Coming from Agrippina of all people this was a preposterous allegation, but oddly the barb seems to have hit home without reviving memories of her younger days.

Anxious to protect his daughter, Claudius' suspicions were easily aroused. Claudius immediately broke off his friendship with Silanus, who was forced to give up what little time was left of his praetorship. On the very same day that Claudius married Agrippina in 49 the discredited Silanus took his own life. With the death of Silanus, whom we should remember was also Agrippina's cousin, one of those rare and valuable lines of descent from Augustus through the female line came close to annihilation. For good measure Silanus' sister Junia Calvina was banished. As it happens, the two had an older brother called Marcus Junius Silanus. Agrippina, who played the long game, would deal with him later.[17]

Agrippina set about expanding her own network of cronies. Unlike Messalina she did this in a calculated and strategic way. Lucius Annaeus Seneca had been exiled by Claudius in 41 for committing adultery with Germanicus' daughter Julia Livilla, sister of Caligula. Caligula had had a dim view of Seneca's literary skills even though or perhaps because Seneca was becoming very popular at the time, dismissing him as 'sand without lime'.[18] Agrippina favoured Seneca, believing that he would be a powerful advocate for her interests and would also attack Claudius on her behalf. She persuaded Claudius to let Seneca come home on the basis that he would be an excellent tutor for her son. She was already preparing Lucius Domitius for power, even allegedly having wealthy victims murdered so she could steal their estates for him.[19] The choice of Seneca proved to be an excellent one. He effectively became her first minister following Claudius' death in 54. The role of Seneca also illustrates how Agrippina had the vision to understand the importance of surrounding the nucleus of imperial power with individuals of high ability. It was part of a process that helped the evolution of the principate. Under Agrippina, Claudius' administration became more effective than it had been in the preceding eight years.

After the wedding Agrippina could do more or less as she pleased. So she did. From the outset she used her position to advantage. She decided by late 49 to tackle Lollia Paulina because she had been a rival candidate to marry Claudius. Perhaps she was worried that Claudius would change his mind. Agrippina invented various trumped-up charges, including one that Lollia had had the cheek to consult the oracle of Clarian Apollo about Claudius' wedding. Claudius declined even to listen to Lollia's defence. After initially complimenting her, he proceeded to condemn her as a threat to the state. To prevent Lollia from ever being able to be such a threat most of her property was confiscated. She was left with five million sesterces, a great deal of money in its own right but she was given scant opportunity to enjoy it.[20]

Agrippina was dissatisfied with the outcome which seemed to her to be altogether far too inconclusive. She had a better idea. A tribune, probably drawn from the Praetorian Guard, was sent to force Lollia Paulina to take her own life. Just to make sure she was dead, Lollia's putrefying head was brought to the new empress to inspect. Unable to recognize this grisly relic, Agrippina inspected the teeth by using her own hands to part the mouth, or so Dio claimed. The story might be true but it also bears the hallmarks of a gratifyingly revolting anecdote invented to help embellish tales of Agrippina's all-round degeneracy.[21] Every tale was used to condemn her for a villain.[22] Another woman, named Calpurnia, whose looks had been good enough to inspire a casual compliment from Claudius, was exiled. What she was accused of and her exact punishment are unknown but at least she survived.[23] Whether either of these women presented real threats is difficult to measure. Agrippina was perhaps simply trying to cover every possible option, but any sense of rationale might easily have been compounded by a more visceral jealousy and resentment.

Agrippina was concerned about a great deal more than just manoeuvring within the confines of the imperial family. She was determined to assert herself on the political stage. This was also part of her understanding of the importance of consolidating and reinforcing imperial power in the interests of the state. She worked in advance of any major decisions to make sure that she had the Senate, soldiers and even the ordinary citizenry onside first.[24] She sought, and was granted, the establishment of a colony of veterans in Germany which was named after her family line. Colonia Claudia Ara Agrippinensium (Cologne) was duly created on the site of a fort where she had been born in the year 15 while it was Germanicus' headquarters. It developed into the principal Roman city in the province of Germania Inferior.[25]

Claudius proceeded to adopt Agrippina's son Lucius Domitius who now became known as Nero, in February 50, even though the boy was three years older than his own son Britannicus. Like a cuckoo Agrippina had started the process of displacing Messalina's line of descent (plate 23). Nero's inheritance, confiscated by Caligula, had already been restored when Claudius became emperor.[26] It was obvious what the adoption would mean. Claudius had acted in contravention of his own brag earlier that no one had ever become a Claudian by adoption (though in fact Nero could claim Claudian descent through his great-grandfather Nero Claudius Drusus).[27] Pallas, who was now allegedly sleeping with Agrippina, was her agent for persuading Claudius that Britannicus would be safer in the presence of someone older. Pallas clinched the argument when he reminded Claudius of how useful Tiberius had been to Augustus. The subtext was that Pallas and the other freedmen were worried about what Britannicus might do to them in revenge for their part in bringing down his mother Messalina.[28]

Nero was inevitably given precedence over Britannicus because of his seniority in years. Suetonius was not impressed by the way Britannicus had been sidelined, who was now to be treated as a 'mere nobody'.[29] For Agrippina it was a triumph that only accelerated her climb to the top. Her son was now the preferred heir, styled officially thereafter Nero Claudius Caesar Drusus Germanicus. She became the Augusta. No previous empress had been named Augusta in her husband's lifetime. Even Livia had had to wait till after Augustus' death. Tacitus used a play on the verb *augere* ('to augment', or 'increase') with the word Augusta to suggest that the title represented a literal augmentation of Agrippina's power and status beyond that of simply being an imperial spouse.[30]

Agrippina appeared to have succeeded brilliantly in her ambitions, at least thus far. It is just as likely that Claudius was making his own plans for the succession. Nero's stellar dynastic credentials also included descent from Livia and Octavia. Britannicus could claim the latter too through his father and his mother, but Messalina's behaviour made it theoretically possible Claudius was not his father. Had Britannicus taken precedence there was the potential for a coup with Nero as the figurehead. Short of removing Nero in advance there was nothing Claudius could do to prevent that other than making his stepson the designated heir, even though he came to have second thoughts about this.[31] Either way, the fact was that Claudius prioritized the female bloodline descent from Octavia, Livia and Augustus via Julia and Agrippina for the succession. Claudius must have suspected that since Nero was a grandson of Germanicus the chances were that when he died the Guard might end up declaring for Nero anyway. Claudius betrayed his own son. He might also have thereby offset the chance of a disputed succession.

In Herculaneum, an elegant seaside town luxuriating in its superb location below Vesuvius in the Bay of Naples, a well-to-do freedman called Lucius Mammius Maximus decided to invest some of his wealth in a display of fealty to the imperial family, past and present. Between 50 and 54 he set up a series of statues *pecunia sua*, 'at his own expense', in and around a porticus he had commissioned which stood beside the basilica. They were dedicated to the deified Augustus and Livia, Tiberius, Germanicus and Claudius and their mother Antonia, the heir-apparent Nero, Claudius' daughter Claudia Octavia, and Agrippina the Younger, styling the latter as 'daughter of Germanicus' as well as wife of Claudius (plate 14).[32] Naturally, Caligula went unmentioned, as did Messalina. The display, which matched the subjects of much of Claudius' dynastic coinage, must have represented a good example of the popular image of the principate and imperial family. The statues also showed how any wealthy and ambitious man positioned himself in his home town as a loyalist. Current members of the imperial family were depicted alongside past luminaries with Augustus and Livia presiding over them benignly as if they were gazing down protectively from heaven above. The inspiration doubtless came from Rome itself where several surviving inscriptions, originally placed on five columns, recorded key members of the imperial family: Germanicus, Antonia, Agrippina, Nero and Octavia. Presumably there were originally several more, commemorating Augustus, Livia and so on. These probably once accompanied statues placed on the triumphal arch dedicated in 51 to celebrate Claudius' conquest of Britain.[33]

The adoption of Nero was a disaster for Britannicus. He knew it, and he was not alone. Nobody's fool, Britannicus could spot Agrippina's maternal posturing towards him for the humbug it was.[34] Nero was soon further promoted, undoubtedly at Agrippina's behest. By 51 Nero was declared a consul designate, an office he would assume at the age of twenty in 57. He would hold proconsular power outside Rome; that is, hold the privileges of a man who had held the consulship. He was also named *princeps iuventutis*, as Gaius and Lucius had been over half a century earlier. Britannicus was allowed to wear the *toga praetexta*, the mark of a senatorial magistrate, at events in the circus. It was a meaningless privilege. He was soon pushed into second place by Nero who was permitted to wear the triumphal clothing of a successful general. The military garb was an utter nonsense since Nero had been nowhere near any kind of military campaign. Nor would he ever, but that was not the point. It was obvious to any onlooker which of the two boys had precedence. That was precisely what Agrippina wanted. It is all too easy to confuse the teenage Nero with the bloated and profligate cur of his late twenties and early thirties; in fact the young Nero had much to recommend him, as well as his ancestry. A talented poet, as a boy he also showed a keen interest in and a critical eye for painting and sculpture.[35]

Nero was not given the tribunician power to indicate his status as intended successor as Tiberius had been under Augustus. The tradition had not yet been fully established in a dynasty that was still exploring ways to manage the succession. Claudius had obviously been unexpectedly made emperor in 41 so the possibility had not even arisen of his being given it prior to Caligula's assassination. Before him Caligula may have been considered by Tiberius too young and inexperienced to warrant it. Nevertheless, the lack of tribunician power for Nero left some residual ambiguity about who would follow Claudius. It also meant that he was denied the chance to have something that might have overshadowed Agrippina. Perhaps Agrippina had used her power over Claudius to prevent Nero being honoured this way.

Nero's succession was still essential to Agrippina's plans. Any member of the Praetorian Guard who was suspected of being sympathetic to Britannicus was relieved of his duties at the palace. So also were any imperial freedmen with similar views. The Praetorian Guard's loyalties were deliberately courted by allowing Nero to present the soldiers with a cash gift. He then led them in a formal parade, thanking Claudius for the privilege in the Senate.[36]

Britannicus resorted to what little ammunition he had left. He unwisely tried sneering at the man of the moment, insisting on calling him Domitius or Ahenobarbus to remind Nero of his true identity. Nero's riposte was to try to persuade Claudius that Britannicus was a changeling, a child substituted at birth. Later, as emperor, he would solve the problem rather more simply by killing Britannicus. In the meantime Agrippina stepped in to complain that

Nero's adoption was being undermined right there within the imperial house-hold even though the Senate and the People of Rome had voted for it. Claudius, inevitably, acquiesced. He let her remove anyone close to Britannicus, beginning with his tutor Sosibius. Sosibius was quickly executed, easily brought down with the simple claim that he was plotting against Nero on Britannicus' behalf though of course the claim might have been true. It was too early in Agrippina's career as empress for anyone to have worked out quite what she was capable of. Britannicus was then kept under the close watch of Agrippina's guards. Most strikingly of all, he was kept away from Nero and not included in any public appearances.[37]

Armed with Seneca as one of her most influential supporters (or so at least she believed), Agrippina began to clear out anyone whom she suspected of potential disloyalty. In 51 two of those singled out for immediate treatment were the prefects of the Praetorian Guard. Her concern was that Rufrius Crispinus and Lusius Geta were not only loyal to the memory of Messalina but also, and more dangerously, to Britannicus and Claudia Octavia. Claudius evidently accepted Agrippina's argument that the two men's conflicting ambitions were dividing the Guard. Both men were dismissed and replaced with one new prefect, Sextus Afranius Burrus. Having identified the 'problem' to Claudius, like all arch manipulators Agrippina had provided a solution in the next breath. The reality was that Crispinus and Geta would not do what Agrippina wanted. She thought Burrus would be more compliant. If so, she was wrong. It was a sign that her judgement was not always reliable. The intention was clearly to bring the imperial bodyguard under her control. In the event, that would also turn out to be a serious miscalculation. Burrus was a man of exceptional military ability. He was also far too intelligent not to realize what Agrippina expected of him. She would, in time, come to regret what she had engineered.[38] That at least is what Tacitus and Dio would have us believe.

It might just as easily be concluded that Agrippina, with Seneca's advice, had found in Burrus a man of the stature and ability commensurate with the job of praetorian prefect in the latter days of Claudius' reign. Agrippina had made a decision that worked well in the interests of the Empire's welfare. Burrus was no Sejanus. He had no designs on greater office and proved to be a remark-ably stabilizing influence when the inevitable transfer of power to Nero took place. It was also true that Burrus would become one of those whose intoler-ance of Agrippina's ambition would play a significant part in her downfall.

Agrippina did not have everything her own way. Since Messalina's death Lucius Vitellius, now advanced in age, had become one of Agrippina's most dedicated supporters. In 51 he was accused of treason, and of having designs on becoming emperor, by a senator called Junius Lupus. It was a dangerous moment. Claudius had suspended the treason (*maiestas*) law on his accession to distance himself from how Tiberius and Caligula had behaved. Now to Agrippina's horror Claudius was bending towards listening to the case against Vitellius. There were only two possible outcomes. Either the *maiestas* law would be brought back into force, potentially making it possible for Britannicus to be charged with treason for undermining Nero; or, if it was not brought back into force, then Junius Lupus would have to have a case of malicious prosecution brought against him. Agrippina seems to have used these points to persuade Claudius to give Vitellius a minimal punishment (denial of fire and water) and leave it at that.[39] She had saved him, but only just.

Agrippina's tentacles of patronage extended beyond the court, and also far beyond Rome. In Palestine a Samarian insurrection in 51 led to a series of violent events in Judaea. The situation was confused. It was made even more confusing by the fact that Tacitus' and Josephus' respective accounts do not tally. What seems to have happened is that Antonius Felix, brother of the imperial freedman Pallas, was appointed procurator of Samaria. Samaria was an area of Judaea that had been separated from the main province as part of an administrative rearrangement to help settle the disturbances. This was a very unusual state of affairs. Procuratorships were normally only given to men of equestrian rank, but Felix was a freedman like Pallas. The rest of Judaea remained under the control of the procurator Ventidius Cumanus. This made the tension worse, thanks to the rivalries and blurred responsibilities. The whole scenario was overseen with difficulty by Ummidius Quadratus, governor of the adjacent province of Syria.

Eventually Quadratus decided to refer the matter to Claudius to settle. The emperor's reliance on his freedmen meant that he only listened to their concerns for the Samarian cause. Agrippa II, then client king of Chalcis, spoke for the Jews. He had also sought the support of Agrippina who intervened on the side of the Jews and insisted that due process was followed and both sides heard.[40] The outcome was that the Samarians were found to be responsible for the trouble, compounded by Cumanus' incompetence. Cumanus of course lost his job and that left a vacancy to which Antonius Felix was now appointed, another promotion for him. It is difficult to believe Agrippina was not behind this twist. Small bronze coins were struck in 54 under Felix in the name of the emperor. This had been normal for procurators of Judaea, but in fact none had been minted since late in the reign of Tiberius. The new coins bore Claudius' name on the obverse, but on the reverse the prominent legend IOULIA AGRIPPINA, 'Julia Agrippina', paralleling the remarkable new joint coins struck in Rome. It was obvious whom he was thanking. Felix did well in his new post, marrying Agrippa II's sister.[41]

The obvious question is that, if helping Felix's advancement was Agrippina's agenda, then what was in it for her? That is a good deal less easy to answer. It has been suggested that since we only have Josephus' word for Agrippina's involvement in Judaea (as well as the coin evidence), then perhaps she was similarly involved in other provincial affairs.[42] There is no evidence whatsoever to substantiate that, including anyone else like Felix who benefited from office. Broadening out speculation from the evidence for one set of circumstances and turning it into evidence for Agrippina's wider policy is a step too far. The only evidence we have is that she intervened in a way that benefited the brother of one of her husband's freedmen, whom she was allegedly having an affair with. Since that is all we have to go on the possibility is that Pallas had exacted this as a favour to himself in return for supporting and facilitating Agrippina's involvement in other affairs of Claudius that were of far greater importance to her. Felix's career suggests he was a man of significant ability but as a freedman that could never have been enough. Pallas, however, was Agrippina's arch 'fixer' in the imperial household and had been from the moment he proposed her as Claudius' new wife.[43] In short, she owed him.

Quite apart from promoting Nero's interests and manufacturing a court faction that supported her, while removing anyone else, Agrippina was unable to resist disporting herself in public as empress in as conspicuous and as elitist a manner possible. She routinely accompanied Claudius on imperial business but was seated on a separate tribunal.[44] She went about Rome in a carpentum, as Livia had done, but it may have been a privilege she adopted of her own accord; there is no suggestion that Claudius had offered her the right himself.[45] One of Agrippina's surely most gratifying experiences was in 50 to receive the captured British chieftain Caratacus along with Claudius. Claudius and Agrippina sat on thrones placed on separate podiums but Caratacus, his wife and his brothers paid Agrippina exactly the same respect and praise as they did to Claudius. This reflected the British tribal tradition that a woman could rule a tribe and also lead it in war in her own right. Tacitus, however, considered that the audience showed how Agrippina was presenting herself in public as co-ruler, and thereby contravening Roman custom.[46] Agrippina, no doubt, regarded the occasion as one on which her true status had been acknowledged, even if it took a captured barbarian to recognize it.

At a naval battle display (*naumachia*) in the Fucine Lake in 52 put on by Claudius and organized by Narcissus, Agrippina sat at her husband's side in a military cloak made of cloth of gold (*aureo textili*). Claudius wore rather less ostentatious conventional military clothes and so did Nero; there is no mention of Britannicus, who was presumably excluded. The battle turned out to be rather less impressive than expected since the rival 'fleets' were not especially keen on losing their lives for Claudius, in spite of greeting him with the acclamation 'we who are about to die salute you'. In the event they had to be forced to destroy each other. Worse was to come. Narcissus' elaborate seating on the lake's banks was damaged during the display, frightening Claudius. The reason was that a water channel designed to carry water away from the lake was not deep enough and had to be dug out further. Unfortunately, when the water surged out it did so with such urgency that the ground was washed away. The flood terrified everybody with the noise and damage, including guests at a dinner party located dangerously close to the torrent. This resulted in a furious confrontation between Agrippina and Narcissus, its origins no doubt lying in Narcissus' failure to back Agrippina as a candidate for empress a few years earlier. Agrippina accused Narcissus of siphoning off the money earmarked for the event into his own coffers while he, for his part, retorted by accusing her of being a woman with excessive ambition and who was out of control.[47] It was a bad sign for Agrippina. That Narcissus felt able to make these accusations so volubly and apparently in public, and get away with it, must be evidence that behind the scenes her conduct was causing serious concern. For the moment though Agrippina proceeded down the route she was determined to follow.

Agrippina's rapid rise to prominence was recorded and advertised on the coinage in the last years of Claudius' reign. As early as 51 she appeared on an unprecedented series of double-headed gold and silver coins minted at Lugdunum (Lyon) that have his bust on one side and hers on the other, Agrippina being labelled as Augusta. A particularly memorable cistophoric silver tetradrachm produced at Ephesus in 51 shows Claudius and Agrippina on the obverse, their busts side by side in the manner of joint rulers (plate 22).[48] Nero was also introduced to the public in the same way, his bust appearing on the reverse of gold and silver coins. He is only identified by name and his title *princeps iuventutis*.[49] The significance of these dynastic issues cannot be overestimated. Agrippina's position was unequivocal and so was Nero's. Britannicus was virtually ignored, confined to a very rare series of sestertii of uncertain, perhaps posthumous, date and possibly only made in a mint in the Eastern half of the Empire.[50]

Given that Messalina had been almost completely omitted by Claudius from his earlier coinage, the Agrippina and Nero series in his reign represent a complete change of policy. It must be the case that Agrippina lay behind the design and issuing of the new coins, the pliable Claudius acceding to her demands. They were certainly a masterstroke in the way they advertised her new place at the heart of the regime's dynastic identity, just as she had been on the Gemma Claudia (plate 23). No other Roman woman had ever created such a blatant message of 'equality of power', which she so craved. The coins could also easily be seen as a means of familiarizing the wider public with her status as a first step towards preparing them for her sole appearance in the coins as ruler in her own right. Indeed, the coins of the closed currency system in Egypt at this time included a series of bronze coins showing only her on the obverse as Agrippina Augusta, but still listing the regnal years of Claudius' reign.[51] To these can be added the Judaean coins issued under Felix that named Claudius and Agrippina (but without portraits), one on each side. The coinage of the first few years of Nero's reign continued in much the same vein. Nothing like the double-headed coins of Ephesus had appeared since Antony's brazen flaunting of Cleopatra on his double-headed silver coinage. Given the scandal and loathing Antony provoked it is, on reflection, remarkable that Agrippina countenanced anything so similarly provocative. That she did was a mark of her audacity.

In 53 imperial affairs were definitely going Agrippina's way. At least that was how it seemed. No opportunity was missed to promote Nero's interests, masquerading as support for Claudius. The origin of her ambitions for Nero lay back when he was born, or so the story went. It was claimed an astrologer had predicted Nero's rule and that he would murder his mother.[52] The story is too symmetrical to be reliable and is surely apocryphal: it not only 'foretold' with uncanny precision but also amplified Agrippina's reputation for over-weening ambition at any price. But in spirit it was true enough. When Claudius fell ill Nero was dispatched by Agrippina to the Senate to offer a public horse race if he recovered. The subtext, because with Agrippina there always was one, was that it was a chance to increase Nero's popularity with the mob. The point was making the promise, rather than wanting to fulfil it; Agrippina of course was hoping that Claudius would die. Claudius did indeed recover and the horse race went ahead as promised. For the moment at least whether Claudius lived or died was beyond even Agrippina's control.

In the meantime Claudius was brought in on the promotional campaign for Nero. When a riot was sparked over sales of bread Claudius was persuaded to announce that should he die Nero was already fully prepared to take over.[53] The truth of course was that Agrippina wanted to make sure that her reign continued without being inconvenienced by a messy succession. Just to be certain, Agrippina put it about that Britannicus was afflicted by epilepsy and mental illness. Given Claudius' original reputation for being mentally impaired, this probably sounded convincing enough to be widely accepted.

Around this time Nero was married to Claudia Octavia, Claudius' daughter, which effectively cemented the succession in his favour. The dynastic credentials were excellent. Nero's descent from Augustus via his mother was the most important. Like Nero, Claudius' daughter was descended from Livia and Augustus' sister too. The only potentially complicating factor was whether Claudius' daughter was really the daughter of one of Messalina's lovers, but since Messalina was descended from Augustus' sister her lineage was not necessarily compromised. Either way the marriage was the logical one and suited Agrippina's purposes perfectly.

Agrippina was now to all intents and purposes operating as a joint monarch.[54] She seems to have been unable to avoid meddling in or exploiting any situation where she had spotted something to her advantage, even if it was for a trivial reason. Just as Messalina had taken a fancy to the Gardens of Lucullus, Agrippina decided she would like the Gardens of Statilius Taurus, a senator of celebrated wealth.[55] Agrippina wasted no time on trying to buy the Horti Tauriani, or on trying to get Taurus to give them to her. Instead she decided to destroy him. It was a blatant abuse of her power and privilege, but that was hardly a new development and seems in itself to have been part of the attraction. Abusing privilege was a means of advertising her power, though reporting such stories was also a useful way of embellishing Agrippina's bad reputation by later historians.[56] Taurus was then serving as proconsular governor of Africa and one of his legates there was a senator called Tarquitius Priscus. Agrippina persuaded Priscus to accuse Taurus of extortion and magic on their return to Rome in 53. Priscus obliged, adopting the routine but rather crass pretext of dressing in faded and damaged clothing while making the accusation to enhance his credibility.

Taurus could see he was finished regardless of his innocence. He honourably committed suicide. Priscus might have won on Agrippina's behalf but it was a pyrrhic victory for him at least. He was driven out of the Senate despite Agrippina's pleas that he be left untouched. That Priscus had complied in the first place must say something about Agrippina's manner in person. She was surely a woman who, despite the distasteful side to her character, was capable of manipulating and playing men with relative ease. At this distance in time, and without a reliable eyewitness account by someone who knew her personally, it is impossible to know really what she was like to be with in person. To achieve what she did, she must have used more subliminal methods than issuing orders and threats. Priscus must have fallen for what passed for her charms. He did what she wanted because she flattered his vanity, offered him her attention and interest, and fooled him into believing she valued him for himself. Agrippina was only interested in playing weak-willed people who could be leaned on. Anyone more resilient would be eliminated.

The Horti Tauriani affair was a clear demonstration of the Senate's disgust at Agrippina's machinations. The reality was that they could do nothing about her, and she had got what she wanted. Was it an 'early warning', as some have suggested, of her fall? This is unlikely. Agrippina was amassing enemies but none of them was in a position to reciprocate by destroying her. She may have been annoying, ruthless, arbitrary, greedy and shameless but the Senate had long since been reduced to a shadow of itself. It was a whingeing collection of frustrated old men emasculated by a woman with no sense of boundaries and an ageing husband without any idea how to contain her or the will to do so. It is unlikely in any case that Agrippina cared very much about Tarquitius Priscus. He had served his purpose. Others would find themselves discarded soon too, including Claudius. In the event Agrippina ended up being wrong footed by the one person whose interests she had so actively pursued for her own purposes.[57]

Claudius became desperate to protect Britannicus. He even planned to announce Britannicus as his heir. The revival of his paternal interests might have unwittingly provoked Agrippina into action to bring about her husband's death before he could marginalize Nero. In the meantime Claudius was worried that history might repeat itself. His marriages had not been triumphs. The one to Messalina had been a catastrophe that might have brought down the principate. In an instance of *in vino veritas*, an intoxicated Claudius had indiscreetly let slip that he had come to believe he was destined by fate to suffer his wives' outrages and then punish them. According to Tacitus this caused Agrippina a great deal of concern, though it is difficult to believe she had not already realized how much of a risk she had been taking. The real problem was that she had a potential rival; if she fell then there was an eligible candidate for Claudius' next wife waiting in the wings. This was Domitia Lepida, the mother of the executed Messalina.[58] She was Nero's paternal aunt, and was descended like his father from Antony and Augustus' sister Octavia. Lepida was also Britannicus' maternal great aunt.[59] Armed with these credentials she regarded herself as Agrippina's equal.

Domitia Lepida seems to have been almost a doppelganger of Agrippina's, sharing the wealth, looks, intelligence, immorality and guile of the empress. For the Julio-Claudians to have produced one woman like Agrippina was a misfortune. Producing two women like Agrippina was much more dangerous. There was scarcely room for Agrippina's ego and ambition already. There was certainly no room for Lepida as well, as far as Agrippina was concerned, especially given the possibility that Lepida might decide to champion Britannicus' cause.[60] Lepida expended a great deal of energy on cultivating her relationship with the pliable young Nero. She presented him with an alternative influence that lacked Agrippina's threatening dominance and autocratic parenting. Lepida also not surprisingly had the support of Agrippina's enemy Narcissus, which meant his death warrant was as good as signed too.[61]

It was clear to Agrippina where Domitia Lepida's interference might lead. She could foresee her own destruction followed by Lepida installed as the next empress and beneficiary of dowager imperial status when Nero succeeded. It was more than Agrippina could bear. All her work would have been for nothing. So Agrippina adopted the usual tactic. She duly drummed up some baseless accusations and set out to destroy Lepida. Tacitus disparagingly said that this incident amounted to a womanish spat.[62] Lepida's eldest sister

Domitia had also engaged in a 'ferocious rivalry' with Agrippina. The allegations on this occasion were that Lepida had been targeting Agrippina with curses, and that she managed her vast collection of slaves so badly they were beginning to threaten civil disorder. It was all absurdly easy. Nero obliged by testifying against Lepida to help his mother.[63] Lepida was finished in an instant and executed. Agrippina had won again. Whatever Claudius' concerns, he had withdrawn into a drunken stoic haze where he was content to let be what would be. Perhaps he regarded Agrippina as no better than Rome deserved. Either way his otiose complacency handed the initiative to Agrippina once again. Narcissus was appalled by developments. He believed the imperial house was being destroyed by Agrippina and placed all his hopes in Britannicus. He was wasting his time.[64]

Although she was helped by the type of man Claudius was, Agrippina had shown herself to be remarkably adept at promoting her own interests. Given her comparatively low profile until she married Claudius, her achievements are all the more remarkable. She had also played a prominent part in making the everyday process of government and administration run more smoothly. Nevertheless, she had been very definitely helped by circumstances. The skill had been in spotting the opportunities and taking advantage of them. By 54 she knew she would have to act in a more drastic way than ever before. This time she had to be the agent of change. It is unlikely that she acted on impulse. If the story is true, the decision to murder Claudius had probably been taken years before, but she waited until the risks of that crime were less than the risks she faced from other quarters. Agrippina wanted a method of killing Claudius that would distance her from his death but not delay it so long that he might realize he was being slowly exterminated. If he did, then he might act to ensure Britannicus' succession.

Agrippina allegedly turned to an expert and convicted poisoner called Locusta. That Locusta was also female helped Tacitus amplify the sense of a conspiracy of 'bad women'.[65] Locusta recommended poisoning Claudius' food. The trick was to have the food presented by the emperor's normal server and taster, a eunuch called Halotus, which ought to assuage any suspicions that something untoward was going on. In another version Agrippina fed Claudius the poisoned mushroom personally, being sure to eat others first to 'prove' they were safe. Obviously the ones she consumed had not been poisoned. Agrippina had taken the precaution of making sure Narcissus was not on hand to smell a rat. She had sent him to Campania to seek the treatment of medicinal waters for his gout. With him away, Claudius was dangerously exposed.

Like all the best-laid plans, Agrippina's scheme went wrong but she was quite capable of improvising. The dish of adulterated mushrooms was presented to Claudius. He was temporarily saved by suddenly becoming ill, apparently vomiting or suffering diarrhoea or both as a reaction. Agrippina all but panicked and abandoned her intention to see Claudius die several hours later as the poison took hold. She resorted to a Plan B that she had already lined up. Claudius was given more poison. Tacitus says that a doctor called Xenophon had agreed to attend Claudius on the basis that he was trying to stop the emperor vomiting, and to use a feather covered with poison that he placed in the emperor's mouth.[66] There is some variation in the detail, Suetonius for example suggesting that a syringe might have been used for the extra poison. But it is clear that no one was subsequently in any doubt that Agrippina was responsible, and that a second phase of poisoning had been necessary, regardless of how or by whom it was administered. Claudius was dead by the morning of 14 October 54. Agrippina had become the first empress of Rome to organize the murder of an emperor, or so at least most of our sources allege.[67] If Agrippina was entirely innocent, and Claudius merely the unlucky victim of bad mushrooms or some other condition, then she had just experienced the most remarkable good fortune. There is no doubt that if he was poisoned then the simplest explanation was that she had been behind his death. An even simpler explanation is that since he was in his mid-sixties it was a natural death, though that means refuting the stories that he was murdered. It made no difference. The end of Claudius could not have come at a better time for Agrippina and Nero. Either way, Agrippina was the first and only living descendant of Augustus ever to see her child become emperor.[68] To make sure this happened, for the moment news of Claudius' death was kept secret.[69] Just as Livia had stage-managed the succession forty years before to ensure her son became emperor, now the great-granddaughter of Augustus would stage-manage another, and with the same purpose.

THE REIGN OF AGRIPPINA THE YOUNGER
PART 2 54–9

The death of Claudius in 54 placed Agrippina exactly where she wanted to be. Her power was unequalled. Just as she had planned, her teenage son Nero was now emperor giving her an unmatched opportunity to rule the Empire through him. Dynastic rivals had been marginalized or removed, along with her enemies. She fully expected to be in total control of Nero's principate. As such Agrippina posed as his co-ruler on the coinage of the new reign, marking continuity in this role from the last. No other Julio-Claudian woman had come so far and so close to ruling in her own right. She took privilege for granted but entirely underestimated Nero's interest in fighting off her influence and control. The years 54–9 became a battle of wits. Agrippina tried to force her son into a corner as her influence began to dwindle. Nero, however, discovered that his power was greater than hers and that he could rule without her whereas she could not rule without him.

Appropriately enough for a woman who had (allegedly) murdered her husband Agrippina expended minimal energy on a display of grief. She did, however, manage to put on an impressive performance as the bereaved stepmother while simultaneously taking control of the palace by posting guards at every entrance. She grasped Britannicus and assured him he was the spitting image of his father, thereby making sure he stayed in his room. She also saw to it that his sisters Claudia Octavia and Claudia Antonia were confined to quarters. This subterfuge, which sounds carefully planned, made it possible for Nero to go straight to the Castra Praetoria before news got out about Claudius' death. There he easily secured the Praetorian Guard's loyalty and support with a gift of fifteen thousand sesterces each, matching Claudius' accession donative. Britannicus was thus in an instant permanently pushed out of the picture. It was a brilliant move. Some of the praetorians on guard at the palace were surprised by Nero approaching them. They asked where Britannicus was. In the absence of any explanation they were easily led off to the Castra Praetoria with Nero and any doubts they might have had evaporated when they saw the money on offer. The Guard could be relied on; their loyalty could always be purchased. With the Guard bought the Senate avoided the suicidal option of rejecting Nero and simply rubber-stamped the praetorians' decision.[1]

Self-serving though Agrippina was she had also seamlessly ensured the successful, safe and stable succession of her son. Nothing would have been worse than a disputed change of emperor. Whether Nero's accession had been Claudius' intention is neither here nor there. The contents of his will, written and sealed not long before, are unknown. At the time the will was deliberately ignored, maybe even destroyed, perhaps to divert attention from the succession of a stepson over a son or possibly because it contained instructions that Britannicus should succeed him.[2] In Egypt Nero's accession was welcomed thirty-five days after Claudius' death as the coming of an emperor 'whom the world expected and hoped for', the new reign oleaginously described as a dream fulfilled.[3] The ship bringing the news must have only just arrived. Agrippina's role had evidently not yet been noted. At Aphrodisias in Asia Minor (Turkey) a full-sized sculpture was created for the Sebasteion in due course showing Agrippina crowning the young Nero with a laurel wreath (plate 24). It is an unequivocal composition in which Agrippina's role as the bestower of imperial power is clearly depicted. She holds a horn of plenty symbolizing her fertility. This presented her as Fortuna or Demeter, implicitly elevating her to quasi-divine status and associating her with the deceased and deified Claudius.[4] In the East this was easier to do. In Italy she was more likely to be shown acting in the politically safer role of priestess.

Agrippina could have sat back and basked in the glory of Nero's accession and limited her interference to subtle and lateral influence as Livia had. In the context of the world in which Agrippina operated this might very well have facilitated sustained and considerable power for her. Instead, she carried on as she had under Claudius. If anything she did whatever she could to increase her power and influence. Since Seneca and Burrus, two men whose appointments she had seen to, were in post Agrippina had every reason to assume they would continue to work in her interests. The daughter of Germanicus had a very clear sense of herself not only as Augusta, but as an empress with executive power. In that respect, if nothing else, she completely marginalized Nero's wife Claudia Octavia who as a fifteen-year-old empress could be simply ignored.

On the day he became emperor in October 54 Nero acknowledged Agrippina's importance by giving the Praetorian Guard tribune the password *optimae matris*, 'the best of mothers'.[5] Perhaps this flattered her vanity. As things turned out, the gesture might have been one of the first instances of Nero playing his mother. If so, it cut right to the heart of the tension between them. Agrippina wanted a full, if not pre-eminent, share of the power she believed she was entitled to. To achieve such dominance meant Agrippina had to have total control over Nero. Not only did that involve making sure no one else had any influence over him, but it also meant he had to have no influence over himself. This created serious problems. Agrippina pushed her role in public affairs further than any woman before her, which meant challenging the establishment to the core. Her possession of power was now blatantly displayed. More significantly, she was allowed to present herself this way, the purpose perhaps being to give her enough rope to hang herself. Tacitus implies that the ingratiating filial password episode was one of several instances of Nero disingenuously flattering her ego.[6]

Nero, for his part, was in the process of growing into adulthood. That resulted in him exploring the extent of his power and seeking to curb his mother's. Similarly, Seneca and Burrus proved very quickly that they had no intention of acting as her obsequious hangers-on, or of facilitating her needs. They also spotted that supporting Nero's independence was the best way to undermine Agrippina, though they had to be careful – she was the only person who had any real ability to control him. This, at any rate, is the picture Tacitus painted. Whether the friction was as bad as he describes is harder to judge. As Nero's true personality became ever clearer the issue of his independence became a very important one. It was the exact reverse of what Agrippina wanted or expected. As far as she was concerned Nero should have been suitably grateful to his mother for this elevation. Agrippina expected Nero to show this through continued dependence, compliance and respect. It was an echo of what Livia had wanted from Tiberius though she was dealing with an embittered middle-aged man, not a conceited and narcissistic adolescent.

The difference between Nero and his mother of course was that his position as emperor was legitimate at least insofar as being *princeps* had any technical legitimacy at all, whereas Agrippina's had none whatsoever. To begin with that did not matter particularly because it was clear that in practice Agrippina's position was dominant; but without any constitutional foundation her role as a ruler was inevitably vulnerable to the effects of any changes. Nero growing up and flexing his muscles was one of those changes. So also was the mobilization of the establishment against her. No sooner had Agrippina placed herself at the heart of power, monarchizing with her state and pomp, than she came under attack.

Any account of Agrippina's life and activities is largely dependent on Tacitus' version of what happened. He painted a remarkably vivid picture of her behaviour and also what happened to her. The story is so extraordinary that it borders on a virulent piece of misogynistic fiction. She 'was burning with a passion for complete evil domination'.[7] Tacitus wrote about Agrippina with a compelling immediacy that almost suggests he had witnessed the events himself and seen the she-devil in person. Of course Tacitus had done neither, though he certainly knew people who had (he was born a year or so before Agrippina's death in 59). He rarely cites his sources and when he does they usually no longer exist and are therefore unverifiable. Nonetheless, a passage in Josephus, and probably written somewhat closer to the time, describes very briefly a broadly similar sequence of events, including Agrippina's culpability, to that found in Tacitus and Dio.

Josephus makes some very interesting observations about the problems presented in his own time by extremely biased historians who wrote either excessively damning or far too flattering accounts of Nero's rule. It is clear that garnering the truth was no less difficult then than it is now. Josephus, alone of our sources, suggests quite clearly that only 'a report had gone about' which implicated Agrippina in Claudius' murder.[8] In other words, it was just a rumour as far as he was concerned. Conversely, Tacitus was very clear about what sort of person Agrippina was. Her decline and fall were in his narrative an inevitable consequence of her malevolent and immoral personality, a victim of herself rather than anyone else. Her freedom to behave this badly was also a comment on Claudius and Nero's inadequacies. His story was surely largely founded in truth but it is important to remember that however much blame is pinned on Agrippina she was also, and perhaps mainly, a victim of the society she operated in and which she had challenged. By Juvenal's time, around fifty to sixty years later, it was clear that Agrippina's guilt was completely established in popular lore. In his sixth *Satire*, an exploration of female immorality, Juvenal favourably compared the *boletus Agrippinae* ('mushroom of Agrippina'), which made her a *venefica* ('she-poisoner') when she used it to kill Claudius, with Caesonia, wife of Caligula. His reasoning was that Agrippina's deed only killed one old man whereas Caesonia had supposedly poisoned Caligula and driven him mad with dreadful consequences.[9]

One of Agrippina's first actions after Claudius' death was to start removing any residual rivals or threats. In 49 Agrippina had engineered the death of Lucius Junius Silanus. He had a brother called Marcus Junius Silanus, then proconsul of Asia. These Silani were descended from Augustus through his daughter Julia. Like any self-respecting despot Agrippina knew that the existence of an aggrieved rival with cast-iron dynastic credentials was a potential focus for any malcontents. Agrippina used her favourite method, sending out an equestrian called Publius Celerius and a freedman called Helius to administer poison at a banquet in Asia. They did this, apparently, quite openly. Perhaps that was deliberate. It showed that the state in the form of Agrippina could and would strike where it pleased.[10] After all, her own brother Caligula had been fond of quoting a line from the tragic poet Accius: 'let them hate so long as they fear'.[11] It was the first murder of what might be regarded as the second phase of the reign of Agrippina the Younger. Pliny attributed the killing to Nero, noting how this Marcus Junius Silanus, great-grandson of Augustus, had been seen by the first emperor in the year of his death (14) and survived to the first year of Nero's reign.[12] His death of course wiped out a line of descent from Augustus.

Narcissus, of all people, knew that when Claudius was murdered he and his personal fortune of over 400 million sesterces were finished too, even though he had notoriously amused himself in the past by publicly mocking the emperor.[13] Like a viper Agrippina went for him immediately, even though she had previously gone to some effort to bring him on side.[14] Oddly, Narcissus burned the correspondence of Claudius which he had in his possession. This included letters incriminating Agrippina and others.[15] Had he not destroyed them Agrippina might have been damaged by the contents. One might have thought Narcissus would have been interested in using them; perhaps as a member of the imperial staff he felt unable to go that far. By chance the beleaguered freedman was executed beside the tomb of Messalina, though Tacitus implies that he was driven to suicide. His death may have had a positive impact on the regime. This may have been part of Agrippina's purpose. Narcissus' corruption had attracted him to Nero who opposed Narcissus' execution precisely because he was interested in learning more about nefarious activities.[16] If that was true, then it is possible the Roman world was saved from Nero's excesses for a few more years.

The funeral of Claudius followed. It featured a suitable degree of humbug in the form of a eulogy read out by Nero. It had been written by his tutor Seneca. His inexperience and youth were painfully obvious. No previous emperor had had a speech written for him.[17] Nonetheless, his address to the Senate went well because of his appeal to tradition and the duties and responsibilities of the senators. Seneca's words had been carefully chosen with the Senate's sensibilities in mind. It is possible to see in this pro-Senate stance a carefully veiled warning to Agrippina that what had prevailed under Claudius had been left behind. The key phrase was: 'the [imperial] house and state are separate'.[18] In other word, state affairs were not to be dealt with in the environment where Agrippina held sway. It was a blatant appeal to the traditional Roman perception of male and female spheres. Unfortunately, this exacerbated the conflict of interests in one key area. Since Claudius had been made a god, and Agrippina the priestess of his cult, it followed that one of her duties was to preserve and protect his legislation, which ought to remain untouched.

Instead, galvanized by Nero's speech, the Senate passed a number of measures including one that had been specifically opposed by Agrippina: exempting quaestors-designate from having to put on gladiatorial productions. She therefore cannot been involved in its composition or agreed to its delivery.[19] An old Republican law, the lex Cincia (204 BC), had been passed to inhibit corruption by preventing lawyers from being paid for pleading a case. By Augustus' time this had been reinforced by the imposition of fines of four times any sum received by a lawyer. Claudius had modified the law to allow a lawyer only to receive up to ten thousand sesterces.[20] Now the reinvigorated Senate wanted to restore the lex Cincia according to its original principles.[21] It was a clear case of overturning one of Claudius' enactments. By behaving as it did the Senate knew very well that there was little or nothing Agrippina could do. Her 'authority' was thus exposed for the sham the senators regarded it as, or at least wanted it to be.

These measures were enacted in spite of the fact that Agrippina was present. The Senate 'kept being summoned' to the Palatium so that she could scrutinize the daily business. She remained behind a curtain (*velo discreta*) so that she was invisible but could hear what was going on. Tacitus presents this as deliberate manipulation on her part. So it might have been, but in reality the Senate often met there and had done so for decades.[22] In any case the Senate was effectively a mobile assembly that met wherever was considered suitable at the time. Temples, theatre porticoes, the imperial palace – all were possible venues in addition to the chamber itself. A woman concealed behind a curtain on such occasions was not particularly radical either. Agrippina was not making any attempt to create a precedent. She was far too clever for that. If a dutiful wife attended her husband's public events she remained decorously out of sight.[23] Pliny the Younger was greatly impressed by his third wife, Calpurnia, who attended her husband's public readings in order to enjoy the praise he was given but remained behind a curtain (*discreta velo*, using the same words as Tacitus). Agrippina's invisible presence at senatorial meetings was simply a development of tradition in her capacity as Claudius' wife or at least could be presented as such. Livia had also avoided entering the Senate chamber but had still been able to assert her power.[24] The real development was the Senate taking the opportunity to be openly defiant.

Agrippina had become accustomed under Claudius to being present and visible on occasions involving deputations from foreign nations. She clearly assumed she could continue to be so under Nero. On one occasion the young emperor was listening to an appeal by Armenians when Agrippina decided to join her son and sit beside him. Seneca spotted her coming and told Nero to go and greet his mother before she committed a faux pas. Publicizing Nero's reliance on his mother would have been a catastrophic sign of weakness on his part. She may have intended that but Seneca knew he had to stop her. Agrippina was already receiving embassies. More worryingly for Rome's male establishment she was even taking charge of the relevant paperwork. This was just part of a broader context in which she was trying to take sole charge of running the Empire.[25] Official positions were also being held in both Nero's name and hers. At Corinth in Greece in 54–5 a prominent local citizen called Gaius Julius Spartiaticus was the first Achaean to be made 'high priest for life of the Augustan house'. The inscription recording this adds to his other titles, including that he was 'procurator of Caesar and the Augusta Agrippina'.[26] Given the location perhaps not too much significance should be attached to a provincial reference to Agrippina's status, but Corinth was an important city and Spartiaticus an important man. If procuratorial authority was held in the names of both Nero and Agrippina then she was clearly gravitating into an unprecedented class of formal female authority. What is less clear is the true extent of Agrippina's real or official autonomy. The murder of Silanus demonstrated that she did act unilaterally where she pleased. But a case such as that was clearly unofficial.

Rare post-accession issues of gold and silver coins featuring Agrippina's portrait with Nero's were struck at Lugdunum in 54 and 55 for use in Rome and the West.[27] Indeed, coins depicting the two instead of just Nero seem to have been the order of the day at the start of the reign. It was not until 55 or 56 that coins depicting just Nero began to appear. The mint of Alexandria struck no coins at all of Nero until 56 at the earliest. Whether this was as a result of Agrippina actively trying to prevent her son overshadowing her is impossible to say but it would not be inconsistent with her determination to control affairs at the start of the reign.[28] A novel design was the depiction of her and Nero's busts facing one another, which appeared on both gold and silver.[29] The design is clumsy and cramped, the two portraits being jammed in and almost touching. Whether this was just an experiment in coin design or a deliberate attempt to evoke some sort of bizarre blurring of maternal and matrimonial relationships is impossible to say. What was unequivocal is that this side of the coin featured only Agrippina's legend, identifying her as 'Agrippina Augusta, wife of the deified Claudius and Mother of Nero'. Nero's titles were placed on the reverse. This was balanced by another type which showed the two as jugate busts, Nero clearly overlying his mother's with his legend, hers being placed on the reverse. This coin therefore presented Nero as having precedence and appears to have followed the type with facing busts once Nero assumed the consulship in 55. A number of eastern mints produced coins depicting mother and son in the manner of co-rulers.[30]

It is too easy to read a lot more into the precise design of these coin types than was necessarily intended.[31] The jugate busts were quite possibly seen as being aesthetically more satisfactory and allowing larger profiles to be displayed on what are fairly small coins. They were also surely easier to engrave into the tiny dies.[32] Claudia Octavia, despite her position as Nero's wife, was ignored for the purposes of the coinage, as she was in every other respect, with the exception of the mint of Alexandria and one or two other provincial mints.[33] The disappearance of the double-bust coins in the West after 55 might seem to be further evidence in their own right of Agrippina's waning influence.

In fact few coins of any type were struck in the West in Nero's name between 56 and 60, though those that were excluded Agrippina. The mint at Alexandria resumed production in 56 with Nero's sole portrait invariably on the obverse, Agrippina featuring as one of the many reverse types. No base-metal coinage appeared under Nero before 64, sustaining a shortage begun under Claudius in about 42.[34] The silver and gold struck between 60 and 64 were confined to a very small number of issues and almost all post-dated Agrippina's death.[35] These latter types include the legend EX SC. Precisely what this means remains a matter for inconclusive debate.[36] SC undoubtedly expands as *Senatus Consulto* and with *ex* means 'from a decree of the Senate'.[37] One possibility therefore is that it indicates a revival in the Senate's power to control gold and silver coinage. If so, it must have been part of the programme of measures to restore the Senate's jurisdiction and autonomy outlined in Nero's accession speech; as such they would have helped further restrict Agrippina's influence. However, it is also possible that EX SC was no more than a formality and just represented the visible traditional senatorial admin-istrative mechanism of instituting a coinage reform rather than any more significant transference of real powers. An alternative interpretation is that the formula meant that the imperial honours and titles on the coins had been awarded by the Senate. In other words it was 'a gesture of deference'.[38] That these, frankly fairly arcane, alternatives cannot be resolved into a definitive conclusion only goes to show how little we know about the technicalities of the way the Roman state operated. What is beyond debate is that the SC had not appeared on imperial gold and silver since Augustus' time (in fact when he was still Octavian). The SC disappeared once more from gold and silver in the later part of Nero's reign, reappeared on Vespasian's precious metal coins and then disappeared permanently but they were featured routinely on base-metal coins into the third century.

The reason for the shortage of coins made under Claudius and Nero (to 64) is unknown today but in 64 a massive new issue of coins was ordered, made at Rome and Lugdunum. Today the vast bulk of Nero's coinage belongs only to 64–8. So it is simply not possible to use the absence of Agrippina on coinage between 55 and 59 as conclusive evidence for her loss of influence, even if her power was indeed in decline, because so little was made. In any case, the continuation of double-headed coinage in the East shows that her presence at the centre of politics remained prominent in popular perception, at least in some places. What is likely to be of far more significance is that when the vast recoinage was commissioned in 64 none of it featured dynastic issues of the types that Caligula and Claudius had produced.[39]

Claudius was deified, causing Nero to joke that mushrooms must be the food of the gods since mushrooms had turned Claudius into one.[40] The apotheosis of Claudius also elevated Agrippina to the dizzying heights of wife of a god, the first dowager empress since Livia to be so. As a priestess of the cult of the deified Claudius, Agrippina had reached the highest official status a Roman woman could achieve. This was further amplified by being given the privilege of an escort of two lictors in the manner of a magistrate. It was another possible example of permitting Agrippina to overstep the mark by offering her a temptation she was quite unable to turn down.

Claudius' funeral was modelled on the obsequies organized for Augustus. Agrippina, who had so generously speeded Claudius on his way to heaven, presided over the event like a praying mantis.[41] After the funeral was over Agrippina set about immediately rearranging the pieces on the chessboard with the exception of herself. In theory Nero was the new emperor, and so he was at least as far as the public face of the regime was concerned. In reality the reign of Agrippina the Younger continued unabated with only the technical difference that she was now the emperor's mother rather than his wife. Nero resented the way she kept him constantly under close watch, sniping at him if he said or did anything of which she disapproved. After her death he felt able to fulfil his dreams to take part in a chariot race and sing with his lyre. The implication was that Agrippina had stopped him from doing such things.[42] He consoled himself for the moment with the occasional disgruntled promise that he would abdicate and take himself off to Rhodes.[43] It was not an entirely empty gesture. He knew full well that without him Agrippina had no position or leverage. In time Nero would come to realize he had the power to dismantle her influence piece by piece.

Agrippina's most serious error was to believe that she could carry on like this in the way she had done while Claudius was alive. The average Roman could have been forgiven for not even noticing to begin with since the coinage of the new reign had continued to feature Agrippina in the manner of a joint ruler. The success of the early part of her reign during Claudius' time seemed to have resulted in her being more powerful than anyone else. This was an illusion, as she was to discover all too soon. Claudius may have been an annoyance and an obstacle to her progress but both thanks to his actions and inaction he had helped facilitate her advance. Now he was gone Agrippina had lost one of her most important assets.[44]

A source of delight to Roman historians was the involvement of key personalities who devoted their time and attention to controlling Nero, inhibiting his excesses, and thwarting Agrippina. These were the new praetorian prefect, Afranius Burrus and Nero's tutor Seneca whom Tacitus credits with having saved Rome from a good many more murders Nero might otherwise have ordered.[45] Neither sought imperial power, but both were men of very high ability and judgement. They were able to work together to govern the state by supporting Nero. They were helped by Nero's growing sense of self-awareness and desire to act as he pleased. The obstacles of course were Agrippina and Pallas but Pallas, far from helping her, was her undoing because Nero – unlike his deceased stepfather – simply refused to defer to an ex-slave.[46] This meant that effectively there were now two factions in the imperial palace, or at least so it suited the Roman historians to claim. The evidence suggests that they were right.

Instability in Parthia and Armenia threatened Rome's eastern provinces. Whether the seventeen-year-old Nero and his mother were capable of managing the state and fending off such a threat proved to be a controversial topic. After all, Octavian had only been a little older at nineteen when he embarked on the civil war, but then he had not been under the control of his mother and nor had he been a preening narcissist. Others wondered whether Burrus and Seneca could step up to the mark if necessary to guide the regime through a difficult time. They consoled themselves with the thought that at least the addled and indolent Claudius was no longer in charge.[47] The speculation illustrated the uncertainty occasioned by having an underage emperor, the youngest yet, and the unique role Agrippina was playing.

Nero was nothing like as compliant as his mother imagined. By 55, despite being married to Claudia Octavia and claiming to be disgusted by his mother's freedman lover, he had found himself an obliging girlfriend called Acte, with a little help from his friends Marcus Otho and Claudius Senecio. Acte was a freedwoman, formerly a slave purchased in Asia. To begin with Agrippina had no idea about Acte, but it is no great surprise that she soon found out. Initially she resorted to innocuous cursing, describing Acte as a 'freedwoman rival' and having a 'maid' effectively for a daughter-in-law.[48] There was something to be said for Nero using up his energy on an irrelevant underling. A tryst with a woman of high status could have been far more politically damaging and, more to the point, destructive to Agrippina's interests; one of Nero's more daring affairs had been with a Vestal Virgin called Rubria. Ironically, Nero initially defended Acte by claiming she was really of royal birth and treated her as if she was his wife, in spite of Claudia Octavia.

Agrippina damaged her own interests by letting her frustration and jealousy of Acte get the better of her. It showed how potentially the greatest threat to a woman's power was another woman. Agrippina could not share Nero with anyone else. Dio and Suetonius also refer to a prostitute mistress of Nero's who was said to have resembled Agrippina. The likeness was the very reason Nero was so fond of her. He even commented that sleeping with her was like sleeping with his mother. Unfortunately, Agrippina's prostitute doppelganger is unnamed. In Agrippina's world order her men had to be unconditionally compliant and under her control. Nero had made it clear he had a mind of his own and his mother was not prepared for that. The reign of Agrippina suddenly started to look under threat. She was increasingly voluble in her criticisms of the relationship with Acte with the result that Nero started to drift away from Agrippina. He turned to Seneca for advice and guidance instead.[49]

The breakdown in relations between Agrippina and Nero over Acte illustrated perfectly how difficult the role of a woman in the context of Julio-Claudian power was. Agrippina had pushed her power and status further than anyone else. She had achieved a remarkable level of equality but it relied entirely on the acquiescence of the male in whom power was legitimately vested. If he withdrew his compliance, just as Nero was now doing, there was literally no legal or constitutional recourse open to a woman in Agrippina's position. She also discovered that she was increasingly isolated. The truth seems to have been that Seneca had deliberately manipulated Nero into the relationship with Acte, in the full knowledge that it would undermine Agrippina in the privacy of the imperial palace. A very close friend of Nero's, Annaeus Serenus, had agreed to pose as an admirer of Acte and to shower her with gifts. This meant that Nero's more discreet presents went unnoticed so that in public it was generally believed that Serenus and Acte were lovers.[50]

Nero found other ways to challenge his mother. He had a favourite freedman called Doryphorus, with whom he developed a sexual relationship, and on one occasion ordered that 10 million sesterces be given to him. This outraged Agrippina who demanded that the cash be piled up into a heap so that Nero would realize how outlandish and unsuitable his gift had been. Nero was far from outfaced by this. With scathing wit he announced to his mother that on reflection he was appalled at how small the present was and ordered it to be doubled.[51] Agrippina could do nothing and had to give way to the mounting realization that she had created a monster. She resorted to rage, frustration and desperation.

What followed was by far and away the most notorious development throughout the history of the Julio-Claudian women but the salacious details belonged to a broader context. Agrippina was already associated with allegations that she and her sisters had had sexual relations with their brother Caligula. It was now in the year 55 that Agrippina allegedly offered to sleep with her son as a way of diverting his interests and doing so in a way that could be more easily concealed than having a mistress.[52] She also offered him some of her substantial fortune. There are several different ways in which this story could be interpreted. One possibility is that she was simply developing something Caligula had experimented with – the idea of descent being contained within the Julio-Claudian family. Such an allegation also fitted perfectly with the Roman tradition of constructing an image of the immoral woman and added to the suite of undesirable characteristics and behaviour attributed to Agrippina both in her lifetime and afterwards. As such it may have been pure invention.

Another possibility is that Agrippina made the offer of incest as a provocative proposition simply to make a point to Nero and with no intention that he should interpret it literally. Her purpose was thus to show Nero that she had made him emperor and therefore could take it away from him. If so, she was quite wrong. As Dio pointed out, once she had given Nero absolute power she by definition had no power to take it away from him. In such a context it was possible that anyone overhearing something to that effect would have been able to repeat the story, which then entered popular lore and was taken at face value. The final possibility is that it really was true. As far as Tacitus was concerned this was simply another example of Agrippina's manipulative and deceitful behaviour. That was an inevitable judgement for him to make, even though it is a legitimate possibility. It may also simply have been panic in a context of the dawning realization that her options were diminishing rapidly. For the moment though it was at least only a suggestion of incest.[53]

Nero was supposed to be an acquiescent pawn but Agrippina had fatally miscalculated. It is easy to see how desperation, and using the only methods left to her, might have coloured her judgement. She did of course have the option of retiring to a matronly distance and allowing Nero and his advisers to rule in their way. That was clearly quite beyond Agrippina. She had come too far to give up now, even though Nero not only smelled a rat but also had plenty of friends who reinforced his suspicions about his mother. It was surely they who advised him to undermine Agrippina by removing her sidekicks. Pallas was the first to go but had the wit to cut a deal which left him immune to any further enquiry into his affairs. Before too long, Agrippina might have wondered whether she should have had the sense to take similar precautions.[54] Acte clearly never disappeared from the scene. In 59 she played an important part in Agrippina's downfall (see next chapter). In 68 she would accompany Nero's nurses to deposit his ashes on the Pincian Hill in Rome.[55]

Agrippina played her trump card, or at least the card she thought would remind Nero permanently whose debt he was in. It was, on the face of it, a bizarre volte-face. While Claudius was still alive she had worked overtime to wheedle her son into prime position as heir apparent. Of course the reason had been also to guarantee her own position once Claudius was dead. Agrippina had steadfastly promoted the cult of Claudius in order to guarantee Nero's legitimacy as his heir. When Nero became emperor and began to challenge his mother she faced being frozen out. Her solution was to use Britannicus as a threat. Agrippina told Nero that Britannicus was beginning to approach his coming of age and was quite clearly the legitimate dynastic heir; he, Nero, was only exercising power as an adopted son because of what she had done, and all the crimes she had committed, to get him there. It was an extraordinary tirade in which she trumpeted how providence had protected Britannicus. She would be the one to take him to the Praetorian Guard and show the soldiers the true heir of Claudius whom they would obviously prefer to Burrus and Seneca whom she abused.[56] She cannot possibly have intended to side with Britannicus. The idea was to worry Nero so much that he would back down and accept her role alongside him.

The episode is a key piece of evidence, perhaps the only evidence, for a breakdown in relations between Agrippina and Seneca and Burrus in Nero's early reign. If it really happened then it turned out to be a fatal gamble. Agrippina was forcing Nero into a corner and to make a choice. If his mother was going to start posing as Britannicus' advocate then there was only one choice Nero could make if he was to survive. He was well aware that as Britannicus grew up he would be an obvious rival or the figurehead of a faction against him, just as Nero could have been used in the same way against Britannicus. He was also well aware that his mother could continue to use Britannicus as a threat. Therefore, his stepbrother had to die. From there it would be a short step to deciding that Agrippina would have to be taken care of too. The counter argument, that this episode is completely implausible, makes it harder to understand why Nero ended up ordering his mother's death in 59.[57]

Britannicus cuts a tragic and embittered figure in the sources, but also someone capable of some dignity and presence of mind. He was depicted as the victim he was, with nobody, once his father was dead, to defend his interests except himself. Agrippina's sudden interest in his cause was a sham and no one knew that better than he did. At a more personal level Britannicus threatened the narcissistic Nero's craving for public attention. On one occasion Britannicus showed that he was all too aware of what was happening. During the festival of Saturn, Nero told the boy to stand up and make a presentation, assuming that as Britannicus was far too young to understand that this was a drunken revel he would make a fool of himself. Britannicus stood and with dignity recited a poem about how he had been pushed out of his rightful position. This provoked an unexpected wave of sympathy from the audience, and Nero was horrified. Britannicus had signed his own death warrant.

The services of Locusta were engaged once again, this time at Nero's behest, through the auspices of Locusta's prison guard, a praetorian tribune called Pollio Julius. The poison provided by Locusta was administered by Britannicus' tutors. The poison was not sufficient to kill Britannicus immediately. This infuriated Nero who thought Locusta and Pollio were trying to divert attention from themselves. He demanded quicker action, even at the risk of showing his hand. A new poison was prepared. At a family meal Britannicus was deliberately handed a scalding hot drink. The drink of course was harmless apart from the heat. Britannicus handed it back and adulterated cold water was added. Britannicus fell into the trap, swallowed the drink and promptly broke into convulsions. Nero dismissed the convulsions as symptoms of his epilepsy, and sat calmly looking on. It seems that Agrippina had had no idea about the second phase of poisoning and was completely wrong-footed by what was happening before her eyes. The horrific truth registered with her, or so Tacitus claimed, that Nero had just set a precedent for murdering a relative, even though she was already allegedly guilty of similar crimes.[58] It was also typical of Nero that he had worked through intermediaries, just as his mother was accustomed to doing.

The body of the wretched Britannicus was smeared with gypsum to conceal the effects of the poison. An inconvenient downpour washed it off while the corpse was being carried through the Forum. The heavy rain seems to have been a fact, the gypsum story possibly a decorative embellishment.[59] It was apparent to one and all, and not just Agrippina, that Nero's reign had taken an important turn for the worse. Agrippina, whom Nero made no effort to please with gifts, appeared now to instigate a separate court of her own. She made overtures to Claudia Octavia to bring her on side, and began to build up a network of supporters amongst the Praetorian Guard and the senatorial nobility as well as securing funds from wherever she could find them. Nero decided to marginalize his mother as much as possible to prevent her from becoming the epicentre of a factional challenge to his rule. She was denied the German bodyguard unit she had been allocated. She had to go about visibly without a praetorian escort too because Nero determined they were for the emperor alone. Since the praetorian escort had been a key part of her publicly visible status, its removal was a calculated and effective way of humiliating her. In addition Nero now established his own household and obliged Agrippina to move to a house once occupied by her grandmother Antonia.[60]

Agrippina felt the impact immediately. Nero only attended her with an escort of centurions. Others simply spurned her, even openly ducking away from her if they encountered her unexpectedly. Only a few female friends remained loyal but even those friendships were fragile. One of these women was the childless Junia Silana, the woman Messalina had forced her lover Silius to divorce. They fell out when Agrippina managed to persuade a suitor of Junia's called Sextius Africanus to abandon his plans to marry Junia by suggesting that she was both immoral and ageing.[61] It was an interesting use of an accusation more usually levelled against Agrippina. Junia reciprocated by accusing Agrippina of plotting to place Rubellius Plautus on the throne instead of Nero. Tacitus describes Plautus as being Nero's equivalent in descent from Augustus. This was not true other than in a legal sense. Rubellius Plautus was Tiberius' great-grandson and thus, by adoption, great-great-grandson of Augustus even though there was no blood descent apart from that through

Augustus' sister Octavia. However, since his grandfather was Tiberius' son Drusus, Rubellius was therefore a cousin of Agrippina and Nero.[62]

Junia Silana knew how to work up an opportunity. While all the members of the imperial family and their associates were inclined to employ agents, it was especially true that the women carried out their intrigues this way. Junia Silana used two of her own clients, Iturius and Calvisius, who obliged her by making the accusation about Rubellius Plautus. They passed it on to Atimetus, a freedman of Nero's aunt Domitia, who immediately engaged the services of one of Domitia's other freedmen, an actor called Paris. Paris went straight off and turned up at a late-night drinking session of Nero's to drop the bombshell. Nero's reaction was exactly what Junia Silana must have wanted. He was instantly petrified and wanted his mother dead. He also wanted Burrus removed since he had been promoted at her behest. Burrus saved himself by promising to have Agrippina executed if the allegation was proved, but reminded Nero that the information had come from one source alone. Nero was advised to wait till the next morning. For the moment the crisis subsided.[63]

The following day Burrus and Seneca presented Agrippina with the charges and from whom they had come. Agrippina was more than equal to the challenge. She dismissed Junia's allegations on the simple basis that, since Junia had had no children and was an adulterous immoral woman, she could not possibly understand that no mother would replace one child with another. Agrippina claimed that Domitia was simply using her freedmen fornicators to make up stories better suited for theatrical performances. She observed that had anyone other than Nero succeeded Claudius there would have been plenty of people accusing her of murdering her husband. Consequently the only person she was likely to have any support or sympathy from was Nero; thus, it was absurd to suggest she would support anyone else against him. It was an effective argument and showed Agrippina's cool and presence of mind to good effect. Rather than importune Nero to accept her innocence she demanded reprisals for her accusers, and rewards for her friends. Nero obligingly agreed.[64] Junia Silana was the principal loser. She was forced into exile. Paris had to be left alone because he was too close to Nero and played too large a part in his decadent activities, though Atimetus, Iturius and Calvisius were all punished. One of the beneficiaries was Faenius Rufus who was made prefect of the corn dole. This was not a bad decision and shows that Agrippina's judgement of people was not necessarily flawed.

Rufus was subsequently appointed joint prefect of the Praetorian Guard by Nero as a sop to the people; Rufus had become popular because he was not corrupt and had not profited from the corn dole job.[65]

By 58 the tension between Agrippina and Nero seems to have subsided. There is little indication of any more difficulties for the next year or so. Agrippina's quick thinking had bought her more time but it was clear her profile and status had been permanently damaged. The easiest way now to try and destroy a person's reputation was simply to accuse him or her of being associated with Agrippina. Seneca was one of the targets, the victim of the notorious Publius Suillius. Since Seneca had once been a lover of Agrippina's sister Julia Livilla it was a short jump to alleging that he had become embroiled with the emperor's mother too.[66] Seneca was discredited by Suillius for a variety of reasons. His wealth accumulated over four years as Nero's tutor seems to have incurred particular anger. Counter accusations followed and in the event Suillius was banished to the Spanish archipelago of the Balearic Islands. Seneca survived for the moment even though his conduct appeared to be completely at variance with his stoic philosophy.

Whatever the truth about Agrippina's marginalization from the centre of power in Rome, out in the Eastern Empire the news had apparently been slow to travel. With so little coinage being manufactured in the West it is difficult to use that evidence to demonstrate her loss of influence. Conversely, in Alexandria billon tetradrachms with Nero's portrait on one side and hers on the other continued in 56–7, together with a similar issue for Claudia Octavia.[67] The Egyptian mint, producing coin for the closed-currency system of Egypt, was extremely active under Nero but the vast majority was produced between 64 and 68. The tetradrachms produced between 56 and 59 are dominated by coins with female reverse types, including Claudia Octavia and Agrippina as well as Demeter, Eirene and Aequitas. Conversely, coins produced for Nero after 60 at Alexandria were much more likely to have male type reverses such as Augustus, Tiberius and Actian Apollo, though his last empress Poppaea made an appearance in 64–5.[68] At Caesarea in Cappadocia in 58 a number of types were struck showing Agrippina with her son in the manner of the Western gold and silver coins of 54–5. These included a silver didrachm produced in 58 with her on the reverse, described as 'Agrippina Augusta, mother of the Augustus [Nero]'.[69] It is likely that some of these coins were produced explicitly to pay Roman troops engaged by then in the Parthian

War, so it is particularly interesting that Agrippina had been deployed as part of the design of many of this series of coins. Her descent from Germanicus may well have been seen as a useful piece of state propaganda to help motivate the Roman forces. Nero, after all, had no military reputation whatsoever. It was the last time Agrippina would appear in so prominent a way. Her time was almost done.

MURDER
AGRIPPINA, CLAUDIA OCTAVIA AND
POPPAEA 59–68

Nero was to cause the death of three empresses in the last decade of his aston-
ishing and notorious reign.[1] Determined to rule as he pleased unrestricted by
his mother, and bitterly frustrated by her attempts to control him, he ordered her
murder in 59. Agrippina's death brought to an end the main Julio-Claudian
female line which stretched back to Julia the Elder. One of Nero's main objections
to Agrippina had been her resistance to his relationship with Poppaea Sabina, a
woman no less ambitious than Agrippina. Poppaea became empress, but only after
Nero had also destroyed his wife Claudia Octavia, daughter of Claudius by
Messalina, in 62. He and Poppaea had a tempestuous marriage leading finally in
a horrible twist to her death in 65 when he kicked her in a rage. Poppaea's death
and that of her unborn child meant that apart from a few desultory and obscure
survivors the Julio-Claudians were no more. From the start the line had been
sustained through the female bloodline and without it there was no dynasty.

The double-headed Caesarea coins of 58 really amounted to Agrippina's
swansong. Within a year she was killed on Nero's orders. A few years after that
Nero's wife and empress Claudia Octavia was also dead, and not long afterwards his new empress Poppaea too. All three died because of Nero's actions,
two on his orders and the other under a rain of his kicks. Agrippina's death in
59 brought to an end the line of Julio-Claudian women whose lives had
defined the progress and even existence of the dynasty. Nero was to reign for

another nine years but during that time he destroyed the last chance for the dynasty to carry on to another generation when he killed his wife Poppaea and their unborn child.

The murder of Agrippina is so notorious an event in Roman history that it has risen up and out of the period to which it belongs. It has become a symbol of moral degeneracy of exceptional proportions and the absolute corruption of power. As the year 59 opened, Tacitus said that Nero decided no longer to put off the audacious act he had been planning for a long time.[2] There is no doubt about what he meant and he knew his readership would know too. The story was so well known that only an allusion was required. That Nero had been planning the death of Agrippina suited Tacitus' purpose but it is no less likely that it came about more spontaneously. On the one hand it is all too easy to see Agrippina as the architect of her own destruction, thanks to her own greed for power. On the other matricide is the epitome of incomprehensible evil. It outranks all of Nero's other crimes, with the possible exception of the death of Poppaea. Characteristically for Nero Agrippina's murder was committed by go-betweens. In that respect he acted like her, always choosing agents to do his dirtiest deeds.

The seeds of Agrippina's demise are not difficult to spot. She was able to identify them for herself. The death of Britannicus showed Agrippina that Nero was just as capable as her of eliminating anyone who looked like a potential obstacle, especially close family members. The unique dynamic that existed between her and Nero was the paradox of a mother who wanted to be the sole dominant female influence in Nero's life yet who could never fulfil the role of an empress and bear him an heir. In that respect the relationship between Nero and Agrippina was doomed. As his power and awareness increased so hers was bound to diminish. By removing Claudius Agrippina had laid the way open for Nero's accession but failed to realize that she had thereby guaranteed the steady decline in her power and influence. Since Nero's power was by definition pre-eminent it followed that any attempt she made to challenge him would be thwarted. She also came gradually to appreciate that Nero had the Roman male establishment on his side. Indeed, this may actually have been the most decisive force involved. It strengthened Nero even more and in the end it was clear that the young emperor's excesses and idiosyncrasies were treated, at least to begin with, as an acceptable price for seeing Agrippina cut down to size.

At this point in Nero's life the catalyst for the final act in Agrippina's was the arrival on the scene of Nero's latest girlfriend, Poppaea Sabina, in the year 58. Tacitus regarded Poppaea as a striking example of a new wave of immorality that presaged 'massive calamities for the state'.[3] Tacitus was, of course, looking back in hindsight several decades later. Part of his agenda was making the most of any useful contrasts he could implicitly draw with the reformed regime of Trajan in the early second century, though it was in his interests to exaggerate the differences. Nero's reckless indulgences and the civil war that followed were the perfect material. Tacitus was not specific but Pliny supplies one example. A particularly fine Chinese cloth had become available in Rome, perhaps some sort of cotton-based muslin. Manufacturing it was labour intensive and it had been transported a vast distance. This was just so that Roman matrons 'can dress in see-through clothes in public', and presumably at horrifying expense.[4] It was clear Pliny disapproved, not least because of all the trouble involved for such a trivial requirement. He also lived through the time he was describing and added elsewhere that the use of depilatories had resulted in women's genitals being exposed, a development no doubt exacerbated by the use of translucent clothing.[5]

Nothing suited a Roman historian more than a likely-looking portent. One of the best options was identifying a cavalcade of immorality and the general all-round annihilation of traditional Roman virtues. Depicting Poppaea as a symbolic cheerleader for decadence, and as a jealous and scheming harridan, made for a compellingly reactionary narrative. It provided a basis for understanding why Nero ended up killing his mother. It did not do to dismiss the significance of Poppaea so glibly; it is possible that Nero found himself at the centre of a remarkable web of tension between two women, with the hapless Claudia Octavia condemned to being an impotent onlooker. Agrippina and Poppaea wanted power and both were denied it within the Roman system. Possession of Nero was their only means to gain that power. In that context, and given Nero's personal defects and complicated weaknesses, it was bound to end in tears. No one, and that included Nero, could possibly have imagined what this would all have led to. Poppaea's murder in 65 at Nero's hands, the only one of his victims to die as a direct result of his personal physical action, was an epoch-changing moment. It was also an integral part of a sequence of events that began with the killing of Agrippina in 59.

Poppaea had an excellent pedigree, though not on a par with the imperial family. Her maternal grandfather was Poppaeus Sabinus, a consul who had been awarded triumphal regalia in 26. Her mother had been a celebrated beauty, an attribute Poppaea seems to have inherited. Poppaeus Sabinus had had a distinguished career as a provincial governor, according to Tacitus because of his friendship with Tiberius rather than any exceptional abilities.[6] The extended family owned extensive property, especially in and around Pompeii. A Quintus Poppaeus is known to have served as an aedile in Pompeii, and a seal of a Q. Poppaeus or Q. Poppaeus Eros was found in the House of the Menander along with various graffiti. That these are a reliable basis for identifying the house's ownership remains open to debate since they may simply be the scattered traces of persons coming to the house for business; nonetheless, they do attest to the presence of the Poppaei in Pompeii.[7]

Poppaea had been married at about fourteen to Rufrius Crispinus, a praetorian prefect under Claudius. Since that marriage had produced a son she had proved her fertility, and this may well have contributed to her appeal. Poppaea proceeded to earn for herself a reputation as a woman who would do whatever would work best to her advantage. She conducted herself in public as if she was a paragon of virtue but was notorious for her lack of private morals. This may be an exaggeration, designed to contrast Poppaea with Nero's first wife, the rather more modest, unassuming and vastly more popular victim Claudia Octavia.[8] Poppaea's reputation endured long after her lifetime. Dio recounted her habit of bathing in the milk supplied by a herd of five hundred asses, and her fear that she might outlive her prime. According to Pliny she had introduced the custom, based on the belief that it prevented wrinkles developing.[9] The story slots neatly into the canon of Roman anecdotes about the grotesque indulgence of rich and powerful women, their profligate expenditure on 'luxury' and all the feminine degeneracy that suggested.[10]

The trend-setting Poppaea attracted the attention of Nero's friend Otho and this brought her directly into the imperial court circle. Around the year 58 she became first Otho's lover and then his wife, divorcing Rufrius Crispinus along the way. Nero would later get rid of both Crispinus and their son.[11] Indeed, Otho's proximity to the emperor may have been the reason Poppaea acquiesced; she must have spotted the opportunity being associated with the emperor's closest friend would offer her. For Otho's part he recognized that the possession of a dazzling and desirable wife could only enhance his standing at court. Otho decided to share Poppaea with Nero, believing this would only serve to his advantage. It both worked and went disastrously wrong. Nero fell headlong into the honey trap, transfixed by Poppaea, but was momentarily frustrated by her tactical refusal to abandon Otho. This was further complicated by Otho's reluctance to give up his wife, to the extent of shutting out anyone Nero sent to collect her and then even Nero himself. This unexpected obstacle was neatly solved by Nero who simply removed Otho from Rome and posted him to the governorship of Lusitania in the Iberian Peninsula. In the event Otho did a good job for the next decade in the post but he was biding his time. In 68 he would support Galba in his efforts to become emperor instead of Nero, before deciding to become emperor himself.[12]

Poppaea became Nero's favourite mistress. The relationship must have been an open secret. Poppaea was already too well known for her liaisons to go unnoticed. She was around seven years older than the emperor, experienced, and sophisticated in political manipulation. Her presence had contributed to mounting tension between Nero and his mother who became particularly agitated at the thought that Nero might seek to marry Poppaea. It was obvious the young woman presented an enormous threat, far more than Acte had. Nero was already thoroughly bored and frustrated with his wife Claudia Octavia, who had failed to bear him a child. More to the point he was becoming obsessed with the idea of marrying Poppaea.[13] Claudia Octavia was quite obviously the main obstacle to that scheme.

Nero had already murdered Claudia Octavia's brother Britannicus, because he was a potential rival and focus for any opposition to his own rule. Britannicus might have gone, but Claudia Octavia was hardly likely to have been especially well disposed towards her husband, making her removal desirable. Together these factors gave Poppaea enormous power. More importantly, and this was typical of the manner in which the senior women of the imperial circle manipulated and exercised their power, Poppaea was able to function in a completely different way from Nero's male advisers and associates by operating outside the system. While women were ostensibly incarcerated in the restrictions imposed on them by Roman society, the reality for some was the freedom to bypass the protocols through which male power structures worked.

By the same token Poppaea had identified immediately that although Nero was married to Claudia Octavia her principal rival was Nero's mother, the one person similarly free from constitutional constraints.[14] The feeling was mutual. Just as Agrippina was an impediment to Poppaea, so also was Poppaea to Agrippina. Agrippina's rise was a source of some official embarrassment, and probably also frustration to Nero's key advisers, Seneca and Burrus, and it certainly offended members of the Roman establishment. As Nero began to emerge from his teenage years so he too began to become irritated by his mother's shameless acquisition and flaunting of privileges that really only belonged to the emperor, such as an escort of praetorian soldiers. Poppaea's influence over Nero, driven by what was clearly a sexual infatuation on his part, began to drive out Agrippina. By keeping her marriage to Otho going to begin with, and therefore holding Nero back while simultaneously enticing him, Poppaea whipped the young emperor up.

Poppaea sneered at Nero. She mocked him as his mother's ward, for being at the beck and call of a person who was obstructing their marriage, and threatened to demand to be restored to Otho's side. Nero's hangers-on were delighted because they were infuriated by Agrippina's domination and wanted her destroyed. Agrippina spotted what was going on. She knew better than anyone else that female power had to be exercised through the medium of a man. If Nero's attention wandered to another woman then her influence would be destroyed. In early 59 Agrippina was forty-three years old. This Roman matron, now entering middle age, had already allegedly decided that the only option remaining to her was to try once more offering her son inces- tuous relations.[15] Given that his father Gnaeus Domitius had been accused of incest with his sister Domitia Lepida perhaps Agrippina felt there was a chance her son would acquiesce.[16] However, Nero moved rapidly from this point to persecute, irritate and humiliate his mother and then commission her murder.

The story of Agrippina's death is well known, but remains mostly remark- able for the farcical way it was carried out. Had it been dreamed up by a novelist it would be roundly dismissed as a hopelessly implausible and idiotic plot twist. In 59, at the height of his obsession with Poppaea, Nero's frustra- tion at not being able to rid himself of Claudia Octavia so long as Agrippina lived began to boil over. He was egged on by Poppaea's taunting. Agrippina, for her part, seems to have been fully aware that Nero was on the brink of having to make a choice. The story goes that she waited until Nero was in a state of at least semi-intoxication at a banquet and then offered herself openly to him for incest. Unusually, Tacitus states his source for this as a history written by a senator called Cluvius Rufus but nothing now is known about Cluvius' work.[17] The story continued that Seneca could see how this move on

Agrippina's part represented a serious threat at so many levels if it were to come off. Seneca decided to utilize the services of Acte, at considerable risk to her. Acte told Nero that Agrippina had been boasting about the incest and that the army would refuse to support a perverted emperor. Tacitus muses over other sources available to him that supported Cluvius' version and another that blamed Nero for instigating the incest but concluded that all the supporting and circumstantial evidence clearly incriminated Agrippina. It is of course impossible now to know.

Nero's response was to start distancing himself from his termagant of a mother. She, for her part, reciprocated by removing herself from public life, withdrawing to her private gardens or her estates. It is improbable that she regarded this as a permanent arrangement. After years of manipulating people and circumstances to her advantage she was unlikely to abandon her ambitions quite so easily. Remembering her relentless interference in his life up to that point Nero must surely have realized it was only a matter of time before Agrippina grew bored of, and frustrated by, her self-imposed exile. Nero concluded therefore that it did not matter where Agrippina was. She would remain a *praegravis*, literally a 'burden' that would weigh him down. He therefore decided to kill her.[18] Given that he had already had Britannicus removed for similar reasons the development was an entirely logical one, at least in Nero's mind.

The disturbing experience of having Britannicus clumsily murdered by a poison that failed to work properly evidently had unsettled Nero. The sources, as ever, diverge on this point of detail. Suetonius says Nero tried three times to poison Agrippina but abandoned the plan when he discovered she had fortified herself with antidotes. The others say that he rejected any idea of poisoning Agrippina for that very reason, not least because he knew she would realize immediately what was happening anyway. A straightforward assault on her with weapons was unlikely to work because not only would it be hard to hide them, but Nero was also worried that anyone ordered to kill Agrippina might refuse. The underlying reason for this was the simple fact that Agrippina was the daughter of Germanicus, a qualification of such exalted esteem that no self-respecting soldier was likely to agree to her murder. Under such circumstances it began to look as if Agrippina was inviolable. Fortunately for Nero, Agrippina had left a number of enemies in her wake and some of them nursed murderous resentment in their hearts. For Nero's purposes this was perfect:

someone else would surely do his dirty work. Anicetus, a freedman who had formerly been Nero's tutor, was currently serving as the prefect of the imperial fleet at Misenum and loathed Agrippina with a passion. To this he added the useful attribute of an imaginative mind. For this mission impossible he came up with the idea of a self-destructing boat which would eject Agrippina into the water. Clearly, Anicetus promised, no one could possibly suspect Nero because it would 'obviously' have been a simple, but tragic, accident. Nero would then be free to observe all the usual obsequies and posthumous respect a woman of Agrippina's status deserved.[19] That at least is Tacitus' version. Dio believed the plot was primarily one dreamed up by Nero and Seneca, the latter either wanting to divert attention from criticisms about his own behaviour or to help accelerate Nero's downfall. They supposedly saw a ship designed to fall apart during a theatrical performance and used that as their inspiration.[20] The exact origins of the idea matter less than the curious subterfuge adopted as a means of avoiding Agrippina's suspicions.

Nero was delighted by the idea of the defective boat, whether he or anyone else had thought of it. He was at the time attending a festival of Minerva called the Quinquatrus, held on 19–23 March at Baiae on the Bay of Naples.[21] The pretext would be to present the occasion as an opportunity for mother-son reconciliation, which he had been working on by pretending to be as devoted a son as possible. Even better, it was nowhere near Rome. Any hare-brained scheme to kill Agrippina in Rome was bound to be exposed. Agrippina duly arrived and was taken by Nero to a nearby villa called Bauli for the period of the festival. A rumour circulated that she had smelled a rat and was on her guard, and was carried to Baiae by road rather than any form of boat or ship. But she seems to have settled into the banquet because Nero had her seated in the place of honour as the most important person there. The banquet over, Nero took her to the rigged boat which duly set sail across the Bay of Naples to take her home. The voyage progressed without incident to begin with until, suddenly, the canopy over Agrippina's area collapsed, thanks to the lead with which it was roofed. This failed to kill Agrippina and her servant Acerronia Polla because the bed they were lying in had such high sides.[22] The farce continued with the boat's failure to disintegrate, leaving the crew arguing over how best to make the vessel sink. In the chaos the selfless Acerronia made a futile gesture by insisting that she was Agrippina. She was promptly beaten to death under a hail of blows from pikes and oars, while Agrippina dived overboard and swam for it. She was picked up by some boatmen nearby and taken to her villa.[23]

Agrippina had the presence of mind to realize that her best tactic now would be to pretend to believe that the disaster had all been a genuine accident, while keeping Nero at a distance. She sent a freedman of hers called Agermus to tell Nero that she was safe but that he should not visit her, however scared he might have been by the danger she had been in. She took care to have Acerronia's will found and her property taken control of.[24] The plan to keep Nero in the dark fell at the first hurdle. He had already been told that Agrippina knew he was the culprit, and was instantly certain she would be looking for vengeance. He turned to Seneca and Burrus. Burrus said there was absolutely no prospect of the Praetorian Guard injuring anyone descended through the imperial family, and a child of Germanicus to boot. It was suggested that Anicetus finish off the job he had started. This was just as well because when he returned from not having killed Agrippina Anicetus was only too happy to take advantage of the offer of a second chance. Agermus arrived with a message from Agrippina but walked right into a trap. A sword was produced and Agermus was immediately framed, accused of having turned up to attack Nero. It was part of a new narrative dreamed up by Nero and his associates: Agrippina had been out to get him by using one of her freedmen, with Agermus conveniently serving as the obliging but unwitting patsy who 'proved' the yarn's veracity. Therefore Agrippina had allegedly chosen death instead out of shame at her own wickedness. Depicting Agrippina as a terminally contrite would-be filicide was certainly a neatly symmetrical way of explaining recent events, but whether this new official explanation would hold any more water than Anicetus' collapsing boat had been supposed to remained to be seen. Coming as it did only a few years after the accusations against Agrippina concerning the Rubellius Plautus plot the story at least had the asset of being moderately consistent and embellished with tenuous plausibility.[25]

In the meantime Agrippina still had actually to be killed. This turned out to be little more than a technicality. A crowd of ordinary people had gathered near Agrippina's villa, distressed at the news of what they had thought was a ghastly accident and believing initially that she was already dead. These rumours turned out to be false, for news broke that she was alive, provoking some misplaced excitement. It was also worrying evidence that Agrippina, for all her political activities and scheming, was clearly still the focus of some general popularity. At that moment Anicetus arrived with an armed band. He broke his way into Agrippina's villa. She knew the game was up. One of her maidservants turned out to be less generous-minded than Acerronia and absented herself immediately. That left Agrippina with an even clearer sense of betrayal. Anicetus beat Agrippina down and then a centurion finished her off, she famously presenting her belly and demanding to be stabbed there in a symbolic swipe to Nero that he was destroying the very place whence he had been born. Dio supplies her acclamation: 'Strike here, Anicetus, strike here, for this bore Nero.'[26] With Agrippina's death the Julio-Claudian line did not come to an end, because Nero still lived and there were others who could trace their descent from one or other of the original dynastic strands. But her death did mark the end of her direct female line from Julia, Augustus' daughter. One might have asked, and people surely did at the time, where Nero was at this crucial moment. The answer is that Otho, Poppaea's cuckolded husband, obligingly provided Nero with an alibi by arranging a banquet for the two of them.[27]

Dio says that Nero literally could not believe what had happened, the enormity of the crime being so great that to begin with he denied it was possible. Of course that might simply have been part of the act since he must have been perfectly well aware of what had happened. Either way, he insisted on seeing Agrippina's corpse. It was said at the time that Nero admired his mother's lifeless body when he looked at it later that night. He inspected the cadaver with unnatural curiosity, commenting that he had had no idea how beautiful she was. Both Tacitus and Dio who report the story with its unnerving overtone of necrophilia knew that it would remind their readers of the tale of the Amazon queen Penthesilea at Troy. Achilles killed her, and removed her helmet only to fall in love with her beauty.[28] Any such allusion was of course suffused with irony, given Nero's limitless lack of heroic qualities. It also provided further amplification, as if any were needed, of Nero's total degeneracy.

It is easy enough to indulge in a search for some coherent explanation for why Nero had his mother killed and therefore to see it as the climax of a sequence of events that led remorselessly to this outcome. Another way of looking at the event is to consider Agrippina's murder as something that was sanctioned by Nero without understanding how he had come to that point or what it would really mean. In other words, he had gravitated from one crime to the next, eventually reaching a position that would have seemed unimaginable at the start but by the end was only an increment further down a long road and therefore easier to take. Selfish, emotionally immature and easily frightened, Nero was floundering around trying to understand his own power. He was also surrounded by people with their own axes to grind and their own ambitions; finding ways of pleasing Nero and alleviating his fears was, in the immediate term, the most expedient route to their own advancement. Agrippina was so potent a force, so assertive and resilient a personality, and such a visible threat to Nero's autonomy and self-indulgence it is not wholly surprising that in a moment of recklessness the unthinkable suddenly turned into what passed for a rational solution. Nero's reaction in the cold light of day only serves to illustrate how little he had understood of all the factors that had coalesced into the bizarre plans to kill his mother.

Agrippina's body was gathered up, placed on the type of couch used at a banquet and cremated that same evening. She was only given a proper burial by some of her loyal staff who interred the ashes in a tomb beside the road to Misenum not far from a villa once owned by Julius Caesar. In a melodramatic moment one of her freedmen, Mnester, committed suicide. It might have been in honour of his former mistress or because he was all too aware what fate Nero might have arranged for him and others like him in Agrippina's orbit.[29] Agrippina had lived to fulfil a prophecy she had once been given long before that Nero would kill her; to this she had declared 'let him kill, so long as he rules'. In the long run the killing of Agrippina would define Nero's memory for generations to come.[30]

Far from Agrippina's bloody demise bringing him peace of mind, Nero spent the rest of the night in fitful apprehension. He continued to have disturbed nights. As a result he proceeded to move from one of his residences to another in search of peace. He was alone in a way he had never been before, and he was also completely exposed. Perhaps this was the time he hunted out the gold bracelet containing the skin of the snake that had saved him from Messalina's assassins when he was a small child.[31] The Neronian spin machine was started up. The only story Nero could put about was the one planned that Agrippina had been plotting against him and so she had paid the penalty for something she had arranged. For good measure Nero threw in various other charges against her. These included her desire to have a partnership in power, that she wanted the Praetorian Guard, Senate and the people to swear allegiance to her, and how much trouble he had had to go to stop her barging into the Senate or speak to embassies from foreign countries. Together with all that Nero then also blamed on Agrippina everything that had been wrong with Claudius' principate. The speech had been composed by Seneca but the mistake was to include a reference to the shipwreck. This was so patently implausible that Tacitus insisted it was tantamount to Nero admitting publicly his culpability.[32]

One of Nero's first moves as he stumbled his way ahead with his cover story like a blind man with a bad case of the jitters was to pay a cash handout to the Praetorian Guard. Their flexible loyalty was always for sale, but crucially Nero was a member of the Julio-Claudian family, which was an essential asset. Agrippina of course had been too but by throwing money at the problem Nero found out how easy it was to sell the official version of what had happened and thereby divert the praetorians' focus onto him. In the event it mattered not one jot whether anyone believed him, just so long as they could be persuaded to accept it in public. So the praetorians were bought, but only for the moment. Next the propaganda wheel was cranked into action with an imaginative public-relations campaign. Nero recalled women and others whom Agrippina had forced out. It was a way of damaging her public reputation by reminding everyone of her vindictive behaviour. The lucky ones included Junia Calvina and Calpurnia who were allowed to return to their family homes, while the ashes of the less fortunate Lollia Paulina, who had expired already, were brought back to be buried properly. Junia Silana missed out on rehabilitation as she too had died while returning from exile at a time when Agrippina had ceased to care much about her.[33] Despite these fake gestures of reconciliation and magnanimity Nero remained extremely worried about whether he would be welcomed at Rome or treated as a pariah. Court sycophants assured him that all would be well because, they said, Agrippina had been hated.[34] It was just what he wanted to hear.

Suitably galvanized, Nero set out for Rome. His reception when he arrived there was distinctly ambivalent. In public nothing seemed untoward because the usual respect due to an emperor was shown. The Senate played along, with the sole exception of a senator called Publius Thrasea who was disgusted by people stupid enough to flatter Nero when it was quite clear they, too, might well be among his future victims. Remarkably he survived for the moment but was forced into suicide in 66. Behind closed doors people were less circumspect because there was no doubt about what had happened. Sinister gestures started being made, reported by Dio. Parricides were normally sealed into leather bags with several animals and thrown into the Tiber to drown. So leather bags were hung on Nero's statues in an open hint that that was what should happen to him. Slightly less plausible is the story that a baby was abandoned in the Forum with a label reading 'I shall not rear you in case you kill your mother'. Even efforts to remove any trace of Agrippina were thwarted. Her statues were taken away when Nero returned to Rome but one remained standing for a while. It was promptly veiled and a label fixed to it reading, 'I am shamed and you are unashamed'. Throughout Rome graffiti named Nero along with the famous mythological matricides Orestes and Alcmaeon, while an actor called Datus taunted him with a song referring to the deaths of Claudius and Agrippina. The anecdotes make a gratifying assemblage. How apocryphal they are it is impossible now to know, but they have the aura of subtle and contrived wit accumulated over time.[35]

Nero pressed on, continuing to act as the innocent party. Short of admitting to being guilty he had little choice. Indeed, apart from committing suicide in public in an act of self-destructive but courageous shame and contrition he could hardly do anything else. Agrippina's birthday was declared to be a day on which no public business could be done because it had now been classified as a bad-omen date. Work on the Temple of the Deified Claudius, a cult that had been presided over by Agrippina as priestess, ceased. Part of what had been built of the temple platform was turned into a nymphaeum by Nero, some of which remains visible today. Construction of the temple would not be resumed until the reign of Vespasian (69–79).[36] Sacrifices were offered in Agrippina's honour but during these Dio claims that a total eclipse of the sun occurred and stars became visible, interpreted as one of several gestures made by the gods on this ominous occasion. Tacitus merely states that the sky was darkened. The eclipse is a rare instance of an unequivocal reference point in a complicated canon of disparate evidence. One did indeed occur on 30 April in the year 59 but it was not total in Italy as Dio clearly implies. The path of totality passed through North Africa, across the Mediterranean almost clipping Sicily and the Peloponnese, and then through Syria. In Rome the eclipse was partial, the moon obscuring an impressive three-quarters of the solar disc in the early afternoon.[37] That was easily enough to provoke disquiet, coming as soon as it did after Agrippina's death, even though it was not enough to allow stars to become visible. That the eclipse happened is a mathematical certainty, even if calling it a 'total eclipse' was an exaggeration of the situation in Rome. Less plausible is the story that a thunderbolt landed on Nero's table and destroyed his meal.[38] Dio had taken what we now know to be an indisputable scientific fact but either modified it deliberately to improve his story or used records that had confused sightings much further south with what happened in Rome.

Nero had uncovered a hitherto carefully guarded secret about his principate. It turned out it was possible to live and be emperor without Agrippina. He was free. Armed with this startling revelation his guilt and fear began to dissipate. His long-repressed desires soon filled the resulting void. Like any self-respecting coward Nero looked around for easy targets. Domitia, his aunt and his mother's bitter rival, was an obvious choice so Nero immediately took aim. He could not miss since she was now into her sixties and was unlikely to have been any sort of real threat. Nero seems by now to have regarded her with the same suspicion he had developed for Agrippina, even though Domitia had brought him up during his mother's banishment and shown him great kindness.[39] Naturally he took care to subcontract the job to his minions. He ordered Domitia to be poisoned, her death facilitating his appropriation of her estates, which had probably been on his mind from the moment he first thought about getting rid of her.[40] By way of compensation he built gymnasia on his aunt's estates and also ordered a festival at vast expense to celebrate Agrippina's life. The entertainments he put on suggest it was more a celebration of his liberation. Of course it was all conducted in the worst possible taste. Equestrians and senators were said to have taken part in the performances in the theatre and circus. Even Nero joined in though that was scarcely a surprise; it is hard to imagine how anyone could have stopped him.[41]

There was no other attempt on Nero's part to expiate his crime by deifying or honouring his mother in some more permanent and public way. Agrippina's immortality subsisted only in her enduring reputation for being unnaturally interested in power, the allegations of incest, the murder of Claudius, and the notorious antics of the last few years of her son's disastrous reign, a man whom she had visited on Rome instead of Britannicus, the rightful heir. Her death deprived Agrippina and the world of finding out what would have happened had she proceeded with her ambitions, and what she would have done about the succession. It would take another female dynasty, the Severans, over 150 years later, to experiment further with the limits of female power in the Roman world.

In the meantime, while Nero still ruled, anyone on record as having been a friend of Agrippina's was liable to find the fact first on any charge sheet brought against him. Faenius Rufus, only recently made one of the praetorian prefects, along with the loathsome Tigellinus, was a man of impeccable character but still fell foul of this tactic. The charge seems to have been instigated by Tigellinus and evidently nothing came of it at this date, Rufus remaining in post for several years but constantly harassed by Tigellinus who continued to try and discredit him.[42]

Agrippina's murder had been followed by the death of Burrus in 62, possibly after having been poisoned. With Burrus gone Seneca found that he had lost his former influence. Nero turned his attention to what Tacitus called *deteriores* ('inferior men').[43] It was these very lesser men who decided to have Seneca removed from the centre of government by making various accusations against him, including one that his acquisition of wealth and estates meant he was deliberately challenging Nero for opulent living. Seneca had the wit to withdraw with dignity and tact, expressing the view that there was no more he could do for Nero as his friend. Nero magnanimously accepted Seneca's decision to retire and said he would appreciate Seneca's return to advising him should he fall short in any way. Tacitus regarded this as simply disingenuous and masking his real hatred for Seneca but that judgement was typical and resembled his perception of Agrippina's duplicitous nature.[44] Seneca was subsequently forced to commit suicide.

Remarkably, by a process of manipulation and guile, Poppaea had indirectly helped achieve the elimination of Agrippina, something that had eluded all Agrippina's other enemies. Even more conveniently, she had had a ringside seat from which to watch the events but had avoided any actual participation in the crime. However, Poppaea's path ahead remained unclear. Claudia Octavia stood in the way so Poppaea still had work to do. Between 59 and 61 Nero began to reconfigure the principate in his own image, but at that time he was still operating under the watchful eyes of Burrus and Seneca. It was not until 62 that Nero made the decision to marry Poppaea. He seems to have been unnerved by what this would mean. Claudia Octavia was popular but Poppaea wanted, indeed needed, Claudia Octavia gone for obvious reasons. Poppaea also allegedly persuaded one of Claudia Octavia's staff to accuse her of having an affair with a slave called Eucaerus. Nero's initial attempts, surely encouraged by Poppaea, to repudiate Claudia Octavia on the basis of infertility, divorce and banish her, led to popular protests, parades supporting Claudia Octavia and even the public desecration of statues of Poppaea. Whether Poppaea was responsible or not, there was no doubt in the mind of the mob whom they blamed. Order was only restored when troops were sent into the streets to chase the protesters out.

The chaos caused by Nero's rejection of Claudia Octavia demonstrated just how febrile Roman mob sentiment was, and the potentially fatal consequences of misjudging it. Perhaps this was why Poppaea's portrait apparently never appeared on coinage produced at either of the imperial mints in the West (Rome and Lugdunum). Poppaea was terrified because she could see her way to becoming Nero's Augusta about to disappear. She knew that Nero, always obsessed with his popularity, was sure to cave into the mob so she tried a different tack with a brilliant piece of lateral manipulation. She managed to convince Nero that Claudia Octavia's popularity was a direct threat to him. Were he to divorce Claudia Octavia, she pointed out, the mob might then seek a new husband for her and thereby displace him as emperor. The appalling thought that he might be pushed aside, however theoretically, was easily enough to prod Nero into action. He invited his favourite assassin Anicetus, the prefect of the fleet at Misenum and incompetent collapsing-boat builder, to confess to adultery with Claudia Octavia, an altogether far simpler scheme than the plot to drown Agrippina.

Presented with the choice of riches for complying or being executed for not agreeing, Anicetus found the decision easy to make. That did the trick though the story did nothing for Nero's reputation. Despite the allegations of treason and infidelity, as well as sterility, Claudia Octavia remained the object of public sympathy while Poppaea was elevated to the position she craved, 'married only for the ruin of a wife'.[45] She and Nero tied the knot just twelve days after he divorced Claudia Octavia.[46] In this way Poppaea Sabina became empress of Rome, initiating the final sequence of events that would end with her own death. Seneca enjoyed himself in his tragedy *Octavia* by having the deceased Agrippina appear at the time of the wedding so that she could curse the rites and wail about Nero's destruction of her monuments.[47] He was buying into the popular tradition of Claudia Octavia as the victim.

Claudia Octavia was promptly banished to the island of Pandateria. Shortly afterwards in 62 she was killed even though a number of people had sworn she was innocent despite being tortured to persuade them to testify otherwise. Also murdered was Doryphorus, Nero's powerful freedman and former lover, who had had the temerity to oppose the marriage. To round off the proceedings, Poppaea was presented with Claudia Octavia's head. It was a pyrrhic victory. Nero was Poppaea's third husband. In 63 Poppaea presented Nero with a daughter, named by him Claudia Augusta and thereby marking her out as implicitly an empress in her own right. It seemed that the Julio-Claudian dynasty now had a future. Poppaea's womb was commended by the Senate to the gods, added to for good measure with a decree that a temple dedicated to Fecunditas (Fertility) be built.[48]

The vital importance of an imperial woman to the imperial line was being publicly acknowledged and Poppaea's status as a Roman matron seemed inviolable. Had she proceeded to bear Nero a son, she would have been the first empress to make it possible that a Roman emperor would be succeeded by his own male offspring. By now she was really beginning to enjoy the fruits of her status though we do not know what estates and other property Nero had given her when she was his mistress.

Within four months, probably in the early summer of 63, the infant Claudia Augusta expired. Nero was devastated though Poppaea, still in her early thirties, was capable of bearing another child. By late 64 or early 65 she was pregnant again. His relationship with Poppaea was becoming increasingly fractious, though in her defence Nero's indulgence in homosexual relationships was hardly likely to have strengthened their union even if these dalliances did not reach their climax until after her death. Nero was now in his late twenties and ever less inclined to tolerate anyone else attempting to control him. He was beginning to discover he had replaced one autocratic and domineering woman with another. Nevertheless, in public at least Poppaea and Nero even seemed to be acting as joint rulers, Poppaea apparently filling the place once held by Agrippina. Gold and silver coins of Nero struck at Rome in 64–5 include one type with a reverse possibly depicting him and Poppaea standing side by side with the legend AUGUSTUS AUGUSTA.[49] Other female virtues and personifications found their way on to Nero's coins at this time including Concordia (Harmony), Salus (Health), Vesta (goddess of the Roman hearth) and Roma. In Egypt the mint of Alexandria turned out tetradrachms with Nero on one side and Poppaea on the other (plate 26).[50]

At Pompeii a number of graffiti refer to the *iudicii* ('judgements') of Nero and Poppaea and wishes of good fortune to them. The judgements are unspecified but it is clear they were regarded as emanating from 'the Augustus and Augusta' jointly.[51] According to two graffiti found in the House of Julius Polybius it seems that at some point the two visited Pompeii and made offerings to the city's patron goddess, Venus. Poppaea presented Venus with a beryl and two pearls, while Nero gave gold.[52] Near Pompeii the palatial villa identified as Oplontis is on a scale that suggests that in its final form it was owned by Nero. It was perhaps subsequently used by Poppaea as empress when out of Rome, though it is no less possible it was already her family's property or that it belonged to someone else (plate 27).[53] Poppaea undoubtedly had estates in the area. The 'Arrian potteries of Poppaea Augusta' are specified as being in Pompeian territory based on information from a writing tablet found at Herculaneum dated to 8 May 63.[54]

In 64 Nero's activities had included organizing an orgy in a pool that formed part of the Baths of Agrippa, a major complex of public facilities in the Field of Mars. Agrippa, Augustus' right-hand man and father of his grandchildren, as well as being Nero's great-grandfather, would have been horrified to see the regime that he had helped to build degenerate into a plaything for a profligate and narcissistic youth. Nero had even engaged in a mock marriage, posing as the wife-to-be with one of the partygoers, a freedman of his called Pythagoras.

Not long after the party Rome was almost destroyed in a catastrophic fire. Naturally enough the sprawling city, with its mazes of tiny alleys that wormed their way through teetering tenements made of wood and packed to the rafters with tenants, was no stranger to fire. One of the buildings destroyed, perhaps at this time, was the Temple of the Deified Augustus and Livia.[55] In the days of the late Republic, the senator Marcus Licinius Crassus had amassed an astronomical fortune simply by virtue of possessing a fire brigade. His gangs waited for fires to break out, which they did with convenient frequency. The firemen attended the blaze and offered the hapless owners or landlords a knock-down price for the plot, and then put out the fire. Similar offers were made to neighbours whose houses were likely to burn down too as the fire spread. Those who accepted walked away with little; those who did not walked away with even less, having had to accept an even smaller sum for what was left of their property since the firemen had declined to put the fire out.[56] Apart from the fact that Augustus had organized an official militarized fire service in the form of the *vigiles*, or 'night watch', little or nothing had changed many decades later.[57] Roman hydraulic engineering was unsurpassed in the ancient world, but the ability to carry astronomical quantities of water across the landscape to feed to baths and fountains of the city did not translate into being able to force a controlled jet of water higher than two or three storeys of an apartment block. When a major fire broke out, leaping from one inflammable structure to another, there was little or nothing the night watch crews could do. Rome, which was now bigger and more overcrowded than ever before, was ripe for devastation.

The fire of 65 broke out in the valley between the Palatine and Caelian Hills, at the southeast end of the Circus Maximus. Here there was a commercial area filled with shops storing inflammable goods which are likely to have included oil and wood. To begin with the fire probably seemed no more dangerous than the blazes that started constantly in Rome. The flames, already ripping through the shops, were intensified by the simple bad luck of a wind that blew them northwest straight down the length of the circus. It was just how London was destroyed in 1666. The fire soon became unstoppable, at least by any of the precautions or equipment available at the time. The majority of the population swiftly abandoned any attempts to stop the fire and ran haywire through the streets, desperate to find a way out. An unknown number were killed in the process while the fire continued to wipe out whole districts.[58]

Nero was at the coastal settlement of Antium (Anzio) some 30 miles (50 km) from Rome. Naturally he had been informed of the catastrophe so he made his way back, especially concerned at the destruction of his house and the imperial palace on the Palatine Hill. His first gesture was to open up the Field of Mars and his personal gardens as a place of refuge. He also ordered the erection of temporary buildings to house the homeless, and announced a reduction in the price of grain.[59]

Unfortunately, the benefits of Nero's efforts were invalidated by a rumour that he had tactlessly decided to put on a private show in order to sing about the fire by comparing it to the destruction of Troy. The fire continued to rage until the demolition of buildings seemed to bring it to an end by creating open spaces the flames could not cross. Mysteriously though, the fire broke out again but this time appeared to favour public buildings. This raised a fresh rumour that Nero was behind it, inspired by the belief that the new fire had started on land belonging to the praetorian prefect, Tigellinus, the emperor's crony-in-chief.

Whether he was responsible for the fire or not, Nero seized the opportunity it offered. He decided to commission the construction of a sprawling and luxurious palace that he named the *Domus Aurea* ('Golden House') (plate 25). This became his new home and it also became home to the pregnant Poppaea, by then aged around thirty-four. Systematically extorting the Roman elite to fund a vast new palace in Rome, performing in public, and indulging in sexual perversion both as a participant and voyeur, Nero was undermining the whole basis of Roman society. Nevertheless, his lack of inhibition, love of showmanship and sheer indulgence delighted the Roman mob. To them Nero's rebellious indifference to protocol and the expectations of a man of his class was a refreshing humiliation of the smug and privileged senatorial elite. To those senators and their families, or at least those he had not yet killed, Nero's rule had turned into a degrading circus and threatened the existence of the Roman state.

At some point in 65 Poppaea chided Nero about going to the races too often. She did not anticipate that her preening, volatile and self-obsessed husband would in a fit of barbaric violence destroy the future prospects of the Julio-Claudian dynasty by kicking her to death. Nero had scarcely exhibited any personal inclination to violence up to that point, even though he showed no restraint in ordering violence to be inflicted on others by his soldiers and staff. The occasion showed how far this young man had degenerated in an environment where his absolute power was no longer under any restraint.

The story of Poppaea's death being explicitly Nero's fault was the story recounted by the historian Suetonius.[60] As so often in Roman history, such a sensationalist account merits a little closer examination. Tacitus, generally somewhat more measured in his judgements, was certain that Nero had been enraged but also that the kicking had been accidental. He also reported that the authorities to whom he had turned for his evidence included some that attributed Poppaea's demise to poison, though he says nothing about who the culprit or culprits were.[61] Dio sat on the fence, reporting that the incident might have been either deliberate or accidental, but that it had involved the emperor jumping on Poppaea with his feet while she was pregnant.[62]

It made no real difference. The outcome was just the same. A woman whom the emperor Nero loved, indeed was once infatuated with, had died at his hands and taken her unborn child with her. Having killed his second wife, Nero promptly set about trying to reincarnate her in a series of inchoate and surreal schemes with tinges of madness and necromancy. The emperor burned so much scent that day in her memory that before long it was put about that he had burned more than the annual scent production of Arabia.[63] Such a story fitted the more general picture of Nero's extravagance; if the story circulated at all it was probably just a scurrilous attempt at withering humour.

Poppaea's body was embalmed instead of being cremated, and her remains interred in the mausoleum built by Augustus.[64] She was deified, identified with Venus, and a temple was built out of funds that according to Dio had been stolen from women. Its location is unknown but Rome or Campania, where her family connections were, are both possible. The choice of Venus was not surprising. The Julian family had prided itself with the conceit that it was descended from Iulus, son of Aeneas, the mythical founder of the Roman race and the son of Venus (plate 1). The dynasty emphatically had its origins in a divine female progenitor. Poppaea's association with Pompeii and the gifts she had made to the goddess there attest to her own interest in Venus.[65] Also deified was Claudia Augusta, recorded on coins issued at Caesarea Paneas in Syria. At Luna (Luni) in Italy a dedication to Nero in 65 was modified in 66 with an additional dedication to 'deified Poppaea Augusta'.[66] Denying Poppaea's divinity could be regarded as an act of treason.[67]

Poppaea was not the first of Nero's female victims, as we have seen, but killing her himself was a development even for Nero. With Agrippina, Claudia Octavia and Domitia already dead, the murder of Poppaea left Nero exposed and completely unrestrained. Turned down by Claudius' other daughter Claudia Antonia, he had her murdered too on the flimsy pretext that she was plotting a coup even though the concept was not recognized in Roman law.[68] By killing these women Nero was systematically annihilating any chance of his dynasty outliving him. He had evidently failed to observe that the single reason there was a dynasty at all was because of a remarkable succession of women who had provided the only durable lines of descent.

Nero proceeded to find himself one more wife. She was the obscure but intelligent and beautiful Statilia Messalina, whose husband, Vestinus Atticus, Nero obliged to commit suicide to facilitate the marriage, which took place by the middle of 66. She was also distantly related to Caligula's empress Lollia Paulina and Claudius' empress Valeria Messalina. Why Statilia Messalina consented first to become Nero's mistress and then his wife is a curiosity in its own right, given her new husband's track record. Perhaps she was too scared to say no. She was another woman in Nero's life who was his senior. The union bore no fruit, at least that which we know. She made a very few appearances on coins issued for Nero at Ephesus in Ionia and Hypaepa in Lydia, the latter showing the emperor and his last empress facing each other on the obverse.[69] Today Statilia Messalina is a footnote in history.

Nero's last years were characterized by increasingly reckless abandon, protracted absence in Greece and an obsessive relationship with a young man who bore a curious resemblance to Poppaea. He ordered the emasculation of Sporus that he might better fulfil the role of a surrogate Poppaea. Nero called him 'Sabina' and in 67 'married' him in Greece. In a bizarre observation of the normal protocols, no doubt out of fear of causing offence, the Greeks even prayed that the happy couple would proceed to have children.[70] The coinage from 64–8 is, bizarrely, magnificent. The quality and plasticity of Nero's brutal and imposing portraits on the brass sestertii and even the smaller base metal denomination of the dupondius and as have been admired and prized since antiquity. Although we know nothing about how and by whom the coins were created, it is generally assumed that Nero himself had taken a significant interest in making sure the finest die-engravers were sought out and employed. The reverse types were original and superbly designed from the seated figure of Roma to the new harbour of Ostia, newly completed, and a mounted Nero with a mounted Praetorian Guard. In an ironic twist they provided a gratifyingly suitable canvas for those inspired by the *damnatio memoriae* that followed his death. Gouging Nero's portrait with a knife or chisel, preferably through the eye and face, was one way of paying him back for what he had done to his mother and two of his wives.

Nero's complacent and self-regarding indifference summed up his personality. It helps explain why even his suicide in 68 was no more than an act of self-destructive narcissism. The succession could not have been further from his mind. Ironically Nero's entire existence had been defined and dominated more by women than any other emperor to date. Unlike Caligula and Claudius, though, Nero ignored the opportunity to produce a series of dynastic coins that included his female relatives. It was patently obvious why he omitted his mother. Her deliberate intrusion on his early coinage was an uncomfortable memory to add to his culpability for her death. Apart from some provincial issues Claudia Octavia and Poppaea were similarly ignored. The main reason surely was Nero's egocentricity and his complete lack of concern for the political interests of his dynasty. Caligula, for all his misguided despotism, understood the importance of positioning himself as a descendant of Augustus through his mother Agrippina the Elder and used the coinage as one means of doing that. Claudius was aware of the need to promote the idea of an imperial family just as much, especially as he was not directly descended from Augustus. Around 150 years later the Severan women would show even better that they understood how to promote the interests of a dynasty.

Statilia Messalina outlived her emperor husband, only to be offered marriage by Nero's friend Otho, the short-lived emperor of 69 (succeeding Galba), who in a curious twist some years before had given up his own wife Poppaea so that Nero could marry her. It made no difference. Statilia had no children by Otho either.[71] Thereafter, Statilia disappeared from our evidence for the period as a dynastic irrelevance.

The deaths of the infant Claudia Augusta in 63 and her mother, together with her unborn sibling, in 65 turned out to mark the end for the Julio-Claudians. Had Poppaea and one of her children lived they might have ensured the continuity of the dynasty, which for the first time would have relied for its Augustan authenticity on the paternal line. At the very least such children might have provided a focal point for the loyalty of the Praetorian Guard. Even Poppaea's son Rufrius Crispinus the Younger, by her first husband, was killed on Nero's orders.[72] Without them there was no one else. There were certainly those who could trace their descent from some of the key women of the Julio-Claudians but these were obscure people. They lacked the ambition, connections or the opportunity to seize power. Rome's first imperial dynasty had turned to dust.

Those who knew their history and its spurious anecdotes and omens of course were in a position to say that this had all been as good as foretold. Had anyone been in two minds about the prospect for the dynasty, a couple of omens ought to have settled the issue. In Nero's last year the descendants of Livia's hens died along with the laurel. For good measure 'a temple of the Caesars' was struck by lightning. The end was nigh.[73] It was all rather circular. The Roman mentality was to start with a recent or current evil and seek some sort of cause and effect explanation in the past. Anything 'odd' might do. Pliny, ever ready with a story, took the demise of the Julio-Claudians all the way back to the fact that Agrippa had had a breech birth. His name alone proved that – it derived from *aegre partus*, 'born with difficulty'. A breech birth was thought to guarantee a problematic life; indeed, in Pliny's view,

Agrippa was exceptional in having been a success though he had suffered lameness as a child. But the real price for his breech birth was the 'unhappiness caused to all the world by his offspring . . . especially the two Agrippinas, who gave birth to the emperors Caligula and Nero, two firebrands to mankind'. Even more inauspiciously, Agrippina herself reported in her memoirs that Nero had been a breech birth as well; we also have Pliny to thank for that since the original is long lost.[74]

No wonder then. At least the blame for the reigns of Caligula and Nero was based on a false premise about something that happens in nature, not just the defects of the two Agrippinas as women. It was a small consolation. Pliny was writing in the early to mid 70s, in the immediate aftermath of Nero's reign. His explanation, which probably reflects thinking at the time, must have allowed those who survived to look back and see the degeneration of the Julio-Claudians as some sort of aberration due to very specific circumstances rather than an inherent defect of the Roman world or being due to chance. The notion proved enduring. England's notorious Richard III was also said to have been born in the breech position (together with other birth peculiarities) by Tudor historians such as Thomas More and others, thus satisfying a similar need to explain Richard's alleged crimes.[75] The story helped imply how much better things had become under the first Tudor king, Henry VII. Similarly, by the time Pliny was writing the reign of Vespasian (69–79) was already being depicted as a vast improvement in security and stability.

When Augustus established himself as the supreme authority in Rome a century before Nero's timely demise he was immediately presented with the problem of how his power would be transferred to a successor. It was apparent from the outset that he instinctively wanted to arrange this within a dynastic context, while at the same time doing so within the curious framework of constitutional powers and his own personal authority. In a sense, having no son of his own was an accidental advantage because it helped obscure the monarchical tendencies of the pseudo-constitutional system he was developing. Augustus turned his attention therefore to male relatives who were linked to him by blood through the female lines of his daughter Julia and his sister Octavia, and through his wife Livia's son Tiberius. His Julio-Claudian successors were all descended from Livia, three of them from Octavia, and two of them from Julia via her daughter Agrippina the Elder and granddaughter Agrippina the Younger. Without these lines of descent there would have been no Julio-Claudian dynasty and once they expired the dynasty effectively came to an end. There were no means of bringing it back.

There was at least one survivor. Junia Calvina, sister of Marcus (murdered) and Lucius (suicide), both Junius Silanus, had been recalled by Nero in 59 from her banishment under Claudius in 49. It was a way in which he tried somehow to rehabilitate himself. A great-great-granddaughter of Augustus, Junia was born probably sometime around 10–14 and had been considered 'handsome and provocative'. Her line of descent from Augustus was entirely through the female line from Julia the Elder. Her reputation as 'the most delightfully jolly of all girls' resonated with Julia's.[76] By 68 Junia Calvina was in her mid to late fifties. She had been married to Lucius Vitellius the Younger, brother of the short-lived post-Nero emperor Aulus Vitellius, but they were divorced in 49. She was apparently still alive in 79, aged around at least sixty-five, when Vespasian was told that part of Augustus' mausoleum had suddenly opened up (probably due to subsidence or a structural fault giving way). He joked that perhaps it was creating space for Junia Calvina. There is no record of her leaving any descendants of her own, or of the exact date when she died.[77] One physical manifestation of her existence was found at Tivoli (ancient Tibur) in the form of a dedication to a freedwoman of Calvina's. It reads 'To Tyrannis, the best of wives and daughter of Spurus, the favourite of Junia Calvina, daughter of Marcus Silanus. Gaius Albius Thymelus Herculaneus, Augustalis and freedman of Livilla [set this up]'.[78] The text is undated but the reference to a freedman of Livilla, who died in 31, means it probably belongs to Junia Calvina's younger years, though it need not have come before Livilla's death. It is a fleeting vignette of Junia Calvina's household, presided over by an affable and engaging woman of the highest rank who enjoyed the companionship and service of her most trusted staff. At the end of her days Junia Calvina, alone of all the Julio-Claudians, was able to look back across her lifetime through the astonishing reigns of Tiberius, Caligula, Claudius and Nero, and the precarious route she had had to tread along the way. Even at that proximity it must have already seemed virtually impossible that such things could ever have happened. No doubt she mused on the extraordinary fact that she had survived and lived to tell the tale.

After Nero's death in 68 power shifted outside the Julio-Claudian orbit and gravitated to those who had the necessary military backing and prestige after the convulsions of a civil war which had showed the alternative on offer to the Roman people without a stable principate. Galba, the first emperor of the civil war year of 68–9, had been well known to Livia and favoured by her, but he was not a relative. One of his first acts was to remove statues of Nero and Poppaea. After his murder in January 69 his successor Otho instructed the Senate to order the restoration of Poppaea's statues, and also some of Nero's as part of considering whether to rehabilitate Nero's memory. It was a sentimental gesture that encouraged a mob reluctant to accept the end of the Julio-Claudians. He was even hailed by the mob as 'Nero Otho' but before he could decide whether to accept the acclamation he had been toppled and committed suicide.[79] His short reign followed by that of Vitellius began to make it look as if the principate was doomed. In the meantime the bizarre emergence of the pseudo-Nero showed that the matricide still had his fans. In 69 a Nero lookalike materialized in Greece, passed himself off as the emperor and gathered supporters in the East until he was killed by forces under the command of the governor of Galatia and Pamphylia.[80] The possibility that news of the demise of the Julio-Claudians had been greatly exaggerated was exposed as a mirage.

Fortunately for Rome the imperial system was reinvented under the Flavians between 69 and 96, beginning with Vespasian, a man who had no familial connection whatsoever with the Julio-Claudians but who did have the good sense to hijack their names and titles. This established an enduring tradition that lasted for centuries. One more tradition that seemed impossible to shake off was the failure of the imperial male line. This would lead in time to another remarkable Roman imperial dynasty of women.

Augustus' court, wife, daughter, descendants, ancestors, sister . . .
The whole court is dead . . .
Of necessity, some one must be the last.[81]

270

II

EPILOGUE
THE SEVERAN AND OTHER EMPRESSES

*T*he story of the Julio-Claudian women covers several decades strung out along a key line of descent from Julia the Elder down to Agrippina the Younger. They established all sorts of precedents but it was the failure of the imperial male bloodline that had magnified their importance and provided opportunities. Once those circumstances changed and discriminating adoption became the mechanism of succession the significance of the women of the imperial family was marginalized. It was not until the Severan period in the early third century that once more the failure of the male bloodline provided an opportunity for a female dynasty. This time several empresses – Julia Domna, her sister Julia Maesa and Maesa's daughters Soaemias and Mamaea – made a much more concerted attempt to rule the Roman world. They quite deliberately modelled their image on that created by the Julio-Claudian women. Like their Julio-Claudian predecessors they still depended on achieving power through men. While much had changed, this factor had not. Their 'temporary projection' onto the Roman stage lasted just a few decades and disappeared almost without trace. Indeed, they discredited the idea of women ruling. The Severan women were followed by a succession of soldier emperors elevated by the army before the Roman Empire evolved into a new type of state, and one in which empresses had until the fifth century scarcely any profile at all, with one or two notable exceptions. This all has much to tell us about how and why the Julio-Claudian women achieved what they did but without establishing permanent change in the Roman world.

After Nero's death in 68 the Roman world was still one dominated by men and in which the political and legal structures were ones from which women were formally excluded. It was only the circumstances of the failed male bloodline that had allowed the Julio-Claudian women so much dynastic significance. The way in which this happened again under the Severans is of crucial importance in helping us understand what circumstances were necessary for women to become powerful in the Roman Empire.

When faced with having to resolve the question of succession Augustus invariably based his decisions on blood, establishing a principle for the dynasty. It was this factor above all that made the Julio-Claudian female line of descent so important to the history of that period. With the end of the dynasty circumstances and political preferences changed. Vespasian (69–79) already had his own two adult sons, Titus (79–81) and Domitian (81–96), obviating the need to consider any alternative succession mechanism until 96 since neither left a son to succeed him. For much of the second century the imperial male line consistently failed but instead of relying on a female bloodline discriminating adoption was used instead. This minimized the chances of a succession crisis and also indirectly ensured that the female line of descent was sidelined.

The Julio-Claudians retained a spectral presence in Rome long after the dynasty all but evaporated with Nero's death. Their buildings and monuments remained conspicuous features, not only in the city but elsewhere in the Empire, even though they often needed repair and were increasingly submerged or absorbed by later projects and structures. Vespasian was probably responsible for reinstating the construction of the Temple of the Deified Claudius, a project begun by Agrippina the Younger but abandoned by Nero after her murder in 59.[1] On the other hand, Vespasian's celebrated Colosseum and his son Titus' baths succeeded in burying much of Nero's Golden House (plate 25). By the early third century so much building and development had taken place in Rome that a great deal of what had been constructed in the Julio-Claudian period would have been difficult to spot.

Agrippina the Elder's destruction at the hands of Tiberius led to a sustained period of posthumous veneration which lasted long after the Julio-Claudian era. In the year 80 Titus reissued the sestertius type which Claudius had commissioned in her honour, with his own titles substituted for those of Claudius on the reverse. It was only one of a long series of restored types issued by Titus that helped present the Flavian emperors as legitimate successors of the Julio-Claudians, but Livia and Agrippina the Elder were the only Julio-Claudian women singled out for inclusion. It said much for these two women that they were the ones who enjoyed the greatest revival. By this time the name Augustus had been adopted as a synonymous term for supreme power, and Caesar for the designated successor. This practice continued for centuries. Antoninus Pius (138–61) restored a temple dedicated to the deified Augustus and Livia and commemorated the fact on a series of coins (plate 28). Livia went unnamed but her figure is shown beside that of Augustus between the columns of the octastyle façade, in the manner of joint monarchs.[2]

No other Julio-Claudian woman was memorialized in the same way; for the most part they were simply too notorious. Their stories were generally confined to the works of Roman historians like Tacitus who indulged themselves by providing as much detail as possible about their shortcomings. This way Julia the Elder, Messalina and Agrippina the Younger entered popular lore as destabilizing and villainous characters. The empresses of the Flavian period (69–96) and the second century are mostly opaque figures. Vespasian's wife Domitilla had died before he became emperor. Only Domitian's wife Domitia Longina came close to significant power when she plotted against her husband. Titus (79–81) had no empress, having divorced his wife Marcia Furnilla some fourteen years or so earlier. Their daughter Julia's husband was executed by Domitian in 82. Remarkably Julia Titi proceeded to become Domitian's mistress and was named Augusta.

The pseudo-Neros had not gone away. Another pseudo-Nero gained some notoriety in the year 79 under Titus, again in the East. This time the Parthians flirted briefly with the idea of 'restoring' the latest 'Nero' to the throne until his true identity was exposed. Suetonius reported another, twenty years after Nero's death in the reign of Domitian and once more among the Parthians. But he too came to nothing despite the disquieting evidence that an emperor who had killed his mother and two wives clung on to some posthumous popularity. After all, his grave was freshly decorated for some time after his death.[3]

When Domitian died in 96 a new solution to the succession had to be found. An ageing senator called Nerva was appointed to the position as a stopgap. For the next century the transmission of the principate followed a more reliable blurring of the dynastic and adoptive routes. Nerva (96–8),

Trajan (98–117), Hadrian (117–38) and Antoninus Pius (138–61) had no sons of their own. Each man therefore adopted a candidate for a successor who appeared to have the necessary attributes. Even so, almost from the outset a potential dynastic line of female descent lurked in the background. Nerva chose for his successor Trajan, a brilliant and popular general who pleased the army and the people alike. He enhanced his authority and legitimacy by symbolically presiding over civil trials in both the Forum of Augustus and the Porticus of Livia.[4] Trajan and his wife Plotina were childless which ended any chance of a direct line dynasty. Nonetheless, Pompeia Plotina was a woman of considerable presence and honour. On one occasion she chastised Trajan for not keeping proper control of tax collectors.[5] Trajan adopted his ward Hadrian whose cause Plotina was particularly keen on promoting. Hadrian was married to a woman called Sabina, Trajan's great-niece. Sabina's grandmother Marciana was Trajan's sister. Trajan had made some headway with constructing the image of a new dynasty in the making, though Hadrian's marriage to Sabina was primarily Plotina's idea.[6] Trajan issued coins in the name of his father, whom he seems to have deified after his death in 100, his wife Plotina, his sister Marciana and Marciana's daughter Matidia. One new trend was the more frequent deification of female members of the imperial family. All three women were also later deified by Hadrian after their individual deaths.

Hadrian and Sabina were also childless. That ended any hopes Trajan might once have nursed of a lateral line of descent resembling that which Augustus managed through his sister Octavia. Sabina loathed Hadrian and professed even to not wanting to bear Hadrian children rather than impose his successor on the Roman people.[7] Hadrian adopted a senator called Antoninus Pius (after a previous choice, Aelius, died in early 138) who was as honourable and honest as his name suggests. His wife Faustina the Elder, whom he loved, died in 141, just three years after her husband's succession, and was deified. As the deified Faustina she posthumously became the subject of one of the largest issues of coins in the entire Roman series with the simple obverse legend DIVA FAUSTINA.

Although these women formed a significant part of the imperial image this was not the same as having the sort of influence and power that Livia and Agrippina the Younger had wielded. Women such as Plotina and Faustina were primarily consort or dynastic figures rather than the sort of empress who directly involved herself in an emperor's actions.[8] Their lack of sons, and the consequent process of discriminating adoption, had reduced their potential importance. Faustina had borne her husband no surviving sons but there was a daughter, Faustina the Younger. She was married by Antoninus Pius to his choice of adopted son and successor, Marcus Aurelius, in 145. Antoninus Pius also adopted a co-successor, Lucius Verus, who was married to Marcus Aurelius' daughter Lucilla in 164. A form of bloodline was being held together through women again but the use of male adoption masked that. Aurelius and Verus ruled as joint emperors until the latter's death in 169 not only restored the Empire to single rule but also led to Aurelius and Faustina's son Commodus being earmarked as the successor. Once more a bloodline from one emperor had passed through the female line.[9] Commodus was the first son of an emperor born during his father's reign to succeed as emperor himself, a quite remarkable fact given that it was more than two centuries since the principate had been established by Augustus.[10] In that time the Roman perception of women and effeminacy had changed little. Marcus Aurelius included 'a womanish character', along with stubbornness, childishness, stupidity, tyranny and the fraudulent, when he compiled a shortlist of human deficiencies.[11] He also mused on the struggle earlier generations had had with sustaining their dynasties. 'Consider what trouble those before them have had that they might leave a successor.'[12]

In 180 on the death of his father Commodus became sole emperor (he had been made co-emperor with Marcus Aurelius in 177). Like Nero he was temperamentally unsuited to power and also lacked the experience and maturity to recognize this. Indulged by corrupt and self-serving officials, just as Nero was in his later years, Commodus virtually abrogated responsibility for rule, preferring to spend his time on games and other amusements. His considerably older sister Lucilla became involved in a plot to unseat Commodus from his disastrous reign but failed and was banished to Capri where she was executed, as was Commodus' wife Crispina. This destroyed any chances of them attempting to seize power through male surrogates. Commodus was murdered on the last day of 192, leaving no offspring. He was briefly replaced by an elderly senator called Pertinax whose efforts to reform the principate were welcomed by the public but not by the Praetorian Guard.[13] They murdered him for his efforts and then decided to auction off the Empire.

When the senator Didius Julianus opted to try and become emperor in the auction in the opening days of 193 it was largely because he had been egged on by his ambitious wife Manlia Scantilla and his daughter Didia Clara. His failure to pay the soldiers what he had promised meant that he was killed after sixty-six days. But the imperial mint had set to work immediately on his accession. Manlia Scantilla appeared on a series of coins in gold, silver and base metal, with a reverse depicting and naming Juno Regina, the queen of the Roman gods. The association was obvious. Didia Clara had her own series, associating her with Hilaritas Temporum, 'the joy of the present age'. When Didius Julianus was toppled after his laughably short and disastrous reign these two women saw their plans evaporate in a trice. Scantilla and Clara disappeared into obscurity. They were lucky to escape with their lives. We can only imagine what sort of empresses they might have tried to be.

Didius Julianus had been destroyed in part because of a far more ambitious and successful candidate for the throne. Septimius Severus, senator and general, was approaching with the armies of the East and became the victor of the civil war that had followed Commodus' death. In tow came his family, presided over by the monumental personality of his Syrian wife Julia Domna, and their sons Caracalla and Geta. Domna brought with her into the imperial circle a sister called Julia Maesa and Maesa's daughters Julia Soaemias Bassiana and Julia Mamaea. They all shared a cultural affinity and expectations with the eastern tradition of monarchy and entitlement, a highly significant difference from the Julio-Claudian women.

In the East monarchies had long been an established part of the world that the Romans absorbed in the days of the late Republic. Syria had been taken into the Empire by Pompey the Great in 66 BC when the Armenian king Tigranes the Great capitulated. Tigranes remained as a client king until around 55/54 BC when he died. Thereafter Syria became one of the richest and most strategically important of all the Roman provinces. Government in Syria relied on the indigenous ruling classes, as it did in much of the Roman East. These wealthy families became Roman citizens and operated local government on a Roman model, engaging in the competitive munificence so characteristic of status in a Romanized community, and establishing powerful dynasties who expressed themselves in a Roman idiom. However, the East remained dominated not only by new Roman identities but also by Greek civilization and local traditions. Antony and Cleopatra, the ultimate hybrid oriental royal couple, had issued coins in Syria showing their portraits on either side in the lead-up to Actium from 34–31 BC, for example at Chalcidice. By the late second and early third centuries the monarchical nature of the emperors was now openly accepted. Dio, a contemporary of the Severans, said it was impossible to see their rulers of Rome as anything other than kings because of the nature of their ultimate authority. There can be no doubt that the Severan women were assisted in their ambitions by this more open acceptance of the reality of male imperial power.[14]

As so often in history it was a twist of fate that resulted in what has been called, with piercing accuracy, a 'temporary projection' of one of these Syrian dynasties on to the Roman stage.[15] The decisive moment in the short-lived era of the Severan women was not the arrival of Julia Domna with Severus in 193, but rather the death of her son Caracalla, followed by her own, in 217. It was then that Domna's sister, Julia Maesa, seized the moment and decided to propel herself and her daughters Soaemias and Mamaea, together with their sons, into the heart of Roman power (plates 29–31). These three women, together and individually, would dominate imperial politics as a matriarchy well into the third century.[16] Despite that, both Soaemias and Mamaea claimed that their sons (Elagabalus, 218–22, and Severus Alexander, 222–35) had been fathered by Caracalla. The need to create the pretence of a male bloodline remained as important as it had been in Julio-Claudian and Antonine times. This time though the reality was even more obvious.

Julia Domna, or Julia Augusta (her official title as empress), was a Syrian woman from Emesa (Homs) of some presence who delighted in the status and prominence imperial life had brought her.[17] She was also educated and highly able though just how her education was managed is not something we know much about.[18] Her father was a wealthy Romanized Arab called Gaius Julius Bassianus, high priest of the Elagabalus (Ba'al or El-Gabal) sun-god cult in Emesa. Her father's name and, therefore, hers had useful associations with the Julio-Claudians; indeed, one can assume that one of his ancestors had been made a Roman citizen under Augustus or Caligula and thereby acquired the 'Gaius Julius' elements. The Domna part of her name was obviously a modification of Domina. Septimius Severus was keen to use every possible avenue to enhance the 'legitimacy' of his dynasty. Julia Domna's name was quite clearly usefully reminiscent of Livia's official name. Severus, given to superstition, had heard that her horoscope had predicted she would marry a king. He used his contacts to meet Julia Domna and take her for his wife in the mid-180s.[19]

It was also claimed that Severus dreamed that Marcus Aurelius' wife Faustina the Younger (who had died in c. 175) had gone so far as to prepare their wedding night bedroom in the Temple of Venus close to the imperial palaces on the Palatine Hill.[20] These added to a portfolio of portents that allegedly foretold his imperial destiny, making Julia an integral component in validating Septimius Severus' entitlement to rule. It also helpfully associated their union with the divine progenitor of the Julio-Claudians. Severus came up with the dynastic conceit of posing as the 'son' of Marcus Aurelius, renaming his eldest son Lucius Septimius Bassianus (Caracalla) as Marcus Aurelius Antoninus to reinforce the spurious claim.[21] Septimius Severus' manufactured lineage was a sleight of hand his wife's sister Maesa and her daughters would deploy in the next phase of the dynasty which began in 218.

Julia Domna was given the title *mater castrorum* ('Mother of the Army') by Severus possibly as early as 193.[22] It was an honour Agrippina the Elder might have been given. Her relationship with the army certainly anticipated such a title, but Tiberius would never have allowed it. He was unable to understand the value to the regime of a woman like that and simply felt threatened. Domna herself happily flaunted the title *mater castrorum*. One of the most unusual records of this title is a small bronze plate found at Rome. Intended to be fixed to a carriage, it announced that the vehicle and its goods were on the business of Julia Augusta Domna, *mater castrorum*, and were therefore immune from liability for payments or duties.[23] Even so, Domna seems to have been a relatively opaque figure earlier in Severus' reign, perhaps because he decided to delay being open about his dynastic plans.[24] Caracalla, for example, was not named successor until 196 when he was eight and co-Augustus with his father two years later. Domna's profile was enhanced too. In 204, while her husband and sons presided over the Saecular Games in Rome, sacrificing and participating in processions, Domna as Julia Augusta with 109 matrons took part in a banquet to female deities called the Sellisternia.[25]

Domna and Plautianus, Severus' ambitious and manipulative praetorian prefect, loathed each other. Plautianus routinely insulted her to Severus and 'conducted investigations into her conduct'. Oddly, Severus seems to have taken the slights to his wife on the chin. His indifference to Plautianus' impertinent disregard for her status infuriated Domna. She withdrew into the background and 'began to study philosophy and passed her days in the company of sophists'. She was, after all, supposedly 'one of Roman history's most famous women of culture'.[26]

Julia Domna's philosophical get-togethers must have been a blissful refuge from the difficulties she experienced at court. To what extent Domna's philosophical group amounted to anything of significance remains unresolved. Almost none of the members is known today though she may well have been an important patron to those who participated. These certainly included the sophist Philostratus. His biographical work about the itinerant first-century Greek Pythagorean philosopher Apollonius of Tyana was supposedly commissioned by Domna, though she did not live to see it finished. The introduction to the work credits Domna but sets her support in the past. Philostratus claimed: 'I belonged to the circle of the empress, for she was a devoted admirer of all rhetorical exercises; and she commanded me to recast and edit these essays.'[27]

Domna's meetings with philosophers may have been far less formal than the reference suggests. Philostratus' work is almost entirely unverified and may be partly or even largely fiction. Apollonius is depicted as a kind of philosopher superhero with miraculous powers, blurring him into quasi-messianic status.[28] The account of his life borders on entertaining mythology, which makes it hard to know what Domna's interest in Apollonius really was. The wildly varying, even bewilderingly different, interpretations available in modern works only serve to show just how futile it is to speculate since it is quite clear no conclusive solution exists or ever will.[29]

Caracalla resolved the problem of the insolent praetorian prefect Plautianus by killing him. He had been married to Plautianus' daughter Plautilla (whom Caracalla loathed, not surprisingly), in 205.[30] In fact Caracalla had set Plautianus up by manufacturing evidence to suggest that the prefect had been planning to kill him and his father. Domna was delighted by the outcome. With Plautianus out of the way there was a better chance she could exert the sort of influence over her husband that a woman of her station and background regarded as her right. Plautilla was dealt with by the usual method of disposing of inconvenient women, pioneered by Augustus and Tiberius. She was sent into exile and eventually killed.

For all her intelligence and eastern sophistication, Julia Domna met her comeuppance in Britain during Severus' campaign there in 208–11. The imperial court was based in York during the protracted and frustrating efforts to conquer Caledonia (Scotland). This involved episodic bouts of negotiation with tribal leaders. During one such encounter Julia Domna mocked British women for being shared amongst tribal men. The wife of the Caledonian leader Argentocoxus supposedly snapped back by announcing that whereas British women were able to consort with the best men, Roman women were secretly debauched by the 'vilest'.[31] The anecdote is so sharp, and so unusual, that it is tempting to believe it is true.[32]

Julia Domna was still in Britain when Severus expired at York in early 211, worn out by illness and war and warned of his impending death by a litany of portents.[33] Domna would soon find herself trying desperately to deal not with a disputed succession but with the fact that her sons could not, would not, rule together. The flaw in Severus' plan for Caracalla and Geta to rule together was that they hated each other. When the two decided to divide the Empire up between them Domna was mortified and asked them how they proposed to divide her between them. She resorted to a melodramatic tirade in which she suggested they kill her and cut her body up.[34] The histrionic display worked, illustrating the enormous influence she could exert, and the scheme was abandoned. However, as the story about Domna is only recounted by Herodian it is possible he based at least some of it on what he had read about the similar one involving Agrippina and Nero.[35] Domna of course had the very different problem of juggling the sensibilities and selfishness of two sons, though between them their existence entitled her to a position of power.

Domna was not acting out of philanthropic concern for the peoples of the Empire, any more than Agrippina the Younger was driven by the same motive. One thing both women valued more than anything else was being at the top and holding on to their exalted status. Keeping their errant sons under control was an essential part of the process. Agrippina at least had only one son to deal with, not that it did her any good in the end. Domna's predicament was altogether more complicated. The sparring between her sons could only end in tears, and so it did. In 212 Caracalla organized the murder of Geta in his mother's arms.[36]

Domna remained as an adviser to Caracalla, and was placed in charge of much of his correspondence as well as being incorporated into acclamations of loyalty by the army. The murder of Geta had left Caracalla content that he was emperor. His mother therefore retained a pre-eminent position in his regime; indeed, she might actually have been relieved. There was no need to continue as adjudicator and she was still Augusta.[37] If Domna was devastated about Geta's death she set her grief to one side, kept calm and carried on. Even if that suited her purpose, it was still a performance that would have gone down well in the grand Roman tradition of stoic matrons. From a modern perspective her behaviour seems almost beyond belief, but the real issue is whether she had any alternative beyond suicide. A bizarre story in the biography of Caracalla, composed probably in the fourth century, has it that she was not only really his stepmother but also that she solicited his sexual attentions resulting in an incestuous marriage between them. Presumably also inspired by the stories about Agrippina and Nero, the tale can be disregarded but still belonged to a tradition in which 'history' was used to damage Domna's reputation.[38]

The deceased Severus had been very keen to make his mark on Roman history. As far as he was concerned the Severans were there to stay; since his rule had apparently been preordained the logical thing to do was to use propaganda to publicize his family so that no one would be left in any doubt. It was precisely this focus on the bloodline that was to provide his sister-in-law Julia Maesa with an opportunity. He issued an important and unusual series of dynastic coins that included either his wife, or his sons, or all three, as reverse types. Severus was the first emperor to oversee a series of coins that promoted the 'concept of the imperial house', though some of the inspiration came from Julio-Claudian issues.[39] One of the most radical designs featured Domna, face-on, in the middle of the reverse, flanked by opposed profile portraits of Caracalla and Geta.[40] The purpose was clearly to advertise the boys as the sons of an honourable and laudable empress, and thereby enhance their own virtues. It recalled some of the coins produced by Augustus depicting Julia the Elder and her sons Gaius and Lucius two centuries earlier. Another used Domna's portrait for the obverse and opposed profile images of her sons on the reverse.[41]

Julia Domna also featured on a wide range of coins struck in her sole name during the reigns of her husband and sons. These advertised her as an integral part of the regime in a way no previous empress had been and also borrowed extensively from ideas pioneered by the Julio-Claudians. The Severan coinage programme reflected a further evolution of the image of empresses begun under the Antonine emperors in which they were much more likely to be represented on issues of coinage in their own names and during their lifetimes. Their qualities and attributes were used to enhance the emperor's by association, and the monarchical nature of his rule, thereby forming part of wider Severan propaganda. Under the Severans the issues for the women were more extensive than ever before, showing how important it was to utilize those virtues. Named as Julia Augusta under Severus, Domna was promoted implicitly as a new Livia, but even Livia had not acquired the title until after Augustus' death. The coin designs and reverse types conflated Domna's identity with key Roman goddesses such as Ceres, Juno and Vesta, as well as eastern divinities.

In Rome, either under Severus or Caracalla, repairs to the Temple of Vesta in the Forum were carried out in Domna's name. This work linked her once more to Livia, Livia's restoration of several other ancient temples associated with female cults, and the wider Severan programme of moral revival propaganda and legislation derived from the Augustan model. The extant (heavily restored) partial structure visible today is largely attributable to her work (plates 17, 18).[42] This was also commemorated on a silver denarius that depicted Domna sacrificing in front of the distinctive round and domed temple.[43] Moreover, these coins publicized more than any other medium Julia Domna's habitual use of elaborate braided wigs, similar examples of which were worn by her sister and nieces (plates 29–31). Domna featured prominently in imperial sculpture and is still visible today on the Arch of Septimius Severus in the imperial forum, and nearby on the Arch of the Moneychangers (Porta Argentarii). The use of Aeternitas (Eternity, Stability) as an associated theme on many of the dynastic coins was an indication of Severus' dynastic expectations.[44]

After Severus' death in 211, Domna was rebranded as *mater augustorum* (Mother of the Emperors) on a coin produced before Geta's murder in 212, depicting her as the eastern mother goddess Cybele. She was later associated with Venus Genetrix on an issue that implied a blatantly fraudulent Julio-Claudian-type descent of her own from Venus.[45] Her titles also changed to an incongruous blurring of traditions. Domna was made *mater senatus mater patriae*, 'Mother of the Senate, Mother of the Nation'.[46] She now became Julia Pia Felix Augusta, the Pia ('dutiful') and the Felix ('fruitful', or 'auspicious') being more normally associated with emperors from the mid-second century on. The Pia Felix title makes it possible to distinguish coins struck in her name under Caracalla from those struck under Severus. Pia Felix was perhaps a way of implying that Domna had absorbed and was continuing her husband's attributes as emperor just as Livia had sought to present herself as the living embodiment of Augustus' qualities after his death. In Britain, amongst other places, military dedications were made both to Caracalla and to her as 'Mother of our Emperor, likewise of the army, Senate and the nation', matched in coin legends.[47] Many of these titles, whether granted her under Severus or Caracalla, were unprecedented.[48]

When Caracalla was murdered in 217, an inevitable outcome given the tyranny of his rule, Julia Domna was dismayed.[49] Rather than being overcome with sadness at the loss of her repulsive and violent son, she was rather more upset about losing the public life she so enjoyed. Her anxiety cut right to the heart of the problem faced by all-powerful Roman imperial women: they never possessed that power and status on their own terms. Those always and only came via a male. Without one to hand the widowed and childless Julia Domna was an irrelevance. The prospect of returning to the obscurity of a private existence appalled her so much that to begin with she promptly struck herself violently, probably exacerbating an existing cancerous breast tumour, and tried to take her own life by starving herself to death.[50]

Domna's suicide attempt failed but the new emperor, the incongruously promoted praetorian prefect Macrinus (217–18), turned out to be surprisingly accommodating, despite the fusillade of abuse that Domna directed at him. Macrinus allowed her to keep all the trappings he considered suitable for a dowager empress, including her retinue and praetorian escort. Unfortunately, that gave Domna the opportunity to start thinking about whether she could use these privileges as the basis of plotting and making herself sole ruler of the Roman world in her own right. She was inspired by the ancient queens of Mesopotamia, Semiramis and Nitocris.[51] This, at least, is what Dio says and it paints an interesting contrast with earlier depictions of her as the victim of her sons' ambitions and evil behaviour.

There was no prospect of a woman holding power in her own right any more now than there had ever been, for all the extravagant titles Domna had enjoyed over the last few years. Had Nero predeceased her, Agrippina the Younger would have found herself in the same situation. In any case, Julia Domna appears to have been dying of breast cancer and allegedly lost the will to live when she realized how unpopular Caracalla had been. She could not even live off his legacy and had no other son to use in his stead. She starved herself to death before the cancer could do its work.[52] It was a sad and ignominious end but at least it had the merit of being one Domna had chosen for herself.

Julia Domna's career left Dio musing on how great power brought no one happiness unless they enjoyed life for itself and had good fortune.[53] It was a lesson her sister Maesa and Maesa's daughters Soaemias and Mamaea took no notice of.[54] Maesa, who until this point had quietly orbited the outskirts of the inner imperial circle, living at the court in Rome since Severus became emperor, spotted that the time was ripe to make a move. Maesa was a determined and ambitious pragmatist as well as being sure of her superior status. As far as she was concerned Macrinus, the former praetorian prefect, was no more than an upstart equestrian. He insulted Maesa by ordering her to leave Rome and return to Syria. That was his first mistake. His second was to allow her to hold on to her huge wealth, acquired through her 'long period of association with imperial power'.[55] The wealth would play a significant part in what happened next. Relocating Maesa to Syria put her close to the vast eastern garrison, giving her the opportunity and means to mount a rebellion, making good Domna's inability to do so. In Maesa's elitist mind the idea of someone like Macrinus ruling amounted to a power vacuum she had every intention of filling, 'maintaining the pre-eminence of the family'.[56] Unlike her deceased sister she had two grandsons available to fill it. In the meantime Macrinus had negotiated a disadvantageous peace with the Parthians, whom Caracalla had been fighting. The terms severely dented his already limited popularity amongst the army. It was relatively easy for Maesa to drum up support for her elder grandson Bassianus, known to history as Elagabalus, who was named after his maternal great-grandfather.

Julia Maesa was, if her coin portraits are anything to go by, a grim-faced and humourless woman with all the charm of an ageing iceberg. The more unforgiving examples show her with a double chin and her hair (or wig) severely tied back and coiled on the back of her head. She had been married to a senator of proconsular rank called Julius Avitus, a man promoted by Severus, now deceased.[57] Having only had two daughters, Maesa's ill-weaved ambition ought to have got no further, but since both daughters had usefully each produced a son the way was open for the accession to jump a generation. Both her daughters were as greedy and as ambitious as Maesa; they were also widowed, which conveniently ruled out any ambitious husbands complicating their plans and was a hugely significant factor in what came next. Together the three proceeded with zealous and unanimous determination to turn the Roman world into their personal dominion.

Julia Soaemias' son was officially known as Varius Avitus Bassianus and had been born at Emesa in Syria in around 204 or 205.[58] The fatherless Bassianus was thus about fourteen years old when his grandmother Maesa decided that the Roman world would be better off under him than Macrinus. Bassianus, or Elagabalus as he is invariably known today, was a fanatical follower of the god Elagabalus (Heliogabalus) and came to believe that he and the deity were one and the same. Elagabalus served in the hereditary priesthood of the eponymous cult which was centred on a large conical sacred black stone, almost certainly the remains of a meteorite. The boy was considered to be extremely handsome and a showman who understood the musical and costumed theatre of the cult.[59] Maesa told the soldiers in the Syrian garrison that he was in reality Caracalla's illegitimate son which, as Elagabalus conveniently bore a passing resemblance to his cousin, was easy to believe.[60] He seemed altogether more appealing to the legions in the East than Macrinus. The soldiers had already been impressed by Elagabalus' religious activities. They were all the more inclined to fall for the scam because there was another rumour that Maesa was fabulously rich and was willing to share that wealth with the army if they restored her family to power.[61] Under the circumstances there was no need for them to consider their options further. On 16 May 218 Elagabalus was proclaimed emperor but with the pseudo-legitimate name of Marcus Aurelius Antoninus (reviving Caracalla's official name). Within a few weeks Macrinus' forces had been defeated and he had been killed. Ironically, the last known reference to the Temple of the Deified Augustus and Livia is dated just a few days later (plate 28).[62]

Perhaps Maesa should have considered the omens in the way the superstitious Severus would have done. On 7 October 218 a total eclipse of the sun commenced in southeastern Gaul and headed across northern Italy, over modern Bulgaria and through the middle of Asia Minor (Turkey) and eastern Syria. It was visible as a substantial partial eclipse over most of the Roman Empire. Dio regarded the event, and the appearance of a comet earlier in the year (which can be identified as the one known now as Halley's Comet, estimated to have appeared closest to Earth on 30 May 218), as clear indications that the 'evil and base' reign of Elagabalus had been foretold; but then he was writing with hindsight.[63] Elagabalus turned out to be an exceptionally loathsome individual and completely unsuited to imperial power. He was also soon spotted as no more than a medium for the women behind the throne.

Maesa embarked on a brazen display of female power. The considerable amount of coinage that now appeared in her name far exceeded the types produced for Agrippina the Younger, as had that of Julia Domna. Unlike Domna, Maesa was not even the wife of an emperor, but she was still styled Augusta on the coins. This was a radical development. The issues in her name began appearing almost as soon as those of Elagabalus and probably continued after his death in 222. The types are conventional but Maesa was being seamlessly associated with a series of appropriate Roman goddesses and divine female personifications such as Juno, Pudicitia and Venus Victrix.[64] The emphasis on Pudicitia was a particularly self-conscious throwback. Soaemias' coinage, which was less extensive than her mother's, was more explicitly divinely dynastic, hers being dominated by Venus Caelestis ('Heavenly Venus').[65] In the province of Moesia Inferior local coins were issued that recalled some of those of Nero and Agrippina, showing Elagabalus facing either his mother or grandmother on the obverse.[66]

A bizarre cavalcade set out for Rome in late 218 and made its way slowly from the East. Elagabalus, bedecked in finery and performing his eccentric rituals, called 'ridiculous motions' by Herodian, was the centrepiece but he had also his mother, his aunt and his grandmother in tow.[67] Maesa and her ostentatious, oriental-deity worshipping homosexual grandson were soon to discover that he had less chance of lasting as an emperor of Rome than she had of serving as a praetorian soldier. Maesa had already anticipated that Elagabalus' habit of wearing jewellery, a tiara and silk while being accompanied with flutes and drums might turn out to be a bad call. She tried to persuade her grandson to dress as a conventional Roman man of high status. But the new emperor had already stopped listening to his grandmother, if indeed he had ever started. He made Nero's resistance to Agrippina look lethargic and surrounded himself with sidekicks who had the same inclinations as himself. Ever the extrovert, Elagabalus sent to Rome in advance a huge picture of himself worshipping his god and ordered that it be placed in the Senate house. He also demanded that the new cult take precedence over all others.[68] Eventually in 219 the new emperor reached Rome, bringing with him the sacred stone of his eponymous cult. As it entered the city the new court and its entourage must have looked and sounded like an avalanche in a seraglio. At least Elagabalus had the wit to travel to the Senate in his grandmother's company, on the basis that she would enhance his own lack of authority.[69]

Sending his picture in advance at least helped to let the Romans know what to expect. They were less shocked than they might have been and meekly accepted Elagabalus' accession donative. A new temple was built and the theatrical cult rituals instigated, which involved vast numbers of animals sacrificed daily and Phoenician women dancing and playing instruments.[70] Overnight Rome started looking like the headquarters of a supercharged oriental despot from some outlandish myth. Appropriately enough the Romans nicknamed him 'The Assyrian'. Elagabalus compounded his weirdness by contemplating having his genitals amputated as part of his preference for effeminacy, but decided in a moment of uncharacteristic restraint to desist. He contented himself instead with his own circumcision and that of his cult associates as part of the rituals.[71]

Like many regimes ruled by someone hopelessly unsuited to power, arbitrary executions followed, as did a fleeting attempt at a conventional marriage (to Julia Cornelia Paula), before Elagabalus disgusted Roman tradition by marrying a Vestal Virgin called Aquileia Severa. For good measure he 'married' Minerva to his Sun God. It was Elagabalus' attempt at a symbolic union of the Roman and Eastern cults. To the Romans it looked like a full-scale assault on all they held dear. Although Elagabalus seems genuinely to have had some interest in Aquileia he allegedly still indulged in his predilection for being the passive member in homosexual relationships. Of course, there is inevitably a need for some caution. Depicting Elagabalus as someone who violated Roman traditions, especially a Vestal Virgin, was a useful symbolic tactic for Dio and Herodian and revived memories of the effeminate moral degeneracy of earlier emperors. It had echoes of how Nero had 'debauched the Vestal Virgin Rubria'.[72]

Elagabalus was in his element. Unfortunately, no one else was, including his grandmother. Spotting the outrage this marriage had caused, together with all the other disturbingly eccentric behaviour, a seriously worried Maesa finally stepped in. She decided to conjure up a face-saving diversion in order to strengthen the dynasty. Maesa forced her eccentric grandson to divorce Aquileia Severa and marry the far more suitable, but older, Annia Faustina in 221. This young woman was descended from Marcus Aurelius, which ought to have helped confer some sort of dynastic integrity and continuity, yet again through the female line. At the very least the union might have given Elagabalus' official name some sort of credibility. Poor Annia turned out to count for nothing. Maesa's plans evaporated when Elagabalus abandoned Annia and returned, in a manner of speaking, to Aquileia.[73]

In the meantime, Soaemias' main interest was increasing her power and influence, regardless of Elagabalus' behaviour. She soon took a seat at centre stage. Soaemias was said to have been the first woman openly to attend the Senate, 'as if she belonged to the senatorial order'. Livia and Agrippina had not needed to. Agrippina listened to senatorial proceedings but was not seen. What might have passed for 'normal' in the East was a scandal in Rome. Soaemias' alleged appearance in the Senate led to the unprecedented establishment of a 'women's senate' which she presided over, ensuring the passage of decrees that determined all sorts of rules of precedence and sumptuary laws for women.[74] The idea of a female senate, if one existed at all, must have been Maesa's and remains therefore an indication of the sheer chutzpah these remarkably ambitious women displayed. Considering that Elagabalus despised senators, sneering at them as 'slaves in togas', it was not perhaps quite the radical honour it might have seemed.[75] Nonetheless, it was all starting to look as if Rome was being ruled by a would-be woman who was under the influence of other women, and who was facilitating a takeover by women. The story was clearly designed to invoke outrage and in that respect is not necessarily wholly true. It may at least in part owe its detail to a general feeling of more nebulous contemporary anxiety at Maesa and Soaemias' behaviour and their intrusion into public affairs.[76]

If Maesa was unlucky in her independent-minded grandson, he was arguably unluckier in his grandmother since she was ambitious in a way he was not. Maesa could see where Elagabalus' antics would inevitably lead. He could not, and nor did he care. Ever able to see what really mattered, at least to her, Maesa knew that if Elagabalus was toppled she would have to return to ordinary private life, not least because there was no line of succession. So appalling was this prospect that she decided to try and persuade her rouge-caked popinjay of a grandson to adopt his cousin, Mamaea's son Alexianus, who was about four years Elagabalus' junior. As an alternative Alexianus was a really rather more appealing option, even if he was still little more than ten or eleven years old.[77] With Maesa and Soaemias on either side of him Elagabalus adopted Alexianus and wittily congratulated himself on suddenly becoming the father of a son already so grown.[78] In fact, unknown to him the adoption was part of Maesa's scheme to get rid of Elagabalus permanently, along with Soaemias who had so actively encouraged the sun-worshipping cult and Elagabalus' freakish behaviour. One might speculate at this point if Agrippina had survived into the latter part of Nero's reign whether she could have come to a similar conclusion. The key difference of course is that Maesa had an alternative available, though Agrippina had taunted Nero with the prospect of transferring her support to her stepson Britannicus before Nero had him murdered. If Elagabalus ever thought of killing his cousin he did not act fast enough.

Elagabalus had high hopes that Alexianus, now renamed more evocatively as Alexander, could be drawn into his own notorious activities. He was to be soundly disappointed even though the boy was easily led. Alexander's mother Mamaea stepped in and made sure her son was properly educated to prepare him for rule. He was already more popular with the army than his flamboyant cousin. Needless to say Elagabalus tried to put a stop to that immediately by expelling his cousin's teachers.[79] Mamaea took precautions to protect her son from poisoning and started secretly sending money to the Praetorian Guard.[80] The ever-watchful grandmother Maesa took steps to thwart any further scheming by the increasingly anxious Elagabalus. The turning point came when the emperor came to the Castra Praetoria and promised to punish any soldier who supported Alexander. He might perhaps have more usefully spent his time commissioning some sort of plan to kill his grandmother and aunt. In the event he had neither the wit nor the henchmen to do that for him. He attempted to placate the suspicious soldiers by putting on a pretence of familial unity, attending the Senate with his grandmother and allowing her to sit in the chamber. But within hours Elagabalus and Soaemias were dead, their bodies allegedly mutilated and ignominiously hurled into sewers that fed into the Tiber. The story may well be true but reporting that the bodies of villains were disposed of in this fashion is fairly routine in ancient sources, and might form part of a rhetorical degradation.[81]

Maesa remained at the helm, albeit at the price of one daughter and one grandson. It was plain to everyone, and especially the Praetorian Guard, that their new emperor was completely under the control of his mother and grandmother. Severus Alexander was 'naturally gentle and docile', making him a far more compliant individual than Nero had proved 180 years earlier.[82] He was by far and away the youngest emperor to accede since the beginning of the principate. It was scarcely surprising therefore that he had no chance of ruling on his own. This was really the reign of Maesa and Mamaea. Nevertheless, doubtless in an effort to reverse the faux pas of the female 'senate' under Elagabalus, a decree was issued that banned in perpetuity a woman ever attending the Senate again, on pain of death for any man who allowed such a thing.[83] This was, therefore, a much more carefully stage-managed accession which had all the appearance and propriety of a conventional reign under an emperor.

A far more appealing boy, Severus Alexander enjoyed a much greater level of popularity than his cousin. Maesa and Mamaea attempted to do a genuinely good job at restoring normal service. This was reinforced by Mamaea's spurious claim that her son was really Caracalla's.[84] A great deal of pressure was applied to Severus Alexander by his mother to focus on judicial business. This prevented him from falling under any bad influences or undesirables. It also had the beneficial effect that the general standard of government improved markedly.[85] The dominance of the two women did not do Severus Alexander any favours with the army in the long run but he was helped by Maesa's death in or around 224–6. By then she and Mamaea had overseen the restoration of the old traditional cults and the installation of government and administration under competent and experienced men.[86] One wonders why this had not been done in the first place. Perhaps it took Elagabalus' reign to make Maesa and Mamaea realize that they had to play the game by the rules; not playing by the rules had been a huge mistake made by Agrippina the Younger.

In the event Julia Maesa died a natural death of old age. She was probably little more than about sixty. As well as being the sister-in-law of Septimius Severus she had managed the remarkable and unique feat of being an aunt to two emperors and grandmother to two more, all four of whom were murdered (the fourth not until a decade later). Maesa was awarded full honours and deification which, given her political machinations, was a considerable achievement. Without Maesa's controlling influence Mamaea was let loose. It was a fatal turn of events that would bring the Severan dynasty to an end, though the rocky road to disaster would take another ten years. Mamaea's behaviour was only one of a series of mounting problems, which most of all involved an arrogant and unruly army increasingly inclined to act as it pleased.

Mamaea's coins, which were produced in vast numbers, portray a kindly looking woman, her hair (or wig) tightly bound up and carefully braided into parallel rows.[87] Despite the positive side of her influence, she proved to be a jealous and domineering mother, which in the context of her family was scarcely unexpected. She was determined to protect herself and her son. Alexander was contained almost under house arrest to keep him safe from bad influences, which meant almost anything or anyone except his mother. Indeed, he was known generally as Alexander Mamaeae ('Alexander, son of Mamaea'),[88] in Roman terms a deliberately demeaning title which evoked the traditional connotations of effeminacy. Even Nero escaped being known as Nero Agrippinae, at least so far as we know. Mamaea was also greedy, hoarding money while claiming she was saving it so her son could make a present of it to the army.[89] Becoming rich seems to have been a preoccupation of the Severan women, though of course accusing powerful women of greed was a favourite pastime of Roman historians since it proved their effeminate degeneracy.

Mamaea forced Alexander to divorce his wife, who enjoyed the epic name Gnaea Seia Herennia Sallustia Barbia Orbiana, and had her banished to Africa. She had also denied Orbiana the title Augusta, which she held herself, even though she had chosen Orbiana personally. Orbiana's father had objected to how she was being treated, which was reasonable enough but earned him his execution. That ended any immediate prospect of a legitimate heir, but Mamaea could not stand the way Orbiana was gaining influence over Alexander. It was the same sort of jealousy that helped destroy Agrippina the Younger when Poppaea appeared on the scene. This illustrated another key problem for women like Agrippina and Mamaea. Their dependence on a male figure through whom to exercise their power meant they could neither share nor lose him without being destroyed. Mamaea was particularly resentful that Orbiana had the title Augusta instead of her.[90] Mamaea's 'pride and avarice', as Edward Gibbon described her failings, were the cause of Severus Alexander's downfall, exposing both him and her to 'public ridicule'.[91] The banishment at least saved Orbiana's life, but Alexander was no Nero. He stood meekly by and acceded to his mother's wishes. It was a bad sign. If he had been more of a Nero, which would not have taken much, he might have lasted longer. But then this was a young man who had built his mother her own dedicated suites of apartments in the imperial palace which remained known for generations later as the 'ad Mammam'.[92]

Alexander's undoing was the outbreak of war in the East when the Persians under Ardashir attacked. He set out with a great expedition to meet the enemy host. Bad luck and a surprise Persian attack were serious problems, compounded by his lack of experience. Herodian wondered whether Alexander had been held back by Mamaea from more daring action.[93] Defeat followed but oddly Ardashir withdrew and the Romans recovered Mesopotamia. A morale-boosting triumph was held in Rome in 233. Nonetheless, Alexander's reputation had been fatally damaged. The following year he and Mamaea headed to the Rhine with the eastern legions to see off a threat from the Alamanni. Alexander's solution was to try and pay the German tribesmen off rather than fight them. That left his army feeling humiliated so they chose a giant of a man called Maximinus Thrax from amongst their own number to be emperor instead. Maximinus effortlessly brought the army onside with an accession donative and offering to double their pay, as well as bonus payments in cash and kind.[94]

These events took the Severan dynasty full circle. A huge former Thracian strongman, Maximinus had been handpicked by Septimius Severus for the Praetorian Guard several decades earlier, so impressed had he been by his size and strength. Some of the eastern troops that Alexander had brought turned against him and killed the young emperor and his mother in 235 in a tent in a military camp near Moguntiacum (Mainz).[95] They also killed anyone else they believed to be friends or favourites of Severus Alexander. The way was now open for Maximinus. Herodian, who otherwise approved of Severus Alexander, said his premature death was down to his mother's greed and meanness.[96] Severus Alexander and Mamaea were, oddly, remembered fondly. The young emperor was deified. His birthday was commemorated with a feast day thereafter in his name and also his mother's.[97]

The 'temporary projection' of the Severan women on to Roman power was over. Like the Julio-Claudian women the Severan empresses had known that their power relied entirely on the possession and control of a male who could hold the formal positions of an emperor. Julia Maesa treated her grandsons like pawns and got away with it, though had she survived another decade it is all but certain she would have been killed along with Mamaea and Severus Alexander in 235. She was an opportunist who saw with precision just how conveniently circumstances had played into her hands. Her daughters were no less ambitious. Like Messalina and Agrippina the Younger though they failed to take account of the factors beyond their control. Elagabalus was not the puppet he was supposed to be, and was so conspicuously unsuitable to be emperor that his reign could not last. Worse, he pushed the army (and that means mainly the Praetorian Guard) beyond its limits of tolerance. By the third century the army was the principal deciding factor when it came to who was emperor; this was a process which had begun under the Julio-Claudians but now it surpassed all other forces. Severus Alexander had a better chance but his acquiescence to his mother's wishes and his military failures signed his death warrant too. Neither Elagabalus nor Severus Alexander, for entirely different reasons, had succeeded in satisfying the soldiers' requirements and expectations.

Maesa and her daughters had been deliberate and concerted in their pursuit of power. They came closer than any of their Julio-Claudian forebears to controlling the state. But the fate of Soaemias and Mamaea showed that nothing really had changed. Roman imperial women could exert enormous power but they could only do so if they had a compliant man available to fill the formal post of emperor. That created a paradox. The sort of emperor they needed was unacceptable to the army, just as Nero had been in the end. By the early third century the army was emerging as consistently the most decisive factor in regime change. Dynasties and blood counted for nothing. As a result the Severan women remained entirely unable to hold onto power in their own right. That was something Agrippina would surely have discovered herself had Nero not killed her. It was a feature of the Roman system that remained more or less a permanent characteristic.

What followed were decades of brutal reigns with one soldier emperor after another and his henchmen wiping out his predecessor before being murdered himself. Even the muscle-bound superman thug Maximinus I (235–8) would barely last three years. Few of their empresses made any impact on the jumbled and disjointed history of the era and those that did are little known to us beyond their names. Maximinus' wife Paulina probably died shortly after his accession. She features only on a small number of posthumous coins tentatively dated to his reign. Furia Sabinia Tranquillina, empress of Gordian III (238–44), was the daughter of the praetorian prefect Timesitheus (or Timistheus) but what happened to her when her husband was murdered remains a mystery. Marcia Otacilia Severa, empress of Philip I (244–9), and Herennia Cupressenia Etruscilla (possibly related to Severus Alexander's wife Orbiana), empress of Trajan Decius (249–51), had no known impact on imperial politics.[98] The respective murders of their husbands and sons terminated any dynastic legacy they might have left and their fates are unknown.

Much the same applies to Cornelia Salonina, empress of Gallienus (253–68), and Ulpia Severina, empress of Aurelian (270–5),[99] the only other third-century empresses about whom we know anything. Cornelia Salonina earned for herself a similar reputation to Domna's, at least according to an ancient biography of the mid-third century Greek philosopher Plotinus, by his pupil Porphyry. Salonina and her husband 'honoured and venerated' Plotinus; they were apparently only stopped from supporting his plan to revive an abandoned 'city of philosophers' in Campania by opposition at court.[100] Gallienus was described elsewhere as an educated man with an interest in poetry and rhetoric.[101] This makes our sole source for Salonina's interest in philosophy marginally more credible but the truth is beyond us; the passage in Porphyry may be little more than a reworking of what had once been said about Domna.

The endless violent regime changes meant that dynasties virtually ceased to exist until the fourth century and the House of Constantine emerged. It is a moot point whether this descent towards anarchy would have happened anyway or whether the Severan women caused or exacerbated the problem. There is no question that seventeen years of being ruled by inexperienced young men whose mothers and grandmothers were really in charge did nothing to help the dynasty's image in the eyes of the soldiers. On the other hand, the Roman army and in particular the Praetorian Guard had been steadily becoming harder to control since the reign of Commodus. Septimius Severus' famous advice to his sons to live in harmony (which they ignored) and enrich the soldiers and scorn everyone else (which they did) had set the tone.[102]

When the Roman world emerged into some sort of daylight a century later it had become a very different place. The 'Dominate', established by Diocletian and which saw the Empire divided into an East and a West for the purposes of government and defence, mutated into a Christian regime under Constantine I (306–37). Imperial women retreated further into the background than ever before. Although Constantine issued many coins in the names of his mother Helena and his wife Fausta, his son Constantius II (337–61) issued none in the names of his empresses. However, the involvement in imperial affairs of Eusebia, empress of Constantius II, is known from comments made by the historian Ammianus Marcellinus and a panegyric composed by the emperor Julian II who was married to her sister-in-law Helena and created Constantius' heir in 355. Despite Julian's praise for Eusebia's learning and wisdom, Ammianus, who explicitly calls her *regina* ('queen'), alleged that in 357 the childless Eusebia had attempted to poison Helena and induce a miscarriage out of jealousy at her fertility. Whether this was true or not remains a matter for debate. Helena's miscarriages may have been natural, but the Roman historical tradition of attributing such events to the machinations of a calculating woman was perhaps too attractive to Ammianus to ignore. The empresses of Valentinian I (364–75) and his brother Valens (364–78) are little known. It would not be until the reign of Theodosius I (379–95) that an empress was honoured on the coinage again. His empress Aelia Flaccilla (d. 386) was, however, featured on coins with only one reverse legend, *Salus Rei Publicae*, 'the Health of the Republic'.[103] In a Christian empire it was impossible to associate her with a portfolio of pagan qualities and attributes, even though her motherhood of Arcadius (383–408, ruler of the Eastern Empire 395–408) and Honorius (393–423, ruler of the Western Empire 395–423) secured the succession.

Nonetheless, women had been restored to a more conspicuous role in the image of the imperial state even if the coins were vapid and innocuous. Arcadius' daughter Aelia Pulcheria (who lived 399–453) proved to be a powerful political player in the Eastern Empire and its capital Constantinople. She ruled as regent for her brother Theodosius II (402–50) who was only seven when his father died in 408. His shortcomings as emperor meant that Aelia Pulcheria effectively ruled the Eastern Empire in his stead throughout the reign. She even chose and married his successor, Marcianus. However, the blandness of her coins gives little indication of her influence or official identity. Honorius struck no coins for either of his empresses but Pudicitia had not been forgotten. The late Roman poet Claudian wrote an *epithalamium* for the first, Maria (who was also Honorius' cousin), on her wedding day in 398. Having described how Maria exceeded 'Livia of old' and other women of the imperial house in beauty, Claudian went on to explain that she had learned from her mother Serena how 'to follow the example of *prisca pudicitiae* ['old world chastity']. Venus 'arrives' shortly afterwards to admire Maria's 'loveliness' and exhort her to be the progenitor of the next generation of the dynasty as the mother of a 'little Honorius'.[104] It is clear that complimenting an imperial woman of late antiquity meant comparing her in the first place to Livia, the enduring template of traditional female moral rectitude.

The most important of the later empresses was Aelia Galla Placidia (lived *c.* 388–450), daughter of Theodosius I, half-sister of Arcadius and Honorius, wife of the short-lived Constantius III (421) when she became Augusta, and mother of Valentinian III (425–55) for whom she ruled as regent till he came of age in 437, making her 'the ruler of the West'.[105] It was the first time a Roman empress ruled alone and unchallenged, though as ever it was only very special circumstances that had allowed this. It is likely she had been brought up in much the same way as Julia the Elder four centuries earlier, but little is known about much of her life.[106] Bearing a dynastic significance unmatched since Agrippina the Younger, the widowed Galla Placidia nonetheless died a natural death after retiring into a life of Christian devotion. In her time she witnessed what amounted to a Christian version of *pudicitia* in which some women renounced sexuality in preference for a life of virtuous virginity, even once widowed.[107] A conspicuous state of piety could be synonymous with power in the late Roman Christian state, just as *pudicitia* had been an integral part of Livia's authority and influence in government.

Galla Placidia's coins, like those of other empresses of the period, served no purpose other than to act as a mechanism of exchange, bearing for the most part just the *Salus Rei Publicae* legends on the reverses.[108] The obverses labelled her clearly as *D(omina) N(ostra)* and *Augusta*. For obvious reasons she was never linked on the coins to the Venus Genetrix lineage claimed by the pagan empresses, even though Claudian's poem to Maria showed that an empress's association with Venus was far from forgotten even if only as an allegorical figure. Instead, on some coins Galla Placidia is shown wearing the Christian chi-rho symbol on her shoulder, showing that her authority and status came from God.[109] Her son Valentinian III's coins dominated those issued at the time and depicted him as an adult emperor from the outset.

Galla Placidia's daughter Justa Grata Honoria (*c.* 417/18–455) turned out to be another imperial princess who failed to live up to expectations. Given her mother's qualities, Honoria's behaviour recalled earlier times. In echoes of Julia the Elder and Messalina she had an affair in 449 with an imperial official called Eugenius. This time though the problem became even more serious. Valentinian III executed Eugenius and forced Honoria to marry a senator called Flavius Bassus Herculanus. Infuriated by this humiliating turn of events Honoria asked Attila the Hun to avenge her. Attila took this to be a proposal of marriage and demanded her along with half the Western Roman Empire as her dowry. Valentinian refused and prepared for war. Attila was defeated in 451 and died in 453, which fortunately ended the crisis. Honoria's fate is unknown but her curious story, depending on how much of it is true, seems to belong to a much older Roman tradition of depicting women as either bastions of perfection or irremediably bad and destabilizing.[110]

In a curious twist of fate a dynastic relief of Claudian date was found close to Galla Placidia's so-called tomb in Ravenna in the late fifteenth or early sixteenth century (plate 32). The stone depicts the deified Augustus, alongside

Livia as Venus Genetrix (she carries Eros on her shoulder), probably her son Nero Claudius Drusus, her grandson Germanicus, and an unknown female relative, perhaps Antonia Minor.[111] The relief is incomplete and it is likely that Claudius was originally depicted to the right of Augustus. It is impossible to prove a connection with Galla Placidia, since the building's identity as her mausoleum has never been confirmed and is disputed with good reason.[112] Nevertheless, the sculpture takes the story full circle. Livia's conspicuous presence on the artefact is a reminder that it was the Julio-Claudian and Severan women who remained the real and most visible phenomena in the imperial Roman state when it came to the public display of female power. Galla Placidia and other later empresses would have been only too aware of that.

The temporary prominence of the women of the Julio-Claudians and Severans, and likewise Galla Placidia, was mainly the result of chance and circumstance. The dynastic aspirations of Augustus and Severus, failed male bloodlines, underage emperors and the ambitions and abilities of the women all provided opportunities to bring them to the forefront of imperial politics. It was Livia above all who managed not only a partnership in power with Augustus but also to outlive him and control her son Tiberius in ways that infuriated him. Like all Roman women she operated within and without the Roman political system. She manipulated it in a way that would have been impossible for a man. Her level of involvement in male political institutions was unmatched and reflected her ability to take advantage of the opportunities fate had presented her with.[113] This is an important consideration. Women suffered from huge disadvantages in the Roman system, but some also enjoyed a lateral access to power and influence precisely because they were women. This is easily overlooked when focusing on the formal exclusion of women from political office. Nevertheless, when they shared power with emperors, sought power in their own right or simply asserted themselves, these women were exposed to the same or greater risks than the men. Both Julias, Messalina, the Agrippinas, Poppaea, Soaemias and Mamaea were variously executed, murdered or committed suicide, outcomes that befell so many of the Julio-Claudian or Severan emperors. It went with the territory. Had these women been the respectful, compliant and appreciative wives and mothers they were supposed to be they might well have died in their own beds instead.

Livia was the one Roman woman who came closest to power in her own right because she understood how to do that without sowing the seeds of her own destruction. She had many imitators but no equals. Livia also managed what she did because she had been able to absorb and radiate some of Augustus' special qualities. She did so with an idiosyncratic and potent brilliance. Nevertheless, Livia relied on the fact that she was the wife of a man who achieved supreme power in his own right and also the mother of his successor. Without those key qualifications Livia would probably have remained just another high-born Roman woman confined to the domestic politics of her household, supporting the political careers of her menfolk and engaging in the everyday pastimes considered suitable for a woman of her status.

Livia's statue alongside that of Augustus in their joint temple must have stood as a tantalizing challenge to women like Messalina, Agrippina the Younger, Poppaea and Julia Maesa (plate 28). Today, much of what we have left to attest to these remarkable individuals is the skewed and judgemental record of the Roman historians who preserved in such disparaging detail how the Roman world perceived women and their place in society. In their accounts these women found their greatest challenge. That says so much about the world they lived in, and by the same token our own where women are still presented with prejudice and obstacles their Roman forbears would recognize only too well. Above all, they understood that power has to be taken. No one was going to give them power, and everything would be done to deny it to them. Despite all the restrictions of Roman society they managed to buck the trends, assert themselves by using the opportunities open to them as women, and change the history of the Roman world for good or ill, even if many were made to pay a terrible price. In that sense they were all worthy of the epithet Venus Genetrix. That association symbolized how women existed at the very heart and essence of all that imperial Rome once was right back to its earliest beginnings. Venus herself gave birth to Aeneas and set the mythical origins of the Roman people on their course towards the future peace and greatness under Augustus that Jupiter had promised was their destiny. But it remained a man's world. Agrippina the Elder's 'impatience for equality' was never fulfilled. She waits still.

APPENDIX 1

KEY DATES

THE JULIO-CLAUDIANS (see Family Trees 1a, 1b, 2, 3)

44 BC	Assassination of Caesar
	Posthumous adoption of Octavian, officially renamed Gaius Julius Caesar
43/42 BC	Livia Drusilla marries Tiberius Claudius Nero
40 BC	Death of Gaius Claudius Marcellus, husband of Octavia
	Death of Fulvia, wife of Mark Antony
	Octavia married to Mark Antony
38 BC	Birth of Julia the Elder, daughter of Octavian/Augustus by Scribonia
	Scribonia, mother of Julia, divorced by Octavian
	Livia Drusilla divorces Tiberius Nero and marries Octavian
36 BC	Mark Antony openly living with Cleopatra VII
32 BC	Octavia divorced by Mark Antony
31 BC	Battle of Actium: Antony and Cleopatra defeated by Octavian
27 BC	Constitutional settlement creates Octavian's basis of power
	Octavian renamed Augustus
25 BC	Julia the Elder married to Marcus Marcellus
23 BC	Death of Marcus Marcellus
21 BC	Julia the Elder married to Agrippa

20 BC	Birth of Gaius Caesar, Julia's son by Agrippa
19 BC	Birth of Julia the Younger, Julia's daughter by Agrippa
18–17 BC	Lex Julia makes adultery a public offence
17 BC	Birth of Lucius Caesar, Julia's son by Agrippa
	Augustus adopts Gaius and Lucius Caesar, Julia's sons by Agrippa
14 BC	Birth of Agrippina the Elder, Julia's daughter by Agrippa
13 BC	Death of Drusus the Younger, Tiberius' son by Vipsania
12 BC	Death of Agrippa, widowing Julia the Elder
	Birth of Agrippa Postumus, Julia's son by Agrippa
11 BC	Tiberius forcibly married to Julia the Elder
	Death of Octavia, Augustus' sister
9 BC	Death of Livia's younger son Drusus the Elder (brother of Tiberius)
7 BC	Porticus of Livia dedicated
6 BC	Tiberius exiles himself to Rhodes, his marriage to Julia in tatters
4 BC	Gaius and Lucius Caesar made consuls-elect and *principes iuventutis*
2 BC	Julia the Elder's adulteries exposed; Julia exiled
1 BC	Tiberius seeks permission to return to Rome, but is denied
AD 2	Tiberius returns to Rome
	Death of Lucius Caesar, son of Julia the Elder and Agrippa
4	Death of Gaius Caesar, son of Julia the Elder and Agrippa
	Augustus adopts Agrippa Postumus and Tiberius
7	Agrippa Postumus banished to Planasia
8	Exile of Julia the Younger
12	Murder of Sempronius Gracchus, lover of Julia the Elder
14	Death of Augustus, accession of Tiberius
	Murder of Agrippa Postumus before Augustus' death announced
	Death (possible murder) of Julia the Elder
	Agrippina the Elder and Germanicus on campaign in Germany
15	Birth of Agrippina the Younger
19	Death of Germanicus
22	Livia falls ill
23	Death of Tiberius' son Drusus
25	Birth of Messalina, granddaughter of Octavia
29	Death of Livia
	Murder of Julia the Younger in exile

31	Murder of Nero Caesar, Agrippina and Germanicus' eldest son
	Fall of Sejanus
33	Death of Agrippina the Elder
	Murder of Drusus Caesar, Agrippina and Germanicus' second son
37	Death of Tiberius, accession of Caligula
	Birth of Agrippina the Younger's son Lucius Domitius Ahenobarbus
	Death of Antonia, mother of Claudius, grandmother of Caligula
37/38	Caligula recovers the remains of Agrippina for reburial
38	Deification of Drusilla, Caligula's sister, the first woman to receive it
39	Marriage of Messalina to Claudius
	Birth of Octavia, Claudius' daughter
41	Assassination of Caligula; accession of Claudius
	Deification of Livia
	Birth of Germanicus (after 43 called Britannicus), Claudius' son
	Execution of Messalina's stepfather Silanus
42	Vinicianus plot against Claudius
	Deification of Livia
43	Claudius invades Britain
48	Execution of Messalina
49	Agrippina the Younger marries Claudius
	Agrippina moves against her 'rival' Lollia Paulina and has her killed
	Recall of Seneca from exile at Agrippina's request
50	Adoption of Lucius Domitius Ahenobarbus, renamed Nero, by Claudius
	Agrippina named Augusta, the first as wife of a living emperor
	Caratacus accords Agrippina equal respect to Claudius
51	Nero named consul designate and *princeps iuventutis*
	Britannicus systematically marginalized at Agrippina's behest
52	Agrippina appears in a gold cloak at a mock naval battle
53	Marriage of Nero to Octavia, daughter of Claudius
54	Murder of Claudius by Agrippina

	Accession of Nero
	Murder of Britannicus
59	Murder of Agrippina on Nero's orders
62	Murder of Octavia, exiled on Pandateria
	Poppaea Sabina marries Nero
63	Birth and death of Claudia Augusta, Nero's daughter by Poppaea
65	Murder of Poppaea by Nero
68	Suicide of Nero: end of the Julio-Claudian dynasty
	Accession of Galba
69	Galba toppled, reign of Otho, reign of Vitellius, accession of Vespasian
69–79	Reign of Vespasian (wife deceased)
79–81	Reign of Titus (no empress)
81–96	Reign of Domitian (empress: Domitia Longina)
96–8	Reign of Nerva (no wife known)
98–117	Reign of Trajan (empress: Plotina)
117–38	Reign of Hadrian (empress: Sabina)
138–61	Reign of Antoninus Pius (empress: Faustina the Elder, d. 141)
161–80	Reign of Marcus Aurelius (empress: Faustina the Younger d. 175)
161–9	Co-ruled with Lucius Verus (empress: Lucilla, executed 182; d. 169)
180–92	Reign of Commodus (empress: Crispina m. after 182)

THE SEVERANS (see Family Tree 4)

192	Murder of Commodus
193	Accession and murder of Pertinax
	Accession and murder of Didius Julianus (empress: Manlia Scantilla)
	Accession of Septimius Severus (empress: Julia Domna)
198	Caracalla made joint emperor with his father Severus
209	Geta made joint emperor with his father and brother Caracalla
211	Death at York of Septimius Severus
	Severus' sons Caracalla and Geta rule on their own
212	Murder by Caracalla of Geta in their mother Domna's arms

APPENDIX 2

FAMILY TREES

The family trees divert from the normal practice with the Julio-Claudians which usually focuses on the emperors. The first four family trees (1a, 1b, 2, 3) show the lines of descent from Octavia, Livia and Julia the Elder, with a fifth tree (4) showing the Severan lines of descent from Julia Domna and Julia Maesa. The emperors therefore appear normally in subsidiary positions. In order to minimize repetition there are cross-references within the trees. For example, Julia the Elder's daughter Agrippina the Elder married Germanicus, grandson of Livia. Their descendants are shown in Tree 2 (the descent from Livia). A sixth family tree (5) has been included to show Galla Placidia's relationships with several emperors of the late fourth and early fifth centuries.

Creating the trees is complicated and involves not only judicious omissions but also a certain amount of guesswork. Some relationships are uncertain and some of the dates are only estimates. Not all dates are shown for space reasons. See the text, Appendix 3, and the Index for others. However, collectively they show the remarkable success enjoyed by Livia, from whom all the later Julio-Claudian emperors were descended, Octavia, from whom three were, Julia, from whom two were, and Julia Domna and her sister Maesa, from whom four Severan emperors were (two each).

Family Tree 1a. Octavia Minor and her descendants by her first marriage

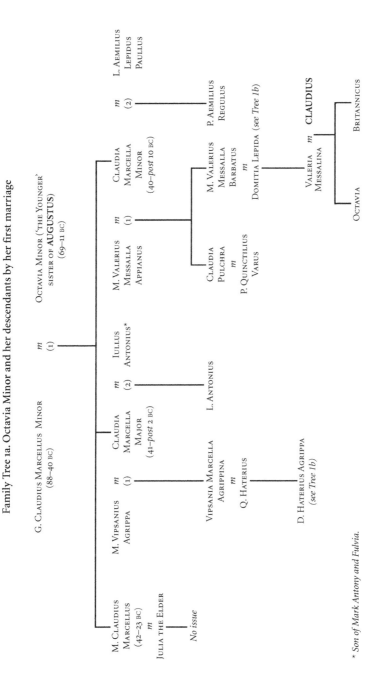

* Son of Mark Antony and Fulvia.

Family Tree 1b. Octavia Minor and her descendants by her second marriage

NERO CLAUDIUS DRUSUS
(see Tree 2 for the descent to CLAUDIUS and CALIGULA)

OCTAVIA MINOR ('THE YOUNGER' sister of AUGUSTUS)
(69–11 BC)

m

m (2)

MARK ANTONY
(83–31 BC)

ANTONIA MINOR
(36 BC–AD 37)

APPIUS JUNIUS SILANUS *m* (3) CLAUDIUS***

FAUSTUS CORNELIUS SULLA *m* (2) AELIA PAETINA

Descent from ANTONIA MINOR (see above and Tree 2)

ANTONIA MAJOR
(39 BC–?)

m

L. DOMITIUS AHENOBARBUS
(49 BC–AD 25)

M. VALERIUS MESSALLA BARBATUS *m* (1) DOMITIA LEPIDA

FAUSTUS CORNELIUS SULLA FELIX

CLAUDIA ANTONIA

m (2)

A boy, died young

D. HATERIUS AGRIPPA *m* (1) DOMITIA *m* (2) G. SALLUSTIUS* PASSIENUS CRISPUS

Gn. DOMITIUS AHENOBARBUS *m* AGRIPPINA THE YOUNGER

DOMITIA LEPIDA *m* (1) VALERIA MESSALINA

CLAUDIUS** (See Tree 1a) *m* VALERIA MESSALINA

D. HATERIUS AGRIPPA (see Tree 1a)

NERO
(37–68, r. 54–68)

---

* He divorced Domitia and married Agrippina the Younger.
(her second marriage). Domitia's full name is uncertain: see Appendix 3.

** The third marriage of Claudius.

*** The second marriage of Claudius between 28–31, before he became emperor.

N.B. Three of the four Julio-Claudian emperors after Augustus could trace their descent from Octavia: Caligula (see Tree 2), Claudius and Nero.

Family Tree 2. Livia and her descendants

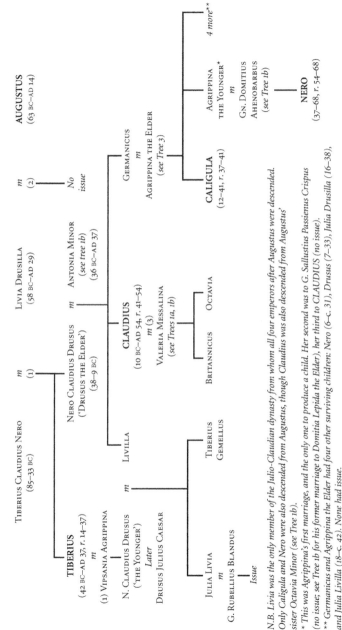

N.B. Livia was the only member of the Julio-Claudian dynasty from whom all four emperors after Augustus were descended. Only Caligula and Nero were also descended from Augustus, though Claudius was also descended from Augustus' sister Octavia Minor (see Tree 1b).

* This was Agrippina's first marriage, and the only one to produce a child. Her second was to G. Sallustius Passienus Crispus (no issue; see Tree 1b for his former marriage to Domitia Lepida the Elder), her third to CLAUDIUS (no issue).

** Germanicus and Agrippina the Elder had four other surviving children: Nero (6–c. 31), Drusus (7–33), Julia Drusilla (16–38), and Julia Livilla (18–c. 42). None had issue.

Family Tree 3. Julia the Elder and her descendants

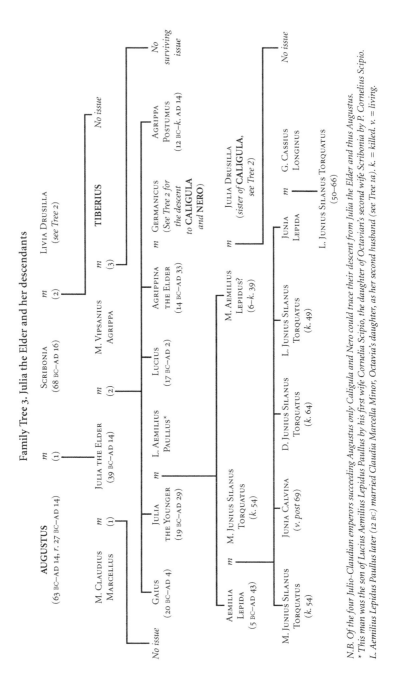

N.B. Of the four Julio-Claudian emperors succeeding Augustus only Caligula and Nero could trace their descent from Julia the Elder and thus Augustus.

* This man was the son of Lucius Aemilius Lepidus Paullus by his first wife Cornelia Scipio, the daughter of Octavian's second wife Scribonia by P. Cornelius Scipio. L. Aemilius Lepidus Paullus later (12 BC) married Claudia Marcella Minor, Octavia's daughter, as her second husband (see Tree 1a). k. = killed. v. = living.

Family Tree 4. The Severan women and their descendants

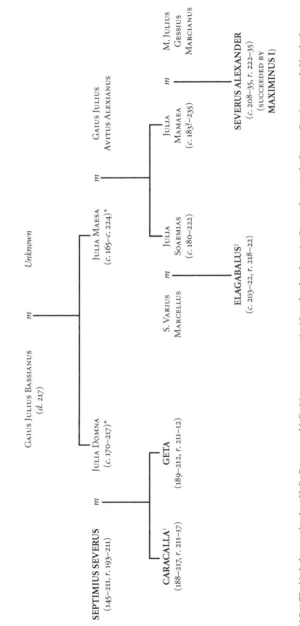

N.B. * The birth dates and order of Julia Domna and Julia Maesa are uncertain. Note also that from April 217 to June 218 the Roman Empire was ruled by the former praetorian prefect Marcus Opellius MACRINUS.

[1] Birth name [Lucius?] Septimius Bassianus. Official name Marcus Aurelius Antoninus.

[2] Birth name Varius Avitus Bassianus. Official name Marcus Aurelius Antoninus.

Family Tree 5. The family of Aelia Pulcheria and Aelia Galla Placidia

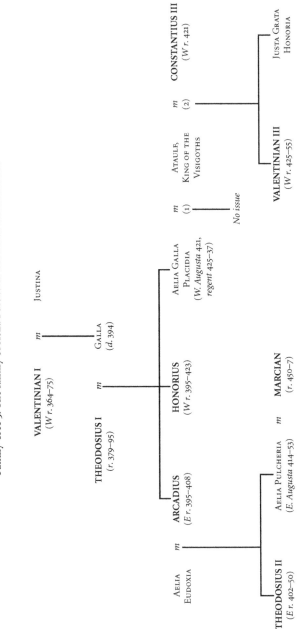

E = Eastern Empire, W = Western Empire

APPENDIX 3

KEY FEMALE PERSONALITIES

This appendix summarizes the dynastic and family connections of the key female personalities mentioned in this book. Some minor characters have been included to help clarify any confusion that might arise from the similarity of so many names. Some of the dates are approximate and some are unknown.

1. The Late Republic (in alphabetical order)

Cleopatra VII (69–30 BC). Rank: pharaoh of Egypt. Marriages: (1) Ptolemy XIII; (2) Ptolemy XIV; (3) Julius Caesar; (4) Mark Antony. Children: Caesarion (by 3), Alexander Helios, Cleopatra Selene, Ptolemy Philadelphus (by 4). Death: suicide or assassination.

Cornelia Africana (c. 190–c. 100 BC). Parents: Publius Cornelius Scipio Africanus and Aemilia Paulla. Marriage: Tiberius Sempronius Gracchus. Children: Tiberius Gracchus, Gaius Gracchus, Sempronia (plus nine others who died in childhood). Death: natural.

Fulvia (83–40 BC). Marriages: (1) P. Clodius Pulcher; (2) Scribonius Curio; (3) Mark Antony. Children: P. Clodius Pulcher, Clodia Pulchra (by 1); M. Antonius Antyllus, I. Antonius (by 3). Death: natural (after 40 BC). Her children were raised by Octavia after her marriage to Antony.

Sempronia (*fl.* first century BC). Marriage: Decimus Junius Brutus (consul 77 BC). Children: Decimus Junius Brutus Albinus (tyrannicide: Caesar). Death: unknown. Not to be confused with the daughter of Cornelia Africana (q.v.), or the mother of Fulvia (q.v.).

2. The Julio-Claudians (in alphabetical order)

Agrippina the Elder (14 BC–AD 33). Daughter of Julia the Elder and Agrippa, granddaughter of Augustus and step-granddaughter of Livia. Marriage: Germanicus. Children: Nero, Drusus, Agrippina the Younger, Julia Drusilla, Julia Livilla. Death: in prison.

Agrippina the Younger (Julia Agrippina) (15–59). Rank: Augusta and Empress of Rome (CLAUDIUS). Daughter of Agrippina the Elder and Germanicus. Sister of Caligula. Marriages: (1) Gnaeus Domitius Ahenobarbus; (2) G. Sallustius Passienus Crispus; (3) CLAUDIUS. Children: L. Domitius Ahenobarbus (the emperor NERO (by 1)).

Antonia Major (39 BC–?). Daughter of Octavia and Mark Antony. Marriage: L. Domitius Ahenobarbus. Children: Domitia, Gn. Domitius Ahenobarbus (father of NERO), Domitia Lepida (mother of Messalina q.v.). Grandmother of NERO. Death: unknown.

Antonia Minor (36 BC–AD 37). Rank: Augusta (applied posthumously under CLAUDIUS). Daughter of Octavia and Mark Antony. Marriage: Nero Claudius Drusus (son of Livia). Children: Germanicus, Livilla, CLAUDIUS. Grandmother of CALIGULA, great-grandmother of NERO. Death: suicide.

Claudia Antonia (30–66). Daughter of Aelia Paetina and CLAUDIUS. Marriages: (1) Gn. Pompeius Magnus (killed on Messalina's orders); (2) Faustus Cornelius Sulla Felix (half-brother of Messalina through his mother Domitia Lepida). Declined a third marriage with NERO after the death of Poppaea. Death: executed for refusing NERO.

Claudia Marcella Major (41–post 2 BC). Elder daughter of Octavia and G. Claudius Marcellus. Sister of M. Claudius Marcellus (first husband of Julia the Elder). Marriages: (1) M. Vipsanius Agrippa; (2) Iullus Antonius (son of Fulvia and Mark Antony). Children: Vipsania Marcella Agrippina (1), Lucius Antonius (2). Death: unknown.

Claudia Marcella Minor (40–post 10 BC). Younger daughter of Octavia and G. Claudius Marcellus. Marriages: (1) M. Valerius Messalla Appianus; (2) L. Aemilius Lepidus Paullus. Children: Claudia Pulchra, M. Valerius Messalla Barbatus (father of Messalina – see Domitia Lepida) (by 1); P. Aemilius Regulus (by 2). Death: unknown.

Claudia Octavia (39–62). Empress of Rome (NERO). Daughter of Messalina and CLAUDIUS. Marriage: NERO. Death: killed in the manner of a suicide.

Claudia Pulchra (14 BC–AD 26). Daughter of Claudia Marcella Minor, grand-daughter of Octavia. Marriage: to the general P. Quinctilius Varus (d. AD 9). Death: natural.

Clodia Pulchra (c. 57–post 38 BC). Daughter of Fulvia and P. Clodius Pulcher. Wife of AUGUSTUS (as Octavian). Children: none. Death: unknown.

Domitia (8 BC–AD 59). Daughter of Antonia Major and L. Domitius Ahenobarbus. Marriages: (1) D. Haterius Agrippa (d. 32); (2) G. Sallustius Passienus Crispus, who divorced her to marry Agrippina the Younger. Children: Q. Haterius Antoninus (by 1). Death: possibly murdered on NERO's orders. N.B. this woman's full name was probably Domitia Lepida (Major) but she is only ever called Domitia by the sources. This distinguishes her from her younger sister Domitia Lepida (q.v.) who was thereby technically Domitia Lepida (Minor). The two are easily confused otherwise.

Domitia Lepida (5 BC–AD 54). Daughter of Antonia Major and L. Domitius Ahenobarbus. Marriages: (1) M. Valerius Messalla Barbatus; (2) Faustus Cornelius Sulla Lucullus (d. before 41); (3) Appius Junius Silanus (executed 42). Children: Messalina (by 1); Faustus Cornelius Sulla Felix (husband of Claudia Antonia) (by 2). Death: murdered on Agrippina's orders. N.B. this woman's elder sister was Domitia (q.v.), probably Domitia Lepida Major, so she is therefore sometimes referred to as Domitia Lepida Minor.

Julia Agrippina: see Agrippina the Younger

Julia Drusilla (16–38). Daughter of Agrippina the Elder and Germanicus. Sister of CALIGULA. Marriage: M. Aemilius Lepidus. Children: none. Death: natural.

Julia Livia (4–43). Daughter of Livilla and Drusus, son of Tiberius. Marriages: (1) Nero (son of Agrippina the Elder and Germanicus); (2) G. Rubellius

Blandus. Children (by 2): G. Rubellius Plautus, Rubellia Bassa. Death: executed by CLAUDIUS at Messalina's behest.

Julia Livilla (18–*c*. 42): Daughter of Agrippina the Elder and Germanicus. Sister of CALIGULA. Marriage: M. Vinicius. Children: none. Death: execution by starvation, though Messalina believed her husband had killed her to save her from further ignominy.

Julia the Elder (39 BC–AD 14). Daughter of AUGUSTUS by Scribonia. Marriages: (1) M. Claudius Marcellus (d. 23 BC); (2) M. Vipsanius Agrippa (d. 12 BC); (3) Tiberius. Children: Gaius, Julia the Younger, Lucius, Agrippina the Elder, Agrippa Postumus (all by Agrippa). Through Agrippina the Elder she was thus the grandmother of CALIGULA, and the great-grandmother of NERO. Death: in exile, from starvation.

Julia the Younger (19 BC–AD 29). Daughter of Julia the Elder and Agrippa. Marriage: L. Aemilius Paullus. Children: Aemilia Lepida, possibly M. Aemilius Lepidus. Death: murdered in exile.

Junia Calvina (*c*. 10–post 69). Great-great-granddaughter of AUGUSTUS via Julia the Elder, Julia the Younger, and Aemilia Lepida. Survived into the reign of VESPASIAN (69–79). Marriage: L. Vitellius the Younger. Children: unknown. Exiled by CLAUDIUS. Recalled by NERO. Death: unknown.

Livia Drusilla (58 BC–AD 29). Rank: Augusta (after AD 14), Empress of Rome. Marriages: (1) Tiberius Claudius Nero (div. 38 BC); (2) AUGUSTUS. Children: Tiberius, Nero Claudius Drusus by (1). No issue by (2). Death: natural.

Livilla (Claudia Livia Julia) (13 BC–AD 31). Daughter of Nero Claudius Drusus and Antonia Minor. Sister of CLAUDIUS and Germanicus. Marriage: Drusus, son of TIBERIUS. Children: Julia Livia, Tiberius Gemellus. Lover of Lucius Aelius Sejanus. Death: execution, or starvation enforced by her mother Antonia Minor.

Messalina (Valeria Messalina) (*c*. 17–48). Empress of Rome (CLAUDIUS). Daughter of Domitia Lepida and M. Valerius Messalla Barbatus, granddaughter of Antonia Major, great-granddaughter of Octavia. Marriage: CLAUDIUS. Children: Claudia Octavia, wife of NERO, Britannicus. Death: executed for bigamy and conspiracy.

Octavia (69–11 BC) (sometimes known as Octavia Minor, or the Younger, to differentiate her from her elder half-sister). Sister of AUGUSTUS (Octavian). Marriages: (1) G. Claudius Marcellus (d. 40 BC); (2) Mark Antony (d. 31 BC). Children: M. Claudius Marcellus (d. 23 BC), Claudia Marcella Major, Claudia Marcella Minor, grandmother of the empress Messalina (by 1); Antonia Major, Antonia Minor (by 2). Ancestress of CALIGULA, CLAUDIUS and NERO. Death: natural.

Octavia Major (mid-first century BC). Daughter of G. Octavian and Ancharia. Half-sister of Octavia Minor and AUGUSTUS. Not to be confused with Octavia Minor. Marriage: S. Appuleius. Death: unknown, probably natural.

Poppaea Sabina (30–65). Rank: Augusta and Empress of Rome (NERO). Daughter of Titus Ollius and Poppaea Sabina the Elder. Marriages: (1) Rufrius Crispinus; (2) M. Salvius Otho, later OTHO (emperor 69); (3) NERO. Children: Rufrius Crispinus the Younger (murdered by NERO), Claudia Augusta (d. 63). Death: as a result of kicking by NERO in a fit of rage.

Scribonia (68 BC–AD 16). Daughter of Sentia and L. Scribonius Libo. Marriages: (1) unknown; (2) P. Cornelius Scipio (div. 40 BC); (3) Octavian (AUGUSTUS). Children: Cornelia Scipio (mother of L. Aemilius Paullus) (by 2); Julia the Elder (by 3). Through Julia she was thus the great-grandmother of CALIGULA and great-great-grandmother of NERO. Death: natural.

Statilia Messalina (c. 35–post 68). Empress of Rome (NERO). Most likely daughter of T. Statilius Taurus Corvinus through whom she was probably related to Messalina. Marriages: (1) M. Julius Vestinus Atticus (murdered by NERO in 65); (2) NERO. No known issue by NERO. Death: unknown (probably natural under VESPASIAN, TITUS or DOMITIAN).

3. The Severan Empresses (in chronological order)

The Severan women were descended from Gaius Julius Bassianus and his unknown wife, parents of Julia Domna and Julia Maesa. Note that of the four Severan women only Julia Domna was the wife of an emperor and as such was an empress in the normal meaning of the word. The others: Maesa, Mamaea and Soaemias, all took the rank of Augusta, making them effectively empresses in a technical sense. Only the spouses of Caracalla, Elagabalus and Severus Alexander were conventional empresses. Less is known about the connections and lives of all these women than for the Julio-Claudians, a reflection of the sometimes less reliable and fewer sources for this period.

a. The Severan Women

Julia Domna (*c.* 170–217). Rank: Augusta and Empress of Rome (SEPTIMIUS SEVERUS). Daughter of Julius Bassianus and mother unknown. Sister of Julia Maesa. Marriage: L. SEPTIMIUS SEVERUS. Children: CARACALLA and GETA. Death: suicide.

Julia Maesa (*c.* 160–225). Rank: Augusta. Daughter of Julius Bassianus and mother unknown. Sister of Julia Domna. Marriage: Julius Avitus. Children: Julia Soaemias, Julia Mamaea. Death: natural.

Julia Soaemias Bassiana (*c.* 180–222). Rank: Augusta. Daughter of Julia Maesa and Julius Avitus. Sister of Julia Mamaea. Marriage: S. Varius Marcellus. Children: ELAGABALUS. Death: murdered by praetorians.

Julia Avita Mamaea (*c.* 183–235). Rank: Augusta. Daughter of Julia Maesa and Julius Avitus. Sister of Julia Soaemias. Marriages: (1) a consul (name unknown); (2) M. Julius Gessius Marcianus (murdered 218 by MACRINUS). Children: Theoclia (also murdered 218), SEVERUS ALEXANDER (by 2). Death: murdered by soldiers.

b. The Empresses of Caracalla, Elagabalus and Severus Alexander

Fulvia Plautilla (d. 211). Rank: Augusta and Empress of Rome (CARACALLA). Daughter of Caius Fulvius Plautianus from Leptis Magna, North Africa, praetorian prefect under Septimius Severus. Marriage: CARACALLA in 202 who divorced her after her father's fall in 207. Children: none. Death: in exile on the Lipari Islands.

Julia Cornelia Paula (*c.* 204–post 222). Rank: Augusta and Empress of Rome (ELAGABALUS). Daughter of the praetorian prefect Julius Paulus. Marriage: to ELAGABALUS in 219. Divorced: 220 or 221. Children: none. Death: unknown.

Aquileia Severa (dates unknown). Rank: Augusta, Empress of Rome (ELAGABALUS) and Vestal Virgin. Marriage: ELAGABALUS 219. Divorced:

221? Marriage resumed later that year after rejection of Annia Faustina. Children: none. Death: unknown.

Annia Faustina (dates unknown). Rank: Augusta and Empress of Rome (ELAGABALUS). Descendant of Marcus Aurelius. Marriage: ELAGABALUS 221. Divorced 221. Children: none. Death: unknown.

Gnaea Seia Herennia Sallustia Barbia Orbiana (dates unknown). Rank: Augusta and Empress of Rome (SEVERUS ALEXANDER). Possibly related to Herennia Etruscilla, empress of Trajan Decius (249–51). Marriage: SEVERUS ALEXANDER 225. Exiled in 227. Fate unknown. Children: none. Death: unknown.

4. Others (in chronological order)

Aelia Galla Placidia (380–450). Rank: Augusta and Empress of Rome. Daughter of THEODOSIUS I and Galla (through whom she was granddaughter of VALENTINIAN I). Marriages: (1) Ataulf, king of the Visigoths; (2) CONSTANTIUS III. Children: Theodosius, VALENTINIAN III, Justa Grata Honoria (by 2). Death: natural.

Aelia Pulcheria (398?–453). Rank: Augusta and Empress of Rome. Daughter of ARCADIUS (through whom she was granddaughter of THEODOSIUS I) and Aelia Eudoxia, sister of THEODOSIUS II in whose stead she ruled until 450. Marriage: MARCIAN. Children: none. Death: natural.

GLOSSARY

as

A copper coin worth one half of a dupondius, and a quarter of a sestertius. The commonest everyday 'small change' in Roman coinage.

Augusta

The formal and honorific title eventually used by the wife of an Augustus, the emperor. It denoted her special association with him and by implication shared status and privileges. Livia was not given the title until after Augustus' death. It was not always awarded to an empress. Messalina, for example, was denied it by Claudius on his accession. Augusta could also be awarded to an imperial woman other than the emperor's wife. Claudius gave his mother Antonia the title posthumously. By the time of the Severan women 'Augusta' was being used in its own right, for example by Julia Maesa as the grandmother of emperors, and her daughters as their mothers. Augusta was also a form of religious dignity that could be attributed to a man. Augusta was therefore an ambiguous label, probably deliberately so.

Augustus

The name adopted by Octavian in 27 BC. It had semi-religious associations and marked him out as of special status with unique authority, but without specifically referring to him as a ruler. It became synonymous with what we would call an emperor.

aureus
Standard Roman gold coin unit, nominally equivalent in value to 25 denarii, or 100 sesterces.

carpentum
Carriage originally used by Roman matrons in processions in Rome. Enjoyed as a specific privilege by some senior female members of the imperial family for private purposes.

cistophoric tetradrachm/cistophorus
Large silver coin originally produced by the kingdom of Pergamum in Asia Minor in the mid-second century BC. The denomination continued to be produced in certain cities after Rome took control. Diameter (under Rome) *c.* 27mm; weight *c.* 10.5g.

client king
Local monarch allowed to continue in power, or placed in power, by the Romans to act as ruler of a frontier buffer state on condition of loyalty to Rome. In return the client king received military, financial and political support. This way Rome exploited local power structures to help smooth the process of absorption into the Empire.

comis
Female elegance, courtesy, and friendliness.

constantia
The quality of reliability and steadfastness, expected of a Roman wife.

damnatio memoriae
'The damnation of memory'. A process enacted by the Senate after the death of an individual, man or woman, who had been vilified for actions in life. This involved the destruction or recarving of sculptures representing the person, the erasure of their name from inscriptions and, if coin issues existed depicting

them, the defacing of the portrait and/or legend. Women subjected to *damnatio memoriae* were Livilla and Messalina.

denarius
The standard Roman silver coin, issued from Republican times regularly up until the mid-third century when it gave way to the double-denarius, the antoninianus. Purity declined during the period. Diameter typically 19mm; weight *c.* 3.9g.

docta
An 'educated' woman, for example *matrona docta*.

domina
Literally means 'mistress of the household', and was linked to the word for the home, *domus*. See also *materfamilias*.

dupondius
Brass coin worth half a sestertius and two asses (q.v.).

duumvir
One of the two annually elected senior civic magistrates (*duoviri*, 'the two men') in a Roman city. They were the local equivalent of the two consuls in Rome. A *duumvir* had to fulfil a property qualification and had previously served as a junior civic magistrate, *aedile*.

effeminare
'To make [someone/something] effeminate'. This pejorative term suggested weakness and degeneration through greed into luxury, vice and decadence. It was used particularly to discredit men, such as Mark Antony, and was often associated with the influence of a degenerate woman, in his case Cleopatra.

epithalamium
A dedicatory poem composed specifically for a bride on her wedding day.

familia
The Roman family household which included the slaves (*famuli*). See also *paterfamilias* and *materfamilias*.

Gemonian Stairs (or Steps)
A flight of stairs that connected the Capitoline Hill and the Forum in Rome. The bodies of executed criminals were cast down them and left there to rot in public view for several days before being thrown into the river Tiber.

imperator
Original meaning was 'general', or 'commander-in-chief', but evolved under the principate into being synonymous with ruling, leading to our word emperor.

imperium
The power of military command awarded usually to a consul by a vote of the Senate. Such powers did not extend to commanding armies in Italy, but this was granted to Augustus as *imperium maius*.

mater castrorum
Literally 'Mother of the Military Camps' and normally translated as 'Mother of the Army'. An honorific title awarded to some empresses conferring on them the status of a benevolent mother figure watching over the army.

materfamilias (also *materfamilias domina*)
Mother, mistress, of the family. The senior female figure in a Roman household with authority over the day-to-day management of the household and its staff, and the education and upbringing of her children.

mater patriae
'Mother of the Nation', a female equivalent of the emperor's position of *pater patriae*. Tiberius denied Livia the title after Augustus' death. Julia Domna used it.

paterfamilias
Father of the family. The senior male who stood at the head of a household with supreme authority over all family members. He determined who married whom, using marriage contracts to form political and social alliances. He might also selectively use adoption to extend his family's interests and contacts.

porticus

The word meant literally a colonnaded walkway but evolved into the generic term for a building complex of some architectural pretensions with elaborate entrances, colonnades, niches, temples, art galleries displaying paintings and sculptures, meeting rooms and facilities such as a library. Livia and Octavia each endowed Rome with a porticus. They remained in use for centuries. Only the porch of the Porticus of Octavia survives today (plates 6, 15).

Praetorian Guard

The imperial bodyguard of elite troops based in the Castra Praetoria in Rome from the reign of Tiberius on. The praetorians protected the emperor and also sometimes served on military campaigns. Some empresses (particularly Agrippina the Younger and Julia Domna) adopted praetorian escorts as a sign of their prestige. They played an intermittent but decisive role in regime change at certain dates. See de la Bédoyère (2017) for a comprehensive history of their activities.

princeps iuventutis

An informal title indicating a youthful imperial heir-apparent, literally 'first amongst the young'.

provincial coinage

Mainstream Roman coinage was struck at the mint of Rome, and under the Julio-Claudians also at Lugdunum in Gaul (the latter was closed after Nero's reign). These coins circulated across the Roman Empire except in Egypt which had its own coinage system. However, a number of cities across the Empire, mainly in the Greek-speaking East but also Spain, produced coins for local or regional use. These were predominantly base metal but some silver coins, such as the cistophori made at Ephesus for Claudius and Agrippina and the tetradrachms made at Alexandria, were minted. These coins are known today as Roman provincial coinage and sometimes also as 'Greek Imperial'. Provincial and Egyptian coins were produced in a huge variety of types and often include dynastic issues which were not featured in the coinage series produced at Rome or Lugdunum. Livia, for example, appeared on such coins during the reign of Augustus but not at Rome. Messalina and Poppaea are only known as portrait types on provincial coins. The provincial series produced under the Severans is one of the largest in the history of Roman coinage.

pudicitia

The semi-divine quality of chastity and sexual virtue, expected of a Roman woman before and during marriage. One published definition is a Roman woman's primary virtue: 'sexual fidelity enhanced by fertility'.[1]

Saecular Games

Games held to celebrate the passing of a *saeculum*, a nominal period of 110 years used as a form of commemorative chronological measurement. A modern equivalent would be something like 'centennial games'.

sestertius

The principal base-metal (brass) coin of the imperial era, produced from the reign of Augustus up till the mid-third century and briefly revived under the Gallic emperor Postumus. The sestertius was also the standard unit of measure cited when sums of money were quoted even though in reality larger amounts were probably paid in silver denarii. Plural sestertii (Latin) normally used for generic references to the coin, e.g. 'Nero's issue of sestertii', sesterces (English) usually used for amounts, e.g. 'it cost 100 million sesterces'. Diameter *c.* 30–33mm; weight *c.* 23g.

toga virilis

The pure white toga worn by a Roman male when he reached puberty, indicating his arrival at manhood. The exact age is uncertain but was around fourteen to sixteen.

tribunician power

The tribune of the plebs was a Republican office created to defend the interests of the plebs against the power of the patrician class through the Senate. During his year of elected office a tribune of the plebs could propose and veto legislation. To ensure his safety his person was inviolable. Augustus devised the idea that he would be voted the powers and privileges of a tribune of the plebs without actually holding the office. He and later emperors normally had these privileges awarded annually in imitation of the annual tenure of the tribunate. These powers and privileges were then enjoyed by certain female members of the imperial family by association.

Venus Genetrix

Venus 'the progenitor', i.e. the mythical divine female ancestor of the Julian family through her son Aeneas and his son Iulus (Ascanius). Celebrated in particular by Julius Caesar, who built a temple to her as a central feature of his forum in Rome, and the Julio-Claudians, and also claimed by the Severan empresses.

NOTES

Unless otherwise specified, the works of Tacitus referred to in this book are restricted to his *Annals*, Pliny is Pliny the Elder and his *Natural History*, and Seneca is the Younger. Owing to considerable confusion in the book numbering of Cassius Dio's history in the Loeb Classical Library series, the exact page number in each volume is noted as well as the book number in the running headers (which for bewildering reasons differs from those given at the start of each book). This precaution should make precisely clear where the relevant reference is to be found. The Loeb Classical Library is the main series used for ancient sources in this book. However, Zonaras is to be found in T. Banchich and E. Lane's edition (2009). For coins I have generally used David R. Sear's excellent catalogues (1982, 2000, 2002, 2014) for the simple reason that they are the only sources generally accessible to a wider readership; I make no apology for this. They contain references to a wide range of academic resources should a reader need them but these latter are to all intents and purposes completely unavailable outside the most specialist libraries.

AE	*L'Annee épigraphique* (Paris, 1888–) (N.B. some of this material is now available on the Internet from the same source as *ILS* below).
CIL	*Corpus Inscriptionum Latinarum* (Berlin, 1863–) in sixteen volumes (N.B. some of this material is now available on the Internet from the same source as *ILS* below).
ILS	H. Dessau (1892–1916), *Inscriptionum latinae selectae* (Berlin) in three volumes (now available on the Internet with full search facilities at http://db.edcs.eu/epigr/epi_en.php).
JRS	*Journal of Roman Studies*, published by the Society for the Promotion of Roman Studies.
L&R	Lewis and Reinhold (1955).
RIB	*The Roman Inscriptions of Britain:* see R.G. Collingwood and R.P. Wright (1965), revised edition R.S.O. Tomlin (1995). Available online at: http://romaninscriptionsofbritain.org.
RPC	*Roman Provincial Coinage.* A. Burnett, M. Amandry and P.P. Ripollès (1992).
SHA	*Scriptores Historiae Augustae* (Loeb Classical Library edition).

Foreword

1. Burns (2007), Freisenbruch (2010) and Chrystal (2015) are typical of the genre.
2. Mullens (1942), 60, did note that 'The history of the Julio-Claudian house is remarkable for the frequency with which the continuance of the line depended upon a woman', and described the relationships and descent.
3. For example, 'women's history is firmly established in the mainstream of historical scholarship and is terrain that no longer needs to be firmly barricaded as the sole preserve of female, or feminist, scholars'. Edmondson (2009), 39.
4. Hemelrijk (2004) uses 'Major' and 'Minor' for the mother-daughter Agrippinas as well. That may be technically more correct but in the present author's view this is unhelpful for some readers. 'Elder' and 'Younger' is a clearer depiction of a parental relationship.
5. An example of the latter is Andrew Wallace-Hadrill (2008), 327ff., who is quite content to draw valid and interesting comparisons between ancient Rome and medieval Italian states concerning sumptuary control.
6. The Lancastrian Margaret of Anjou (queen of Henry VI), and the Yorkist Elizabeth Woodville (queen of Edward IV). They were of course conversely championed by other contemporary historians who supported their causes.
7. See for example Beard (2017) where these comparisons are explicitly drawn.

Introduction

1. The first emperor to be so was Vespasian (69–79), by Titus (79–81). The first emperor to be succeeded by a son born during his father's reign was Marcus Aurelius (161–80), by Commodus (180–92).
2. For example, Alston (1998), 135, notes the loss of wife and heir but sees the event only in the context of Nero's decline rather than as the dynastic disaster it represented. Griffin (1984) devotes a whole chapter to the problem of the imperial succession at Nero's death but does not discuss how the Julio-Claudian female line had hitherto provided the key spine to sustaining the dynasty. Shotter (2008) similarly prefers a more conventional look at this aspect of the period, as does Holland (2015), for example at pp. 404–5. Chrystal (2015) tells the individual stories of some of these women well but not in the sense of them driving a narrative of the period. An exception is Mullens (1942), see Foreword, note 2.
3. There are several instances, especially in the third century, of sons and even grandsons serving as joint rulers. None of the latter, for example Valerian II (d. 258) and Saloninus (d. 259), the sons of Gallienus (d. 268) and grandsons of Valerian I, survived their fathers. In the fourth century Constantine I (306–37) followed his father Constantius I (295–306), and was succeeded by his sons Constantine II (337–40), Constantius II (337–61) and Constans (337–350). Theodosius II (402–50) was the son of Arcadius (383–408) and grandson of Theodosius I (379–95) and ruled in his own name from 408 to 450. But see p. 295 for his sister Aelia Pulcheria.
4. After that date the nature of imperial rule changed dramatically and led shortly afterwards to a permanent administrative division between the East and the West. Known today as the 'Dominate', the Roman Empire was a very different institution by then and beyond the scope of this book.
5. He is sometimes incongruously known today as Alexander Severus for no good reason. Coin legends invariably place the Severus before Alexander. This is also the normal formula for inscriptions. His full name as emperor was Marcus Aurelius Severus Alexander Pius Augustus.
6. Such as Aelia Galla Placidia (388–450), see pp. 295–6.
7. Strabo, *Geography* 6.4.2; Tacitus, *Histories* 1.1.
8. Bauman (1992), 219.
9. Tacitus (1.2) acidly observed that Augustus gradually absorbed into his own person the functions of the Senate, magistracies and legislature. This is usually regarded as his inherent

senatorial bias against the way in which the Senate's importance and influence were diminished.

10. The quote is from Barrett (1996), XII.
11. Suetonius, *Augustus* 39.2.
12. Appian, *Civil Wars* 2.68. The cost of the land alone for the new forum was an epic 100 million sesterces, Pliny 36.24.103.
13. Appian, *Civil Wars* 2.102. See also Walker and Higgs (2001), 277.
14. I am particularly grateful to Joann Fletcher for drawing my attention to the subtleties of the terminology. See also Tait in Walker and Ashton (2003), 7, and Southern (2001), 123.
15. The only statue we know of from the late Republic of an important Roman woman was of Cornelia. The voting of statues of Livia and Octavia in 35 BC was a major innovation. See p. 55, and Chapter 1, n. 48
16. Plutarch, *Caesar* 49 recounts the story of the way Cleopatra allegedly seduced Caesar. Suetonius, *Caesar* 52.1–2 describes the visit to Rome, and that Mark Antony told the Senate that he had acknowledged the child.
17. Cicero, *Letters to Atticus* 15.15.2.
18. Plutarch, *Caesar* 57.4.
19. Sear (2000), no. 1421.
20. This was not entirely a problem for women. An emperor faced with an unsuitable son of his own blood was still likely to give him precedence as an heir. The most notorious example was Marcus Aurelius and Commodus. Commodus could not have been more ill suited to the role.
21. Tacitus 6.25.1 provides these comments about Agrippina the Elder.
22. With a statue in the Porticus of Octavia as well as a wider reputation for her learning and literary skills. See p. 28. Also Fantham et al. (1994) incisively comment that Cornelia was 'not the only deceased woman commemorated for virtues she neither possessed nor esteemed'.
23. Tacitus 1.1.
24. See for example Rutland (1978) who analyses Tacitus' preoccupation with Livia's role in seeing Tiberius succeed Augustus and her alleged culpability for the fates of Germanicus and Agrippina the Elder.
25. Strong (2016), 109, notes that 'it is impossible' to separate the historical personalities of a woman like Messalina from the portraits painted by, for example, Tacitus.
26. Herodian 1.2.5. It is impossible to say whether Herodian was a senator, equestrian, freeborn or even a freedman. Likewise, we do not know if he wrote in a personal capacity or because he was on the immediate staff of one of the emperors of the period.
27. The proportionate difference is reflected in the structure of this book.
28. Edwards (2010), 28, notes that *both* should be read with the same degree of caution. In addition, the reign of the despotic Domitian (81–96) was also treated as a useful contrast with the new era.
29. The problem is not confined to Tacitus. Charles, Prince of Wales, wrote to the then president of the United States, Ronald Reagan, to say that 'if you happen to find yourself in a public position it becomes progressively more impossible to operate without every move being regarded as having an ulterior motive'. Quoted in the *Daily Mirror*, 5 June 2017 (Stephen White).
30. Syme (2002), vii–viii; ibid., 5, for Sallust's influence on Tacitus.
31. Balsdon (1962), 64, does just that, arguing that the historians' concern was to create 'brilliant caricatures' rather than portraits. Conversely, see n. 00 below on the alternative idea that Tacitus might have been right.
32. See below, pp. 257–8 for the solar eclipse of 59 as a case in point.
33. Barrett (1996), xix–xx, managed to compile a list of the 'Whereabouts of Agrippina [the Younger]' but the inclusion in that list of 'would have lived', 'possibly', 'probably', 'may well have been', 'uncertain', 'apparent absence', 'may have', and 'almost certainly', combine to show that the list is as much based on guesswork as any hard evidence. It is therefore of

dubious value though that should not be taken as a criticism of his well-intentioned efforts to try to marshal the evidence there is.

34. An epitome was written by the monk Xiphilinus in Constantinople in the eleventh century, and another by Zonaras in the early twelfth century. Only around one-third of Dio's original work has survived. Quotations or extracts in other authors fill some gaps.

35. Aulus Gellius, *Attic Nights* 15.7.3 (see p. 110). There are of course some obvious exceptions from earlier or later dates, such as the correspondence of Cicero or Pliny the Younger but it is impossible to know how much those were edited prior to publication in antiquity. Some letters were transcribed into inscriptions, which occasionally survive, for example a letter from Tiberius refusing divine honours in AD 15, see Sherk (1988), no. 31.

36. See for example de la Bédoyère (1997), 17–25, demonstrating the unreliability of some later editions of seventeenth-century correspondence. The process of corruption is demonstrated, as well as discrepancies between drafts, letters-sent and retained copies. Similarly, one of the most extensive collections of Roman correspondence is that of Cicero. It is clear this was compiled from retained copies of letters-sent and cannot be verified against the actual manuscripts dispatched to his correspondents.

37. Barrett (1996), 240, rejects a particularly dramatic episode in Tacitus at 13.14.3 involving Agrippina the Younger as 'hardly believable' and 'histrionic', largely it seems because it is inconsistent with his thesis, itself mainly based on an absence of other evidence.

38. See Birley (1999), 115, and Burns (2007), 186, where the latter has taken the former's speculation about Domna's return to Emesa after Severus had seized power and turned her visit into a fact.

39. Calhoon (1994) suggests that Tacitus should not automatically be seen as a 'bad' historian; it is equally possible to consider whether in fact he managed a brilliant depiction of evil in action. See, for example Mellor (1993). Beard (2015, 400) observes that Tacitus 'regularly rests his case on the character and the crimes of the individuals on the throne'.

40. See below, p. 130, for a detailed discussion of this building and its association with Livia.

41. It is very important to appreciate that while the 'main' Roman coinage was struck at Rome and/or Lugdunum for circulation across the Empire, a number of cities mainly in the East were permitted to strike generally base-metal issues for local use. Some cities, and Ephesus is a good example, struck large silver denominations based on earlier Greek types for a part of the world that was accustomed to their availability. These various provincial coins frequently feature a much wider range of dynastic and innovative types than would ever have been seen in the Western Empire. Egypt remained 'closed' and had its own coinage, again with a wider range of imperial Roman dynastic issues.

42. For the importance of *pudicitia*, see pp. 23–4.

43. Both Livia and Julia the Elder are attested as having kept dwarfs, Livia as having also a collection of small boys. See in particular Pliny 7.16.75 and below, p. 131.

44. See Richlin (1992).

1 Virtue, Honour and Chastity

1. 3.8.6. Valerius Maximus wrote during the reign of Tiberius.

2. 'In the official decrees of Tiberius and his predecessor Augustus, the divisions between different types of women were clear and absolute.' Strong (2016), 2.

3. Livy 1.13.

4. Ovid, *Amours (Amores)* 1.10, 'You'll have no good outcome from sordid presents. Sabine bracelets weren't worth so much when weapons pressed down upon the sacred virgin's head.' Propertius, *Elegies* 4.4, covered the story in terms of a moral warning to his own times. See also Strong (2016), 35.

5. Varro, *Latin Language* 6.3.18; Macrobius, *Saturnalia* 1.11.36–40, 3.2.14.

6. Livy 34.1ff. The account of Cato's speech is of course in Livy's words and reflects as much his own take on the argument as whatever was actually said at the time. See also Williams (2010), 150. It is interesting that Varro made a point of recording a specific word for

women acting in unison, *axitiosae*; his implication is that such behaviour constituted a form of threat. *Latin Language* 7.3.66. See also Valerius Maximus 2.1.5b for the suggestion that modest use of purple and gold was supposed to provide chaste women with a degree of elegance.

7. 9.1.3. Valerius Maximus only brought the point up because he was, as he said, more concerned about men going down the same route.

8. See Kiefer (1976).

9. Corbeill (2015), 144. The notion that effeminacy was synonymous with degeneracy and a lack of manliness and masculine pre-eminence endured well into early modern times, and probably reflects a consequence of a classical education. In his *London Journal* on 12 January 1763 James Boswell bragged of his sexual prowess which he called his 'godlike vigour', noting that 'sobriety had preserved me from effeminacy and weakness'. Pottle (1950), 141.

10. Cicero, *Orations* 2.68.277. *Famosas* = 'infamous women', i.e. women with bad reputations.

11. Dio 62.3–5 (Loeb vol. VIII, pp. 93–5).

12. See, for example, the letter of the Younger Pliny when his advice was sought about a wife, p. 30.

13. Cicero, *Murena* 12.27; Lucretius, *De Rerum Natura* 5.1355–6.

14. Valerius Maximus 7.8.3 when referring to Quintus Metellus who failed to make any provision for his kinsmen in his will, preferring a proscribed supporter of Marius called Carrinas.

15. *De Re Republica* 3.10.17, where the injustice of the daughter of Publius Crassus being able to inherit far more than the law permitted is noted.

16. Dio 56.32.1 (Loeb vol. VII, pp. 71–3).

17. A particularly memorable instance is the lengthy funerary eulogy of Turia(?), written by her husband. *CIL* 6.1527, *ILS* 8393, most readily accessed in Shelton (1998), 292–4. Valerius Maximus 4.6.1–3 admiringly recounts a number of examples of men who either sacrificed themselves to save their wives or who committed suicide after their wives' deaths rather than go on without them. For Pliny the Younger and Calpurnia see p. 232. For Murdia see *CIL* 6.10230, *ILS* 8394. Her son seems in part to have been influenced in his judgement by the terms of his mother's will in which she had treated all her sons equally, except that he received an additional bequest because he was the product of an earlier marriage; she was, he said, honouring the inheritance she felt he was due also from his real father.

18. Tacitus, *Agricola* 6.1. The play on the word 'impenetrable' is fairly obvious. For Agrippina, see Tacitus 4.12.1. See also Baldwin (1972), 83–101, and Rutland (1978).

19. Pudicitia did not appear on Julio-Claudian coinage, but was later a very popular part of the Antonine and Severan women's coinage repertoire to the extent that it became a dominant type. For the association of *pudicitia* and *fecunditas* see Valerius Maximus 7.1.1.

20. Valerius Maximus 6.1.1.

21. For the ancient cult and comparison of *virtus* to *pudicitia* see Livy 10.23.3–10; also Langlands (2009), 2. The patrician shrine was in the Forum Boarium, best known today for the extant temples of Portunus and Hercules Victor. The plebeian version may have been on the Quirinal Hill. Nothing is known of either Pudicitia shrine now.

22. Langlands (2009), 13.

23. Langlands (2009), 37ff. provides a particularly useful discussion of *pudicitia*'s powerful force.

24. Valerius Maximus 2.1.3, 8.15.12. Flaccus was consul in 179 BC.

25. Propertius 4.11.70–2.

26. 'Propertius portrays *pudicitia* above all as susceptible to disturbances in the social order.' Langlands (2009), 196. A century later Juvenal looked back to Propertius' time and bemoaned the passing of *pudicitia* while at the same time mocking it (see the opening lines of the 6th *Satire* and also lines 286ff. for the 'good old days' of chastity and poverty). Ibid., 56. For Tarpeia see Propertius, *Elegies* 4.4 passim.

27. 6.1.3. In modern parlance these would be called 'honour killings'. It should be noted that an unchaste youth could be punished too. See 6.1.5.

28. See the case of Caesar at Clodius Pulcher's trial, below, p. 46, and also Sallust's judgement of Sempronia, p. 32.
29. Plutarch, *Caesar* 5.
30. Cornelius Nepos, *preface* 6–7, quoted and discussed by Wallace-Hadrill (2008), 216.
31. Dixon (2007), xv, 34–5.
32. This Sempronia should not be confused with Sempronia, wife of Decimus Junius Brutus (consul 77 BC). The sister of the Gracchi earned praise from Valerius Maximus at 3.8.6.
33. Cornelius Nepos, *fragment* 2.
34. Plutarch, *Gaius Gracchus* 4.2–3.
35. Plutarch, *Gaius Gracchus* 4.4. See also Corbeill (2015), 148.
36. *Brutus* 104, 211, written *c.* 46 BC. See also Best (1970).
37. Plutarch, *Gaius Gracchus* 19; Valerius Maximus 4.4 *praef.* A reputation for intellectual patronage was an attribute often ascribed to women of high standing. Julia Domna (see Chapter 11) was also described this way. The extent of the literal truth is harder to discern. Quintilian 1.1.6. recorded in the late first century AD how Cornelia's 'extremely learned speech' had been handed down.
38. Horace, *Odes* 4.4.19–30. See Corbeill (2015), 77, note 72.
39. See below, p. 161, and Suetonius, *Claudius* 3.2. She called him a 'monster of a man' and used him as a benchmark by which to judge the stupidity of others. See also Hemelrijk (2004), 64, on this general topic.
40. See p. 183 for how Antonia was regarded by later Roman historians.
41. Valerius Maximus 6.7.1.
42. Plutarch, *Caesar* 7.
43. Livy 4.44.11.
44. Flower (2011), 160. The *pontifex maximus* was acting as the symbolic equivalent of the *paterfamilias*.
45. Both had their monuments and inscriptions officially destroyed in the process of *damnatio memoriae* (literally 'damnation of the memory [of a person]').
46. The son of the triumvir of the same name killed at Carrhae in 53 BC.
47. For the story of a Caecilia Metelli, i.e. wife of Metellus, see Valerius Maximus 1.5.4, who had taken it from Cicero, *On Divination* 1.104, and 2.83.
48. *CIL* 6.10043; Pliny 34.14.31. The base of the statue of Cornelia has survived, found in the Porticus in 1878. Now in the Capitoline Museum at Rome. For the modification of the text see Fantham et al. (1994), 220 and 265. The word GRACCHORVM is still visible on the base, but may be itself a later restoration. AFRICANI.F is far more prominent. The statue might have been of bronze; if so it was probably the posthumous one mentioned by Plutarch, *Gaius Gracchus* 4.3, which he says was inscribed 'Cornelia, Mother of the Gracchi'. See also Flory (1993), 290.
49. For Julia's death: Seneca, *To Marcia on Consolation* 14.3; Cicero, *Letters to Quintus* 3.1.25. For the games: Suetonius, *Caesar* 26.2; Dio 43.22.3–4 (Loeb vol. IV, p. 251).
50. Caesar may have been married previously to a woman called Cossutia. Plutarch appears to imply there was a wife before Cornelia, *Caesar* 5.7, in addition to Cornelia, Pompeia (whom Plutarch calls the 'third' wife), and Calpurnia. See also Goldsworthy (2006), 49.
51. Plutarch, *Caesar* 5; Suetonius, *Caesar* 6.1.
52. Suetonius, *Caesar* 6.1. See also Corbeill (2015), 84.
53. For example, if a man had been widowed, or simply out of political expediency.
54. Valerius Maximus 2.1.4.
55. See Skinner (2011), in particular Chapter 3. Fantham et al. (1994), 271, comment on Terentia's financial manipulations, citing Cicero's *Letters to Atticus* 11.24.3.
56. Treggiari (2007), 34–5.
57. Valerius Maximus 2.1.6. The goddess Viriplaca is otherwise unknown.
58. The girl's father, Arulenus Rusticus, had been executed by Domitian in AD 93. Pliny the Younger, *Letters* 1.14.

59. Tacitus 4.34–35 (who makes no reference to Marcia's role), and Seneca, *To Marcia on Consolation passim* but particularly Foreword 1–5 where he heaps praise on her for her actions.

60. Hemelrijk (2004), 19, 26; Suetonius, *Grammarians* 16.

61. Hemelrijk (2004), 27.

62. Quintilian 1.1.6, 'read not merely as an honour to her sex'. Quintilian specifies other women whose learning and literary skills had earned them enduring reputations, including Cornelia, mother of the Gracchi. See also Valerius Maximus 8.3.3.

63. Valerius Maximus 8.3.1–3, writing in the reign of Tiberius; Ulpian is cited by Justinian, *Digest* 3.1.1.5. There is some doubt about the names. Gaia Afrania is given as Carfania, which is assumed to be a garbled miscopying of G. Afrania, though Justinian calls her Carfania too. Lucretius 1.839 described the *androgynus* as 'between man and woman, yet neither'. Pliny 7.3.34 devoted a section to 'hermaphrodites, formerly called *androgyni* and considered as portents, but now as entertainments'. Other uses of the word are innocuously descriptive and do not seem pejorative in tone. On the importance for a man of not sounding like a woman, see Quintilian 11.3.19. Also, Hillary Rodham Clinton describes the issues raised by women speaking in public in political contexts during her candidacy for the US presidency in 2016, even describing the female voice as being perceived as 'discordant', 'screaming', 'screeching' (2017), 121–5.

64. 8.3, the opening sentence.

65. Sallust, *Catiline War* 25.1–5. She should not be confused with Sempronia, wife of Scipio Aemilianus.

66. *quae multa saepe virilis audaciae facinora commiserat*, '[Sempronia] who had often committed many crimes of the boldness of men', Sallust, *Catiline War* 25.1. Sallust's sanctimonious judgement of Sempronia can be partly attributed to an 'obsession with morality' resulting from his own conversion from being an 'evil-doer'. See Balsdon (1962), 48, and also 53–6 for the stories of Praecia and Volumnia Cytheris, and other notorious women of the late Republic.

67. Livy 1.1.12.

68. *Catiline War* 11.3, 12.1.

69. Suetonius, *Augustus* 44.2. Livia was excepted from this restriction, Dio 60.22.2 (Loeb vol. VII, p. 423), and it became a mark of distinction for empresses.

70. Ulpian, *Rules* 11.1.

71. Beard (2015), 378, describes Julia appropriately as Augustus' 'favourite instrument in his plans'.

72. Discussed in more detail below, pp. 123–4.

73. This did not stop Seneca from depicting Claudius as the villain of the piece, and Messalina as the victim. See p. 260.

74. Following an adulterous affair with a senator called Decimus Junius Silanus. See also Dio 55.7.3 for a reference to Augustus' affair with Maecenas' wife.

75. For a more detailed discussion of P. Clodius Pulcher and the identity of Lesbia, see below, p. 333, n. 28, and Chapter 2, n. 28.

76. Martial, *Epigrams* 2.49. Martial's feelings were ambivalent. He went on to admit that he would sleep with Telesina (*volo*, 'I want her') precisely because of her adulterous activity, something he evidently found titillating. For the possible further connotations of Martial's comments see Williams (2010), 25–6.

77. See Lyne (1981), especially 118.

78. Suetonius, *Caesar* 50.2, 52.1. Servilia was the mother of Brutus, one of his assassins. Also, Macrobius 2.2.5.

79. Suetonius, *Augustus* 69.1–2.

80. The decree was displayed on bronze tablets in Italian cities. One from Larinum seems to refer to this measure though the relevant section is incomplete. See Sherk (1988) no. 35, n.1, and also Suetonius, *Tiberius* 35.2. Tacitus 2.85.1–3; Suetonius, *Tiberius* 35.2. Strong (2016), 2.

81. Strong (2016), 10, 42, citing *CIL* 9.2029, 116 and 238. The modern Spanish *ramera*, literally 'whore', appears to preserve part of the Latin term but rather less ambiguously. *Meretrix* is the origin of the English word 'meretricious', meaning 'worthless' or 'undeserving of praise'.
82. *CIL* 6.37965, described and illustrated by Strong (2016), 54–5, and fig. 1.
83. Tacitus 11.29.3–30.1.
84. These attributes are praised on a tombstone recording a woman called Claudia at Rome. *CIL* 1.2.1211, *ILS* 8403.
85. See particularly Pliny the Younger, *Letters* 4.19.2ff.
86. Tacitus 16.7.1.
87. Valerius Maximus 2.1.5b.
88. Valerius Maximus 6.3.7 and 9. Also called Egnatius Maetennus by Pliny at 14.14.89; Augustine, *Confessions* 9.9.
89. Juvenal, *Satires* 6.346–7. His discussion of the problem runs on to line 365.

2 Age of the Imperators

1. Soranus, *Gynaecology* 1.34.1, a doctor of Greek origin who worked in Rome around the beginning of the second century explained this priority in a very matter of fact way.
2. Plutarch, *Caesar* 61.2–3. Lupercus was the god of fertility. His festival had originally been celebrated by shepherds in connection with their flocks. See also Varro, *Latin Language* 5.15.85, 6.3.13 (the latter including the detail about the goat hide thongs). The Roman date was XV Kal. Mar, i.e. the 15th day before and including 1 (Kalends of) March.
3. Fantham et al. (1994), 304. For the postpartum deaths of the Helvidiae sisters, see Pliny the Younger, *Letters* 4.21.1–2.
4. Pliny 35.2.6–11.
5. Polybius 6.7; Cicero, *Republic* 3.13.23.
6. See Rutland (1978), 15.
7. Cicero, *Republic* 2.27.49.
8. Plutarch, *Caesar* 11, 60.1ff.
9. Suetonius, *Caesar* 85.1.
10. Velleius Paterculus 2.75.3 refers to Tiberius as the 'son of Caesar' (Octavian), making no reference to the fact that this was only by adoption.
11. Fletcher (2015), 356. 'Both were flamboyant, both pragmatic, and, when necessary, both were completely ruthless.'
12. Suetonius, *Caesar* 83.2, *Augustus* 6.2; Plutarch, *Caesar* 83.2; Dio 44.35.2 (Loeb vol. IV, p. 367). Two other grandsons of Caesar's sister inherited the remaining 25 per cent of his estate.
13. Suetonius, *Augustus* 8.1.
14. Suetonius, *Caesar* 8.1.
15. Dio 48.44.1–3 (Loeb vol. V, p. 313); Barrett (2012), 26 and note 21 cites the *Fasti Verulani*, a Roman calendar found in Veroli of which only January–March survive, as the source for the date.
16. Suetonius, *Tiberius* 1–3.
17. Marcus Livius Drusus' reforms had primarily been in the interests of the Senate and followed in the aftermath of the radical Gracchi brothers, tribunes whose challenges to senatorial privilege had so outraged the Senate in the late second century BC.
18. Velleius Paterculus 2.71.2, 75.3.
19. Suetonius, *Tiberius* 5; Velleius Paterculus 2.75.1.
20. Suetonius, *Tiberius* 5.
21. Pliny 10.27.154; the story was later repeated by Suetonius, *Tiberius* 14.2.
22. Fulvia was Antony's third wife.
23. *For Milo* (*Pro Milone*) 40 (published in the mid-first century AD by Quintus Asconius Pedianus).
24. Cicero used the term *inpudicissimus* ('very lewdness') to refer to Antony, for example in *Philippics* 2.70, and also challenged his *pudicitia* at, for example, 2.3. See also Langlands

(2009), 315, on how Cicero at 2.99 made an unsubstantiated allegation that Antony had made a charge of immorality against a *pudicissima* ('very chaste') woman simply so that he could marry Fulvia. See also Corbeill (2015), 148.

25. Velleius Paterculus 2.45.1.
26. Suetonius, *Caesar* 6.2; Plutarch, *Caesar* 10.9; Dio 37.45 (Loeb vol. III, p. 171).
27. Plutarch, *Caesar* 8–10. The account includes a detailed description of the affair.
28. It has been suggested that Catullus immortalized Clodia Metelli in in his works as 'Lesbia'. Apuleius, *Apologia* 10 says that Catullus used 'Lesbia' as a pseudonym for Clodia but this is not enough to specify which of the three sisters of Clodius named Clodia she was. Wiseman (1969), 59, and (1985), 2, 131, considered the identification as unlikely, if not implausible. Hejduk (2008), 6–7, Skinner (2011), Chapter 7, and Dunn (2016), ix, are content to identify Clodia as Lesbia. As so often with these cases of disputed identity in antiquity there is simply insufficient evidence to provide a definitive and indisputable conclusion. The reader is invited to consult the works cited here and decide which is the more convincing argument and whether it really matters.
29. *For Caelius* (*Pro Caelio*) 31ff. See also Hillard (1992).
30. See, for example Skinner (2011), in particular Chapter 2.
31. Dio 47.8.2–3 (Loeb vol. V, p. 131). For Hortensia, see pp. 31–2.
32. Dio 48.4.1 (Loeb vol. V, p. 225).
33. See, for example, Sear (2000), nos 1511–13 (Antony and Octavia), and 1516–19 (Fulvia). Two of the issues, both made at Lugdunum, gave Antony's age at the time of issue on the reverses, thus dating them.
34. Suetonius, *Augustus* 62.1. Claudia, daughter of Publius Clodius, was so young she was barely of marriageable age. Dio 46.56.3 (Loeb vol. V, p. 113), 48.5.1ff. (Loeb vol. V, p. 229). They divorced in 40 BC so that Octavian could marry Scribonia as part of his alliance with Sextus Pompey, who was married to Scribonia's niece.
35. Dio 48.54.4 (Loeb vol. V, p. 337). This was not her only betrothal as a child.
36. Appian 5.14.1, 19.1.
37. Suetonius, *Augustus* 14; Dio 48.10.4 (Loeb vol. V, p. 241).
38. Appian 5.59.1.
39. Dio 48.28.3–4 (Loeb vol. V, p. 279).
40. See for example Virlouvet in Fraschetti (2001), 68. Suetonius, *Rhetoricians* 5, provides the description of her appearance, *bucca inflatior*.
41. 'If . . . she developed into a virago, she was at least an infinitely loyal virago.' Balsdon (1962), 49.
42. *Philippics* 2.11, 2.113, 5.11; and 2.48, 99.
43. Dio 47.8.4 (Loeb vol. V, pp. 131–2). The use of a hairpin seems to have played a powerful symbolic role in female retribution. See Fletcher (2016); Velleius Paterculus 2.74.3; Plutarch, *Antony* 10.3.
44. Velleius Paterculus 2.75.1.
45. Velleius Paterculus 2.75.3.
46. Dio 48.15.3–4 (Loeb vol. V, p. 251).
47. Dio 54.7.2 (Loeb vol. VI, p. 299); Suetonius, *Tiberius* 6.1.
48. Valerius Maximus' description of Octavia, which can be found at 9.15.2.
49. Had Messalina not attempted to overthrow Claudius through the medium of a bigamous marriage then their son Britannicus might have acceded as emperor after Claudius, making Octavia the primary line of descent in the Julio-Claudian family.
50. In 43 BC. Dio 47.7.4 (Loeb vol. V, pp. 129–31).
51. See Sear (2000), nos 1511–13.
52. Sear (2000), nos 1489–94.
53. Dio 48.54.5 (Loeb vol. V, p. 337).
54. Suetonius, *Augustus* 69.2, *uxor mea est*. In Egyptian terms they were married.
55. Velleius Paterculus 2.77.2.

56. Dio 48.34.3 (Loeb vol. V, p. 291).
57. Suetonius, *Augustus* 69.1.
58. Edward IV of England married in 1464 the widowed Elizabeth Woodville, Lady Grey, who like Livia already had two sons. It was widely recognized as a love match then and since, but her proven fertility may well have been an important, even decisive, factor.
59. Dennison (2011), 2. It is amusing to note in the context of the present book that Mazzini's claim was inherited only via the female line through his mother.
60. Tacitus 5.1.2 says that they immediately cohabited even though Livia was heavily pregnant. Since he was referring to a detail of personal affairs that took place around 140 years before he wrote we cannot assume he is reliable on this.
61. Tacitus 1.10.5; Dio 48.44.1–2, 55.2.5–6 (Loeb vols V, p. 313, and VI, p. 385).
62. For the stillbirth or miscarriage, see Suetonius, *Augustus* 63.1. Pliny (7.13.57) attributed their childless marriage to the known phenomenon of physical incompatibility between two specific people who were otherwise manifestly fertile. This is now known sometimes as 'incompatibility at conception' and is recognized as having either a genetic or immunological cause in any one case.
63. Velleius Paterculus, for example, says that 'she was conducted' to the ceremony by Tiberius Nero, 2.79.2. Later he says she was 'promised in marriage by Tiberius Nero', 2.94.1. There is some confusion in the sources concerning the exact sequence of events since for example Suetonius implies the birth took place after the marriage (*Augustus* 62.2).
64. Velleius Paterculus 2.79ff.
65. Velleius Paterculus 2.79.5–6. Naulochus was on the north coast of Sicily but its exact location is unknown. It may have been an anchorage rather than a town.
66. Dio 49.34.1 (Loeb vol. V, p. 409), Suetonius, *Augustus* 17.
67. Plutarch, *Antony* 10.3
68. Sear (2000), no. 1515.
69. Butcher (2004), 57, fig. 8.2.
70. Dio 50.5.3–4 (Loeb vol. V, p. 445).
71. Dio 49.38.1 (Loeb vol. V, p. 419). For the innovation of public statues of important women see Flory (1993).
72. In AD 28 Tiberius oversaw the marriage of Agrippina the Younger to Gnaeus Domitius Ahenobarbus. His descent from Octavia was specifically cited as his prime qualification. Tacitus 4.75.
73. Dio 50.2.2 (Loeb vol. V, p. 439).
74. *Res Gestae* 25.
75. Dio 50.3.4–5, 26.1–3 (Loeb vol. V, pp. 443, 491).
76. The account of this remarkable episode is mainly in Dio 50.2–6 (Loeb vol. V, pp. 437–47).
77. Appian, *Civil War* 5.9.
78. Pliny, *Natural History* 33.14.50.
79. Dio 50.8.6 (Loeb vol. V, p. 453).

3 Women in the Augustan State

1. Dio 51.1.1–2 (Loeb vol. VI, pp. 3–4).
2. Dio 51.13.1–3 (Loeb vol. VI, p. 37).
3. Suetonius, *Augustus* 17.5.
4. Horace, *Odes* 1.38 *passim*, *Epodes* 9.11ff.
5. *Aeneid* 8.688.
6. Appian, *Civil Wars* 2.102; Dio 51.22.3 (Loeb vol. VI, p. 65).
7. This division of women into polar opposites is not in any sense peculiar to the Romans. To take just one random example it has been said of the American statesman Alexander Hamilton (*c.* 1755–1804) that he 'could fancy young women as chaste goddesses or naughty little vixens', R. Chernow (2016), *Alexander Hamilton*, Head of Zeus, London, 94.
8. Suetonius, *Augustus* 28.

9. As early as 39 BC as Octavian he had betrothed Julia to his nephew Marcus Marcellus. Dio 48.38.3 (Loeb vol. V, p. 301). In 37 BC he betrothed her to Antony's son Antyllus. Ibid. 48.54.4 (p. 337).

10. *Aeneid* 4.569.

11. Johnson (2015), 45.

12. Johnson (2015), 73.

13. Hardie (2014), 65.

14. *Aeneid* 11.480. See also Brannon (2010), 50, who provides a well-substantiated discussion of the role of key players in the *Aeneid* and the foundation of Rome. Moreover, although Lavinia and Cleopatra could not be further removed from one another, it is clear that Roman tradition was content to attribute much of the evil of the civil war to Cleopatra.

15. Virgil, *4th Eclogue* line 6; Ovid, *Fasti* 6.265–9.

16. *The Art of Love (Ars Amatoria)* 1.135ff.; *Amours (Amores)* 1.4; and above, p. 18 for Tarpeia.

17. *Amours (Amores)* 1.4.

18. See especially Langlands (2009), 196, on Propertius' stance.

19. Edwards (2010, 36), who points out that we cannot know whether adultery had increased or not, warns that 'These colourful characters are not real people but resonant metaphors for the women they claimed to represent', and discusses the way in which suppressing sexual licence was seen as a route to political stability. It should also be noted that Clodius' daughter Claudia was the first wife of Octavian, married to him as part of reinforcing the relationship between him and Antony in *c.* 43–42 BC. She was divorced by him in 40 BC.

20. Dio 58.2.3 (Loeb vol. VII, p. 189). The Greek word for 'chaste women' used by Dio is σωφρονούσαις which has a variety of meanings including discreet, prudent, restrained and having control over sensual desires. We can assume that all were meant in this context. The word comes from σωφρων which means 'of sound mind'. In other words, chastity and restraint were indicators of good mental health in a woman. For this word, see Liddell and Scott (1940), vol. II, 1751–2.

21. 8.5. See also Raditsa (1980).

22. It 'made adultery a public offence'. Edwards (2010), 39.

23. Richardson (2012), 120.

24. This mainly concerned his daughter Julia, and her daughter Julia the Younger. See pp. 96, 101 and 113.

25. Tacitus 3.25, 3.28.

26. Dio 54.16.7 (Loeb vol. VI, p. 125). The legally determined marriageable age was twelve. Suetonius, *Augustus* 34.1 refers generally to laws designed to encourage marriage amongst all classes and outlaw adultery. Augustus had betrothed his own daughter Julia when she was a very small child, though both of her prospective husbands (Antyllus and Marcus Marcellus) were children themselves.

27. In 131 BC Q. Metellus Macedonicus, censor, had spoken (*de prole augenda*, 'On increasing the population') about the need for families to procreate, though his concern was more about the general population. Augustus cited this speech to demonstrate that he was not the first to express his concerns. Suetonius, *Augustus* 89.2, and Scullard (1982), 30. See also Devine (1985) on the interesting idea that excessive heat in baths must have had a serious impact on male fertility.

28. Dio 54.16.1–2 (Loeb vol. VI, pp. 321, 323).

29. Suetonius, *Augustus* 69; Ovid, *Tristia* 2.131–2. Ovid seems to have committed some sort of transgression involving Augustus' family, presumably a 'last straw'. He was not formally 'exiled' but was sent away from Rome and not allowed to return. He was able to stay in contact with friends.

30. Tacitus 3.33.1–34.3.

31. Quintilian 3.7.2.

32. *Natural History* 33.14.50.

33. See, for example, Edwards (2010), 1ff., on the background to this.

34. *Odes* 3.24.25ff.

35. Vegetius 3.
36. Claridge (2010), 133–4.
37. See the case involving her friend Urgulania, below, pp. 123–4.
38. 'By chance or design', Claridge (2010), 208. See also Rossini (2009) for an excellent photographic and historical record and discussion of the Ara Pacis.
39. Rossini (2009), 36.
40. Roma was not worshipped as a deity in her own right in Rome until Hadrian's construction of the Temple of Venus and Rome, though a cult of Roma had existed in the eastern provinces earlier.
41. Seneca, *To Marcia on Consolation* 1.1–2.
42. Suetonius, *Augustus* 30.1; *AE* 1980, 54. Friggeri et al. (2012), ix, 36, 587–8. The inscription probably dates from after *c.* AD 5. Found on the Caelian Hill at the site of San Stefano in Rotondo.
43. Galinksy (1996), 308, and fig. 145.
44. See, for example, Livia as Ceres, and 'an Augustan goddess' with Livia's features in Zanker (1990), 236, fig. 185, and 251, fig. 196.
45. Ungaro (2007), 126.
46. Suetonius, *Augustus* 29, refers to 'colonnades of Livia and Octavia' as well as a colonnade and basilica of Gaius and Lucius, Julia's sons. See also Richardson (1976).
47. Pliny 34.14.31, 36.4.15, 24. For the statue of Cornelia see above, p. 28. A few other traces of the Porticus of Octavia survive but its layout is otherwise only known from the Severan Marble Plan of Rome. See Claridge (2010), 256, fig. 107.
48. Claridge (2010), 339–40. See also Flory (1984) for a discussion of the evidence for the complex. Dio 55.8.2 (Loeb vol. VI, p. 399) records the dedication of the Porticus in 7 BC by Livia and Tiberius. Ovid, *Fasti* 6.637–40, refers to Livia's sole dedication of the shrine to Concordia, and the palace that once stood on the site of the Porticus.
49. Claridge (2010), 77.
50. For a plan, see Cooley and Cooley (2004), 99, fig. 5.2. It can be seen that although the layout was essentially rectangular, a trapezoidal modification had been included to allow it to fit Pompeii's eccentric street plan. The Porticus of Livia had a very similar feature (see plate 15).
51. For translations of all three inscriptions see Cooley and Cooley (2004) nos E42, E44 and E45 (*CIL* 10.808–10).
52. For example, at Veleia in northern Italy, a young woman called Baebia Basilla paid from her own resources for the chalcidicum porch of the city basilica in the late first century BC. *CIL* 11.1189, *ILS* 5560.

4 Forging the Future

1. Valerius Maximus 2.1.4, recounting the story of Spurius Carvilius who in *c.* 223 BC divorced his wife for barrenness. For this Carvilius was heavily criticized.
2. Tacitus 6.22.
3. Tacitus 5.1.
4. Suetonius, *Tiberius* 50.
5. His official name was Drusus Julius Caesar. The marriage to Livilla followed in the aftermath of the death of Augustus' grandsons. See below, p. 119.
6. Tacitus 3.34.6. For a more detailed account of this debate see above, Chapter 2. Barrett (2012), pp. 34ff. draws together the evidence and argues that there must have been a 'basic truth' in Drusus the Younger's assertion.
7. Dio 53.22.5 (Loeb vol. VI, pp. 253ff.). For his illness in Spain see 53.25.7. Barrett (2012), 35, argues that Livia must have been available to nurse him but merely cites this as a probability, his supporting evidence being confined to suggesting that Livia was so self-effacing we should not be surprised if she is absent from the sources. This is totally unconvincing.
8. Suetonius, *Augustus* 24.1.
9. *Odes* 3.14.4–7.

10. See below and Dio 54.19.1–3 (Loeb vol. VI, p. 329).
11. Dio 54.6.4 (Loeb vol. VI, p. 297).
12. *CIL* 10.07340.
13. Josephus, *Jewish Antiquities* 18.31.
14. Dio 54.6ff. (Loeb vol. VI, pp. 295ff.); Goldsworthy (2014), 299, acknowledges only that 'it is quite possible' Livia accompanied Augustus.
15. *CIL* 10.07464.
16. Barrett (2012), 38, states Livia's presence as fact based on an inscription that refers to Livia alone. Conversely, Freisenbruch (2010), 40, recognizes that the evidence is not conclusive for Livia being there. The Aphrodisias inscription (*AE* 1984.867) is available in Greek and English at http://insaph.kcl.ac.uk/iaph2007/iAph080032.html. Freisenbruch (op. cit.) reproduces the English.
17. Dio 54.9.7 (Loeb vol. VI, p. 305).
18. Compare Barrett (2012), 38, 'As Augustus and Livia travelled overland to Rome' with Dio 54.10.2, 'he [Augustus] hastened on to Rome itself'.
19. Suetonius, *Tiberius* 6.4.
20. Suetonius, *Augustus* 64.2, 73.1. Augustus' granddaughters Julia the Younger and Agrippina the Elder, Julia's daughters by Agrippa, received the same education.
21. Vitruvius 7.1–2; see also Wallace-Hadrill (2008), 190–1.
22. Macrobius 2.5.2.
23. Hemelrijk (2004), 53; Kokkinos (2002), 53.
24. Antonia was presented with a book collection of the works of five lyric poets, commemorated in an epigram by Crinagoras of Mytilene, 'The sweet company of the five lyric poets united in this volume offer the work of the inimitable Graces. We come on her festal morning to Antonia, supreme in beauty and mind.' *Greek Anthology* 9.239. This is most readily accessed at the time of writing online at http://www.attalus.org/poetry/crinagoras. html; for Onomaste, see Kokkinos (2002), 61, and *CIL* 6.4434 where Onomaste Laricis(?) is named as a *bibliot(heca) Antoniae*, alongside her seamstress Athenais, indicating the relative status of a librarian.
25. F. Scott Fitzgerald (1925), *The Great Gatsby*, Chapter 3. There is also Anthony Burgess's anecdotal comment that 'the possession of a book becomes a substitute for reading it' (widely attributed). The present author possesses the British prime minister David Lloyd George's personal copy of Seebohm Rowntree's important 1911 report *Unemployment: A Social Study*. The pages have remained uncut, proving that the copy was not read by Lloyd George or anyone else.
26. One is reminded of the fictional Caroline Bingley's remark: 'I declare after all there is no enjoyment like reading! How much sooner one tires of any thing than of a book! When I have a house of my own, I shall be miserable if I have not an excellent library.' Jane Austen (1813), *Pride and Prejudice*, Chapter 11, written in an era when women were similarly constrained.
27. Juvenal, *Satires* 6.434, described how 'annoying' such a woman was. For *lingulaca*, which also means the fish sole, see Varro, *Latin Language* 5.12.77 in the Loeb edition, and the associated note 'f'.
28. Suetonius, *Augustus* 44.2.
29. Dio 54.16.5 (Loeb vol. VI, p. 323).
30. Dio 53.27.5 (Loeb vol. VI, p. 265).
31. Dio 53.28.3 (Loeb vol. VI, p. 267). This flagrant breach of the normal age limits might seem an unreasonable abuse of the system. However, the age limits for office even in provincial towns were ignored shamelessly when it suited the interests of the ruling elite as several instances from Pompeii attest involving children being elected to the town council (see Cooley and Cooley (2004) nos C5, G21, G24). In short, ignoring or bypassing the rules was quite normal in the Roman world.
32. Dio 53.30 *passim* (Loeb vol. VI, pp. 271–3).
33. While 'hardly more than a boy', Suetonius, *Augustus* 63.1.

34. Dio 53.31 *passim* (Loeb vol. VI, pp. 273–5).
35. Suetonius, *Tiberius* 10, though the statement may also be simply a means of enhancing Agrippa's reputation as a man of honour and humility.
36. *Aeneid* 6.860–3, 875–6.
37. Seneca, *To Marcia on Consolation* 2.3–4.
38. Dio 53.33.4 (Loeb vol. VI, p. 279).
39. Seneca, *To Marcia on Consolation* 2.3.
40. Seneca, *To Marcia on Consolation* 2.4; of course at the time Tiberius' brother Drusus was also still alive.
41. Dio 54.3.5 (Loeb vol. VI, p. 289); Plutarch, *Antony* 77–9; Pliny 36.59.183.
42. Tacitus 4.40.
43. Discussed by Bauman (1992), 102–3, who unconvincingly suggests that the stomach pains gave Livia the idea.
44. Suetonius, *Augustus* 63.1.
45. Dio 53.6.5 (Loeb vol. VI, p. 297).
46. See below, p. 142.
47. Dio 54.8.5 (Loeb vol. VI, p. 301).
48. Dio 54.10.4, 19.5, 22.1ff. (Loeb vol. VI, pp. 307, 331, 337). Raetia was a central European Roman province that covered territory now occupied by parts of Switzerland and southern Germany.
49. In total they had nine children (Pliny 7.13.57), but three did not survive infancy.
50. Dio 54.18.1 (Loeb vol. VI, pp. 327–9); Suetonius, *Augustus* 64.1, 3.
51. Claridge (2010), 94–5.
52. Sear (1982), no. 173.
53. Sear (1982), no. 213.
54. Sear (2000), no. 1599; also illustrated by Zanker (1990), 216, fig. 168.
55. Sear (2000), no. 1812, and also restitution versions of this issue produced under Titus and Domitian, ibid. nos 2589 (AD 80), 2894 (AD 81–2). The latter bear reverse legends that confirm their dates, unlike the Caligulan coin.
56. Zanker (1990), p. 217, figs 169–70.
57. Dio 54.12.2–5 (Loeb vol. VI, pp. 313–5); turns down triumph, 54.24.7 (ibid. p. 345).
58. Dio 54.28 *passim* (Loeb vol. VI, pp. 355–7).
59. Pliny 36.24.121 admiringly listed some of them. They included the Aqua Virgo, 500 fountains, 130 water-distribution reservoirs, as well as free entry to 170 public baths.
60. Suetonius, *Augustus* 71.3.
61. Suetonius, *Augustus* 63.2; Dio 54.31 *passim* (Loeb vol. VI, pp. 363–5).
62. Octavia refused to hear his name or have a portrait of Marcellus. Seneca, *To Marcia on Consolation* 2.4.
63. Dio 54.35.4–5 (Loeb vol. VI, pp. 373–5).
64. Suetonius, *Tiberius* 7.2.
65. Tacitus 1.53.3; Pliny, *Natural History* 7.8.45.
66. Dio 54.19.1–3 (Loeb vol. VI, p. 329); Suetonius, *Augustus* 69.1–2, 71.1.
67. Tacitus 1.53.1.
68. Bauman (1992), 112, suggests that Julia claimed superiority because of the divine blood of Augustus that flowed in her veins. This is misleading. Augustus did not pose as a god. To do so would have been political suicide. It was only possible for later descendants to refer to Augustus being divine after his deification by Tiberius. See Tacitus 4.52.4.
69. Tacitus 1.53.3.
70. Suetonius, *Tiberius* 7.3.2–3; Dio 55.2.1 (Loeb vol. VI, pp. 383–5).
71. Flory (1993), 287.
72. Dio 55.2.3–5 (Loeb vol. VI, pp. 385–7). For Livia's third child, see p. 53 and p. 334 n. 62.
73. Purcell (2009), 165, quoting the *Consolatio ad Liviam*. There has been some debate about this poem's authenticity.
74. 2.94.2ff.

75. Suetonius, *Tiberius* 9.1.
76. Dio 55.8.1–2 (Loeb vol. VI, p. 399)
77. Pliny 7.45.149; Suetonius, *Tiberius* 10.1.
78. Velleius Paterculus 2.99.1–2; Tacitus, 1.53.1; Suetonius, *Tiberius* 11.5.
79. 55.9.7 (Loeb vol. VI, p. 405)
80. Goldsworthy (2014), 390, suggests that it is easy to overlook the fact that Roman public and military life was extremely exhausting and that Tiberius was particularly uninterested in the work of an emperor.
81. Tacitus 6.51.2.
82. Dio 55.9.4–8 (Loeb vol. VI, pp. 403–5).
83. Suetonius, *Tiberius* 12.1.
84. See p. 81.
85. For example, a silver denarius issued by the mint of Lugdunum. Sear (2000), no. 1596.
86. See Cooley (2003), no. J56, pp. 219–20.
87. *ILS* 8897. See also Keppie (1991), 55 and fig. 27.
88. See Chapter 3.
89. Suetonius, *Augustus* 65.1.
90. Velleius Paterculus 2.100.3; Dio 55.10.12 (Loeb vol. VI, p. 411).
91. Jones (1970), 164.
92. Suetonius, *Augustus* 71.4.
93. Fantham (2006), xi.
94. Seneca, *On Benefits* 6.1.
95. Suetonius, *Augustus* 29.3, 94.4.
96. Ovid 6.382ff.
97. Pliny, *Natural History* 21.6.10. However, the Latin is ambiguous and may refer simply to 'a letter' written by someone now unknown. Goldsworthy (2014), 398, speculates that it was commonly assumed Augustus had known but turned a blind eye to indulge his daughter.
98. Seneca, *On the Shortness of Life* 4.5, said this was the second time that Augustus had had to fear a woman in league with an Antony.
99. Dio 55.10.15 (Loeb vol. VI, p. 413).
100. Pliny, *Natural History* 7.8.46.
101. Tacitus 1.53.3.
102. Available contraceptive techniques were limited and of dubious reliability. See p. 191.
103. The sayings about Julia can be found at Macrobius 2.5.2ff. He supplies evidence to substantiate his anecdotes.
104. On the advice to emulate Livia, see Macrobius 2.5.3, 6.
105. See above, p. 27 and Livy 4.44.11.
106. Bauman (1992, 110) describes them as 'direct evidence' but provides no basis for making this judgement concerning their reliability. Seneca, *On Benefits* 3.2, describes how dinner guests recorded Augustus' words but it is highly improbable he witnessed this personally though his father, Seneca the Elder, may have done. Nor do we know whether any of these found their way into the histories we possess.
107. *In defence of Plancius* 14.35 where Cicero complained that he was angered when 'the sayings of other men' were attributed to him, not least because he considered himself unworthy of them. This gripe also occurs in a letter of his to Volumnius Eutrapelus (*Letters to his Friends* 7.32.1). See Corbeill (2015), 213.
108. See p. 351, n. 100 and the way Seymour, Lady Worsley, was compared to Messalina in the eighteenth century. Roman knowledge of venereal disease was sketchy, and consequently our knowledge of its prevalence and the forms is limited. The evidence for whether syphilis was known in antiquity is particularly uncertain and disputed (see Gruber el al. 2015). However, in general see for example Martial, *Epigrams* 7.71 referring to the common affliction of the *ficus* or tuberous excrescence characteristic of some sort of sexually transmitted infection. Celsus, *On Medicine* 4.28.1–2, described a male symptom of gonorrhoea, an unusual discharge from the penis (mistaking it for 'an excessive outflow

of semen') and appropriate treatment, but did not apparently recognize that the condition was associated with sexual activity. Pliny the Elder, 20.20.39, recommended the application of onions 'to sores of the genitals', evidently unaware of what had caused the symptoms. Later literature provides more evidence of the probable reality in antiquity. One of Christabel Pankhurst's principal gripes about the philandering habits of men of her era was the consequent infection of their wives with venereal disease, many of whom were unaware of what had happened to them (*The Great Scourge and How to End It*, London 1913). James Boswell had found gonorrhoea, 'the poisonous infection raging in my veins', to be an occupational hazard of his philandering in the early 1760s though he automatically blamed his female partners (Pottle 1950, 157).

109. See above, p. 106.
110. Suetonius, *Augustus* 58.1–2.
111. Tacitus, 3.24.2, adding that Augustus described Julia the Younger's actions in AD 8 the same way.
112. Suetonius, *Tiberius* 11.4; Velleius Paterculus 2.100.5; Dio 55.10.14 (Loeb vol. VI, p. 411).
113. There is some doubt about exactly when this happened. Goldsworthy (2014), 431.
114. Dio 55.13.1 (Loeb vol. VI, p. 425).
115. Suetonius, *Augustus* 65.3.
116. Tacitus 1.53.4–5.
117. Tacitus 4.44.3 and Dio 55.10.15 (Loeb vol. VI, p. 413) say he was killed; Velleius Paterculus says that he committed suicide, 2.100.4. Others were executed or banished to islands. Pliny 7.45.149 states that Julia was found to be plotting to kill Augustus.
118. Dio 55.10. 16 (Loeb vol. VI, p. 413).
119. Propertius 4.11.60. Cornelia's father was Publius Cornelius Scipio. His son of the same name, her brother, claimed descent from Scipio Africanus and served as consul in 16 BC with Lucius Domitius Ahenobarbus, grandfather of the emperor Nero.
120. Seneca, *On Benefits* 6.32.1.
121. Tacitus 1.53.2. Tacitus alleges that Tiberius thought it was so long after she was exiled that no one would notice if she was killed. He had also killed her youngest son, Agrippa Postumus (1.6.1.).
122. Suetonius, *Tiberius* 11.4.
123. Suetonius, *Tiberius* 11.5.
124. Suetonius, *Augustus* 63.1; Augustus, *Res Gestae* 14.
125. *ILS* 8897 (inscription over the entrance to the agora).
126. Zanker (1990), 218–19 and fig. 172.
127. Dio 55.10.8 (Loeb vol. VI, pp. 413–15).
128. Aulus Gellius *Attic Nights* 15.7.3. Augustus' letter, which he wrote partly in Latin and partly in Greek, referred to ὑμῶν ('you' in the plural form), making it clear that both Gaius and his brother Lucius were meant.
129. Tacitus 3.22.1, 23.1. Aemilia Lepida was also descended from Sulla. She should not be confused with another Aemilia Lepida who was Augustus' great-granddaughter through his granddaughter Julia the Younger. See n. 145 below.
130. *CIL* 11.1420; *ILS* 139.
131. Suetonius, *Augustus* 63.1; Florus, *Two Hundred Years of War* 2.32.42–44; Velleius Paterculus 2.102.2–3.
132. Cooley (2003), no. J60. An inscription from Cupra in Picenum referring to the suspension of legal proceedings in Rome until Gaius' remains were deposited in the 'Mausoleum'.
133. *CIL* 11.1421; *ILS* 140.
134. Claridge (2010), 94–5.
135. Tacitus 1.3.3. See Chapter 5.
136. *Res Gestae* 14; Seneca the Elder, *Controversies* 4, preface 5.
137. *CIL* 6.36908, dating the dedication to Lucius' fourteenth year, i.e. 3 BC. It was 'one of the most magnificent buildings in the Roman world' (Claridge, 2010, 69, who cites 2 BC for

the dedication). For Augustus' role in rebuilding the basilica see Dio 54.24.3 (Loeb vol. VI, pp. 343–5).

138. Suetonius, *Augustus* 65.1.
139. Suetonius, *Augustus* 65.1, 4.
140. Suetonius, *Augustus* 19.2.
141. Tacitus, 4.57.3; Dio 57.3.3 (Loeb vol. VII, p. 199).
142. Valerius Maximus 4.3.3.
143. Pliny 7.13.57. Fischer (2016), 43ff., discusses the Gemma Augustea cameo (created no later than AD 12) which depicted Augustus with Tiberius and Germanicus, celebrating the military successes of the latter two. The cameo has been cut down and may also have originally included Tiberius' son Drusus. Either way it undoubtedly reinforced the dynastic descent through Livia.
144. Tacitus 1.33.3; Suetonius, *Augustus* 14.2; Hemelrijk (2004), 27.
145. The betrothal was broken off in 48 when Claudius' last wife, Agrippina the Younger, claimed he had been plotting against the emperor. See below. This Silanus had a brother called Marcus Junius Silanus (14–54) who, Pliny noted with interest, had been born in his great-grandfather Augustus' reign (just) and survived to Nero's when he was poisoned (7.13.58). Aemilia Lepida was also temporarily betrothed to Claudius when both were children. See below, p. 176.
146. Suetonius, *Augustus* 72.3. Aemilia Lepida was to survive until the year 43. She served as a peripheral member of the dynasty; some of her children were to die as a result of their descent from Augustus and the potential threat they posed, for example to Nero (54–68).
147. Suetonius, *Augustus* 64.2. Augustus subjected all his female descendants to the same programme.
148. Suetonius, *Augustus* 19.2.
149. Tacitus, 3.24.2, 4.71.4; Suetonius, *Augustus* 65.4 (the identity of the child Julia was not allowed to bring up is unknown but was obviously a descendant of Augustus); see also Levick (1976).
150. Suetonius, *Augustus* 65.4, 101.3; Tacitus 3.24.2.
151. Julia the Younger died in exile in 28. Tacitus, 4.71.4.
152. Tacitus 3.24.4.

5 The Dowager Empress and Matriarch

1. Purcell (2009), 192.
2. Dio 57.12.2–3 (Loeb vol. VII, p. 141); also Purcell (2009), in particular 168–9. However, his paper argues overall that the Roman matron establishment under Augustus was intended to be a significant and integral political force. Tiberius vetoed the title *mater patriae* for Livia. See below, p. 134.
3. Dio 58.2.3 (Loeb vol. VII, pp. 187–9).
4. ΛΙΟΥΙΑ ΣΕΒΑΣΤΟΥ / ΠΑΤΡΟΣ ΠΑΤΡΙΔΟΣ. The denomination was a diobol (*c.* 25mm in diameter), a small change coin. Sear (2000), no. 1743. Mint of Alexandria. The coins are rare now, usually worn and poorly preserved.
5. Pliny 13.23.74. The original word 'hieratica' became relegated to third-grade paper.
6. Pliny 15.40.136–7. The story is repeated with variations by Suetonius, *Galba* 1.1 and Dio 48.52.3–4 (Loeb vol. V, p. 333).
7. For example 3.3; Dio 53.34.4 (Loeb vol. VI, p. 279) also mentions how suspicion about Livia first surfaced when Marcellus died.
8. Tacitus, 4.71.4; see also 1.3.3 and 1.6.2.
9. 1.3.3–4.
10. Suetonius, *Caligula* 7. Two died as babies, one 'just as he was reaching the age of boyhood'.
11. Syme (1958), 627–8. *CIL* 14.2610.
12. Pliny, 7.45.149; Tacitus, 1.3.3; Velleius Paterculus 2.102.2.
13. *RPC* I 1708.

14. This is discussed in Chapter 2. The principal reference to Livia's participation with Augustus in tours abroad was made during her lifetime in AD 21 by her grandson, Drusus the Younger. Tacitus 3.34.6.
15. Bauman (1992), 124, particularly notes this disparity.
16. Dio 54.19.4 (Loeb vol. VI, p. 329).
17. See above, p. 66.
18. Dio 58.2.4 (Loeb vol. VII, p. 189).
19. Dio 54.16.5 (Loeb vol. VI, p. 323).
20. Tacitus 5.1.3. The words used are *cum artibus mariti, simulatione filii.* The word *ars* can mean skill or profession as well, but there seems no doubt that Tacitus was using one of its other meanings to suggest guile or cunning, just as he used *simulatio* to suggest Tiberius' inclination to pretence or hypocrisy.
21. Dio 55.14.8, 15.3 (Loeb vol. VI, pp. 431–3). The 'soldiers' must be the Praetorian Guard. A shorter, but much earlier, version of the story is in Seneca, *On Mercy* 1.9.6–7.
22. Dio 55.16.2–3, 19.4 (Loeb vol. VI, pp. 443–5).
23. Zanker (1990), 231, fig. 182.
24. For the Pudicitia shrines, see above, p. 122. For Bona Dea Subsaxana and Livia's restoration see Ovid, *Fasti* 5.153–8 and Purcell (2009), 181. Saxum was a part of the Aventine Hill on its north side at the east end of the Circus Maximus. The temple was on the present site of the church of S. Balbina but no trace of it has survived.
25. Fantham (2011), 450. See also below when Livia took it upon herself to encourage fire-fighters trying to douse the flames consuming the Temple of Vesta.
26. Such as compensating victims of fires. Dio 57.16.2 (Loeb vol. VII, pp. 153–5).
27. Stories suggesting someone being preordained to rule are not uncommon in histories written after the event seeking to justify a later regime. Henry VI of England is reputed to have said to Henry Tudor, on being presented with the boy, that he was destined to become king as indeed he did in 1485, seizing the crown to become Henry VII. Alternatively that story may have been inspired by the one about Galba.
28. Suetonius, *Galba* 4, 5.2. Tiberius amended the will and drastically reduced the legacy from 50 million to 500,000 sesterces, i.e. to 1 per cent. See Barrett (2012), 174.
29. Scardigli (1982).
30. Seneca, *On Anger* 1.18.3–6, recounting Piso's ordering a soldier to be executed which turned into the execution of three soldiers simply because Piso would not back down after an initial misunderstanding had been resolved.
31. Urgulania's son Marcus Plautius Silvanus had served as consul with Augustus in 2 BC, and in a military command under Tiberius in Illyricum in AD 7. Her granddaughter Plautia Urgulanilla was the first wife of the future emperor Claudius, Livia's grandson. Her closeness to Livia explains why she believed she was entitled to be protected from the law.
32. Tacitus 2.34.2–4 covers the Urgulania story.
33. Suetonius, *Augustus* 44.3; Tacitus 4.16.4. Note also that Julia Domna is attested as having enjoyed exemption from duties normally paid by vehicular traffic; see p. 278. Also Dio 60.22.2 (Loeb vol. VII, p. 423) on Livia's privileged use of front row seats in the theatre.
34. Suetonius, *Augustus* 34.2.
35. Tacitus 1.5.1–2.
36. Dio 56.30.1 (Loeb vol. VII, pp. 69–71).
37. Tacitus 1.4.2–5; Suetonius, *Tiberius* 52.1.
38. Dio 56.30.2–3 (Loeb vol. VII, p. 71); Tacitus 1.10.5.
39. Suetonius, *Augustus* 98.1–5.
40. Tacitus 1.5.4; Dio 56.31.1 (Loeb vol. VII, pp. 69–71).
41. Tacitus 1.6.1; Suetonius, *Tiberius* 22.1.
42. For Apicadus and Telephus, see above, p. 112. Oddly, the city of Corinth in Achaea issued a small bronze coin in Agrippa Postumus' honour in *c.* AD 4–5. Sear (2000), no. 1752. This was most unusual.

43. Suetonius, *Tiberius* 50.1.
44. Suetonius, *Tiberius* 23.1–24.1.
45. Balsdon (1962), 222. This also relates to the lex Voconia of 169 BC which prevented a man worth more than 100,000 sesterces from making a woman his heir. The provisions were, however, complicated and ambiguous and seem to have been more concerned with making sure that the male heirs were the principal beneficiaries of estates in order to keep them intact.
46. Dio 56.32.1 (Loeb vol. VII, pp. 71–3); Tacitus 1.8.1–2.
47. Rehak (1990) discusses the funerary symbolism of the dedication of a cinnamon root in a golden bowl by Livia, mentioned by Pliny at 12.29.94.
48. Dio 56.46.1–2 (Loeb vol. VII, p.105).
49. Dio 59.30.1 (Loeb vol. VII, p. 361).
50. *CIL* 10.7501. See also plate 10; Hemelrijk (2015), 136, 428. The inscription is illustrated and described by Bonanno (2005), 205.
51. *CIL* 15.7264.
52. Claridge (2010), 135. Barrett (2012), pp. 177ff. seems to assume or at least imply that the house was Livia's without supplying any additional evidence to substantiate her ownership.
53. Known today as the Primaporta villa. Suetonius, *Galba* 1.1.
54. See for example Braund (1985) no. 753 concerning an estate of Livia's in the Arsinoite nome in Egypt where crops had been damaged by stray livestock in 28–9. The land had previously belonged to a Gaius Julius Alexander. It is not known when, how or why Livia acquired the estate but Alexander's full name might be evidence that he was an imperial freedman.
55. Barrett (2012), 181–4, provides a useful survey of Livia's property.
56. Joshel (1992), pp. 101–2; Treggiari (1975), 48–77; see also Barrett (2012), 180.
57. Dio describes Livia's 'prattling boys' at 48.44.3 (Loeb vol. V, p. 313). For Andromeda, the female dwarf, see Pliny 7.16.75 who adds that Julia the Elder had a 'pet' dwarf called Conopas who was 2ft 5 in. high (71.5 cm).
58. See Barrett (2012), 182.
59. This remained a characteristic of Julio-Claudian coinage. In later periods, for example under the Severans, coins issued solely in the name of an empress did not carry male imperial titles, making it impossible to date them precisely.
60. Sear (2000), nos 1739–41. See also Bartman (1999) and Jessen (2013) on the evolving portraiture of Livia reflecting the emergence of the imperial state.
61. Sear (2000), no. 1738.
62. Pliny 7.43.141.
63. Sear (1982), no. 189. This coin of the Deified Augustus and Livia, being struck only for provincial use, is now rare.
64. Sear (1982), nos 199 (Aphrodisias, Aphrodite), 202 (Aezani, Cybele).
65. Tacitus 4.57.3; Dio 57.3.3 (Loeb vol. VII, p. 199).
66. Suetonius, *Tiberius* 26.2. The relationship between Julia Soaemias and the Senate in the early third century took this to a whole different level (see p. 288). Tacitus 1.14.1.
67. Dio 56.47.1 (Loeb vol. VII, p. 107).
68. Tacitus 1.14.1–2. Coins of Livia had been issued under Augustus in Egypt between AD 1 and 5 with another sidestepping version of the title. See p. 116. Also Suetonius, *Tiberius* 50.3, Dio 57.12.4, 58.2.3 (Loeb vol. VII, pp. 141, 187–9). For the *parens patriae* coins of Caesar see Sear (2000), no. 1422, struck shortly after his assassination.
69. Ovid, *Letters from Pontus* 4.13.29; Newlands (1995), 131, discusses the Augustan association of the cult with womanly virtues and with Livia. Ovid's *Fasti* also showed the very close proximity in the Roman religious calendar between Vesta (6.249ff.) on 9 June and Matralia, the cult of good mothers (6.475ff.), on 11 June.
70. Suetonius, *Tiberius* 50.3.
71. Tacitus 1.72.4.
72. Suetonius, *Tiberius* 59.1.

73. The fall of the praetorian prefect Sejanus, owing to his affair with Antonia's widowed daughter Livilla, once married to Tiberius' son, also Drusus (who died in AD 23).
74. Tacitus 6.25.1.
75. Tacitus 1.33.3; Suetonius, *Tiberius* 52.1.
76. Dio 54.19.6 (Loeb vol. VI, p. 331).
77. Cooley (2003), M81.
78. Suetonius, *Augustus* 64.2.
79. Alston (1998), 30.
80. This Nero should *not* be confused with the emperor Nero who was born Lucius Domitius Ahenobarbus, the only child of Agrippina the Younger. This Drusus should also not be confused either with the brother of Tiberius, Drusus the Elder, or Tiberius' son Drusus the Younger.
81. Suetonius, *Tiberius* 50.
82. Tacitus 1.33.1–3.
83. Dio 57.3.1–2 (Loeb vol. VII, p. 119).
84. Suetonius, *Caligula* 8.1–5. Suetonius provides ample evidence to dismiss the idea. Agrippina, however, did give birth to some of her other children while away from Rome.
85. The main part of the story is at Tacitus 1.40–44 *passim*. It is worth noting that Velleius Paterculus makes no mention of Agrippina at all in his brief notice of this war. See 2.125. This either means that Tacitus had exaggerated her role or that Velleius was reluctant to acknowledge it.
86. Dio 57.5.6–7 (Loeb vol. VII, pp. 125–7).
87. Tacitus 1.69.1–5, who states that his main source was Pliny the Elder in a now-lost work.
88. Sear (2000), no. 1827.
89. Tacitus 1.69.5.
90. Suetonius, *Augustus* 100.3, 101.2.
91. Suetonius, *Tiberius* 23.1.
92. Tacitus 1.24.1, using the term 'first citizens', which must mean senators.
93. Tacitus 1.52.1–3.
94. Tacitus 1.76.3–4.
95. Tacitus 2.26.2–5.
96. Tacitus 2.43.1, 44.1.
97. Suetonius, *Caligula* 10.1. See below for the evidence there were two.
98. Tacitus 2.54.4. The extant manuscripts allow for two readings. The alternative is *exitium*, 'extermination'. The ambiguity would have pleased the oracle since uncertainty of interpretation was ideal.
99. Tacitus 2.55.1–6.
100. Tacitus 2.55.5; Rutland (1978), 16.
101. Tacitus 2.59–61 *passim*.
102. It becomes apparent from Agrippina's return to Italy (see below) that only two children were with them.
103. Tacitus 2.69–70 *passim*.
104. Tacitus 2.73.4.
105. Dio 57.18.6 (Loeb vol. VII, p. 163); Tacitus 2.82.1–2.
106. Tacitus 3.1–2.
107. 'The senate and a large section of the people filled the route, scattered in disarray and weeping.' Tacitus 3.2.3. The image resembles that seen in Britain after the death of Diana, Princess of Wales. It was a modern event that does attest to the possibility of a form of mass hysteria resulting from the death of a popular and extremely prominent figure.
108. Tacitus 3.4 *passim*.
109. Tacitus 3.5–6 *passim*.
110. Sherk (1988), no. 36, Part A.
111. 3.12.2.

112. Suetonius, *Tiberius* 52.3. Dio 57.18.9 backs up some of this and adds his belief that Tiberius brought the charge against Piso only to distance himself from suspicion.
113. Tacitus 3.14.3–16.1. See also Alston (1998), 34–5.
114. Tacitus 3.14.3–17.2.
115. Tacitus 3.29.1.
116. Tacitus 4.4.1.
117. Tacitus 3.29 *passim*.
118. Tacitus 3.56.4. For the award of the tribunician power see Tacitus 3.56.1, and also 59.2. This did not become a routine means of designating a successor until after the Julio-Claudian period.
119. Tacitus 3.64.1.
120. Suetonius, *Tiberius* 54.1.
121. Dio 57.18,6–8, 19.1 (Loeb vol. VII, pp. 163–5).
122. Tacitus 4.12.2.
123. Tacitus 4.3.3.
124. The story was later confirmed in a suicide note written by Sejanus' betrayed wife Apicata when Sejanus was exposed in 31. Dio 57.22.1–4, 58.11.6–7 (Loeb vol. VII, pp. 177, 217).
125. Dio 57.22.4 (Loeb vol. VII, p. 217); see also Fantham et al. (1995), 313, on the prioritizing of dynastic propaganda.
126. Fischer (2016), 44–51. The Grand Camée is 31 x 26 cm, making it exceptionally large. It is most likely to have been made between 19 (the death of Germanicus) and 29 (the year of Livia's death) though obviously Agrippina's involvement in its manufacture is entirely speculative.
127. Sear (2000), nos 1793, 1794.
128. See above, p. 88.
129. Tacitus 4.39–40.
130. Tacitus 4.17 *passim*.
131. Bauman (1992), 145, 154–6 becomes deeply involved in 'what Tacitus means' by *partes Agrippinae* because Tacitus also uses the word *partes* in connection with Agrippina the Younger at a later date (13.8.3–5). Since the term was one either in existence in 24 or coined by Sejanus, Tacitus was merely reporting it. He is unlikely to have invented it in the context of Agrippina the Elder, making speculation about his meaning irrelevant. Bauman is also unconvincing in suggesting that the use of *partes* in connection with Agrippina the Younger is somehow 'no accident'. The context is completely different and there is no reason to believe that the word could only be used for one exclusive meaning.
132. Tacitus 4.18.1–3. Gaius Silius was the father of Messalina's lover of the same name.
133. Tacitus 4.19.1–20.2.
134. He also went on to accuse a friend of Agrippina the Elder's, provoking Caligula's ire. See below.
135. Bauman (1992), 146, constructs a convoluted but completely unsubstantiated argument to suggest that Agrippina was genuinely guilty.
136. Tacitus 4.52.3; Suetonius, *Tiberius* 53.1.
137. Tacitus 4.53.
138. Tacitus 4.54.1–2; Suetonius, *Tiberius* 53.1.
139. Tacitus 4.57.1–3.
140. Tacitus 4.59.1–2.
141. Tacitus 4.2; Dio 58.4.3 (Loeb vol. VII, pp. 195–7).
142. Tacitus 4.67.3–4. The text is rather cryptic and the translation not wholly clear. But the suggestion appears to be that Sejanus and his agents wanted Agrippina and Nero to act very publicly to save themselves in a way that might look treacherous. They were too clever to fall into the trap, so Sejanus' stooges just spread the story that Agrippina and Nero were planning that anyway.
143. Tacitus 4.68.3–4.

144. Tacitus 4.70.4.
145. Tacitus 4.74.1–4.
146. Suetonius, *Tiberius* 43, rounds up a selection of the most salacious and revolting anecdotes, thereby guaranteeing himself a perpetual readership.
147. Tacitus 3.24.2, 4.71.4; Seneca, *Octavia* 944–46.
148. Tacitus 4.75. Gnaeus Domitius Ahenobarbus nearly lost his life at the end of Tiberius' reign. See Tacitus 6.47–48.1.

6 Impatient for Equality

1. Tacitus 5.1.1.
2. Dio 58.2.1 (Loeb vol. VII, p. 187); Velleius Paterculus 2.130.4–5.
3. Suetonius, *Tiberius* 51.2.
4. Dio 58.2.2 (Loeb vol. VII, p. 187). This was later reversed.
5. Dio 58.2.6 (Loeb vol. VII, p. 189). An arch from Superaequum (Castelvecchio Subequo in L'Aquila) was dedicated to Livia as 'Augusta, Daughter of Drusus, Mother of Tiberius Caesar and Drusus Germanicus'. This gives an indication of the dedication that might have appeared on the lost Rome arch, had it ever been executed. *CIL* 9.3304.
6. Suetonius, *Tiberius* 51.2; Dio 58.2.3 (Loeb vol. VII, p. 189).
7. Dio 57.22.4 (Loeb vol. VII, p. 177).
8. Tacitus 5.3.1.
9. Tacitus 5.3 *passim*; Suetonius, *Caligula* 7.
10. Cotta Messalinus was related to Caligula's wife Lollia Paulina, and also Nero's last wife Statilia Messalina.
11. Tacitus 5.4.1–2.
12. Philo, *Against Flaccus* 3.9, 19.158. Flaccus was later executed on Caligula's orders, 21.185.
13. Seneca, *On Anger* 3.21.5, referring to how Caligula later had the villa destroyed because it had been his mother's place of incarceration. For her exile to Pandateria, see Suetonius, *Tiberius* 53.1.
14. Suetonius, *Tiberius* 54.2; Dio 58.8.4 (Loeb vol. VII, p. 209).
15. Dio 58.3.8 (Loeb vol. VII, p. 195); Tacitus 6.40.3.
16. Suetonius, *Tiberius* 55.1. Alston (1998), 45, subscribes to the view that Sejanus was being used by Tiberius who knew that withdrawal of his support would bring about Sejanus' downfall.
17. Dio 58.7.4–5 (Loeb vol. VII, pp. 205–7).
18. Dio 58.9–11 *passim*. Livilla's involvement is at 58.11.7 (Loeb vol. VII, p. 217).
19. Tacitus 6.23.2 doubted its veracity.
20. Tacitus 6.10.1.
21. Dio 58.13–14 (Loeb vol. VII, pp. 223–5); Livilla's death is at 58.11.7 where Dio notes that it took place some time later.
22. Tacitus 6.2.1. Flower (2011), 174ff. Very few monuments of Livilla survive. On one to Antonia Minor found at Ilion, the site of Troy, Livilla is described as 'the divine Aphrodite of Anchises' (Anchises being the father of Aeneas in myth), ibid. 176.
23. Marcus Junius Silanus was consul in 15. Tacitus was unable to find out any more about the story. 5.10.1–3. His daughter Junia Claudilla was Caligula's first wife. He should not be confused with Marcus Junius Silanus Torquatus, the son-in-law of Julia the Younger (see Family Tree 3).
24. Tacitus 6.23.2–24.1–2.
25. Suetonius, *Tiberius* 53 *passim*; Tacitus 25.1–3.
26. Tacitus 6.10.1.
27. Seneca, *Octavia* 935–7.
28. Dio 59.6.3–4 (Loeb vol. VII, p. 277).
29. Caligula's sister Drusilla was married to Lucius Cassius Longinus (Suetonius, *Caligula* 24.1; Tacitus 6.15.1.), and subsequently Aemilius Lepidus (Josephus, *Jewish Antiquities* 115.20, 49); Caligula's other sister Julia Livilla was married to Marcus Vinicius (Tacitus

6.15.1); Tiberius' granddaughter Julia Livia was married in 33 to Gaius Rubellius Blandus; she was later killed after a false accusation of incest by Messalina.

30. Tacitus 6.40.3.
31. The story comes from Pliny 10.60.121–123.
32. Tacitus 6.38.1.
33. Tacitus 6.45.1–2, 51.3; Dio 57.16.2 (Loeb vol. VII, pp. 153–5).
34. Tacitus 6.20.1, 45.3; Suetonius, *Caligula* 12.2.
35. Tacitus 6.45.3; Suetonius, *Caligula* 12.2.
36. Tiberius was quite wrong in this judgement as post-68 events proved. Honouring Augustus became an essential ingredient in the profile of all future emperors.
37. Tacitus 6.46 *passim*. For Tiberius' concerns that Gemellus was not really his grandson see Suetonius, *Tiberius* 62.3.
38. Suetonius, *Tiberius* 73.2.
39. Tacitus 6.50 *passim*.
40. Suetonius, *Caligula* 13.
41. Dio 56.46.3, 59, 7.4 (Loeb vol. VII, pp. 105 and 279). See also, Jones (1993), 91, for a discussion of the evidence, and also Fishwick (1992). Construction was far enough advanced under Tiberius for him to use it as a place to display artworks; see Pliny 35.40.131.
42. Dio 59.8.1 (Loeb vol. VII, p. 283); Suetonius, *Caligula* 23.3.
43. Suetonius, *Caligula* 10.1, 15.2.
44. Suetonius, *Claudius* 11.2; Sear (1982), no. 347.
45. Dio 59.3.4 (Loeb vol. VII, pp. 267–9).
46. Josephus, *Jewish Antiquities* 18.236–7. Dio also suggests that Caligula was annoyed at being rebuked by her, 59.3.6.
47. Suetonius, *Caligula* 29.1. For Antonia's death see Dio 69.3.6 (Loeb vol. VII, p. 269), Smallwood (1967), 28, no. 31.
48. Suetonius, *Caligula* 16.3.
49. Sear (2000), no. 1803. The coin is comparatively common today. The seated depiction of Vesta was used by Galba and the Flavians. Later empresses more often used a standing figure of Vesta. The probable connection of the type with Livia is not normally noted. For the statue by Scopas see Pliny 36.4.25. The Gardens also displayed statues of Flora and Ceres, ibid. 23.
50. Suetonius, *Caligula* 23.1–2.
51. See Mullens (1942), 62.
52. Sear (2000), no. 1812. Since Claudius was not descended from Agrippa it is difficult to see how the type could be attributed to his reign.
53. Dio 59.3.5 (Loeb vol. VII, p. 269).
54. *CIL* 6.40372; *ILS* 180. The inscription is prominently displayed in the Tabularium section of the Capitoline Museum, Rome.
55. Flower (2011), 138.
56. Dio 59.19.1–6 (Loeb vol. VII, pp. 319–23).
57. Sear (2000), nos 1823–7. Claudius also struck coins in Agrippina's name, but only identified as Germanicus' wife, and with a reverse bearing Claudius' imperial titles. This type is somewhat less rare than Caligula's issue. Ibid. no. 1906.
58. Sear (2000), nos 1813–22. The gold and silver identify Germanicus as Caligula's father.
59. Sear (2000), nos 1828. The design was used on the reverse of some of Nero's coins.
60. Sidonius, *Letters* 5.7.7.
61. Dio 59.3.4. (Loeb vol. VII, p. 269); Suetonius, *Caligula* 15.3.
62. Suetonius, *Caligula* 24.1, 29.1; Dio 59.3.6. (Loeb vol. VII, p. 269).
63. Josephus, *Jewish Antiquities* 19.204. Probably Drusilla.
64. Suetonius, *Caligula* 22.1, 'And he came near assuming a crown at once and changing the semblance of a principate into the form of a monarchy.'
65. 'If contemporary gossip was the first cause, the historians' lack of integrity was the second.' Balsdon (1962), 64, who attributed this all to the 'salacious imagination' of contemporary Roman society.

66. Seneca, *On Firmness* 18.2. Asiaticus was under Claudius accused falsely of leading a plot against the state. Tacitus, 11.1–3 *passim*. His wife Lollia Saturnina was sister of Caligula's third wife Lollia Paulina.
67. Suetonius, *Caligula* 36; Vout (2009), 1–4.
68. Suetonius, *Augustus* 69.1, 71.1.
69. Unfortunately, we do not possess the section in Tacitus' *Annals* that covered the reign. This might have offered either some balance, or at least more clarification of detail.
70. Sear (2000), no. 1800. Septimius Severus issued a similar type depicting the Three Monetae, Sear (2002), no. 6416.
71. M. Aemilius Lepidus was the son of Julia the Younger and therefore descended from Augustus himself.
72. Sherk (1988) no. 42 B12.
73. See above, p. 129. The stories are so similar that one has to question whether both are true. It is possible that one is a confused rehash of the other.
74. Dio 59.11.1–6. (Loeb vol. VII, pp. 293–5).
75. Dio 59.8.7–8 (Loeb vol. VII, p. 285), Suetonius, *Caligula* 25.1.

7 Self-Destruction

1. Suetonius, *Caligula* 26.5; Dio 59.13 *passim*. For the recall of those who had been banished, see Suetonius, *Caligula* 15.4.
2. Alston (1998), 63.
3. Dio 59.19.1–6 (Loeb vol. VII, pp. 319–23); Suetonius, *Caligula* 23.1.
4. Suetonius, *Caligula* 22 *passim*.
5. Alston (1998), 63.
6. Suetonius, *Caligula* 15.2., 23.2; Dio 59.6.5 (Loeb vol. VII, p. 277).
7. See p. 210 for the fact that a descendant of this line was later betrothed to Claudius' daughter, Claudia Octavia.
8. Suetonius, *Claudius* 26.1.
9. Suetonius, *Claudius* 27.1.
10. Suetonius, *Claudius* 26.2; Levick (1990), 55.
11. Suetonius, *Claudius* 26.1–2. For Claudia Pulchra, sister of Messalla Barbatus, see Tacitus 12.52.1 and above, p. 152.
12. Suetonius, *Claudius* 3.2.
13. Suetonius, *Caligula* 24.3.
14. Caligula had forced Drusilla to divorce her first husband and marry Lepidus. Dio 59.22.6 (Loeb vol. VII, p. 329). Lepidus' execution is at Seneca, *Letters* 4.7.
15. Dio 59.22.6–23.2 (Loeb vol. VII, pp. 329–31); Suetonius, *Caligula* 24.3, 39.1.
16. Dio 59.12.1, 23.7 (Loeb vol. VII, pp. 295, 333); Suetonius, *Caligula* 25.2.
17. After he had had Messalina executed. Suetonius, *Claudius* 26.3.
18. Dio 59.23.7 (Loeb vol. VII, p. 333); Suetonius, *Caligula* 25.3–5. Barrett (1989), 62, suggests that Macro had influenced Caligula to limit Antonia's powers since it was clear she had played a part in Sejanus' downfall.
19. Tacitus 4.47.2–48.1.
20. Juvenal, *Satires* 6.614–17.
21. Suetonius, *Caligula* 33.
22. Suetonius, *Caligula* 59.
23. Dio 60.1–3 (Loeb vol. VII, pp. 367–75); Suetonius, *Claudius* 10; Josephus, *Jewish Antiquities* 19.212–21. See also de la Bédoyère (2017), 94–5.
24. Dio 60.12.5 (Loeb vol. VII, p. 399). It is not clear why he did this but it was probably linked to the elevation of his mother Antonia posthumously to Augusta and a wish to avoid Messalina enjoying parity (see p. 183). He also denied his son the title Augustus. See also Saunders (1994).
25. For the cameos, see the Index for the Grand Camée de France and the Gemma Claudia, and also Fischer (2016).

26. Dio 60.4.1 (Loeb vol. VII, p. 375).
27. Suetonius, *Galba* 5.1. Galba came from an old noble family. He was consul in 33 and had enjoyed the favour of Livia. He would be the first of the non-Julio-Claudian emperors after the death of Nero in 68. Augustus, allegedly, foretold that he would try his hand at becoming emperor, ibid. 4.1. So also did Tiberius, see Tacitus 6.20.2.
28. Suetonius, *Nero* 6.3–4.
29. Suetonius, *Nero* 6.4.
30. Zanker (1990), 303, fig. 234.
31. Crinagoras in *Greek Anthology* 9.239. See above, p. 337, n. 24. Echoed in Plutarch, *Antony* 87.3.
32. Valerius Maximus 4.3.3; Pliny 7.19.80. The Loeb translation calls her 'Drusus's daughter Antonia' but it is clearly in error. The Latin states '*Antonia Drusi*', i.e. 'Antonia [wife of] Drusus', thereby distinguishing her from her elder sister Antonia Major.
33. Sear (2000), nos 1851, 1868–9, 1898–1907. *RPC* 495, 2430 (plate 21).
34. Tacitus 6.45.1; Suetonius, *Claudius* 11.2; Dio 60.5.2 (Loeb vol. VIII, pp. 377–9). See also Fraschetti (2001), 117.
35. Sear (2002), no. 4235 (sestertius; silver versions were also issued). The inscription is *CIL* 6.4222 and *ILS* 4995. See Fishwick (1992) for an extensive discussion of the available evidence for the temple's history. The temple was possibly originally hexastyle if the sestertius of Caligula showing him sacrificing in front of a temple depicts the same building. See Sear (2000) no. 1802.
36. Dio 60.5.1–2 (Loeb vol. VII, pp. 377–9).
37. Claudius was born on 1 August 10 BC in Lugdunum (Lyon). Suetonius, *Claudius* 2.1.
38. Sear (2000), nos 1853, 1855–60.
39. Sear (1982), no. 496. Fantham et al. (1994), 313, make much of the Caesarea coin of Messalina as a mechanism for Claudius emphasizing his legitimacy. This completely misses the point – it is the virtual absence of Messalina from Claudius' coinage other than a few provincial issues that raises more questions about her relative standing at his court.
40. Dio 60.8.4–5 (Loeb vol. VII, pp. 387–9), 61.10.1 (ibid., vol. VIII, p. 57); Suetonius, *Claudius* 29.1. Messalina came to believe that Julia Livilla's husband, Marcus Vinicius, had killed her. Dio 60.27.4 (ibid. vol. VII, p. 437).
41. Dio 61.10.2 (Loeb vol. VII, p. 57).
42. Tacitus 13.43.2–3; Suetonius, *Claudius* 29.1; Dio 60.18.4 (Loeb vol. VII, p. 415).
43. Dio 60.14.2 (Loeb vol. VII, pp. 401–3); Suetonius, *Claudius* 37.2; Tacitus, his murder noted at 11.29.1.
44. Levick (1990), 58–9.
45. Dio 60.15–16.3 (Loeb vol. VII, pp. 403–3).
46. Dio 60.17.4–9 (Loeb vol. VII, pp. 411–13).
47. Dio 60.18.1–4 (Loeb vol. VII, pp. 413–15); Tacitus 13.43.2; Seneca, *Octavia* 941ff.
48. Dio 60.22.3–5 (Loeb vol. VII, p. 423).
49. Dio 60.18.3 (Loeb vol. VII, p. 415).
50. Suetonius, *Claudius* 17.
51. Dio 60.22.1–2 (Loeb vol. VII, p. 423). Augustus had ordered that women normally be seated in the upper tiers; Suetonius, *Augustus* 44.2.
52. Suetonius, *Claudius* 36. He suggests that it was not until Silius came on to the scene that Claudius' 'ardent love' for Messalina diminished. See below, p. 195. Messalina's activities, and Claudius' use of prostitutes, may well have exposed them both to the barely understood consequences of venereal disease; see Chapter 4, n. 108, for a discussion of this in connection with Julia the Elder.
53. Soranus, *Gynaecology* 1.61.1–3; Pliny 29.27.85 quoting 'the commentaries of Caecilius'. Another plant, *silphium*, possibly associated with contraception and certainly many other medicinal uses, had led to its being harvested into extinction in Cyrenaica, its main source, by Pliny's time (19.38–40). See also Riddle (1992).
54. Dio 60.26.1–2 (Loeb vol. VII, p. 33); eclipse details accessed from NASA at https://eclipse.gsfc.nasa.gov/SEsearch/SEsearchmap.php?Ecl=00450801.

55. Dio 60.27.4 (Loeb vol. VII, p. 437).
56. Dio 60.28.2 (Loeb vol. VII, p. 439).
57. Pliny 29.5.8.
58. Dio 60.28.3–5 (Loeb vol. VII, pp. 439–41).
59. Dio 61.29.3–4 (Loeb vol. VIII, pp. 3–5).
60. Claudia Antonia was married to Faustus Cornelius Sulla Felix, son of Domitia Lepida by her second husband (of the same name). He was thus Messalina's half-brother.
61. Sear (2000), no. 1907. These coins formed part of a longer series which included more conventional types just showing Claudius.
62. Details of the career of Asiaticus can be found in Sijpesteijn (1989).
63. Tacitus 11.1–3. Tacitus says at 4.14.3 that Suillius was 'powerful and venal . . . and immoral' though a friend of Claudius'.
64. Dio 61.29.4–6 (Loeb vol. VIII, p. 5).
65. Dio 60.5.8–9 (Loeb vol. VII, p. 381); 61.29.6 (Loeb vol. VIII, p. 5); Suetonius, *Claudius* 29.2.
66. Dio 61.30.6 (Loeb vol. VIII, p. 9).
67. Tacitus 11.4–7 *passim*.
68. I.e. from Livia, Octavia, Augustus (via Julia the Elder, Agrippina the Elder and Agrippina the Younger) and Antony.
69. Tacitus 11.11–12; Suetonius, *Nero* 6.4.
70. Pliny 10.83.172.
71. Dio 60.30.6–31.3 (Loeb vol. VIII, pp. 9–11).
72. Strong (2016), 109, refers to 'fantastic allegations of uncontrolled, unorthodox promiscuity'. Tacitus 11.26.1 has her 'drifting to hitherto unrecognized lusts'.
73. Riddle (1992), 19.
74. Tacitus 11.12.2.
75. Suetonius, *Claudius* 29.3.
76. Tacitus 11.12–13.
77. Tacitus 11.26.1.
78. Dio 60.31.1–4 (Loeb vol. VIII, p. 11); Tacitus 11.26.1, 5.
79. Dio 60.31; Tacitus 11.26.
80. Juvenal, *Satires* 10.329–45.
81. Tacitus 11.28.
82. Tacitus 11.29; Dio 61.31.4–5 (Loeb vol. VIII, pp. 11–13). Both refer to more than one prostitute being involved but only Calpurnia was used to speak to Claudius in person.
83. Tacitus 11.30. There are problems with the exact meaning of Tacitus in some of this passage.
84. Tacitus 11.31.
85. Tacitus 11.32. For the 'immunity' conferred on an empress's vehicle, see the plate once affixed to one of Julia Domna's carriages, p. 278.
86. Tacitus 11.33–4.
87. Tacitus 11.3.1. Co-consul with Claudius in 47. Smallwood (1967), 3.
88. Gaius Silius senior had been prosecuted for extortion and treason under Tiberius. Tacitus 11.35.2, and also Velleius Paterculus 2.130.3.
89. Tacitus 11.35; Suetonius, *Claudius* 36.1.
90. Tacitus 11.36; Dio 61.31.5 (Loeb vol. VIII, p. 13).
91. Tacitus 11.37–8; Dio 61.31.5 (Loeb vol. VIII, p. 13). Few now exist. See Flower (2011), 184ff. for a list of some of the erasures.
92. Flower (2011), 182ff.
93. Suetonius, *Claudius* 39.
94. Alston (1998), 93–4.
95. For example Virgil, *Aeneid* 4.101; Tacitus 4.12.1.
96. Juvenal, *Satires* 6.118; Cleopatra was the 'whore queen of incestuous Canopus', Propertius 3.11.39; also Pliny 9.58.119. Courtney (2013), 237. Juvenal's snipe was also based on the fact that Messalina was not granted the official title Augusta.

97. Alston (1998), 94.
98. *Octavia* 258–9. Seneca depicted the killing of Messalina as a result of Claudius falling into a rage in his (probably) *Apocolocyntosis* (11), a scathing satire of Claudius.
99. Scullard (1982), 302.
100. Tacitus 11.26.1. One should not assume that Messalina's behaviour, or the way it was perceived by contemporaries and later historians, was unique to the Roman period. The notorious Seymour, Lady Worsley (1758–1818), famously had more than two dozen lovers and proved herself in court more than equal to her husband's attempts to punish her through the law. The parallel is not inappropriate. In her own time Lady Worsley was explicitly compared to the promiscuous Messalina, being described as the Messalina of 'the Modern Age' in *The Rambler* (quoted by Rubenhold, 2009, 142).
101. Flower (2011), 184, likens what happened to Messalina as a 'kind of coup', resembling the process of one emperor being deposed and replaced with another.

8 The Reign of Agrippina the Younger: Part 1

1. Pliny 7.16.71.
2. Scullard (1982), 303–4.
3. Polydore Vergil, cited in Dockray (2000), 14, said of Henry VI's queen Margaret of Anjou that she was 'much given to mutability and change', a direct allusion to Virgil, *Aeneid* 4.569, though he sympathized with her. See also the far more critical English Chronicle, also cited on p. 16 by Dockray, and its allegations of greed and adultery. Like Agrippina, Margaret of Anjou had a role model in a very assertive mother in Isabella, Duchess of Lorraine.
4. The date is inferred from the fact that by 47 the gap in Tacitus affecting the reign of Caligula and first few years of Claudius' reign ends. The resumed extant text makes no mention of Crispus' death which would be expected if it had happened then, given that he was Agrippina's husband. It must have happened before. Agrippina maintained a ferocious rivalry with Passienus' former wife, Domitia, and her sister-in-law (Tacitus 13.19.4).
5. See above, p. 182.
6. Suetonius, *Life of Passienus Crispus*. His life and relationship with Agrippina are discussed in some detail by Barrett (1996), 84–6.
7. Dio 61.31.6 (Loeb vol. VIII, p. 13).
8. Tacitus 12.1.
9. Dio 61.31.8 (Loeb vol. VIII, p. 15).
10. Ironically, later Agrippina would try insisting to Nero that Britannicus was the true heir as a threat in order to manipulate him.
11. Tacitus 12.3; Suetonius, *Claudius* 27.3, 39.2.
12. Pliny 10.43.84, 59.120. The conspicuous consumption of the super-rich remains a timeless fascination, as witnessed by modern television documentaries salaciously recounting the absurd and outrageous indulgences of today's multi-millionaires and billionaires.
13. Suetonius, *Galba* 5.1, *Vespasian* 4.2.
14. Fischer (2016), 55, describes the cameo as 'private propaganda' for Agrippina the Younger. There is a possibility the pair on the right are Tiberius and Livia, though the similarity of the profiles makes this far less likely. Claudius and Agrippina would have been far more interested in emphasizing the connection to the descent from Augustus as well as Livia. The cameo is in the Kunsthistorisches Museum, Vienna. Barrett (1996), 103, refers to the cameo but sees no more significance in it other than as a 'visible commemoration of the marriage'. For the Aezani coin of the Agrippinas, see Sear (1982), no. 532 or *RPC* 3102.
15. See Family Tree 3 (Julia the Elder's descendants) for Lucius Junius Silanus Torquatus' parents and siblings.
16. Tacitus 12.3.
17. Tacitus 12.4, 8.1; Dio 61.31.8 (Loeb vol. VIII, p. 15). Junia Calvina was recalled by Nero after Agrippina's death. See Tacitus 14.12.3.

18. Suetonius, *Caligula* 53.2.
19. Tacitus 12.8.2; Dio 61.32.1–3 (Loeb vol. VIII, p. 17).
20. Tacitus 12.22.1ff.
21. Nero subsequently recalled Lollia's remains for a proper burial in the aftermath of Agrippina's death. See Tacitus 14.12.4.
22. *Richard III* 5.3.196, similarly depicted as a caricature villain, Shakespeare no doubt being inspired by the way Roman historians vilified such figures, using every possible pretext and twist to do so.
23. Tacitus 12.22.1–3; Dio 61.32.3 (Loeb vol. VIII, p. 17). Calpurnia was recalled by Nero after Agrippina's death. See Tacitus 14.12.3.
24. Dio 61.32.1–2 (Loeb vol. VIII, p. 17).
25. Tacitus 12.27.1.
26. Suetonius, *Nero* 6.3.
27. Suetonius, *Claudius* 39.2.
28. Tacitus 12.9.2; Dio 61.31.8 (Loeb vol. VIII, p. 17); Suetonius, *Nero* 7.1.
29. Suetonius, *Claudius* 39, 43.1; Dio 61.32.1 (Loeb vol. VIII, p. 17).
30. Shotter (2008), 51.
31. Suetonius, *Claudius* 43.
32. *AE* 1979.172 (Augustus); *CIL* 10.1413 (Livia); *AE* 1979, 173 (Tiberius); *CIL* 10.1415 (Germanicus); 1417 (Antonia); 1418 (Agrippina); *AE* 2009.225 (Octavia); *AE* 1979.175 (Nero). The dedication to Nero as Claudius' son is what pins the group to the period 50–4.
33. *ILS* 222; Smallwood (1967) no. 100. Dio 60.22.1 records the enactment that two arches be erected.
34. Tacitus 12.25.1–26.2; Suetonius, *Claudius* 39.2.
35. Suetonius, *Nero* 52, who notes also that Agrippina denied Nero the chance to study philosophy on the grounds that it was disadvantageous to a ruler. No explanation is offered for this prejudice.
36. Suetonius, *Nero* 7.2.
37. Suetonius, *Nero* 7.1; Tacitus 12.41.3; Dio 61.32.5–6 (Loeb vol. VIII, p. 21).
38. Tacitus 12.42.1; Dio 61.32.6 (Loeb vol. VIII, p. 21 – the numbering in Dio is particularly confusing at this point in the published text).
39. Tacitus 12.42.3; Bauman (1992), 183–4.
40. Barrett (1996), 126. Josephus, *Jewish Antiquities* 20.134–6, 'Agrippa . . . had earnestly entreated Agrippina, the emperor's wife, to persuade her husband to hear the cause.'
41. See Barrett (1996), 284 note 108, for relevant references.
42. Barrett (1996), 127.
43. Tacitus 13.2.
44. Dio 61.33.7 (Loeb vol. VIII, p. 25).
45. Tacitus 12.43.2.
46. Tacitus 12.37.4; Dio 61.33.3 (Loeb vol. VIII, p. 23).
47. Pliny 33.19.63, who apparently witnessed this in person; Dio 61.33.3–5 (Loeb vol. VIII, pp. 23–5); Tacitus 12.57.1–2.
48. Sear (2000) nos 1885–6 (Lugdunum – still the main mint for imperial gold and silver in the West), 1888 (Ephesus).
49. Sear (2000) nos 1889–90. These coins do not show Nero having the tribunician power (abbreviated to TR P) that would be expected had he had the award.
50. Sear (2000) nos 1908–9. The date of these coins is in dispute. They may even have been minted under Titus (79–81).
51. Sear (2000), nos 1911–13, with the obverse ΑΓΡΙΠΠΙΝΑ ΣΕΒΑΣΤΗ. 'Closed currency' means that the Egyptian coins only circulated in Egypt.
52. Tacitus 14.9.3 and Dio 61.2.2 (Loeb vol. VIII, p. 35). See below, p. 255.
53. Dio 61.33.9 (Loeb vol. VIII, p. 27).
54. Dio 61.33.12 (Loeb vol. VIII, p. 27).

55. The Horti Tauriani were on the Esquiline Hill but the exact location is not now known. They were later given to two imperial freedmen, Pallantes and Epaphroditus. Hartswick (2013), 12, 156. For Agrippina's designs on the gardens see Tacitus 12.59. Statilius Taurus' sister was Statilia Messalina, mother of Nero's third and final empress, also named Statilia Messalina.

56. There are numerous other instances at different periods. Accusations of embezzlement and peculation seem to have been a popular way of denigrating powerful women. Elizabeth Woodville, queen of England's Edward IV, was notorious for using intimidation and pressure for financial or material gain, as was her mother Jacquetta, the dowager duchess of Bedford, and Henry VI's queen, Margaret of Anjou. Weir (1998), 343–4, provides a particularly distasteful example involving the appropriation of a tapestry.

57. Dio 61 34.1 (Loeb vol. VIII, p. 29); Tacitus 12.59.1–2. Bauman (1992), 185, suggests this was an early warning of a change in Agrippina's position. This is not really convincing for the reasons cited here.

58. Tacitus 12.64. Domitia was later killed by Nero in 59.

59. Not to be confused with her elder sister Domitia, killed by Nero in 59.

60. Shotter (2008), 53, suggests that the destruction of Lepida was part of a broader campaign by Agrippina to whittle away any potential supporters of Britannicus.

61. Tacitus 12.64–65.1.

62. Tacitus 12.64.1 *muliebribus causis*, literally 'with womanish causes', where womanish could also be 'effeminate' in a derogatory sense.

63. Suetonius, *Nero* 7.1; also Tacitus 13.19.4 for the 'ferocious rivalry' between Agrippina and Domitia.

64. Tacitus 12.65.

65. See Baldwin (1972), 89, 'female poisoners decorate the narrative of the Annals'.

66. Tacitus 66–67; Suetonius, *Claudius* 44; Dio 61.34. Not all modern historians are entirely convinced. Beard (2015, 415) for example says Agrippina 'is supposed' to have killed Claudius with poisoned mushrooms.

67. See p. 229 for a discussion of Josephus' implicit scepticism about the story.

68. Caligula's mother Agrippina the Elder had died four years before her son's accession.

69. Suetonius, *Claudius* 45.

9 The Reign of Agrippina the Younger: Part 2

1. Tacitus 12.68–69.

2. Tacitus 12.69; Suetonius, *Claudius* 44.1; Dio 61.1.2 (Loeb vol. VIII, p. 35).

3. Proclamation 17 November 54. *Select Papyri Volume II* no. 235 (Loeb series).

4. Ginsburg (2006), 84. Claudius and Agrippina were depicted on another panel, this time Agrippina appearing in more obviously mortal form with her husband. The Sebasteion was a large monument commemorating the Julio-Claudian emperors, and is possible evidence for an imperial cult there.

5. Tacitus 13.2.3.

6. 13.2. Shotter (2008), 59, suggests that Tacitus was revisiting the process by which Tiberius allowed Sejanus to destroy himself through excessive self-aggrandisement.

7. Tacitus 13.2. *cunctis malae dominationis cupidinibus flagrans habebat*.

8. Josephus, *Jewish Antiquities* 20.148–51.

9. Juvenal, *Satires* 6.610–626.

10. Tacitus 13.1.1–2. There are echoes here of the murder by poison of Kim Jong-nam, half-brother of North Korean dictator Kim Jong-un, at Kuala Lumpur airport in February 2017.

11. Suetonius, *Claudius* 30.1 citing Accius, *Tragedies* 203, also quoted by Cicero, *On Duties* 1.28.97.

12. Pliny 7.13.58.

13. Dio 61.33.6, 34.4 (Loeb vol. VIII, pp. 25, 31).

14. Dio 61.33.3 (Loeb vol. VIII, p. 21).
15. Dio 61.34.4–6 (Loeb vol. VIII, p. 31).
16. Tacitus 13.1.3.
17. Tacitus 13.3.1.
18. Tacitus 13.4.2, *discretam domum et rem publicam*, literally 'a separate house and public affairs'.
19. Griffin (1984), 39.
20. Tacitus 11.5.3, 7.4; Dio 54.18.2 (Loeb vol. VI, p. 327)
21. Tacitus 13.5.2. In fact even this was undone later in Nero's reign, with fees allowed again, see Suetonius, *Nero* 17.
22. Tacitus of course treated this as a clear sign of Agrippina's manipulative intentions, 13.5.1–2. 'Palatium' means the portico of the Temple of Apollo on the Palatine 'in which the Senate is accustomed to meet', from Sherk (1988), 36B, the Tabula Hebana AD 19–20. This of course placed the Senate in close proximity to the imperial palace, conveniently for Agrippina but it would probably have met there anyway. Just what the rules were concerning women in this sort of context is not entirely clear (as usual). At the Trial of Isidorus and Lampon in 41 or 53, presided over by Claudius, the presence of women as well as senators is recorded on a papyrus. See Sherk (1988) 45, 25–30. Much later, Julia Soaemias would take this a stage further and attend the Senate openly in person in an act that was clearly regarded as unprecedented. See p. 288.
23. *Letters* 4.19.3–4. Pliny the Younger was writing over half a century later but it is clear he was describing behaviour that was considered established and normal for a dutiful wife.
24. Dio 57.12.3 (Loeb vol. VII, p. 141).
25. Dio 61.33.7, 3.2–4 (Loeb vol. VIII, pp. 25, 38–9); Tacitus 13.5.2.
26. Smallwood (1967), no. 264. The full text in translation is also cited in Winter (2015), 201.
27. These coins are generally believed to have been made at Lugdunum where gold and silver could be kept firmly under imperial control, rather than the Senate's. The only specific evidence for striking gold and silver at the Lugdunum mint comes from Strabo (4.3.2) under Augustus; it is not known when bullion striking returned to Rome (Burnett 1987, 30) though some assume it had done so by Nero's early years.
28. Sadek (1966), 132. In fact, no tetradrachms had been struck in Egypt for a decade so whether Agrippina was really responsible is debatable.
29. Sear (2000), nos 2041, 2043.
30. Mostly in Asia Minor and Antioch. See Sear (1982), nos 642–53, and (for example) *RPC* 4175.
31. Shotter (2008), 57, for example argues, without any substantiation, that this is evidence for a 'power struggle'.
32. The gold aureus and silver denarius were similar in size to a modern British 5p piece or a US dime.
33. Sear (2000), no. 1990. Octavia was also featured on coins made in Crete and Sinope in Paphlagonia. Sear (1982), nos 655, 656.
34. This shortage was partly compensated for by drawing in worn Claudian base-metal coins and weighing them to see if they still met the standard. These were stamped PROB or NCAPR and reissued. The latter is normally read as 'Nero Caesar Augustus Probavit' ('Nero Caesar Augustus has approved [this coin]') but it could equally well read 'Nero Caesar (et) Agrippina Probaverunt' (Nero Caesar [and] Agrippina have approved [this coin]'). With no parallel for the abbreviation in any other context it is impossible to say.
35. Only a very few coins giving Nero's second tribunician power can be attributed to 55–56. These have only his portrait and no reference to Agrippina.
36. See, for example, Barrett (1996), 243 (Appendix IX).
37. From *senatus consultum*, 'Decree of the Senate'.
38. See, for example, Griffin (1984), 58–9; Sutherland (1974), 159; and Burnett (1987), 18–19. Griffin in particular discusses the topic with a completely unwarranted conclusive certainty that the formula represents a gesture of deference. It is quite plain that no firm

conclusion can be drawn: the evidence does not exist to answer the point. Quite apart from anything else the significance of SC may have been different at different times. The Roman world was notoriously inconsistent.

39. See below, p. 266.
40. Dio 61.34.4 (Loeb vol. VIII, p. 33).
41. Tacitus 12.69.3, 13.3.
42. Tacitus 14.14.1.
43. Suetonius, *Nero* 34.1.
44. Barrett (1996), 150, argues that these early days of Nero's rule were 'the acme of Agrippina's achievement'. She was, however, also laying the foundations of her destruction.
45. Tacitus 13.2.1.
46. Suetonius, *Nero* 15.2 noted that Nero also denied the sons of freedmen admission to the Senate.
47. Tacitus 13.6.2–4.
48. Tacitus 13.13.1.
49. Tacitus 13.12–13.1; Suetonius, *Nero* 28; Dio 61.6.7, 62.11.4 (Loeb vol. VIII, pp. 47, 61).
50. Tacitus 13.13.2.
51. Dio 61.4.3 (Loeb vol. VIII, p. 43); Suetonius, *Nero* 29.1; Tacitus 14.65.
52. Tacitus 13.13.2. She offered him 'her own bedroom and lap'.
53. See below, p. 248.
54. Tacitus 13.14.1; Dio 61.7.3 (Loeb vol. VIII, p. 49).
55. Suetonius, *Nero* 50.
56. Tacitus 13.14.2–3.
57. Barrett (1996), 240, simply dismisses the speech as 'histrionic' and 'hardly believable', preferring to argue that there is no convincing evidence to support the idea of a rift between Agrippina and Seneca and Burrus.
58. Tacitus 13.15.1–16.4. Dio 61.6.5, 7.5 (Loeb vol. VIII, pp. 47, 49) makes no such reference to a dinner or to Agrippina's horror.
59. Tacitus 61.17.1; Dio 61.7.4 (Loeb vol. VIII, p. 49).
60. Tacitus 13.18; Dio 61.8.4, 6 (Loeb vol. VIII, p. 53); Suetonius, *Nero* 34.1.
61. Tacitus 13.19.2.
62. Tacitus 13.19.3–4.
63. Tacitus 13.19–20. Domitia is Nero's aunt, the elder sister of Domitia Lepida (mother of Messalina).
64. Tacitus 13.21.1–6.
65. Tacitus 13.22, 14.51.2. The other prefect was the notorious Tigellinus, principal organizer of Nero's most nefarious exploits. He and Rufus could not have been more different.
66. Dio 61.10.1 (Loeb vol. VIII, p. 55); Tacitus 13.42.3.
67. Sear (2000), nos 1989–90. Both are labelled as Augusta.
68. Sear (2000), nos 1989–2015 (Egyptian tetradrachms only). It is possible that the female personifications are representations of Agrippina in those respective guises. After her death in 59 the change to more male types may have been deliberate and pointed.
69. Sear (2000), no. 2045.

10 Murder

1. Agrippina, Octavia and Poppaea.
2. This is the literal meaning of Tacitus' words *vetustate . . . coalita audacia*, 14.1.
3. Tacitus 13.45.1.
4. Pliny 6.20.54. The Latin phrase is *ut in publico matrona traluceat*, which literally means 'so that in public a matron may go see-through'. He refers to it being a woollen cloth but this cannot be correct.
5. Pliny 29.8.26.
6. 6.39.3.

7. *CIL* 10.827, *ILS* 6384 for the aedile (undated). The seal (now lost, and of which the reading and interpretation are uncertain) is at Allison (2006), 135, no. 799, with further discussion at 328, 334 and 399.
8. 13.45.1ff.
9. 62.28.1–2 (Loeb vol. VIII, p. 135). Pliny, 28.50.183.
10. One might note here the decision of the British prime minister Theresa May to wear expensive leather trousers for a photoshoot which prompted a 'political row' (BBC News 12 December 2016). Perhaps little has changed for women in power.
11. Crispinus was pushed into suicide in 66 (Tacitus 16.17.1–2).
12. 13.45–46.3; Suetonius, *Otho* 3.2–4.1.
13. Tacitus 14.1.1.
14. Her exceptional pedigree included descent from Augustus via his daughter Julia, Livia and Augustus' sister via their mutual grandson Germanicus, and Agrippa via her mother.
15. Tacitus 14.2–3. See above, p. 238.
16. Suetonius, *Nero* 5.2.
17. Tacitus 14.2.1. This time it seems to have been a specific offer rather than the suggestion that had been made by her in 55. See also Mullens (1942).
18. Tacitus 14.3.1.
19. Suetonius, *Nero* 34.2; Tacitus 14.3.3–4.1–2.
20. Dio 62.12.2–3 (Loeb vol. VIII, p. 63).
21. 'Rites are performed in honour of Minerva, which get their name from a group of five days.' Ovid, *Fasti* 3.809–10. They occurred on the fifth day after (and including) the Ides of March on the 15th.
22. In Suetonius' account the collapsing canopy is relocated to an actual bedroom on land. Its failure then, according to him, led to the quite separate scheme to design a boat that would fall apart (*Nero* 34.2).
23. Tacitus 14.5; Dio 62.13.2–5 (Loeb vol. VIII, p. 65).
24. Tacitus 14.6.
25. Tacitus 14.6–7, 10.3.
26. Tacitus 14.8; Dio 62.13.5 (Loeb vol. VIII, p. 67). The account probably owes more to theatrical tragedy than the truth.
27. Suetonius, *Otho* 3.1.
28. Tacitus 14.9.1; Dio 62.14.1–2 (Loeb vol. VIII, p. 67). This part of the Penthesilea myth is reported by the Bibliotheca of Pseudo-Apollodorus, a collection of Greek myths.
29. Tacitus 14.9.1–2.
30. Tacitus 14.9.3 and Dio 61.2.2 (Loeb vol. VIII, p. 35). For a late (fifth-century) Roman reference to Nero purely for killing his mother see Rutilius Claudius Namatianus, *Concerning His Return* 2.57. The poet compares the death of the mortal Agrippina to the destruction of the immortal Rome by the Vandal general Stilicho who persuaded the Senate to give in to Alaric the Goth's demands, leading to the sack of Rome in 410.
31. Suetonius, *Nero* 6.4. Nero had discarded it when he grew to hate his mother, but looked for it again 'in his extremity'.
32. Tacitus 14.13; Dio 62.11.2–4 (Loeb vol. VIII, p. 67 – the book numbering of Dio at this point is exceptionally confusing).
33. For earlier references to these three, see pp. 211, 212 and 241.
34. Dio 62.1.3 (Loeb vol. VIII, p. 67); Tacitus 14.12.3–13.2.
35. Dio 62.15.1–4, 16.1–3 (Loeb vol. VIII, pp. 69–71); Suetonius, *Nero* 39.3.
36. Suetonius, *Vespasian* 9.1 who says that Nero almost completely destroyed the work Agrippina had overseen; also, Claridge (2010), 349. Substantial parts of the temple platform remain visible today in the Piazza dei SS Giovanni e Paolo. They exhibit the distinctive rusticated finish characteristic of the 40s and 50s which seems to have survived Nero's damage. The arcading is probably the only significant extant structure in Rome associated with Agrippina the Younger. The remains of Nero's nymphaeum on the east side can be seen in the Via Claudia.

37. Considerably more than the eclipse of 45 which Claudius had been worried about. See p. 191.
38. Dio 62.16.4–5 (Loeb vol. VIII, p. 73); Tacitus 14.12.1–2; https://eclipse.gsfc.nasa.gov/SEsearch/SEsearchmap.php?Ecl=00590430. The partial eclipse reached its maximum in Rome at about 1318. Accessed 7 April 2017. This is an excellent example of how one of our key sources is both accurate and inaccurate.
39. Suetonius, *Nero* 6.3.
40. Dio 62.17.1 (Loeb vol. VIII, p. 73); Suetonius, *Nero* 34.5. Curiously the murder goes unmentioned by Tacitus even though he had drawn attention to the ferocious rivalry between Domitia and Agrippina at 13.19.4.
41. Dio 62.19–20.1 (Loeb vol. VIII, p. 75).
42. Tacitus 14.57.1, 15.50.3.
43. Tacitus 14.51–52.
44. Tacitus 14.53–57.
45. Tacitus 14.63.3.
46. Suetonius, *Nero* 35.3.
47. *Octavia* 593–645.
48. Suetonius, *Nero* 35.2–3; Tacitus 14.65.1. Other freedmen were killed but apparently for different reasons, see 14.65.2. For Poppaea's fertility honours, see Tacitus 15.23.1.
49. Sear (2000), nos 1926, 1940. The figures are sometimes identified as Augustus and Livia but it is no less possible the design was deliberately ambiguous and intended to conflate Nero and Poppaea with their illustrious forebears.
50. Sear (2000), no. 2002.
51. For example *CIL* 4.3726, *ILS* 234: Iudici(i)s Augusti P P Et Poppaea Aug(ustae) Feliciter.
52. *AE* (1985), 283, 284.
53. Various graffiti and inscribed amphorae attest to the presence of Poppaea's family. However, it is simply not possible to be certain.
54. Smallwood (1967), no. 433b. Also cited in Braund (1985), no. 767 (b), and Keppie (1991), 113. The text seems to have concerned the sale of a slave. Those involved in the sale seem merely to have conducted their business at the Arrian works. Their relationship to Poppaea is unspecified.
55. Pliny 12.42.94. He does not specify the date of the fire. See Fishwick (1992), 233.
56. Plutarch, *Crassus* 2.4.
57. See Suetonius, *Augustus* 25.2, 30.1; Strabo 5.3.7; and Dio 55.26.4 (Loeb vol. VI, p. 461).
58. The fire is described by Tacitus at 15.38.1–7. It is probable Tacitus witnessed the disaster as a small child (he was born in *c.* 58).
59. Tacitus 15.39ff.
60. *Nero* 35.3.
61. Tacitus 16.6.1.
62. Dio 62.28.1 (Loeb vol. VIII, p. 135).
63. Pliny 12.40.83.
64. Tacitus 16.6.1. Nero may have been inspired by an interest in the customs of the Egyptian Ptolemaic pharaohs. See Counts (1996).
65. For the deification of Poppaea and the construction of her temple see Dio 63.26.3 (Loeb vol. VIII, p. 183), calling her 'Sabina'; and also Kragelund (2010) who discusses the likely location of the temple.
66. For the coin of Claudia Augusta see RPC 4846 (see Sear 2000, 400, no. 2058). For Luna see *ILS* 233, Sherk no. 70 B.
67. Tacitus 16.22.3.
68. This Antonia was Claudius' daughter by his wife Paetina. Suetonius, *Nero* 35.4. Tacitus 6.10.1 '[women] could not be accused of grasping at sovereignty'.
69. Sear (1982), nos 665–6.
70. Dio 62.28.3 (Loeb vol. VIII, p. 137), 63.13.1 (ibid., p. 159).
71. Suetonius, *Otho* 10.2.

72. Suetonius, *Nero* 35.5.
73. See above, p. 118. Suetonius, *Galba* 1.
74. Pliny 7.8.45.
75. See M. Hicks (2015), *The Family of Richard III*, Amberley, Stroud, 51.
76. Tacitus 12.4; Seneca, *Apocolocyntosis* 8.2. Junia Calvina's mother was Aemilia Lepida, daughter of Julia the Younger by Lucius Aemilius Paullus. Her father was Marcus Junius Silanus Torquatus.
77. Tacitus 14.12.3; Suetonius, *Vespasian* 23.4.
78. *CIL* 14.3661; *ILS* 6239. Although 'Livilla' is not more explicitly identified this is presumably the sister of Germanicus and Claudius, daughter of Nero Claudius Drusus and Antonia Minor. The word for 'favourite' is the neuter noun *delicium*, here as *delicio* 'to the favourite . . .'
79. Tacitus, *Histories* 1.78.1.
80. Tacitus, *Histories* 2.8–9.
81. Marcus Aurelius, *Meditations* 8.31.

11 Epilogue

1. Barrett (1996), 148.
2. For Livia see Sear (2000), nos 2586–8, Agrippina no. 2600. For the Antoninus Pius temple coins of 159 see Sear (2002) nos 4020, 4235.
3. Dio 66.19.3 (Loeb vol. VIII, p. 301 text and note 1). He was called Terentius Maximus. For the pseudo-Nero of 88 see Suetonius, *Nero* 57.1–2, who may have confused himself with the one of 79 under Titus though he specifically refers to remembering the event personally. See also Shotter (2008), 171–2.
4. Dio 68.10.2 (Loeb vol. VIII, p. 379).
5. Cited by Birley (1976), 44.
6. Trajan may even have opposed it. *SHA (Hadrian)* 2.10.
7. Aurelius Victor 14.8; she was said to be ill tempered and irritable. *SHA (Hadrian)* 11.3.
8. See Boatwright (1991) on this interesting contrast.
9. Faustina the Younger's life, and reputation as a 'new Messalina', is outside the scope of this book but Burns (2007), 155ff., provides a useful modern survey of the evidence.
10. Titus and Domitian were adults by the time their father Vespasian became emperor in 69. Commodus was born on 31 August 161, his father having become emperor after the death of Antoninus Pius in March 161.
11. Marcus Aurelius, *Meditations* 4.28.
12. Marcus Aurelius, *Meditations* 8.31.
13. Dio 74.5.1ff. (Loeb vol. IX, p. 131ff.). See also de la Bédoyère (2017), 1–3, 216–18.
14. Dio 53.17.2 (Loeb vol. VI, p. 237). For the coins, e.g. *RPC* 4771. Also, Butcher (2004), 57, fig. 8.2.
15. Millar (1981), 213.
16. Freisenbruch (2010), 217. 'Two empresses – Julia Domna . . . and Julia Mamaea . . . surpassed all others who bore the name Augusta in the dignity of their titles, in the public honor they received, and in the extent to which they participated in the actual administration of the government', Williams (1902), 259 – a very useful survey of the epigraphic evidence.
17. Dio suggested incongruously that Domna was of low birth: 'sprung from the people and raised to a high station', 79.24.1 (Loeb vol. IX, p. 395).
18. Balsdon (1962), 153, describes her as a woman of 'strong and imperious character', imbued with Eastern 'credulous mysticism', but also exhibiting the 'ballast of calm reasoning' thanks to her interest in philosophy. Levick (2007), 107–8, considers the possibilities open to Julia Domna when it came to education (comments that therefore must also apply to Julia Maesa) but it is quite clear there is no useful substantive evidence other than the fact that as empress she exhibited all the interests and traits attributed to educated elite Roman women.

19. *SHA (Septimius Severus)* 3.9. He was a 'fantastically superstitious man', Balsdon (1962), 151, who also gives the date of marriage to Domna as 185.
20. Dio 75.3.1 (Loeb vol. IX, p. 167). That it was a dream is only implicit from Dio's text, though the death of Faustina in 175 demonstrates it cannot actually have happened.
21. For Aurelius' birth name see *SHA (Marcus Aurelius)* 1.9–10; it was changed when he was adopted by Antoninus Pius (ibid. 5.5). Marcus Aurelius Antoninus is the name that appears on Caracalla's coins. The name 'Caracalla' is a contemporary nickname by which he is always known today to avoid confusion with Marcus Aurelius and other Severan emperors. It was derived from the word for a hooded tunic of Gaulish origin that he favoured. It was equivalent to a modern monarch being known as 'Anorak'.
22. Originally awarded to Faustina the Younger in 174 in recognition of her care for soldiers on campaign. See Sear (2002), no. 5280. For Domna's award see *CIL* 8.26498 (Thugga).
23. *CIL* 6.2149. See Friggeri et al. (2012), 311. IVLIA.AVG.DOMINAE.MATRI.CAS. IT.IMVNIS.
24. Langford (2013), 11, 13. For an example, see *RIB* 1235 (Risingham, Britain) dated to 213 under Caracalla.
25. So named because *sellae* (seats) were provided for female deities to sit on. Tacitus 15.44.1, and for Domna's participation, see *CIL* 6.32327 (translated at *L&R* II, pp. 558–60).
26. Levick (2007), 107.
27. Philostratus, *Life of Apollonius of Tyana* 1.3. See also Bowersock (1969), 101–9, on this topic, and Anderson (1986); the latter (p. 253) discusses what he regards as Philostratus' real interest in promoting his correction of Homer.
28. This kind of gushing biography helped form the basis of hagiographies of Christian saints and clearly belongs to a broader collective tradition. Domna's role here is akin to that of high-status Christian women who patronized the careers of saints. One is also reminded of Bede's account of the exploits of St Germanus of Auxerre in Britain in the early fifth century (1.17–21).
29. Freisenbruch (2010), 229–30, discusses the conflicting evidence and concludes that Domna was probably an intellectual whose support for philosophy and rhetoric provided an important service to learning. Hemelrijk (2004), 120, points out that the sources say nothing about organized meetings and that the arrangements may have been no more than informal. Levick (2007), 122, even speculates whether Domna's real interest was in 'Apollonius' occasionally picaresque adventures' or whether it was because Apollonius' life provided a sort of 'guide to life', compensating for any shortcomings in her education.
30. Dio 76.15.6–7 (Loeb vol. IX, p. 233), 77.4.1–5 (ibid., pp. 245–7).
31. Dio 77.16.5 (Loeb vol. IX, p. 275).
32. Freisenbruch (2010), 235, regards the story as a 'fictitious piece of reportage'. Levick (2007), 85–6, accepts it as true, even speculating that the conversation may have had a more serious element to it about culture and philosophy. In the end any judgement about the authenticity of this story can only be a matter of opinion at this distance in time, but surely its idiosyncratic tone and authentic context (Domna was undoubtedly in Britain) point to it being true or at least close to the truth. If it is untrue then one might as well discount every other anecdote we have about the empress and perhaps everyone else too. The only specifically questionable detail is the Latinate nature of the Caledonian leader's name, perhaps simply a Latinized version of his native name.
33. *SHA (Severus)* 19.1, 22 *passim* for the portents.
34. Herodian 4.3.8–9. Dio makes no mention of the incident.
35. See above, pp. 239 and 254.
36. Langford (2013), 2; Dio 78.2.1–6 (Loeb vol. IX, p. 283); Herodian 3.15.6. 4.3.4, 4.11.8–9.
37. Dio 78.18.2–3 (Loeb vol. IX, p. 327), 79.4.3 (ibid., p. 347).
38. *SHA (Caracalla)* 10.1–4.
39. Sutherland (1974), 217.
40. Sear (2002), no. 6511.

41. Sear (2002), no. 6517.
42. Claridge (2010), 205. See also Gorrie (2004) on Domna's building patronage.
43. Sear (2002), no. 6613, but also illustrated by Claridge (2010), 206, fig. 37.
44. Sear (2002), nos 6511ff., especially 6511 and 6517.
45. Sear (2002), nos 7117 (212), 7120–1 (215).
46. Langford (2013), 21.
47. *RIB* 1278 from Risingham, in the name of the First cohort of Vangiones, Raetian spearsmen, and scouts. Coins under Severus had already identified her as Mater Castrorum, see Sear (2002), no. 6629, 6644.
48. Balsdon (1962), 151.
49. The unpopularity was in spite of the fact that Caracalla had lived and fought as an ordinary soldier when on campaign. Dio 78.13.1–2 (Loeb vol. IX, p. 313).
50. Dio 79.23.1 (Loeb vol. IX, p. 391).
51. Herodotus 1.183ff.; Dio 79.23.3 (Loeb vol. IX, p. 393).
52. Dio 79.23.1–24.3 (Loeb vol. IX, pp. 391–5).
53. 79.24.3 (Loeb vol. IX, p. 395).
54. Whether Maesa was older or younger than Domna is unresolved. Some authorities are not troubled by the lack of evidence and simply state as a fact that Maesa was the younger. Balsdon (1962), 156, says that Maesa was Domna's younger sister but provides no evidence to support the claim. Likewise Burns (2007), 181, 'her younger sister Julia Masea'.
55. Herodian 5.3.2; *SHA (Macrinus)* 9.1–2.
56. Faulkner (2008), 248.
57. Dio 79.30.3.
58. Dio 79.30.2 (Loeb vol. IX, p. 409). An inscription specifies that Soaemias was his wife. *ILS* 478.
59. Herodian 5.3.6–8.
60. The story was repeatedly put about by Maesa and became widely believed. *SHA (Elagabalus)* 2.1.
61. Herodian 5.3.9–11; Dio 79.32.2–3 (Loeb vol. IX, p. 413).
62. *CIL* 6.2104, 27 May 218 referring to the '(templum) divor(um)' (though in fact the exact date relies on reconstructing part of the text). See Fishwick (1992), 250, who does not mention the necessary restoration of the text.
63. Dio 79.30.1 (Loeb vol. IX, pp. 407–8). For the eclipse of 7 October 218, see https://eclipse.gsfc.nasa.gov/SEsearch/SEsearchmap.php?Ecl=02181007. For the appearance of Halley's Comet, see D.A.J. Seargent (2008), *The Greatest Comets in History*, Springer, New York, 40.
64. Sear (2002), nos 7750, 7764, and 7759 (all 218–20). See Langlands (2009), pp. 37ff., and above, pp. 23–4, for the power of *pudicitia*.
65. Sear (2002), for example no. 7717 (220–2).
66. Sear (1982), nos 3146, 3147.
67. Herodian 5.5.3.
68. Herodian 5.5.6–7.
69. *SHA (Elagabalus)* 12.3.
70. Herodian 5.5.8–9.
71. Dio 80.11.1–2 (Loeb vol. IX, p. 457).
72. Suetonius, *Nero* 28.1.
73. Dio 80.9.3–4 (Loeb vol. IX, p. 459).
74. *SHA (Elagabalus)* 4.2–4 records Soaemias' attendance of the Senate. See Dio 57.12.2 (Loeb vol. VII, p. 141), who describes Livia's ability to rule from her own house without having to consider attending the Senate or anywhere else. Agrippina's attendance of the Senate is at Tacitus 13.5.1, but see also p. 360, n. 75.
75. *SHA (Elagabalus)* 20.1; remarkably, the idea of a female senate was not abandoned entirely after Elagabalus' reign. It was recreated under Aurelian, *SHA (Aurelian)* 49.6.
76. See Purcell (2009), 171–3 on this passage and how it relates to Livia's relationship with the Senate.

77. Herodian 5.6.9–7.1. His father was a Syrian called Marcus Julius Gessius Marcianus, another Syrian equestrian who had held a number of procuratorial posts but had been killed in 218 after Macrinus seized power in 217. Dio 79.30.3 (Loeb vol. IX, p. 409).
78. Dio 80.17.2 (Loeb vol. IX, p. 473).
79. Herodian 5.7.5–6.
80. Herodian 5.8.2.
81. Herodian 5.8.7–9; *SHA (Elagabalus)* 15.6. The same was said by some (e.g. John Speed in 1611) of England's Richard III (1483–85). The 2012 discovery of the king's remains at Leicester friary's ruins shows the story was not true.
82. Herodian 5.8.10, 6.1.1–2, 6.
83. *SHA (Elagabalus)* 18.3.
84. Herodian 5.7.3.
85. Herodian 6.1.6.
86. Herodian 6.1.4; Zonaras 12.15.571.
87. Her portraits were characterized by 'gentleness and dignity'. Sutherland (1974), 224.
88. *SHA (Severus Alexander)* 5.2.
89. Zonaras 12.15.572.
90. Herodian 6.1.5–9. Another, otherwise unknown, wife called Memmia is mentioned at *SHA (Severus Alexander)* 20.3.
91. Gibbon (1776–89) IV, Part IV, 79.
92. *SHA (Severus Alexander)* 26.9, 60.1.
93. Herodian 6.5.8.
94. Herodian 6.8.8.
95. Herodian 6.8.8; *SHA (The Maximini)* 7.4; Zonaras 12.15.574.
96. Herodian 6.9.7–8, 7.1.9; *SHA (Severus Alexander)* 60.1.
97. 1 October. *SHA (Severus Alexander)* 63.3–4. The source refers to this annual ceremony still going on when it was written so in all probability this observation is true. The so-called 'Sarcophagus of Alexander Severus' displayed in the Capitoline Museum did not belong to the emperor but other members of the family. See Claridge (2010), 463.
98. Otacilia Severa's father was called Otacilius Severus/Severianus. There is no reason to suggest that there was any connection between her and the Severan family though it remains a tenuous, but completely unsubstantiated, possibility. Severus was not an uncommon name.
99. See above, p. 326, n. 3.
100. Porphyry, *Life of Plotinus* 12. This goes unmentioned in any other source and seems to be the sole basis for Salonina's reputation as a learned woman interested in patronage.
101. *SHA (The Two Gallieni)* 11.6ff.
102. Dio 77.15.2 (Loeb vol. IX, pp. 271–3).
103. For Ammianus on Eusebia's conspiracy to cause Helena to miscarry see 16.10.18. For a recent discussion of Constantius and Eusebia (who died in 360) see Crawford (2015), Chapter X. For the Theodosian coins see Sear (2014), nos 20603–20628.
104. Claudian, *Epithalamium* 12–13, 232, 241–2, 252ff. Maria's father was the Vandal general Stilicho. Serena was the niece of Theodosius I. Maria bore no children and died in 407.
105. Bury (1958) (i), 198. 'Her authority was not threatened or contested.' She was formerly married to Ataulf, king of the Visigoths from 414 until his death the following year.
106. Freisenbruch (2010), 286. Sivan (2011), 2, notes that Galla Placidia had no contemporary biographer, meaning that a modern life of the empress has to be constructed only from passing references. This of course in practice is true of all Roman empresses and other imperial women.
107. Sivan (2011), 13–14, and 58, discussing 'Jerome's vigorous promotion of virginal ascetism' in the Rome of the 380s. He was particularly keen on the idea of women who had been married never being so again. The state was known as *univira* or *univiria*, literally 'a one-husband woman'.
108. Sear (2014), no. 21343 and many others.

109. Sivan (2011), 197, fig. 20 and, for example, Sear (2014), no. 21343 (illustrated).
110. Sivan (2011), 153ff. The main original source is John of Antioch, an approximate contemporary.
111. Now in Ravenna Museum. See Cooper and Leino (2008), 278, fig. 80, and Wood (1999), 133.
112. Johnson (2009), 167–74, suggests remains found in the chapel of St Petronilla by St Peter's in Rome in 1458 were more likely Galla Placidia's because the chapel appears to have contained the dynastic mausoleum for the Western Empire.
113. Purcell (2009), 165–96, but especially 194 (also published in 1986, see Bibliography).

Glossary

1. Fantham et al. (1994), 225.

SELECT BIBLIOGRAPHY

The available modern literature on the women of Imperial Rome, whether in the form of books or articles, is enormous. The works cited here are those that were most useful to the writing of this book but do not form in any sense a definitive list. The reader will find that the bibliographies in many of the works listed below are an invaluable resource for further reading. It is also worth bearing in mind that a great deal has appeared in recent years and will continue to do so.

Allison, P.M. (ed.) (2006), *The Insula of the Menander at Pompeii. Volume III: The Finds, A Contextual Study*, Clarendon Press, Oxford

Alston, R. (1998), *Aspects of Roman History AD 14–117*, Routledge, Abingdon

Anderson, G. (1986), *Philostratus: Biography and Belles Lettres in the Third Century AD*, Croom Helm, London

Baldwin, B. (1972), 'Women in Tacitus', *Prudentia* 4 (2), 83–101

Balsdon, J.P.V.D. (1962), *Roman Women: Their History and Habits*, Bodley Head, London

Banchich, T., and Lane, E. (2009) (trans.), *The History of Zonaras: From Severus Alexander to Theodosius the Great*, Routledge, Abingdon

Barrett, A.A. (1989) *Caligula: The Corruption of Power*, Batsford, London

Barrett, A.A. (1996), *Agrippina: Sex, Power, and Politics in the Early Empire*, Routledge, London

Barrett, A.A. (2008), *Lives of the Caesars*, Blackwell, Oxford

Barrett, A.A. (2012, revised edition from 2002), *Livia: First Lady of Imperial Rome*, Yale University Press, New Haven and London

Bartman, E. (1999), *Portraits of Livia: Imaging the Imperial Woman in Augustan Rome*, Cambridge University Press, Cambridge

Bauman, R. A. (1992), *Women and Politics in Ancient Rome*, Routledge, London

Beard, M. (2015), *SPQR: A History of Ancient Rome*, Profile, London

Beard, M. (2017), *Women & Power: A Manifesto*, Profile, London

Best, E.E. (1970), 'Cicero, Livy, and Educated Roman Women', *Classical Journal* 65, 199–204

Birley, A.R. (1976), *Lives of the Later Caesars*, Penguin, Harmondsworth

Birley, A.R. (1999), *Septimius Severus: The African Emperor*, Routledge, London

Boatwright, M.T. (1991), 'The Imperial Women of the Early Second Century AC', *American Journal of Philology* 112 (4), 513–40

Bonanno, A. (2005), *Malta: Phoenician, Punic, and Roman*, Midsea Books, Santa Venera

Bowersock, G.W. (1969), *Greek Sophists in the Roman Empire*, Clarendon Press, Oxford

Brannon, R. (2010), 'Founding Fathers: An Ethnic and Gender Study of the Iliadic Aeneid', graduate thesis, University of South Florida Scholar Commons

Brauer, G. (1995), *Decadent Emperors: Power and Depravity in Third Century Rome*, Gazelle Book Services (originally published in 1967 as *The Young Emperors: Prelude to the Fall of Rome, AD 193–244*, Crowell, New York)

Braund, D.C. (1985), *Augustus to Nero: A Sourcebook of Roman History 31 BC–AD 68*, Croom Helm, Beckenham

Brent, A., Rev. (1995), *Hippolytus and the Roman Church in the Third Century: Communities in Tension before the Emergence of a Monarch-Bishop (Vigiliae Christianae, Supplements)*, Brill, Leiden

Burnett, A. (1987), *Coinage in the Roman World*, Spink, London

Burnett, A., Amandry, M. and Ripollès, P.P. (1992), *From the Death of Caesar to the Death of Vitellius (44 BC–AD 69)*, vol. 1, British Museum Press, London

Burns, J. (2007), *Great Women of Imperial Rome: Mothers and Wives of the Caesars*, Routledge, Abingdon

Bury, J.B. (1958), *History of the Later Roman Empire*, Dover, New York

Butcher, K. (2004), *Coinage in Roman Syria*, Royal Numismatic Society, London

Calhoon, C.G. (1994), 'Livia the Poisoner: Genesis of an Historical Myth', doctoral thesis, University of California, Irvine

Chrystal, P. (2015), *Roman Women: The Women Who Influenced the History of Rome*, Fonthill, Stroud

Claridge, A. (2010), *Rome: An Oxford Archaeological Guide*, Oxford University Press, Oxford

Clinton, H.R. (2017), *What Happened*, Simon & Schuster, London

Collingwood, R.G., and Wright, R.P. (1965), *Roman Inscriptions of Britain*, Clarendon Press, Oxford (revised edition ed. R.S.O. Tomlin (1995)), Oxbow Books, Oxford

Cooley, A.E. and Cooley, M.G.L. (2004), *Pompeii: A Sourcebook*, Routledge, London

Cooley, M.G.L. (ed.) (2003), *The Age of Augustus*, London Association of Classical Teachers LACTOR no. 17, London

Cooper, D., and Leino, M. (2008), *Depth of Field: Relief Sculpture in Renaissance Italy*, Verlag Peter Lang, Bern

Corbeill, A. (2015), *Controlling Laughter: Political Humor in the Late Roman Republic*, Princeton Legacy Library, Princeton University Press, Princeton (reprint of 1996 text)

Counts, D. (1996), 'Regum Externorum Consuetudine: The Nature and Function of Embalming in Rome', *Classical Antiquity* 15 (2), 189–202

Courtney, E. (2013), *A Commentary on the Satires of Juvenal*, California Classical Studies, Berkeley

Crawford, P., (2015), *Constantius II: Usurpers, Eunuchs and the Antichrist*, Pen & Sword, Barnsley

de la Bédoyère, G. (1997), *Particular Friends: The Correspondence of Samuel Pepys and John Evelyn*, Boydell, Woodbridge

de la Bédoyère, G. (2017), *Praetorian: The Rise and Fall of Rome's Imperial Bodyguard*, Yale University Press, New Haven and London

Dennison, M. (2011), *Empress of Rome: The Life of Livia*, Quercus, London

Devine, A.M. (1985), 'The Low Birth-rate in Ancient Rome: A Possible Contributing Factor', *Rheinisches Museum für Philologie* 128, 179–82

Dixon, S. (2007), *Cornelia: Mother of the Gracchi*, Routledge, Abingdon

Dockray, K. (2000), *Henry VI, Margaret of Anjou and the Wars of the Roses: A Sourcebook*, Sutton, Stroud

Dunn, D. (2016), *The Poems of Catullus*, William Collins, London

Edmondson, J. (ed.) (2009), *Augustus*, Edinburgh Readings on the Ancient World, Edinburgh University Press, Edinburgh

Edwards, C. (2010), *The Politics of Immorality in Ancient Rome*, Cambridge University Press, Cambridge

Everitt, A. (2007), *The First Emperor*, John Murray, London

Fantham, E. (2006), *Julia Augusta: The Emperor's Daughter*, Routledge, Abingdon

Fantham, E. (2011), *Roman Readings: Roman Responses to Greek Literature from Plautus to Statius and Quintilian (Beitrage zur Altertumskunde)*, De Gruyter, Berlin

Fantham, E., Foley, H.P., Kampen, N.B., Pomeroy, S.B. and Shapiro, H.A. (1994), *Women in the Classical World*, Oxford University Press, New York and Oxford

Faulkner, N. (2008), *Rome: Empire of the Eagles*, Pearson Education, London

Fischer, J. (2016), 'A Woman's Weapon: Private Propaganda in the Large Imperial Cameos of the Early Roman Empire' in J. Fischer (ed.) (2016), *More Than Mere Playthings: The Minor Arts of Italy*, Cambridge Scholars Publishing, Newcastle-upon-Tyne

Fishwick, D. (1992), 'On the Temple of Divus Augustus', *Phoenix* (Classical Association of Canada) 46 (3), 232–55

Fletcher, J. (2015), *The Story of Egypt*, Hodder & Stoughton, London

Fletcher, J. (2016), 'The Egyptian Hair Pin: Practical, Sacred, Fatal', *Internet Archaeology* 42, http://dx.doi.org/10.11141/ia.42.6.5

Flory, M.B. (1984), '*Sic Exempla Parantur*: Livia's Shrine of Concordia and the Porticus Liviae', *Historia* 33, 309–30

Flory, M.B. (1993), 'Livia and the History of Public Honorific Statues of Women in Rome', *Transactions of the American Philological Association* 123, 287–305

Flower, H. (2011), *The Art of Forgetting: Disgrace and Oblivion in Roman Political Culture. Studies in the History of Greece and Rome*, University of North Carolina Press, Chapel Hill

Fraschetti, A. (ed.) (2001), *Roman Women*, University of Chicago Press, Chicago

Freisenbruch, A. (2010), *The First Ladies of Rome: The Women Behind the Caesars*, Jonathan Cape, London

Friggeri, R., Cecere, M.G.G. and Gregori, G.L. (2012), *Terme di Diocleziani. La Collezione Epigrafica*, Electa, Milan

Galinsky, K. (1996), *Augustan Culture: An Interpretive Introduction*, Princeton University Press, Princeton

Gardner, J.F. (1986), *Women in Roman Law and Society*, Routledge, London

Garlick, B., Dixon, S. and Allen, P. (eds) (1992), *Stereotypes of Women in Power: Historical Perspectives and Revisionist Views*, Greenwood, New York

Giacosa, G. (1977), *Women of the Caesars: Their Lives and Portraits on Coins*, Edizioni Arte e Moneta, Milan

Gibbon, E. (1776–89), *The Decline and Fall of the Roman Empire*, Strahan and Cadell, London (and innumerable subsequent editions)

Ginsburg, J. (2006), *Representing Agrippina: Constructions of Female Power in the Early Roman Empire*, American Philological Association, Oxford

Goldsworthy, A. (2006), *Caesar: The Life of a Colossus*, Weidenfeld & Nicolson, London

Goldsworthy, A. (2010), *Antony and Cleopatra*, Weidenfeld & Nicolson, London

Goldsworthy, A. (2014), *Augustus*, Weidenfeld & Nicolson, London

Gorrie, C. (2004), 'Julia Domna's Building Patronage, Imperial Family Roles and the Severan Revival of Moral Legislation', *Historia: Zeitschrift für Alte Geschichte* Bd. 53, H. 1, 61–72

Grant, M. (1975), *The Twelve Caesars*, Michael Grant, London

Grant, M. (1985), *The Roman Emperors*, Weidenfeld & Nicolson, London

Graves, R. (2006), *I Claudius*, Penguin, London

Griffin, M. (1984), *Nero: The End of a Dynasty*, London

Gruber, F., Lipozenčić, J. and Kehler, T. (2015), 'History of Venereal Diseases from Antiquity to the Renaissance', *Acta Dermatovenerol Croat* 23 (1), 1–11

Hardie, P. (2014), *The Last Trojan Hero: A Cultural History of Virgil's Aeneid*, I.B. Tauris, London

Hartswick, K. (2013), *The Gardens of Sallust: A Changing Landscape*, University of Texas Press, Austin

Hejduk, J.D. (2008), *Clodia: A Sourcebook (Oklahoma Series in Classical Culture)*, University of Oklahoma Press, Norman

Hemelrijk, E. (2004), *Matrona Docta: Educated Women in the Roman Elite from Cornelia to Julia Domna*, Routledge, London

Hemelrijk, E. (2015), *Hidden Lives, Public Personae: Women and Civic Life in the Roman West*, Oxford University Press, Oxford

Hillard, T. (1992), 'On the Stage, Behind the Curtain: Images of Politically Active Women in the Late Republic' in Garlick et al. (1992), 37–64

Holland, R. (2004), *Augustus: Godfather of Europe*, Sutton, Stroud

Holland, T. (2015), *Dynasty*, Little, Brown, London

Jessen, K.E. (2013), 'Portraits of Livia in Context: An Analysis of Distribution Through the Application of Geographic Distribution Systems', PhD thesis, University of Iowa, Iowa City

Johnson, M.J. (2009), *The Roman Imperial Mausoleum in Late Antiquity*, Cambridge University Press, Cambridge

Johnson, W.R. (2015), *Darkness Visible: A Study of Virgil's 'Aeneid'*, University of Chicago Press, Chicago

Jones, A.H.M. (1970), *Augustus*, Norton, New York

Jones, B. (1993), *Domitian*, Routledge, London

Joshel, S.R. (1992), *Work Identity, and Legal Status at Rome: A Study of the Occupational Inscriptions*, University of Oklahoma Press, Norman

Keppie, L. (1991), *Understanding Roman Inscriptions*, Batsford, London

Kiefer, O. (1976), *Sexual Life in Ancient Rome*, Abbey, London

Kokkinos, N. (2002), *Antonia Augusta: Portrait of a Great Roman Lady*, Libri, London

Kragelund, P. (2010), 'The Temple and Birthplace of Diva Poppaea', *Classical Quarterly* New Series, 60 (2) (December), 559–68

Langford, J. (2013), *Maternal Megalomania: Julia Domna and the Imperial Politics of Motherhood*, Johns Hopkins University Press, Baltimore

Langlands, R. (2009), *Sexual Morality in Ancient Rome*, Cambridge University Press, Cambridge

Lefkovitz, M.R., and Fant, M.B. (1992), *Women's Life in Greece and Rome: A Source Book in Translation*, Johns Hopkins University Press, Baltimore

Levick, B. (1976), 'The Fall of Julia the Younger', *Latomus* 35, 301–39

Levick, B. (1990), *Claudius*, Routledge, London

Levick, B. (1999), *Tiberius the Politician*, Routledge, London

Levick, B. (1999), *Vespasian*, Routledge, London

Levick, B. (2007), *Julia Domna: Syrian Empress*, Routledge, Abingdon

Levick, B. (2010), *Augustus: Image and Substance*, Longman, London

Lewis, N., and Reinhold, M. (1955), *Roman Civilization. Sourcebook II: The Empire*, Harper & Row, New York

Liddell, H.G., and Scott, R. (1940), *A Greek–English Lexicon*, Clarendon Press, Oxford

Lyne, R.O.A.M. (1981), *The Latin Love Poets from Catullus to Horace*, Oxford University Press, Oxford

Mellor, R. (1993), *Tacitus*, Routledge, London

Millar, F. (1981), *The Roman Empire and its Neighbours*, Duckworth, London

Mullens, H.G. (1942), 'The Women of the Caesars', *Greece and Rome* 11, 59–67

Newlands, C.E. (1995), *Playing with Time: Ovid and the Fasti*, Cornell Studies in Classical Philology, Cornell University Press, Ithaca

Potter, D. (2008), *The Roman Emperors*, Metro Books, New York

Pottle, F.A. (ed.) (1950), *Boswell's London Journal*, Heinemann, London

Purcell, N. (2009), 'Livia and the Womanhood of Rome', in Edmondson (ed.) (2009). Also published in *Proceedings of the Cambridge Philological Society* 32 (1986), 78–105

Raditsa, L.F. (1980), 'Augustus' Legislation Concerning Marriage, Procreation, Love Affairs, and Adultery', *Aufstieg und Niedergang der römischen Welt* vol. 2.13, 278–339

Rehak, P. (1990), 'Livia's Dedication in the Temple of Divus Augustus on the Palatine', *Latomus* 40, 117–25

Richardson, J.S. (2012), *Augustan Rome, 44 BC to AD 14: The Restoration of the Republic and the Establishment of the Empire,* Edinburgh History of Ancient Rome, Edinburgh University Press, Edinburgh

Richardson, L. (1976), 'Evolution of the Porticus Octaviae', *American Journal of Archaeology* 80, 57–64

Richlin, A. (1992), 'Julia's Jokes, Galla Placidia, and the Roman Use of Women as Political Icons', in Garlick et al. (1992), 65–91

Riddle, J.M. (1992), *Contraception and Abortion from the Ancient World to the Renaissance*, Harvard University Press, Boston

Rossini, O. (2009), *Ara Pacis*, Musei in Comune, Electa, Milan

Rubenhold, H. (2009), *The Lady in Red: An Eighteenth-Century Tale of Sex, Scandal, and Divorce*, St Martin's Press, London

Rutland, L.W. (1978), 'Women as Makers of Kings in Tacitus' *Annals*', *Classical World* 72, 15–29

Sadek, M. (1966), 'On the Billon Output of the Mint of Alexandria under Nero', *Phoenix* (Classical Association of Canada) 20 (2), 131–47

Saunders, T. (1994), 'Messalina as Augusta', *La Parola de Passato* 49, 456–63

Scardigli, J. (1982), 'La sancrosanctitas tribunicia di Ottave e Livia', *Atti della facoltà di Lettere e Filiologica della Università di Siena, Perugia* 3, 61–4

Scullard, H.H. (1982, 5th edn), *From the Gracchi to Nero*, Routledge, London (reprinted on numerous occasions)

Sear, D. (1982), *Greek Imperial Coins and their Values*, Seaby, London

Sear, D. (2000), *Roman Coins and their Values, Volume I: The Republic and Twelve Caesars 280 BC–AD 96*, Spink, London

Sear, D. (2002), *Roman Coins and their Values, Volume II: The Accession of Nerva to the Overthrow of the Severan Dynasty AD 96–AD 235*, Spink, London

Sear, D. (2014), *Roman Coins and their Values, Volume V: The Christian Empire: The Later Constantinian Dynasty and the Houses of Valentinian and Theodosius and their Successors, Constantine II to Zeno, AD 337–491*, Spink, London

Shelton, J.A. (1998), *As the Romans Did*, Oxford University Press, Oxford

Sherk, R. (ed.) (1988), *The Roman Empire: Augustus to Hadrian*, Cambridge University Press, Cambridge

Shotter, D. (2000), 'Agrippina the Elder – a Woman in a Man's World', *Historia* 49

Shotter, D. (2008), *Nero Caesar Augustus, Emperor of Rome*, Pearson Longman, London

Sijpesteijn, P.J. (1989), 'Another οὐσία of D. Valerius Asiaticus in Egypt', *Zeitschrift für Papyrologie und Epigraphik* 79, 194–6

Sivan, H. (2011), *Galla Placidia: The Last Roman Empress (Women in Antiquity)*, Oxford University Press, New York

Skinner, M.B. (2011), *Clodia Metelli: The Tribune's Sister (Women in Antiquity)*, Oxford University Press, New York

Smallwood, M. (1967), *Documents Illustrating the Principates of Gaius, Claudius and Nero*, Cambridge University Press, Cambridge (later reissued by Routledge 2011)

Southern, P. (2001), *Julius Caesar*, Tempus, Stroud

Strong, A.K. (2016), *Prostitutes and Matrons in the Roman World*, Cambridge University Press, New York

Sutherland, C.H.V. (1974), *Roman Coins*, Barrie & Jenkins, London

Syme, R. (1958), *Tacitus*, Oxford University Press, Oxford

Syme, R. (2002), *The Roman Revolution*, Oxford University Press, Oxford

Tait, J. (2003), 'Cleopatra by Name' in Walker and Ashton (eds) (2003)

Treggiari, S. (1975), 'Jobs in the Household of Livia', *Proceedings of the British School at Rome*, 43, 48–77

Treggiari, S. (1991), *Roman Marriage: Iusti Coniuges from the Time of Cicero to Ulpian*, Oxford University Press, Oxford

Treggiari, S. (2007), *Terentia, Tullia and Publilia: The Women of Cicero's Family*, Routledge, Abingdon

Turton, G. (1974), *The Syrian Princesses: The Women Who Ruled Rome, AD 193–235*, Cassell, London (reissued in 2009 as an ACLS Humanities E-Book)

Ungaro, L. (2007), 'The Forum of Augustus', in L. Ungaro (ed.) (2007), *The Museum of the Imperial Forums in Trajan's Market* (English edition), Electa, Milan

Virlouvet, C. (2001), 'Fulvia the Woman of Passion', in Fraschetti (ed.) (2001), 66–81

Vout, V. (2009), *Power and Eroticism in Imperial Rome*, Cambridge University Press, Cambridge

Walker, S., and Ashton, S. (eds) (2003), *Cleopatra Reassessed*, British Museum Publications, London

Walker, S., and Burnett, A. (1981), *The Image of Augustus*, British Museum Publications, London

Walker, S., and Higgs, P. (2001), *Cleopatra of Egypt: From History to Myth*, British Museum Publications, London

Wallace-Hadrill, A. (2008), *Rome's Cultural Revolution*, Cambridge University Press, Cambridge

Weir, A. (1998), *Lancaster & York: The Wars of the Roses*, Pimlico, London

Wiedemann, T. (1989), *The Julio-Claudian Emperors*, Bristol Classical Press, London

Wilkinson, S. (2005), *Caligula*, Routledge, London

Williams, C.A. (2010), *Roman Homosexuality*, Oxford University Press, Oxford

Williams, M.G. (1902), 'Studies in the Lives of Roman Empresses', *American Journal of Archaeology* 6 (3), 259–305

Winter, B.W. (2015), *Divine Honours for the Caesars: the First Christians' Responses*, William B. Erdmans Publishing Co., Grand Rapids

Wiseman, T.P. (1969), *Catullan Questions*, Leicester University Press, Leicester

Wiseman, T.P. (1985, reprinted 2008), *Catullus and his World: A Reappraisal*, Cambridge University Press, Cambridge

Wood, S. (1988), 'Agrippina the Elder in Julio-Claudian Art and Propaganda', *American Journal of Archaeology* 92, 80–99

Wood, S. (1999), *Imperial Women: A Study in Public Images, 40 BC–AD 68*, Brill, Leiden

Zanker, P. (1990), *The Power of Images in the Age of Augustus*, University of Michigan Press, Ann Arbor

INDEX

Names are generally indexed by their most familiar and convenient form. Valeria Messalina, empress of Claudius, is indexed under Messalina, for example. References in the Notes are not generally indexed.

Index of Women

Index of empresses and other mortal women. Divine and mythological women are in the General Index.

Index of Emperors

General Index

Male names are indexed by their most familiar form, e.g. Marcus Tullius Cicero is under Cicero, Publius Cornelius Scipio Africanus is under Scipio, and so on. Ancient sources are only indexed where they are specifically referred to in the text; references in the notes are generally not included. Individuals or places who appear in passing are not normally indexed.